The New Cambridge Handbook of
Contemporary
China

COLIN MACKERRAS

CAMBRIDGE
UNIVERSITY PRESS

PUBLISHED BY THE PRESS SYNDICATE OF THE UNIVERSITY OF CAMBRIDGE
The Pitt Building, Trumpington Street, Cambridge, United Kingdom

CAMBRIDGE UNIVERSITY PRESS
The Edinburgh Building, Cambridge CB2 2RU, UK
40 West 20th Street, New York, NY 10011–4211, USA
10 Stamford Road, Oakleigh, VIC 3166, Australia
Ruiz de Alarcón 13, 28014 Madrid, Spain
Dock House, The Waterfront, Cape Town 8001, South Africa

http://www.cambridge.org

First published 2001

Printed in Singapore by Craft Print International Ltd

Typeface Berkeley (*Adobe*) 10/12 pt. *System* QuarkXPress® [DOCUPRO]

A catalogue record for this book is available from the British Library

National Library of Australia Cataloguing in Publication data
Mackerras, Colin, 1939– .
The new Cambridge handbook of contemporary China.
Bibliography.
Includes index.
ISBN 0 521 78143 4.
ISBN 0 521 78674 6 (pbk).
1. China – Politics and government – 1949– .
2. China – Social conditions – 1949– .
3. China – Economic conditions – 1949– .
I. Title II. Title: Handbook of contemporary China.
951.05

ISBN 0 521 78143 4 hardback
ISBN 0 521 78674 6 paperback

CONTENTS

TABLES, FIGURES AND MAPS

FIGURES

M A P S

PREFACE

This work aims to present useful and accurate information, dates and statistics concerning contemporary China in a manageable and accessible form. 'China' has been used to refer to the People's Republic of China, except for Hong Kong and Macau, so although Taiwan and these two places are mentioned occasionally, none of them has, for reasons of manageability, been considered systematically or in detail.

This aim has dictated many of the decisions made about what to include and what to omit. Contemporary China is so large a subject that it is quite impossible to be comprehensive. The material included is that with greatest relevance to China's political economy. I decided to omit the chapter on society and culture in *The Cambridge Handbook of Contemporary China* because it did not fit well with the rest of the present volume and to make it so would have required expansion so great as to become unmanageable.

In other respects this book has a structure very similar to the earlier book. Yet the situation has changed in China so much since that book was completed in April 1990 that this one can be described as a new book. The main focus is on the period 1990 to 2000, which was only just beginning when the original *Handbook* was completed, although there remains a great deal of material concerning earlier years of the PRC. There is only one main author of *The New Cambridge Handbook of Contemporary China*. Chapters written by the other author of the original *Handbook* have, like all chapters, been greatly changed and updated for this *New Cambridge Handbook*. Dr Kevin Bucknall, formerly of the School of Modern Asian Studies, Griffith University, wrote Chapter 6 on China's economy.

Every attempt has been made to keep the information up to date. However, in dealing with contemporary times, it is always neces-sary to establish a cut-off date. In this case that date is August 15, 2000, since that was when the compilation of the book was completed. It has been possible to include the initial results of the 2000 census, though not the details.

The two systems of romanization in most widespread use for English-language material are the British-developed Wade-Giles and the *Hanyu pinyin*, which was devised in the 1950s and came into almost universal use in PRC foreign-language publications on January 1, 1979. Nowadays both systems are in common use for Western European-language books published outside China, but for books about the PRC, pinyin has become much more standard and is the system we have adopted in this book. The only exceptions are for people who are usually known in the West by names not expressed in standard Chinese, such as Chiang Kaishek. However, in Chapter 3 I have given the Wade-Giles equivalent in parentheses for each biographee's name following its presentation as a heading in *pinyin*.

Below are shown some of the most important differences between the two systems.

Pinyin	Wade–Giles	Approximate English sound
c	ts'	ts
ch	ch'	ch
d	t	d
g	k	g
j	ch	j
k	k'	k
p	p'	p
q	ch'	ch
r	j	r
t	t'	t
x	hs	sh
z	ts	dz
zh	ch	j

ABBREVIATIONS

ADB	Asian Development Bank
APEC	Asia-Pacific Economic Cooperation
ARATS	Association for Relations Across the Taiwan Straits
ASEAN	Association of South-East Asian Nations
CAAC	Civil Aviation Administration of China
CP	Communist Party
CCP	Chinese Communist Party
CCPCC	Chinese Communist Party Central Committee (Central Committee)
CCYL	Chinese Communist Youth League
CITIC	China International Trust and Investment Corporation
CMC	Central Military Commission
CPPCC	Chinese People's Political Consultative Conference
CPG	Central People's Government (more commonly referred to as the State Council)
(C)CYL	(Chinese) Communist Youth League
DPRK	Democratic People's Republic of Korea
ESCAP	Economic and Social Commission for Asia and the Pacific
FDI	foreign direct investment
GATT	General Agreement on Tariffs and Trade
GDP	gross domestic product
GNP	gross national product
GITIC	Guandong International Trust and Investment Corporation
HKSAR	Hong Kong Special Administrative Region
JPRS	Joint Publication Research Service
LegCo	Legislative Council of Hong Kong
MFN	most-favoured nation (see NTR)
MIT	Massachusetts Institute of Technology
NPC	National People's Congress
NCNA	New China News Agency
NMD	National Missile Defence
NTR	normal trading relations (formerly MFN)
PLA	People's Liberation Army
PRC	People's Republic of China
RMB	*renminbi* ('people's currency')
ROC	Republic of China
SAR	Special Administrative Region
SEF	Straits Exchange Foundation
SITC	Standard International Trade Classification
SOE	state-owned enterprise
TMD	Theatre Missile Defence
TVEs	township and village enterprises
UNESCO	United Nations Educational, Scientific and Cultural Organization
WHO	World Health Organization
WTO	World Trade Organization
XUAR	Xinjiang Uygur Autonomous Region

General map of China

RUSSIAN FEDERATION

MONGOLIA

KAZAKHSTAN

KYRGYZSTAN

TAJIKISTAN

PAKISTAN

INDIA

NEPAL

BHUTAN

MYANMAR

LAOS

THAILAND

VIETNAM

NORTH KOREA

SOUTH KOREA

JAPAN

TAIWAN

PHILIPPINES

Sea of Japan

Yellow Sea

East China Sea

Pacific Ocean

South China Sea

Bay of Bengal

Lake Baikal

Lake Balkhash

ALTAI MOUNTAINS

TIAN SHAN

PAMIRS

KARAKORUM RANGE

KUNLUN SHAN

GANGDISE SHAN

HIMALAYAS

Lake Qinghai

QILIAN SHAN

TANGGULA SHAN

QINGHAI–TIBET PLATEAU

Nam Co

NYAINQENTANGLHA SHAN

Lhasa

Yarlung Zangbo River

Brahmaputra

HENGDUAN SHAN

Lancang River

Nijiang (Salween)

Changjiang

Yangzi River

(Mekong)

Chindwin

XINJIANG

Urumqi

TIBET

QINGHAI

Xining

GANSU

Lanzhou

NINGXIA

Yinchuan

INNER MONGOLIA

Hohhot

Baotou

Yellow River

HEILONGJIANG

Heilongjiang (Songhua) River

Songhua River

Qiqihar

Harbin

JILIN

Changchun

Jilin

LIAONING

Liao River

Shenyang

Fushun

Anshan

Dalian

HEBEI

Beijing

Tianjin

Tangshan

Shijiazhuang

Handan

SHANXI

Taiyuan

(Huanghe)

Yellow River

SHAANXI

Xi'an

Luoyang

HENAN

Zhengzhou

SHANDONG

Ji'nan

Qingdao

Xuzhou

Shanghai

JIANGSU

Nanjing

ANHUI

Hefei

Huai River

Yangzi River

Taihu

ZHEJIANG

Hangzhou

Wenzhou

HUBEI

Wuhan

Yueyang

Dongting Lake

CHONGQING

Chongqing

Neijiang

SICHUAN

Chengdu

JIANGXI

Nanchang

Poyang Lake

HUNAN

Changsha

Changde

GUIZHOU

Guiyang

YUNNAN

Kunming

GUANGXI

Nanning

West River (Xijiang)

GUANGDONG

Guangzhou

Kowloon

HONG KONG

FUJIAN

Fuzhou

Haikou

HAINAN

500 km

0

This chronology of significant events in China extends from 1949 to August 2000.[1] The events are divided, for ease of reference, into seven categories: **A.** Foreign Affairs Events; **B.** Domestic Political and/or Military Events; **C.** Economic Events; **D.** Appointments, Dismissals, etc.; **E.** Cultural and Social Events; **F.** Births and Deaths; **G.** Natural Disasters, or Natural Disasters, Accidents.

1949 DEFEAT OF THE GUOMINDANG; MAO AND THE CHINESE COMMUNIST PARTY (CCP) ASSUME POWER

A Foreign Affairs Events

July 1. Mao Zedong declares in his 'On the People's Democratic Dictatorship' ('Lun renmin minzhu zhuanzheng'), published on this day, that China will 'lean to one side', that of the Soviet Union.

August 5. The US State Department publishes its China White Paper, *United States Relations with China*, in Washington.

December 16. Mao Zedong arrives in Moscow and meets Stalin on his first trip outside China.

B Domestic Political and Military Events

January 10. The Huaihai campaign ends in a People's Liberation Army (PLA) victory.

January 15. Tianjin falls to the PLA.

January 31. The PLA peacefully takes over Beiping, concluding the Tianjin–Beiping campaign.

April 23. Chiang Kaishek's capital, Nanjing, falls to the PLA.

May 27. Shanghai falls to the PLA.

September 21–30. The Chinese People's Political Consultative Conference (CPPCC) takes place in Beiping/Beijing. On September 27, it renames Beiping 'Beijing' and declares it China's capital. On September 29 it adopts the Common Program, a provisional constitution which

stipulates the policies of the Central People's Government (CPG).

October 1. The People's Republic of China (PRC) is formally established.

D Appointments, Dismissals, etc.

August 27. Gao Gang is inaugurated as chairman of the Northeast People's Government, established the same day.

September 30. The CPPCC elects Mao Zedong as chairman of the CPG.

October 1. The CPG Council, at its first meeting, appoints Zhou Enlai as the CPG's premier of the Government Administrative Council and minister of Foreign Affairs, Mao Zedong as chairman of the CPG's Revolutionary Military Affairs Committee, and Zhu De as commander-in-chief of the PLA.

E Cultural and Social Events

March 15. *People's Daily* formally moves to Beiping.

March 24–April 3. The first National Women's Congress takes place in Beiping.

June 16. *Guangming Daily* (*Guangming ribao*) begins publication.

October. The periodical *People's Literature* (*Renmin wenxue*) begins publication.

1950

A Foreign Affairs Events

February 14. The Sino-Soviet Treaty of Friendship, Alliance and Mutual Assistance is signed in Moscow.

March 4. Mao Zedong arrives back in Beijing from Moscow.

June 28. Mao Zedong denounces the United States for aggression in Korea, where war had broken out on June 25, and in Taiwan.

October 25. The Chinese People's Volunteers publicly enter Korea in support of the troops of the Democratic People's Republic of Korea (DPRK).

B Domestic Political and Military Events

October 19. PLA forces take Changdu, in Xikang, as they advance towards Tibet.

October 30. In a note to India, China states that 'Tibet is an integral part of Chinese territory' and that the Tibetan problem is a 'domestic problem' for China.

C Economic Events

March 22. The CPG orders that the Bank of China be brought under the control of the People's Bank.

E Cultural and Social Events

January 1. The English-language fortnightly *People's China* begins publication in Beijing.

April 2. The Central Drama Institute (*Zhongyang xiju xueyuan*) is formally set up.

April 4. The Central Conservatorium of Music (*Zhongyang yinyue xueyuan*) is set up.

May 1. The CPG promulgates the *Marriage Law of the PRC*.

June 29. The CPG promulgates the *Trade Union Law of the PRC*.

June 30. The CPG promulgates the *Agrarian Reform Law of the PRC*.

1951

A Foreign Affairs Events

January 4. Chinese People's Volunteers and DPRK troops take Seoul.

February 1. The UN General Assembly condemns China as an aggressor in Korea.

B Domestic Political Events

May 23. The Agreement of the CPG and the Local Government of Tibet on Measures for the Liberation of Tibet is signed in Beijing. It recognizes Tibet as part of the PRC but gives the Tibetans the right to regional autonomy.

October 24. The Dalai Lama cables Mao Zedong, signifying his support for the May 23 Agreement.

D Appointments, Dismissals, etc.

February 28. Peng Zhen is made Mayor of Beijing.

E Cultural and Social Events

October 12. Volume 1 of *The Selected Works of Mao Zedong* (*Mao Zedong xuanji*) is published in Beijing.

F Births and Deaths

May. Mao Zedong's son Mao Anying is killed in the Korean War.

1952

A Foreign Affairs Events

March 8. Zhou Enlai denounces the United States for intrusions by its aircraft in China's air space and for using germ warfare in northeast China.

B Domestic Political Events

January 1. Mao Zedong calls for struggle against corruption, waste and bureaucratism (the Three-Antis Movement).

February 1. The CPG launches the Five-Antis Movement against five types of corruption.

C Economic Events

September 29. The long-projected Longhai railway, linking Jiangsu with Lanzhou, capital of Gansu Province, opens to traffic.

D Appointments, Dismissals, etc.

October 10. Gao Gang is appointed chairman of the newly established State Planning Commission.

E Cultural and Social Events

July 5. The New China News Agency (NCNA) announces the virtual completion of land reform.

1953

A Foreign Affairs Events
July 27. The Korean armistice is signed.

B Domestic Political Events
March 1. Mao Zedong promulgates the *Electoral Law of the PRC*.

June 30–July 1. The PRC's first census is taken.

C Economic Events
January 1. A *People's Daily* editorial announces the beginning of the First Five-Year Plan as one of the tasks for 1953.

December 16. The CCPCC adopts a resolution in favour of developing Agricultural Producers' Cooperatives.

E Cultural and Social Events
August 21–October 6. The Chinese Youth and Children Corps is renamed the Chinese Young Pioneers.

F Births and Deaths
September 26. Painter Xu Beihong dies.

1954

A Foreign Affairs Events
April 20–August 1. Premier Zhou Enlai visits many countries in Europe and Asia for various diplomatic purposes.

June 28. In India, Zhou Enlai and Indian Prime Minister Jawaharlal Nehru agree to the five principles of peaceful coexistence in a joint communiqué.

July 21. In Geneva, China's representative Zhou Enlai agrees to the Final Declaration of the Geneva Conference on Indochina.

October 12. A visiting Soviet delegation, led by Party First Secretary Nikita Khrushchev, and CPG leaders issue several joint communiqués, including one that the Soviet Union will withdraw all its troops from Lüshun before May 31, 1955.

October 19–30. Prime Minister Nehru visits China.

C Economic Events
January 31. Formal inauguration of direct Beijing–Moscow passenger rail service.

D Appointments, Dismissals, etc.
March 31. Gao Gang and Rao Shushi are expelled from the CCP and dismissed from all posts.

September 27. The First National People's Congress (NPC) elects Mao Zedong as chairman of the PRC and Liu Shaoqi as chairman of the NPC's Standing Committee; it also approves Mao's recommendation to appoint Zhou Enlai premier of the State Council.

F Births and Deaths
Spring. Gao Gang commits suicide.

G Natural Disasters
August 4. NCNA reports the level of the Yangzi River at Wuhan to be even higher than in 1931, an indication of extremely severe flooding.

1955

A Foreign Affairs Events
April 18–24. Zhou Enlai heads the Chinese delegation at the Afro-Asian Conference held in Bandung, Indonesia, addressing the plenary session on April 19.

April 22. The Sino-Indonesian Treaty Concerning the Question of Dual Nationality is signed in Bandung.

August 1. Sino-American talks at ambassadorial level begin in Geneva.

C Economic Events
March 1. The People's Bank begins issuing a new people's currency at the rate of 10 000 old to one new yuan. The bank announces the completion of the changeover on June 10.

July 30. The NPC adopts the First Five-Year Plan for the Development of the National Economy (1953–57).

D Appointments, Dismissals, etc.
March 9. The Dalai Lama is appointed chairman of the Preparatory Committee for the Tibetan Autonomous Region.

May 25. Writer and poet Hu Feng is expelled from all posts in literature and art circles for bourgeois and idealist thinking on literature and art.

October 1. Saifudin is appointed chairman of the Xinjiang Uygur Autonomous Region, set up on this day at a ceremony in Ürümqi.

E Cultural and Social Events

January 10. The Peking Opera Company of China is formally set up.

December. The first volume of Lenin's complete works, *Liening quanji*, is published; the remaining 37 volumes follow by 1959.

F Births and Deaths

August 29. Dramatist Hong Shen dies.

1956

A Foreign Affairs Events

September 30–October 14. Indonesian President Sukarno visits the PRC.

November 1. The Chinese government issues a statement denouncing British and French aggression against Egypt.

November 6. Zhou Enlai cables congratulations and support to Janos Kadar. Soviet troops had just entered Hungary and Budapest to replace the government of Imre Nagy with that of Kadar.

B Domestic Political Events

April 25. Mao Zedong makes his speech 'On the Ten Major Relationships'.

C Economic Events

March 17. Mao Zedong orders that the Model Regulations for the Agricultural Producers' Cooperatives be promulgated.

D Appointments, Dismissals, etc.

September 26. The Eighth Congress of the CCP elects the Eighth CCPCC, including Mao Zedong as chairman.

September 28. The First Plenum of the Eighth CCPCC elects Liu Shaoqi, Zhou Enlai, Zhu De and Chen Yun as vice-chairmen of the CCPCC, and Deng Xiaoping as secretary-general.

E Cultural and Social Events

January 1. The *Liberation Army Daily* (*Jiefang jun bao*) begins publication.

May 2. Mao Zedong calls for greater artistic and academic freedom with the slogan 'let a hundred flowers bloom, and a hundred schools of thought contend'.

October. The magazine *Chinese Cinema* (*Zhongguo dianying*) begins publication.

1957

A Foreign Affairs Events

October 15. Sino-Soviet Agreement on New Technology for National Defence. According to a Chinese statement of August 15, 1963, the Soviet Union had promised China a sample atomic bomb under this agreement.

November 2–21. Mao Zedong heads a Chinese delegation to the Soviet Union. On November 17, he declares in Moscow that 'the east wind is prevailing over the west wind'.

B Domestic Political Events

May 1–June 7. Open criticisms of the CCP reach their height in the period of the 'Hundred Flowers'.

June 8. An editorial in the *People's Daily* states that rightists are trying to overthrow the CCP. This signals the end of the Hundred Flowers Movement and the beginning of an Anti-Rightist Campaign.

C Economic Events

October 15. The road-railway bridge over the Yangzi River at Wuhan is formally opened. The bridge links the Beijing–Wuhan and Wuhan–Guangzhou lines, creating the Beijing–Guangzhou railway.

E Cultural and Social Events

July 15–August 2. A conference establishes the Chinese Catholic Patriotic Association. It recognizes the Pope's authority in religious matters, but not over political issues.

December. The novel *Keep the Red Flag Flying* (*Hongqi pu*) by Liang Bin is published.

F Births and Deaths
September 16. Painter Qi Baishi dies in Beijing.

1958 THE GREAT LEAP FORWARD

A Foreign Affairs Events
July 31–August 3. Nikita Khrushchev, First Secretary of the Communist Party of the Soviet Union, visits China. On the last day he and Mao Zedong issue a joint communiqué expressing unanimity on all matters, but making no mention of Taiwan.

October 6. The Chinese announce the suspension of the bombardment of the offshore island of Quemoy, begun on August 23.

October 26. The Chinese People's Volunteers complete their withdrawal from Korea.

B Domestic Political Events
March 15. The Guangxi Zhuang Autonomous Region is established.

April 29. The Sputnik Federated Cooperative, China's first people's commune, is established in Henan Province.

May 5–23. The Second Session of the Eighth Congress of the CCP endorses the Great Leap Forward.

August 29. An enlarged conference of the CCPCC's Politburo, the Beidaihe Conference, adopts a decision in favour of establishing people's communes in the countryside. In less than two months, all rural China has been organized into 26 000 communes.

October 25. The Ningxia Hui Autonomous Region is established.

November 28–December 10. The Sixth Plenum of the Eighth CCPCC, held in Wuchang, reverses some of the most radical policies of the Great Leap Forward.

C Economic Events
January 1. The Second Five-Year Plan (1958–62) moves into operation, but is overtaken and superseded by the Great Leap Forward.

D Appointments, Dismissals, etc.
February 11. Mao Zedong appoints Chen Yi as minister of Foreign Affairs, replacing Zhou Enlai.

E Cultural and Social Events
January. The novel *The Song of Youth* (*Qingchun zhi ge*) by Yang Mo is published.

March. Tian Han's spoken drama *Guan Hanqing* is published in the periodical *Play-Scripts* (*Juben*).

March 4. *Peking Review* begins publication.

June 1. *Red Flag* (*Hongqi*) begins publication.

June 29. Pope Pius XII issues the encyclical *Ad Apostolorum Principis*, in which he condemns the Church of the Catholic Patriotic Association and declares its bishops invalid.

September 2. Beijing Television begins broadcasting.

F Births and Deaths
March 9. Peking Opera performer Cheng Yanqiu dies.

October 17. Chinese literature specialist Zheng Zhenduo dies in an aircraft accident.

1959

A Foreign Affairs Events
February 9–12. Ho Chi Minh, president of the Democratic Republic of Vietnam, visits Beijing.

October 21. An armed clash between Chinese and Indian border guards on their mutual border in Ladakh results in casualties on both sides.

B Domestic Political Events
March. On March 10, armed rebellion begins against the Chinese government in Lhasa, Tibet. By March 23, the revolt is suppressed in Lhasa, and on March 31, the Dalai Lama flees Tibet and enters India.

April 28. The First Session of the Second NPC directs that democratic reforms be carried out in Tibet.

June 5. The International Commission of Jurists issues a statement in Geneva that 'deliberate violation of fundamental human rights' has taken place in Tibet.

C Economic Events

February 7. The Guizhou–Guangxi railway, linking Guiyang to Liuzhou, opens to traffic.

November 1. The Luoyang Tractor Plant, China's first such factory, is completed.

D Appointments, Dismissals, etc.

March 28. The State Council appoints the Bainqen (Panchen) Lama to chair the Preparatory Committee for the Tibetan Autonomous Region.

April 27. The NPC appoints Liu Shaoqi as president of the PRC in succession to Mao Zedong, with Song Qingling and Dong Biwu as deputies.

August 16. The Lushan Plenum dismisses Peng Dehuai.

September 17. President Liu Shaoqi proclaims the appointment of Lin Biao as minister of National Defence (replacing Peng Dehuai).

E Cultural and Social Events

September. The Guangdong People's Press publishes Ouyang Shan's novel *Three Family Lane* (*Sanjia xiang*).

September 9–October 3. The PRC's First National Games take place.

G Natural Disasters

June. Serious flooding occurs in Guangdong.

July–August. Extremely serious drought reaches a peak in vast areas of China, affecting about 30 per cent of China's land under cultivation.

1960

A Foreign Affairs Events

April 16. An exchange of polemics between China and the Soviet Union begins with an article in *Red Flag* warning against changing Lenin's notion of the nature of imperialism.

April 25. In New Delhi, Zhou Enlai and Indian Prime Minister Nehru sign a joint communiqué that both governments should study problems on their mutual border.

May 31. In Ulan Bator, Zhou Enlai and Mongolian Prime Minister Y. Tsedenbal sign the Sino-Mongolian Treaty of Friendship and Mutual Assistance.

July 16. The Soviet Union notifies China of its decision to withdraw all its experts from China within a month.

October 1. In Beijing, Burmese Prime Minister U Nu and Zhou Enlai sign the Sino-Burmese Boundary Treaty.

C Economic Events

April 21. The double-track railway bridge over the Yellow River at Zhengzhou, Henan Province, is formally opened to traffic.

E Cultural and Social Events

March 17. The Catholic Bishop of Shanghai, Gong Pinmei, is sentenced to life imprisonment.

May 25. Chinese mountaineers reach the summit of Mt Everest (Jomo Lungma) for the first time.

F Births and Deaths

May 23. Former Shanxi warlord Yan Xishan dies.

May 29. Politburo member Lin Boqu dies.

G Natural Disasters

December 29. NCNA claims the 1960 natural disasters—drought, floods, typhoons and insect pests—as the worst for a century. It claims that over half China's total farmland has been affected and states that only Tibet and Xinjiang have escaped the disasters. Widespread and extremely serious famine results.

1961

A Foreign Affairs Events

April 1. The Sino-Indonesian Treaty of Friendship is signed in Jakarta.

May 16. At the fourteen-nation Geneva Conference on Laos, Foreign Minister Chen Yi demands the abolition of the South-East Asian Treaty Organization.

June 13–15. Indonesian President Sukarno visits China, and ratification of the Sino-Indonesian Treaty of Friendship is exchanged on June 14.

July 11. In Beijing, Zhou Enlai and Kim Il Sung sign the Sino-Korean Treaty of Friendship, Cooperation and Mutual Assistance.

October 19. At the Twenty-second Congress of the Communist Party of the Soviet Union in Moscow, Zhou Enlai defends Albania, publicly censured by Khrushchev two days earlier.

December 15. The UN General Assembly adopts a resolution that the PRC's admission should be regarded as an 'important question' requiring a two-thirds majority. China denounces the resolution on December 21.

E Cultural and Social Events

January 9. The original version of Wu Han's play, *Hai Rui's Dismissal* (*Hai Rui baguan*), is published in the periodical *Beijing Literature and Art* (*Beijing wenyi*).

July 1. The Museum of Chinese History and the Museum of the Chinese Revolution are both opened in the same building in the centre of Beijing.

December. China Youth Press publishes the novel *Red Crag* (*Hong yan*) by Luo Guangbin and Yan Yiyan.

F Births and Deaths

August 8. Peking Opera performer Mei Lanfang dies.

G Natural Disasters

March 6. A spokesman for the Central Meteorological Bureau claims that the 1959–60 drought was among the worst in more than three centuries, and the worst since 1877. Meanwhile, drought persists in Shandong, Henan, Hebei, Shanxi and Shaanxi, and floods ravage Guangdong, Fujian, Zhejiang and Jiangxi, causing widespread and serious continuing famine, resulting in the death of millions from starvation.

1962

A Foreign Affairs Events

July 23. In Geneva, China, the Soviet Union, the United States, Britain and other states sign the Declaration on the Neutrality of Laos.

October 11. A serious clash occurs at Tseng Jong on the Sino-Indian border. The next day Nehru states that he has instructed the Indian army to free Indian territory of Chinese troops.

October 20. Chinese troops launch major offensives on the Sino-Indian border.

November 9. In Beijing, Liao Chengzhi and Takasaki Tatsunosuke sign a memorandum for long-term and comprehensive trade between China and Japan: the Liao–Takasaki memorandum. Trade established through this memorandum is later known as 'L–T trade'.

November 20. China declares a unilateral ceasefire in the Sino-Indian war and announces that its troops will withdraw behind the 'line of actual control' as of November 1959.

December 26. The Sino-Mongolian Boundary Treaty is signed in Beijing.

B Domestic Political Events

September 24. Mao Zedong makes a speech at the Eighth CCPCC's Tenth Plenum, calling for greater emphasis on class struggle. The plenum marks the beginning of the Socialist Education Movement.

E Cultural and Social Events

August. The People's Literary Press publishes the last of fourteen volumes of *Ba Jin's Collected Works* (*Ba Jin wenji*), the first having been released in March 1958. Deng Tuo's *Evening Talks at Yanshan* (*Yanshan yehua*), a collection of essays originally appearing in three Beijing newspapers from

March 1961 to September 1962, is published in four volumes.

F Births and Deaths
February 24. Hu Shi dies.
September 21. Actor and dramatist Ouyang Yuqian dies.

1963
A Foreign Affairs Events
May 16. In Hanoi, Liu Shaoqi and Ho Chi Minh sign a joint statement that includes an attack on revisionism and calls for struggle against 'imperialism headed by the United States'.
July 5. Sino-Soviet talks open in Moscow in an unsuccessful attempt to resolve the bilateral differences. Deng Xiaoping and Peng Zhen lead the Chinese delegation.
July 31. The Chinese government issues a statement supporting the total destruction of nuclear weapons and denouncing the Partial Nuclear Test Ban Treaty, initialled on July 25.
November 22. The Sino-Afghan Boundary Treaty is signed in Beijing.
December 14–31. Zhou Enlai and Chen Yi visit the United Arab Republic, Algeria and Morocco in a large-scale African tour.

B Domestic Political Events
May 20. A Central Work Conference held in Hangzhou issues the 'First Ten Points'. Drafted by Mao Zedong and stressing class struggle, the action is designed to give impetus to the Rural Socialist Education Movement in the countryside.
September. The CCPCC issues the Later Ten Points on the Socialist Education Movement in the countryside, drafted by Peng Zhen.

E Cultural and Social Events
April 3–26. A meeting of heads of CCP Cultural Bureaux discusses the content of dramas and literary works. A circular by Jiang Qing 'on Suspending the Performance of Ghost Plays' is distributed, calling for the banning of traditional drama.
December. The People's Literary Press publishes *Poems of Chairman Mao* (*Mao zhuxi shici*).

F Births and Deaths
August 9. Economist Ji Chaoding dies.

1964
A Foreign Affairs Events
January 9. Zhou Enlai and Chen Yi arrive in Tunis from Albania to continue their large-scale African tour. They visit Tunisia, Ghana, Mali, Guinea, Sudan, Ethiopia and Somalia, leaving on February 4.
August 6. The Chinese government protests against the United States' bombing of northern Vietnam the day before and denounces the United States for fabricating the Tongking Gulf incidents of August 2 and 4. It states that aggression against Vietnam is equivalent to aggression against China.
April 29. The inaugural flight of the Pakistan International Airline to China lands in Shanghai.

B Domestic Political Events
September 10. The 'Revised Later Ten Points' are issued, ushering in a new phase in the Rural Socialist Education Movement.
October 16. China carries out her first nuclear test; the Chinese government declares that China will never be the first to use nuclear weapons.

E Cultural and Social Events
June 5–July 31. The Festival of Peking Operas on Contemporary Themes is held in Beijing.
September. The first part of *Bright Sunny Skies* (*Yanyang tian*), a novel by Haoran, is published in Beijing, with the second part following in March 1966.
October 2. *The East is Red* (*Dongfang hong*), a 'large-scale historical poem with

music and dancing', is premiered in Beijing.

1965
A Foreign Affairs Events
February 11. Soviet Prime Minister Aleksei Kosygin meets Mao Zedong and Liu Shaoqi when he visits Beijing on his return trip from Hanoi to Moscow.

March 12. The Chinese government denounces the arrival of American marines in Vietnam on March 8 and 9.

June 2–8. Zhou Enlai visits Pakistan and Tanzania.

June 19. Zhou Enlai and Chen Yi arrive in Cairo on their way to attend the Second Afro-Asian Conference. This was to start in Algiers on June 29, but never took place because of a change of government in Algiers.

November 4. The PRC Embassy in Jakarta protests over a raid on the Chinese consulate in Medan the day before and the persecution of Chinese in Indonesia in general. This was the first of many such protests by the PRC Embassy and signalled a drastic decline in Sino-Indonesian relations since the coup of October 1 that brought Suharto and the army to power.

B Domestic Political Events
January 14. A Central Work Conference held by the Politburo of the CCP's Central Committee adopts 'The Twenty-three Articles on the Socialist Education Movement'.

September 3. *Red Flag* publishes Lin Biao's article 'Long Live the Victory of the People's War' to commemorate the twentieth anniversary of the War of Resistance against Japan.

September 9. The Tibetan Autonomous Region is formally established.

D Appointments, Dismissals, etc.
September 8. Ngapoi Ngawang Jigme is elected chairman of the Tibetan Autonomous Region.

E Cultural and Social Events
June 1. The decision abolishing ranks in the PLA comes into effect.

June 26. Mao Zedong issues an instruction to put stress on the rural areas in the field of medical and health work.

November 10. In the Shanghai newspaper *Wenhui bao*, Yao Wenyuan denounces Wu Han's drama *Hai Rui's Dismissal* as an anti-Party poisonous weed. The article leads on to fierce denunciations in the press of this and other literary works in the following months.

December. Jin Jingmai's novel *The Song of Ouyang Hai* (*Ouyang Hai zhi ge*) is published in Beijing.

F Births and Deaths
April 9. Vice-premier Ke Qingshi dies.

December 21. Educationalist Huang Yanpei dies.

1966 OUTBREAK OF THE CULTURAL REVOLUTION
A Foreign Affairs Events
February 24. Ghanaian President K. Nkrumah is overthrown the same day as he begins a visit to China. The event signals a deterioration in relations between China and Ghana, the most important of several African countries to split with China in 1966.

April 15. A large-scale anti-Chinese demonstration takes place at the Chinese Embassy in Jakarta, with demonstrators ransacking the building.

B Domestic Political Events
May 7. Mao Zedong writes to Lin Biao calling on the PLA to be 'a great school': the May 7 directive.

May 9. China carries out a nuclear test, its first containing thermonuclear material.

May 16. The Politburo announces its decision to set up the Cultural Revolution Group, and calls for attacks on 'all representatives of the bourgeoisie who have infiltrated the

Party, government, army and cultural world'.

July 16. Surrounded by enormous publicity, Mao Zedong takes a swim in the Yangzi River at Wuhan.

August 8. The Eleventh Plenum of the Eighth CCPCC adopts its Sixteen Points, a decision in favour of the Cultural Revolution.

August 18. Mao Zedong, Lin Biao, Zhou Enlai and others preside over a gigantic rally in support of the Cultural Revolution in Tiananmen Square in the centre of Beijing. The rally reveals the existence of the Red Guards, the vanguard of the Cultural Revolution until mid–1968. Mao Zedong attends several similar enormous rallies over the next few months.

C Economic Events

January 1. *People's Daily* declares China to be completely free of foreign debt.

D Appointments, Dismissals, etc.

May 16. Luo Ruiqing is dismissed as chief of the General Staff of the PLA.

June 3. NCNA announces the decision to appoint Li Xuefeng as first secretary of the Beijing Municipal CCP Committee in place of Peng Zhen, under severe attack as a revisionist in the Cultural Revolution.

July 10. NCNA reveals that Chen Boda is the head of the Cultural Revolution Group.

August 1–12. The Eleventh Plenum of the Eighth CCPCC elects Lin Biao as the only vice-chairman of the Central Committee.

August 31. NCNA reveals that Jiang Qing is Chen Boda's first deputy in the Cultural Revolution Group.

E Cultural and Social Events

August 20. Red Guards in Beijing begin destroying 'bourgeois and feudal remnants' by forbidding various types of dress and literature, ransacking bookshops, private houses and other places. On August 22 they begin the closure, and often also ransacking, of Beijing's churches and other religious establishments.

September. *Quotations from Chairman Mao Zedong* (*Mao zhuxi yulu*), also known as *The Little Red Book*, is published in Shanghai.

F Births and Deaths

March 22. Philosopher Ai Siqi dies.

May 18. Writer Deng Tuo dies.

August 24. Writer and dramatist Shu Qingchun (pen-name Lao She) dies.

1967

A Foreign Affairs Events

August 22. Red Guards attack and ransack the office of the British chargé d'affaires in Beijing, burning down the main building.

September 5. China, Tanzania and Zambia sign an agreement in Beijing under which China will assist in the construction of the Tanzania–Zambia railway.

B Domestic Political Events

January 23. The CCPCC, Cultural Revolution Group and other bodies issue an urgent notice calling on the PLA to intervene in the Cultural Revolution on the side of the 'broad left-wing masses'.

January 31. The Heilongjiang Provincial Revolutionary Committee is set up. An alliance of revolutionary rebels, the PLA and revolutionary CCP cadres, it becomes the model for the Cultural Revolution's administrative system.

June 17. China explodes its first hydrogen bomb.

August 4. A rally in Wuhan celebrates the victory of the central forces in a civil war that had broken out in the city about two weeks earlier, after Zhou Enlai had attempted, on August 20 and 21, to mediate a complicated struggle between factions supporting and opposing Chen Zaidao, the regional commander of the Wuhan Military Region.

D Appointments, Dismissals, etc.

August 4. Zeng Siyu replaces Chen Zaidao as commander of the Wuhan Military Region.

F Births and Deaths

June 22. Former CCP leader Li Lisan dies.

August 15. Former Finance minister Kong Xiangxi (H. H. Kung) dies in the United States.

October 17. The last Emperor, Puyi, dies.

1968

A Foreign Affairs Events

August 23. China strongly denounces the Soviet Union for its invasion of Czechoslovakia, which began during the night of August 20–21.

B Domestic Political and Military Events

June 13. The CCPCC issues an urgent general cable, demanding an end to violent clashes on the railway at Liuzhou in Guangxi, where the system has come to a halt and military materials on their way to Vietnam have been stolen.

July 28. In the early hours of the morning, Mao Zedong and others meet with Red Guard leaders and criticize their indulging in armed struggle. The meeting signals the effective end of the most radical phase of the Cultural Revolution.

September 7. A rally in Beijing celebrates the setting up of revolutionary committees in all provinces, municipalities and autonomous regions, except Taiwan.

C Economic Events

October 1. The rail section of the bridge over the Yangzi River at Nanjing is formally opened to traffic. The road section is formally opened on December 29.

D Appointments, Dismissals, etc.

October 31. The communiqué of the Twelfth Plenum of the Eighth CCPCC announces that Liu Shaoqi has been expelled from the CCP once and for all and dismissed from all posts both inside and outside the Party.

E Cultural and Social Events

December 22. A Mao directive urging that 'educated young people' be sent to the countryside for 're-education by the poor and lower middle peasants' is broadcast.

F Births and Deaths

December 10. Playwright Tian Han dies.

December 18. Historian Jian Bozan dies.

December 26. Peking Opera actor Xun Huisheng dies.

1969

A Foreign Affairs Events

March 2. An armed clash takes place between Chinese and Soviet forces at Zhenbao (Damansky) Island in the Ussuri River on the eastern border.

March 15. A second major clash takes place on Zhenbao Island.

June 10. A major clash takes place between Chinese and Soviet forces on the Sino-Soviet border at Yumin in Xinjiang, the most serious of many clashes on the western border at about this time.

June 14. Zhou Enlai sends a statement of support to Huynh Tan Phat, president of the Provisional Revolutionary Government of the Republic of South Vietnam, set up on June 6.

September 11. Zhou Enlai and Soviet Prime Minister Kosygin meet at Beijing airport and discuss a number of matters, including the Sino-Soviet border.

December 22. A partial lifting of the United States trade embargo against China takes effect. Among other points, it allows American tourists to make unlimited private purchases of Chinese goods.

B Domestic Political Events

April 14. The Ninth CCP Congress adopts a new CCP Constitution that reaffirms

Marxism–Leninism–Mao Zedong thought as the theoretical basis of the Party.

September 23. China carries out its first successful underground nuclear test.

D Appointments, Dismissals, etc.

April 28. The First Plenum of the Ninth CCPCC elects Mao Zedong as chairman and Lin Biao as vice-chairman of the Politburo. Also on the Standing Committee are Chen Boda, Zhou Enlai and Kang Sheng.

E Cultural and Social Events

October 29. *Red Flag* publishes the first of the revised scripts of the 'model dramas': *Taking Tiger Mountain by Strategy* (*Zhiqu Weihu shan*).

F Births and Deaths

January 30. Li Zongren, former vice-president and then president of the Republic of China (ROC), dies in Beijing.

July 29. Historian and CCPCC member Fan Wenlan dies in Beijing.

October 11. Historian Wu Han dies.

November 12. Former PRC president Liu Shaoqi dies in Kaifeng in prison.

1970

A Foreign Affairs Events

May 4. Norodom Sihanouk, overthrown as head of the Cambodian state by a coup d'état on March 18, sets up his Royal Government of National Union of Kampuchea in Beijing. On the same day, the Chinese government denounces the United States troop movements into Cambodia, which were announced by US President Nixon on April 30, as a 'provocation to the Chinese people'.

May 5. China formally recognizes Sihanouk's Royal Government of National Union of Kampuchea.

B Domestic Political Events

April 24. The first Chinese space satellite is successfully launched into orbit.

August 23–25. At the Second Plenum of the Ninth CCPCC, held on Lushan, Jiangxi Province, several supporters of Lin Biao oppose an instruction of Mao Zedong, causing him to doubt Lin's loyalty.

November 24–December 4. The Third Hunan Provincial CCP Congress takes place; it is the first Party congress at provincial level since the Cultural Revolution began.

C Economic Events

July 1. The Chengdu–Kunming railway is formally opened to traffic.

D Appointments, Dismissals, etc.

December 13. NCNA reports that Hua Guofeng was elected first secretary of the Hunan Provincial CCP Committee by the Third Hunan Provincial CCP Congress.

F Births and Deaths

September 20. Vice-minister of Foreign Affairs Gong Peng dies.

September 23. Writer Zhao Shuli dies.

1971

A Foreign Affairs Events

April 10–17. An American table tennis team visits China, the first United States group at official or semi-official level to visit the country for many years. Zhou Enlai receives the delegation on April 14.

July 9–11. US President Nixon's Assistant for National Security Affairs, Dr Henry Kissinger, visits Beijing secretly, holding talks with Zhou Enlai.

July 15. President Nixon announces that he has accepted an invitation from Zhou Enlai to visit China before May 1972.

September 29–October 1. Minister of Foreign Trade Bai Xiangguo leads a delegation to France, the first PRC group at full ministerial level to visit Western Europe since 1949.

October 25. The PRC is admitted to the United Nations.

B Domestic Political Events

September 12. Lin Biao's alleged assassination attempt against Mao Zedong fails.

D Appointments, Dismissals, etc.

January 10. Zhang Chunqiao is elected first secretary of the Shanghai Municipal CCP Committee.

E Cultural and Social Events

November. The People's Literary Press publishes *Li Bai and Du Fu* (*Li Bai yu Du Fu*) by Guo Moruo, the first book on classical literature to be released in China since before the Cultural Revolution.

December 1. NCNA reports that over 340 well-preserved bronzes from about the eleventh century BC were excavated in September 1967.

F Births and Deaths

April 29. CCPCC member Li Siguang dies.

June 21. Historian Chen Yuan dies in Beijing.

September 13. CCP vice-chairman Lin Biao dies.

1972

A Foreign Affairs Events

February 21–28. US President Nixon visits China. On the last day a joint Sino-US communiqué is issued in Shanghai which declares, among other points, that the United States does not challenge the position held by all Chinese 'on either side of the Taiwan Strait' that 'there is but one China and that Taiwan is a part of China'.

August 16. Japanese air services between Japan and Shanghai begin.

September 9. China contracts with the US Boeing Aircraft Corporation to buy ten 707 civilian jet airliners.

September 25–30. Japanese Prime Minister Tanaka Kakuei visits China.

December 29. China signs a contract with the Tokyo Engineering Company of Japan to purchase an ethylene

manufacturing plant, the first whole-factory import by China for many years.

B Domestic Political Events

July 28. Reuter reports that the Chinese government has, through its embassy in Algiers, given the official Chinese account of the Lin Biao affair for the first time.

C Economic Events

October 1. The longest highway bridge over the Yellow River, at Beizhen in Shandong Province, is formally opened to traffic.

E Cultural and Social Events

May. The People's Literary Press publishes *The Bright Golden Road* (*Jinguang dadao*), a novel by Haoran.

July 31. NCNA reports the excavation of a well-preserved tomb near Changsha; over 2000 years old, it contains a female corpse and burial accessories.

F Births and Deaths

January 6. Chen Yi, former minister of Foreign Affairs, dies.

February 21. Zhang Guohua, first secretary of the Sichuan Provincial CCP Committee, dies.

March 26. Xie Fuzhi, former minister of Public Security, dies.

September 1. He Xiangning, chair of the Revolutionary Committee of the Chinese Nationalist Party, dies at the age of 92.

1973

A Foreign Affairs Events

January 29. Chairman Mao Zedong and others send a message of congratulations to the leaders of the Democratic Republic of Vietnam, the Provisional Revolutionary Government of South Vietnam and others on the signing of the Paris Peace Accords (January 27).

February 22. The United States and China announce their intention to establish a liaison office in each other's capitals. Air services, the first between China and Africa, are inaugurated between Shanghai and Addis Ababa.

September 11–17. The President of France, Georges Pompidou, visits China, the first West European head of state ever to have done so, and meets Chairman Mao on September 12.

B Domestic Political Events

August 24. On the first day of the Tenth National CCP Congress, Zhou Enlai gives the official version of the Lin Biao affair and Wang Hongwen reports on the revision of the CCP Constitution, saying that cultural revolutions will recur.

D Appointments, Dismissals, etc.

April 12. Deng Xiaoping is mentioned as a vice-premier.

August 30. The First Plenum of the Tenth CCPCC elects Mao Zedong as chairman and Zhou Enlai, Wang Hongwen, Kang Sheng, Ye Jianying and Li Desheng as vice-chairmen.

E Cultural and Social Events

April 11–16. The Vienna Philharmonic Orchestra visits China.

1974

A Foreign Affairs Events

January 19–20. Chinese troops seize the Xisha Islands from the Republic of Vietnam.

April 10. Deng Xiaoping addresses the UN General Assembly. He declares that the United States and the Soviet Union are seeking world hegemony, but that the international situation is favourable to the developing countries, and that China belongs to the Third World.

May 28–June 2. The Malaysian Prime Minister, Tun Abdul Razak, visits China, his visit resulting in the establishment of diplomatic relations.

August 21. At the UN World Population Conference held in Bucharest, the Chinese representative, Huang Shuze, attacks the Malthusian theory of the population explosion as a fallacy.

October 29. The Beijing–Karachi–Paris route of the Civil Aviation Administration of China (CAAC) is formally begun.

B Domestic Political Events

January 1. An editorial in *People's Daily* and other major newspapers declares the criticism of Confucius to be part of the criticism of Lin Biao. This launches a mass movement known as the Campaign to Criticize Lin Biao and Confucius.

E Cultural and Social Events

January 30. *People's Daily* launches public criticism of the film *China* directed by the Italian M. Antonioni.

September 1–16. The Asian Games take place in Teheran, with China sending its largest sports team ever to go abroad.

F Births and Deaths

April 19. Fu Zuoyi dies.

November 29. Former minister of National Defence, Peng Dehuai, dies.

1975

A Foreign Affairs Events

April 7. Swissair inaugurates its Zurich–Geneva–Athens–Bombay– Beijing–Shanghai air service.

April 30. Mao Zedong and others cable a message of congratulations to leaders of the Democratic Republic of Vietnam, Provisional Revolutionary Government of South Vietnam and others on the liberation of Saigon, which took place the same day.

June 7–10. Philippines President Ferdinand Marcos visits China, resulting in the establishment of diplomatic relations.

June 30–July 6. Thai Prime Minister Kukrit Pramoj visits China, resulting in the establishment of diplomatic relations.

December 1–5. US President Gerald Ford visits China and meets Mao Zedong on December 2.

B Domestic Political Events

May 3. At a meeting of the Politburo, Mao Zedong warns Jiang Qing, Wang Hongwen, Zhang Chunqiao and Yao Wenyuan against 'functioning as a gang of four'.

D Appointments, Dismissals, etc.

January 8–10. The Second Plenum of the Tenth CCPCC elects Deng Xiaoping as vice-chairman of the CCPCC.

December 19. Zhao Ziyang is identified for the first time as first secretary of the Sichuan Provincial Party Committee.

E Cultural and Social Events

August 23. *Guangming Daily* carries articles attacking the classical novel *Water Margin (Shuihu zhuan)*.

F Births and Deaths

March 8. Peking Opera actor Zhou Xinfang dies.

April 2. NPC Deputy Chairman Dong Biwu dies.

April 5. Chiang Kaishek dies.

December 16. Kang Sheng dies.

G Natural Disasters

February 4. A large-scale earthquake strikes the Haicheng–Yingkou region of Liaoning Province.

1976 THE DEATH OF MAO ZEDONG AND THE FALL OF THE GANG OF FOUR

A Foreign Affairs Events

May 27. Pakistan's Prime Minister Z. A. Bhutto meets Mao Zedong, the last high-ranking foreigner to do so and the last of numerous world leaders to visit Mao in the final years of his life.

July 14. The Tanzania–Zambia railway, China's largest foreign aid project, is formally opened to traffic.

B Domestic Political Events

February 10. A poster campaign commences at Beijing University against 'a capitalist roader', clearly Deng Xiaoping, and gathers momentum over the next months.

April 5. Demonstrators in mourning for Zhou Enlai in Tiananmen Square, central Beijing, clash with police; serious violence erupts: the Tiananmen Incident. Similar incidents occur in numerous other parts of China just after this one.

April 7. NCNA condemns the Tiananmen Incident as a 'counter-revolutionary political incident'.

October 6. Four Politburo members, Jiang Qing, Zhang Chunqiao, Yao Wenyuan and Wang Hongwen, are secretly arrested and imprisoned: the fall of the 'gang of four'.

October 24. A gigantic demonstration takes place in Tiananmen Square in support of Hua Guofeng's appointment as CCP chairman and against the 'gang of four'. Wu De claims that Mao specifically chose Hua as his successor and attacks the 'gang of four' for attempting to split the CCP and seize power.

December 10–27. The Second National Conference on Learning from Dazhai in Agriculture is held in Beijing. Hua Guofeng makes a speech on December 25, claiming that major civil war would have broken out had the 'gang of four' not been suppressed.

December 25. For the first time in the PRC, NCNA publishes Mao Zedong's speech of April 25, 1956, 'On the Ten Major Relationships'.

C Economic Events

April 23. NCNA reports the sinking of China's deepest oil well to this point, in Sichuan Province.

August 23. China's first 50 000-tonne oil tanker, the *West Lake (Xihu)*, is launched in Dalian.

D Appointments, Dismissals, etc.

February 3. Hua Guofeng is appointed acting premier of the State Council, in succession to Zhou Enlai.

April 7. Hua Guofeng is appointed first vice-chairman of the CCPCC and premier of the State Council; Deng Xiaoping is dismissed from all posts inside and outside the Party.

October 7. The CCPCC appoints Hua Guofeng as its chairman and also as chairman of its Military Affairs Committee in succession to Mao Zedong.

E Cultural and Social Events

November 5. A *People's Daily* editorial points to a less rigid policy on the arts in the wake of the fall of the 'gang of four'.

F Births and Deaths

January 8. Premier Zhou Enlai dies of cancer in Beijing.

July 6. NPC Standing Committee chairman Zhu De dies in Beijing.

July 27. Musical composer Ma Ke dies.

September 9. CCP chairman Mao Zedong dies in Beijing at 12.10 a.m.

G Natural Disasters

July 28. An extremely severe earthquake, in terms of human casualties among the worst in world history, strikes the Tangshan–Fengnan area of Hebei Province.

1977

A Foreign Affairs Events

November 1. A *People's Daily* article of over 35 000 characters extols Mao Zedong's theory of the three worlds as 'a major contribution to Marxism–Leninism'.

December 31. The Kampuchean Ambassador in Beijing issues a statement charging Vietnam with having launched systematic aggression against Pol Pot's Kampuchea since September 1977.

B Domestic Political Events

May 24. The Chairman Mao Memorial Hall is completed in Tiananmen Square, Beijing.

August 18. The Eleventh National Congress of the CCP (held August 12–18) adopts

the Party Constitution, under which Marxism–Leninism–Mao Zedong thought remains the 'guiding ideology and theoretical basis' of the CCP.

C Economic Events

April 20–May 13. The National Conference on Learning from Daqing in Industry is held first in Daqing and later in Beijing.

D Appointments, Dismissals, etc.

July 21. The Third Plenum of the Tenth CCPCC confirms Hua Guofeng as chairman of the CCPCC and its Military Affairs Committee, restores Deng Xiaoping to vice-chairmanship of the CCPCC and other posts, and expels Zhang Chunqiao, Jiang Qing, Yao Wenyuan and Wang Hongwen from the Party, dismissing them from all posts.

August 19. The First Plenum of the Eleventh CCPCC elects five members to the Politburo's Standing Committee: Hua Guofeng, Ye Jianying, Deng Xiaoping, Li Xiannian and Wang Dongxing.

E Cultural and Social Events

April 15. The People's Press publishes Volume 5 of *The Selected Works of Mao Zedong* (*Mao Zedong xuanji*).

F Births and Deaths

June 17. Literary figure Aying dies.

1978 THE THIRD PLENUM INTRODUCES THE POLICIES OF REFORM

A Foreign Affairs Events

February 16. China and Japan sign a long-term trade agreement, under which exports from each side over the period 1978 to 1985 will total US$10 000 million.

May 24. A spokesman of the State Council accuses Vietnam of persecuting Chinese residents in Vietnam, signalling a public split between China and Vietnam.

July 3. The Chinese government informs the Vietnamese government of its decision to cease all economic and technical aid to Vietnam, and recalls its experts from Vietnam.

August 12. China and Japan sign their Treaty of Peace and Friendship in Beijing.

August 25. A Sino-Vietnamese armed clash occurs at Friendship Pass on their mutual border.

November 8. At a press conference in Bangkok, Deng Xiaoping declares that the Soviet–Vietnamese Treaty of Friendship and Cooperation, signed on November 3, is a threat to China and to peace and security in the Asia–Pacific region.

December 13. The Coca-Cola Co. reaches an agreement with China to sell Coca-Cola there and to open a bottling plant in Shanghai.

December 16 (15 in the United States). China and the United States simultaneously issue a joint communiqué of their decision to establish diplomatic relations as from January 1, 1979.

December 19. In Seattle in the United States, Boeing announces that China has purchased three Boeing 747 airliners.

B Domestic Political Events

November 19. In the first batch of posters on 'democracy wall' in Beijing, one appears accusing Mao Zedong of supporting and buttressing the 'gang of four'.

December 18–22. The Third Plenum of the Eleventh CCPCC shifts the entire stress of the Party on to socialist modernization and begins the reform period of Chinese history.

C Economic Events

October 12. Air services begin between Hong Kong and Guangzhou.

December 18–22. The Third Plenum of the Eleventh CCPCC takes the first steps towards restoring the use of market mechanisms in rural China.

D Appointments, Dismissals, etc.

March 5. The NPC elects Hua Guofeng as premier of the State Council and Deng Xiaoping, Li Xiannian, Chen Yonggui and others as vice-premiers.

December 22. The Third Plenum of the Eleventh CCPCC announces that Chen Yun has been elected as a vice-chairman of the Central Committee and that Hu Yaobang and others have been elected to the Politburo.

E Cultural and Social Events

April 22–May 16. The Ministry of Education convenes a National Conference on Education Work in Beijing.

May 27–June 5. The Chinese National Federation of Literature and Art Circles holds a major conference on literature and art.

June 15. Prominent Japanese conductor Seiji Ozawa conducts the Central Symphony Orchestra at a concert in Beijing, the first public concert by a Chinese symphony orchestra conducted by a foreigner since 1949.

September 8–17. The Fourth National Women's Congress is held in Beijing.

September 11. *Chinese Youth* (*Zhongguo qingnian*) resumes publication after a twelve-year break, one of many periodicals to do so at about this time.

October 11–21. The Ninth National Congress of Chinese Trade Unions is held in Beijing.

October 16–26. The Tenth National Congress of the Chinese Communist Youth League (CCYL) is held in Beijing.

F Births and Deaths

June 12. Scientist, writer and CCPCC member Guo Moruo dies.

August 3. Luo Ruiqing, former chief of the General Staff, dies.

G Natural Disasters

November 2. NCNA reports a nationwide drought in 1978 that is more severe 'in length of time, breadth of scope and seriousness of extent' than the great droughts of 1934, 1959 and 1966.

1979

A Foreign Affairs Events

January 7. The Chinese government denounces Vietnam for aggression against Democratic Kampuchea. Vietnam had invaded Kampuchea, beginning on December 25, 1978, and took Phnom Penh on January 7, 1979.

January 28–February 5. Deng Xiaoping visits the United States, the first visit there by a senior PRC leader.

February 7. In Tokyo, Deng Xiaoping tells Japanese Prime Minister Ohira Masayoshi that Vietnam must be punished for its invasion of Kampuchea. Deng returns to Beijing the next day.

February 17. Chinese troops launch attacks into Vietnamese territory. Both China and Vietnam issue statements, the Chinese claiming that they want only a peaceful and stable border and will withdraw after counterattacking the Vietnamese aggressors; the Vietnamese denouncing the Chinese authorities for starting a war of aggression against Vietnam.

March 5. Chinese troops complete the seizure of Langson in Vietnam; China states that its troops will begin withdrawal the same day (March 5).

March 16. Chinese Foreign Minister Huang Hua announces that Chinese troops have completed their withdrawal from Vietnam the same day (March 16).

May 14. An NCNA commentary gives China's case for claiming ownership of the Nansha and Xisha Islands, a claim also made by Vietnam.

October 15–November 6. Hua Guofeng visits France, West Germany, Britain and Italy, the first tour of Western Europe by a PRC head of government.

December 30. The Chinese government issues a statement denouncing the Soviet Union for its invasion of Afghanistan, which began on December 27.

B Domestic Political Events

July 1. The Second Session of the Fifth NPC adopts seven laws, including China's first *Criminal Law* and the *Organic Law of the Local People's Congresses and Local People's Governments*.

March 30. In a speech at a forum on the principles for the CCP's theoretical work, Deng Xiaoping proposes 'four cardinal principles': 'keeping to the socialist road, upholding the dictatorship of the proletariat, upholding the leadership of the CCP and upholding Marxism-Leninism and Mao Zedong Thought.'

December 6. The Beijing Municipal Revolutionary Committee bans big- or small-character posters in public places, except in one part of one specified park, signifying the end of the 1978–79 pro-democracy movement.

C Economic Events

October 4. The China International Trust and Investment Corporation (CITIC) is formally established in Beijing.

D Appointments, Dismissals, etc.

February 23. Peng Zhen is appointed Director of the Commission for Legal Affairs of the NPC Standing Committee.

E Cultural and Social Events

January 1. All publications appearing in China in languages using the Roman alphabet begin using the *Hanyu pinyin* system of romanization.

February. Wu Han's play *Hai Rui's Dismissal* is restaged.

June. The literary periodical *The Present* (*Dangdai*) begins publication.

October 16. Democracy and human rights activist Wei Jingsheng is sentenced to a prison term of fifteen years for passing on military intelligence to a foreigner, and for counter-revolutionary agitation. (An appeal to a higher court was rejected on November 6.)

October 30–November 16. The Fourth Congress of the Federation of Literature and Art Circles of China takes place in Beijing, the first since 1960.

F Births and Deaths
September 25. Author Zhou Libo dies in Beijing.
December 3. Former CCP leader Zhang Guotao dies in Toronto.

1980

A Foreign Affairs Events
March 24. The Chinese Olympic Committee decides to boycott the Moscow summer Olympic Games.
April 17. The International Monetary Fund admits China as a member.
May 15. The World Bank admits China to representation in the World Bank Group.
May 18. China successfully launches its first carrier rocket, to the Pacific Ocean.
October 27–30. Thai Prime Minister Prem Tinsulanond visits China.
December 3. The Chinese government makes an unsuccessful attempt to persuade the Dutch government to reconsider its decision of November 29 to sell two submarines to Taiwan.

B Domestic Political Events
January 1. Six new laws come into operation, including the *Organic Law of the Local People's Congresses and Local People's Governments*, under which the posts of provincial governors and mayors are restored.
February 29. The Fifth Plenum of the Eleventh CCPCC adopts a communiqué which, among many other matters, rehabilitates Liu Shaoqi posthumously.
May 15. A CCPCC circular is published calling for more consideration of Tibet's special needs and more efforts to train Tibetan cadres and those of other minority nationalities.
May 22–31. Hu Yaobang and others make an inspection tour of Tibet.

October 20–December 29. A trial is held in Beijing concerning the activities of the 'gang of four', six other living people and six deceased. The charges fall under four headings, including plotting to overthrow the 'political power of the dictatorship of the proletariat', persecuting many cadres and others, and plotting to assassinate Mao Zedong.
December 22. *People's Daily* declares that Mao Zedong made great mistakes during his last years, and that the Cultural Revolution which he led was a great disaster.

C Economic Events
June 20. The Tibetan government announces new economic policies, including exemption from all taxes on agriculture and animal husbandry for two years.
September 10. The NPC approves the Income Tax Law Concerning Joint Ventures with Chinese and Foreign Investment of the PRC, and the Individual Income Tax Law of the PRC.
November 4. Inauguration of direct flights between Beijing and Hong Kong.

D Appointments, Dismissals, etc.
February 29. The Fifth Plenum of the Eleventh CCPCC announces the election of Hu Yaobang as secretary-general of the CCPCC; the election of Hu Yaobang and Zhao Ziyang as members of the Standing Committee of the Politburo; and agreement to the requests of Wang Dongxing, Wu De and others to resign from the Central Committee.
September 10. The Third Session of the Fifth NPC approves many changes in the leadership. They include: Zhao Ziyang's replacing Hua Guofeng as premier of the State Council; the resignation of Deng Xiaoping, Li Xiannian, Chen Yun and others as vice-premiers due to old age; and Chen Yonggui's dismissal as vice-premier.

E Cultural and Social Events

February 12. The NPC Standing Committee approves regulations for the award of the academic degrees of Bachelor, Master and Doctor.

August. The PRC's first encyclopedic yearbook, *Chinese Encyclopedic Yearbook 1980 (Zhongguo baike nianjian)*, is published in Beijing and Shanghai.

September 10. The NPC approves the revised *Marriage Law of the PRC*, which, among many other points, raises the marriage age for men to 22 and for women to 20; and the *Nationality Law of the PRC*, which prohibits dual nationality for any Chinese national.

F Births and Deaths

March 8. Poet Li Ji dies.

July 10. Journalist Chen Kehan dies in Beijing.

October 10. Film actor Zhao Dan dies.

December 25. Historian Gu Jiegang dies in Beijing.

G Natural Disasters

June 26–27. Hurricanes, wind and hailstorms strike coastal Zhejiang, killing 151 people and causing severe damage to houses and crops.

1981

A Foreign Affairs Events

January 7. CAAC formally begins its Beijing– New York air service.

January 19. China asks that Sino-Dutch diplomatic relations be demoted to chargé d'affaires level, because of the Netherlands' public reaffirmation, on January 16, of its decision to sell two submarines to Taiwan. The dispute culminates in the withdrawal of ambassadors on February 27.

October 21. Premier Zhao Ziyang meets US President Reagan at the Cancun Summit, an international conference held in Mexico to discuss the North–South relationship.

October 29. In Washington, Foreign Minister Huang Hua criticizes the United States' policy of selling advanced armaments to Taiwan.

December 16. A conference of Chinese and Japanese officials concludes with an announcement of US$1.37 billion of Japanese financial aid to Chinese industry, including the first stage of the Baoshan steel mill.

B Domestic Political Events

January 25. The special court trying the 'gang of four' and others holds its last session. It condemns Jiang Qing and Zhang Chunqiao to death with two-year reprieves, Wang Hongwen to life imprisonment, and the others to long terms of imprisonment.

June 29. The communiqué of the Sixth Plenum of the Eleventh CCPCC reevaluates the role of the CCP since 1949; it attacks the Cultural Revolution as a total disaster, and criticizes Mao Zedong for initiating and leading the Cultural Revolution, as well as many of the other initiatives he took in his later years.

September 30. Ye Jianying calls for negotiations, on the basis of reciprocity, with the Guomindang over Taiwan. He states that after reunification, Taiwan could enjoy a high degree of autonomy and retain its own armed forces.

D Appointments, Dismissals, etc.

June 29. The Sixth Plenum of the Eleventh CCPCC announces that Hu Yaobang has replaced Hua Guofeng as chairman of the CCPCC, with Deng Xiaoping as chairman of its Military Commission; it also announces the election of Zhao Ziyang and Hua Guofeng as vice-chairmen of the Central Committee.

E Cultural and Social Events

January 1. The People's Press publishes Volume I of *Selected Works of Zhou Enlai (Zhou Enlai xuanji)*, with the final volume following on December 14, 1984.

June 1. *China Daily*, the PRC's first English-language daily, begins publication.

September 25. At a meeting to commemorate the centenary of Lu Xun's birth, Hu Yaobang criticizes bourgeois liberalization and other 'currently widespread' unhealthy tendencies in literature and art work.

F Births and Deaths

March 27. Famous writer Shen Yanbing (pen-name Mao Dun) dies in Beijing.

May 29. Song Qingling, former vice president of the PRC, dies in Beijing.

G Natural Disasters

July 9–14. Torrential rain in Sichuan causes serious flooding, killing over 700 people and rendering 150 000 homeless.

1982

A Foreign Affairs Events

March 24. In a major speech in Tashkent, Soviet President Leonid Brezhnev appeals for better Sino-Soviet relations 'on the basis of mutual respect for each other's interests, non-interference in each other's affairs, and mutual benefit'.

April 13. The US government formally notifies Congress of the decision to sell military spare parts to Taiwan. The following day the Chinese Foreign Ministry issues a strong protest against 'this act of infringing upon China's sovereignty'.

May 31–June 5. Zhao Ziyang visits Japan, meeting the Emperor on June 1.

June 11. Chinese Foreign Minister Huang Hua puts forward China's position on disarmament to the Second Special Session of the UN General Assembly on Disarmament.

June 25. *People's Daily* expresses China's strong support for the Coalition Government of Democratic Kampuchea, set up on June 22.

August 17. The United States and China sign a joint communiqué on the issue of arms sales to Taiwan. The United States promises that it will not actually increase the level of sales, either in quality or quantity, and states its intention 'gradually to reduce its sale of arms to Taiwan, leading, over a period of time, to a final resolution'.

September 22–26. British Prime Minister Margaret Thatcher visits China. On September 24 China and Britain agree to begin discussions on the future of Hong Kong.

September 26. Soviet President L. Brezhnev calls normalization of relations with China a top priority.

September 27. In Hong Kong, Margaret Thatcher states her belief that the unequal treaties of the nineteenth century are still valid and both sides should continue to abide by them. The Chinese Foreign Ministry strongly criticizes the statement on September 30, arguing that the unequal treaties are invalid, that Hong Kong is part of Chinese territory, and that China will recover Hong Kong when conditions are ripe.

November 14. Before leaving Beijing for the funeral of Soviet President Leonid Brezhnev, Chinese Foreign Minister Huang Hua describes Brezhnev as 'an outstanding statesman of the Soviet Union'.

December 20. Zhao Ziyang arrives in Egypt at the beginning of an African tour, leaving Cairo for Algeria on December 24, and going to Morocco on December 27 and to Guinea on December 30.

B Domestic Political Events

January 11. Deng Xiaoping sums up the notion of 'one country, two systems' for the first time, saying that it should apply to both Taiwan and Hong Kong. It means that specific territories should be allowed to maintain their own social system while being recognized as part of China.

March 2. Zhao Ziyang gives a report on the restructuring of the government, including reducing the current number of vice-premiers from thirteen to two.

July 1. The PRC begins its third national census, mainly completing enumeration by July 10. The main figures are released on October 27.

September 6. The Twelfth National Congress of the CCP adopts a new CCP Constitution, under which the position of Party chairman is replaced by that of general secretary, and a Central Advisory Commission is established.

December 20–30. The Eleventh National Congress of the CCYL is held in Beijing.

C Economic Events

February 15. The China National Offshore Oil Corporation is officially set up to take charge of the exploitation of offshore petroleum resources, in cooperation with foreign enterprises.

March 8. The NPC Standing Committee adopts provisions for the severe punishment of criminals who do great damage to the national economy.

November 30. Zhao Ziyang gives his report on the Sixth Five-Year Plan to the NPC.

D Appointments, Dismissals, etc.

May 4. As part of the restructuring of the government, the NPC Standing Committee resolves that Wan Li and Yao Yilin will remain vice-premiers, but that the other eleven are to be removed from their posts.

July 27. *People's Daily* reports the dismissal of Yang Yibang, vice-minister of Chemical Industry, for corruption and for violating Party discipline.

September 12. The First Plenum of the Twelfth CCPCC elects Hu Yaobang as general secretary and, in addition, Ye Jianying, Deng Xiaoping, Zhao Ziyang, Li Xiannian and Chen Yun as the members of the Politburo's Standing Committee. It also elects Deng Xiaoping as chairman of the Military Commission of the Central Committee.

September 13. The First Plenum of the Twelfth CCPCC approves the election of Deng Xiaoping as chairman of the CCP Central Advisory Commission; and of Chen Yun as first secretary of the Central Commission for Discipline Inspection.

E Cultural and Social Events

January 10. Volume 1 of *The Selected Works of Liu Shaoqi* (Liu Shaoqi xuanji) is released to the public.

November 5. The drama *Warning Signal* (Juedui xinhao), by Gao Xingjian, is premiered in Beijing.

F Births and Deaths

May 10. Demographer Ma Yinchu dies, aged 101 years.

G Natural Disasters

May 20. Beijing Radio reports that 506 people have been killed in floods in Guangdong Province.

July. Floods in Sichuan Province result in 718 dead and over 6000 injured, according to a report of August 20.

1983
A Foreign Affairs Events

January 1–17. Zhao Ziyang continues his official visit to Africa, arriving in Gabon on January 1, in Zaire on January 2, in the Congo on January 4, in Zambia on January 5, in Zimbabwe on January 9, in Tanzania on January 11 and in Kenya on January 15.

March 18. A United Nations spokesperson announces that Qian Xinzhong, Chinese minister in charge of the State Family Planning Commission, is one of the first two winners of the 1983 UN population awards.

May 3–7. French president François Mitterand visits China.

May 17. A *People's Daily* editorial hails Hu Yaobang's first visit to Eastern Europe as CCP general secretary as a success. Hu had arrived in Bucharest on May 5 and in Belgrade on May 10 for official visits to Romania and Yugoslavia.

October 1. A Burundi student is beaten up and injured in Beijing by two hotel attendants. The incident provokes African students into demonstrating shortly afterwards. On October 8, the Beijing Municipal Public Security Bureau arrests the two attendants.

October 11. China's application to join the International Atomic Energy Agency is approved.

November 23–30. Hu Yaobang visits Japan, the first time a CCP general secretary has visited a non-socialist country. On November 25 he addresses the Japanese Diet, the first Chinese leader ever to have done so.

B Domestic Political Events

January 25. The death sentence on Jiang Qing and Zhang Chunqiao (see January 25, 1981) is commuted to life imprisonment.

October 11. The Second Plenum of the Twelfth CCPCC adopts its decision 'on Party Consolidation', beginning a campaign against 'spiritual pollution'.

C Economic Events

April 10. China's deepest offshore oil well to this point, the Pinghu in the East China Sea, is completed.

July 12. A meeting in Beijing marks the inauguration of the China Petrochemical Corporation.

July 15. Guangdong provincial official sources reveal plans for a very large-scale Pearl River Delta economic zone based on Guangzhou, which will eventually include Hong Kong and Macau.

October 31. The first business in China wholly run by Japanese investment, the Sanyo (Shekou) Company, begins operating in Guangdong Province.

December 14. A ceremony marks the formal commencement of work on the massive Three Gorges Dam Project.

D Appointments, Dismissals, etc.

June 18. The Fourth Session of the Sixth NPC elects Li Xiannian as president of the PRC, and Peng Zhen as chairman of the NPC Standing Committee.

E Cultural and Social Events

May 5. The Chinese premiere of Arthur Miller's play *Death of a Salesman* takes place, directed by the author.

May 27. China confers doctoral degrees on the first batch of postgraduate research students trained in China by its own educators.

July 1. The People's Press publishes *The Selected Works of Deng Xiaoping* (*Deng Xiaoping xuanji*).

July 15. *People's Daily* reveals that in Anyang, Henan Province, police had seized a gang on November 25, 1982 for engaging in kidnapping and selling women and children. Later investigations by police in Sichuan, Henan, Shandong and Gansu Provinces resulted in the arrest of over 50 people. The gang had kidnapped more than 150 women.

July 25. The secretary of the CCP's Central Commission for Discipline Inspection, Han Guang, reveals that economic crimes, including smuggling, graft, bribery, speculation and fraud, have reached a record high since the founding of the PRC.

August 1. The People's Press publishes *The Selected Works of Zhu De* (*Zhu De xuanji*).

September 2–12. The Fifth National Women's Congress is held in Beijing.

September 18–October 1. China's Fifth National Games are held in Shanghai.

December 22. The feminist drama *A Friend Comes in a Time of Need* (*Fengyu guren lai*), by Bai Fengxi, is premiered in Beijing.

F Births and Deaths

February 22. Economist Sun Yefang dies.

June 10. Sino-Japanese relations authority Liao Chengzhi dies of a heart attack.

September 22. Former Foreign minister Qiao Guanhua dies.

September 30. Tan Zhenlin, vice-chairman of the Central Advisory Commission of the CCP, dies.

G Natural Disasters

July 21. A State Council directive on flood prevention makes reference to a serious situation along the Yangzi River and dangerously high water levels in other rivers, such as the Yellow, Huai and Hai. Serious flooding is reported in many parts of China, especially Sichuan, at about this time.

1984

A Foreign Affairs Events

January 1. China formally becomes a member of the International Atomic Energy Agency.

January 10. Zhao Ziyang arrives in Washington for an official visit to the United States.

January 16–23. Zhao Ziyang visits Canada, the first Chinese premier to do so.

February 1. China and the Netherlands agree to upgrade their relations to ambassadorial level, after the Netherlands decides not to grant a permit for the further export of arms to Taiwan (see January 19, 1981).

April 26–May 1. US President Reagan pays an official visit to China.

May 30–June 16. Zhao Ziyang makes a visit to Western Europe, which takes him to France (May 30–June 3), Belgium (June 3–6), Sweden (June 6–8), Denmark (June 8–10), Norway (June 10–13) and Italy (June 13–16).

December 19. In Beijing, British Prime Minister Margaret Thatcher and Chinese Premier Zhao Ziyang sign the Sino-British Joint Declaration on Hong Kong (already initialled on September 26). It states that sovereignty will be resumed by the PRC over Hong Kong with effect from July 1, 1997. However, for 50 years, Hong Kong 'will enjoy a high degree of autonomy, except in foreign and defence affairs', as well as 'executive, legislative and independent judicial power', with the current laws remaining basically unchanged.

B Domestic Political Events

June 22–23. Deng Xiaoping meets with business and other leaders from Hong Kong. He tells them that China's policy on Hong Kong is firm and that Hong Kong's current socioeconomic system 'will remain unchanged after China resumes the exercise of its sovereignty over Hong Kong in 1997': the 'one country, two systems' formula.

July 20. *People's Daily* reports a decision by the CCPCC that a 'major decentralization' of power should be implemented.

October 30. The State Bureau of Nuclear Safety is formally established.

November 27. Yang Jingren, head of the CCP's United Front Work Department, tells three representatives of the Dalai Lama in Beijing that he is welcome to return to China, either on a short- or long-term basis, but requiring, among other points, that he and his followers 'will contribute to upholding China's unity and promoting solidarity between the Han and Tibetan nationalities, and among all nationalities, and the modernization programme'.

December 7. A *People's Daily* article calls for the study of the general laws and methodology of Marxism, but deplores regarding Marxism as dogma. It states that 'we cannot look to the books of Marx or Lenin to solve our problems today'; the last four words were amended the following day to 'solve *all* our problems today'.

C Economic Events

July. Measures aimed at stimulating the Tibetan economy take effect, including the shifting of emphasis from agriculture to animal husbandry, the provision by the People's Bank of China of more interest-free and low-interest loans for Tibet, and exemption from taxation for some enterprises there.

August 7. The 476 km South Xinjiang railway, linking Turpan and Korla, is opened to traffic.

September 1. NCNA reports that China's first nuclear reactor has been declared operational.

October 20. The Third Plenum of the Twelfth CCPCC adopts its decision 'on reform of the economic structure'. It shifts the focus of reform to urban enterprises, calls for the conscious application of the law of value and for the establishment of a rational price system, and urges 'a deep-going transformation of the socialist superstructure' through 'the separation of the functions of government and enterprises as well as simpler and decentralized administration'.

E Cultural and Social Events

February 15. The first volume of *The Selected Works of Chen Yun* (*Chen Yun xuanji*) is published, with Volume 2 following on July 15.

March 12. The Standing Committee of the Sixth NPC adopts the *Patent Law of the PRC* to encourage inventions and creations and to protect patent rights.

April 8. China launches its first experimental communications satellite.

May 31. The Second Session of the Sixth NPC adopts the Law on Regional Autonomy for Minority Nationalities of the PRC.

July 28. At the 23rd Summer Olympic Games in Los Angeles, China wins the first gold medal of the Games and the first ever won by China when marksman Xu Haifeng wins the free pistol-shooting event.

F Births and Deaths

February 5. Senior General Su Yu dies.

April 19. He Zizhen, Mao Zedong's former wife, dies.

May 17. Educator and social scientist Cheng Fangwu dies.

August 11. Theoretician Li Weihan dies.

1985

A Foreign Affairs Events

February 7. China's first trade centre in Western Europe is opened in Hamburg.

March 13. Li Peng attends the funeral of the Soviet President Konstantin Chernenko in Moscow. The next day he meets Mikhail Gorbachev, the new Soviet Party general secretary, and shares with him the hope for major improvements in Sino-Soviet relations.

March 21. The Standing Committee of the Sixth NPC adopts the *Foreign Economic Contract Law of the PRC*.

March 30. The American Agency for International Development announces its decision to cut US$10 million from its donation to the UN Fund for Population Activities, because of the Fund's support for China's population and abortion policies.

May 15. Direct air services between China and Singapore begin.

June 8. A Chinese government statement denounces American attacks on China's family planning program as interference in its domestic policies. The statement disputes allegations that the population policies infringe human rights.

October 28–November 12. Premier Zhao Ziyang makes a visit to Colombia, Brazil, Argentina and Venezuela, the first ever trip by a Chinese premier to Latin America.

B Domestic Political Events

June 4. Deng Xiaoping, chairman of the Central Military Commission, announces China's intention to reduce the size of its army by one million within two years.

September 18–23. A National Conference of the CCP takes place, with closing session speeches by Deng Xiaoping, Chen Yun and Li Xiannian.

C Economic Events

March 27. Zhao Ziyang's report on the work of the government, given at the Third

Session of the Sixth NPC, emphasizes that the two major tasks in the reform of China's economic structure in 1985 are changes in the wage and price systems.

September 23. The National Conference adopts the CCPCC's Proposal for the Seventh Five-Year Plan for National Economic and Social Development (1986–90).

D Appointments, Dismissals, etc.

March 21. Chen Muhua is appointed president of the People's Bank of China; Zheng Tuobin replaces her as minister of Foreign Economic Relations and Trade.

June 18. The NPC Standing Committee announces the appointment of nine new ministers, including Li Peng as minister in charge of the State Education Commission; all ministers have received a higher education degree.

July 30. A CCPCC report is released stating that the Hainan Administrative Region Party vice-secretary and Hainan People's Government head Lei Yu and his colleague Chen Yuyi have been dismissed for organizing a large-scale smuggling network for the corrupt import and resale of cars, minibuses, television sets, video recorders and motorcycles.

September 16. The Fourth Plenum of the Twelfth CCPCC approves the resignations of 64 of its members (18 per cent of the total) on the grounds of old age. Among these are ten members of the Politburo, including Ye Jianying, Wang Zhen, Li Desheng and Deng Yingchao.

September 24. The Fifth Plenum of the Twelfth CCPCC elects six new members to the Politburo: Tian Jiyun, Qiao Shi, Li Peng, Wu Xueqian, Hu Qili and Yao Yilin; they replace the ten who had sent their resignations to the Fourth Plenum. The appointments

implement a policy of putting younger and better educated people into senior leadership positions.

E Cultural and Social Events

May 19. China's defeat by Hong Kong in a football match in Beijing results in a destructive riot, the most serious over a sporting loss since 1949, and the sentence (on June 18) of five people to prison terms ranging from four to 30 months.

May 28. The CCPCC's 'Decision on the Reform of the Educational System' is released by NCNA. The Decision calls for education to be geared to the modernization program, the world and the future, and urges the universalization and improvement of basic education.

October 18. The Bolshoi Ballet performs in Beijing for the first time for more than two decades.

November 20. Students march in Beijing to oppose Japanese politicoeconomic influence in China.

December 10. Some 4000 students rally in Beijing in support of the open-door policy.

December 22. In China's first public anti-nuclear demonstration, several hundred students, including many Uygurs, protest in central Beijing against nuclear testing in Xinjiang.

F Births and Deaths

June 8. Literary and art critic Hu Feng dies.

June 12. Mathematician Hua Luogeng dies in Tokyo.

August 12. General Xiao Hua dies.

October 22. Xu Shiyou, vice-chairman of the CCP's Central Advisory Commission, dies.

G Natural Disasters, Accidents

July–August. Torrential rains and flooding in Liaoning, Guizhou and Sichuan kill some 1000 people, leave thousands homeless and inundate millions of hectares of farmland.

December 24. The main dam of the
   Tianshengqiao Hydroelectric Power
   Station in Guangxi collapses while still
   under construction. Fifty-five workers
   are buried and 48 other people killed.

1986
A Foreign Affairs Events
March 10. China becomes a member of the
   Asian Development Bank.
March 21. Premier Zhao Ziyang announces
   that China has ceased atmospheric
   nuclear tests and will not undertake
   them in the future.
April 7. US President Reagan formally
   notifies the US Congress of an
   agreement with China for the sale of
   high-technology electronic aviation
   equipment worth $550 million to help
   China's military modernization.
July 11. China delivers a note to the General
   Agreement on Tariffs and Trade
   (GATT) secretary-general, formally
   applying for restoration of its status as a
   founding member of the GATT,
   negated in 1950.
July 12. An armed clash takes place along
   the Sino-Soviet border, but both
   countries adopt a low-key attitude
   towards it.
July 28. In a major policy speech in
   Vladivostok, the Soviet leader Mikhail
   Gorbachev calls for a good-neighbourly
   atmosphere in Sino-Soviet relations and
   for the Sino-Soviet border to 'become a
   line of peace and friendship in the near
   future'.
September 20–October 5. The Tenth Asian
   Games take place in Seoul; China
   participates and wins the most gold
   medals of any country.
September 28–30. The first secretary of the
   Polish Communist Party Central
   Committee, Wojcieck Jaruzelski, visits
   China, the first high-ranking Polish
   official to do so for over two decades.
October 12–18. British Queen Elizabeth II
   visits China.

October 21–26. Erich Honecker, general
   secretary of the German Democratic
   Republic's Society Unity Party and
   chairman of the State Council, visits
   China, the first high-ranking East
   German party and state official to do so.

B Domestic Political Events
September 28. The Sixth Plenum of the
   Twelfth CCPCC adopts a resolution 'on
   the guiding principles for building a
   socialist society with an advanced
   culture and ideology'. Among many
   other points, it attacks 'bourgeois
   liberalization', which it defines as a
   trend 'negating the socialist system in
   favour of capitalism'.

C Economic Events
March 25. At the NPC, Zhao Ziyang gives a
   report on the Seventh Five-Year Plan,
   adopted on April 12.
April 12. The NPC adopts the *Law on
   Enterprises Operated Exclusively with
   Foreign Capital*.
May 26–29. In Tianjin a conference of
   mayors of fourteen cities and regions
   decides to establish a special economic
   region around the Bohai.
August 3. NCNA reports that the Shenyang
   Explosion-Prevention Equipment
   Factory has been declared bankrupt,
   the first bankruptcy case in the history
   of the PRC.
September 15. The CCPCC and State
   Council issue regulations on the
   implementation of a responsibility
   system in publicly owned industrial
   enterprises, which gives more power to
   factory directors.
September 26. The Shanghai Stock Market
   reopens, for the first time since
   Liberation.
December 2. The NPC Standing Committee
   approves the *Bankruptcy Law* for trial
   implementation.

E Cultural and Social Events
April 21. The NPC adopts the *Law of the
   PRC on Compulsory Education*, which

stipulates nine years' compulsory education in the cities and developed areas by 1990, and almost everywhere by the end of the century.

May 5. NCNA reports that the People's Press has simultaneously published all 50 volumes of the first Chinese edition of the *Complete Works of Marx and Engels* (*Makesi Engesi quanji*).

May 24–25. A clash between African and Chinese students at Tianjin University leaves several people injured.

July 5–7. The first national Chinese conference of lawyers takes place in Beijing. On the last day the Chinese National Lawyers' Association is set up.

December 5. Several thousand students march in Hefei, the capital of Anhui Province, demanding greater democracy, an early major rally in a series of student demonstrations in many Chinese cities in November, and especially December.

December 19–21. Large-scale demonstrations for greater democracy take place in Shanghai, involving tens of thousands of students and others. They continue on December 22, but with fewer participants, authorities having warned that permission would be required for further rallies.

December 23. In Beijing, some 4000 students demonstrate for an end to authoritarianism.

December 26. The Beijing Municipal People's Congress Standing Committee bans student demonstrations that lack police approval.

F Births and Deaths

March 4. Author Ding Ling dies.

March 26. Former Dazhai 'model' peasant Chen Yonggui dies.

May 3. Linguist and educator Wang Li dies.

July 29. Nuclear scientist Deng Jiaxian dies.

October 7. Marshal Liu Bocheng dies.

October 22. Marshal Ye Jianying dies.

December 28. CCPCC Secretariat Member Huang Kecheng dies.

G Natural Disasters

July 11. Typhoons begin in southeast China; in Guangdong Province alone they result in the deaths of 172 people and cause injuries to 1250.

1987

A Foreign Affairs Events

January 8. Several hundred African students march to the headquarters of the African diplomatic quarter in Beijing to protest against racist attitudes towards them as expressed in a letter written by a body calling itself the Chinese Students Association.

March 26. Chinese and Portuguese representatives initial a joint declaration that sovereignty over Macau will be transferred to the PRC on December 20, 1999, and that thereafter it will be administered as the Macau Special Administrative Region on the basis of the 'one country, two systems' principle.

April 13. In Beijing, the Portuguese Prime Minister Anibal Cavaco Silva and Zhao Ziyang sign the Joint Declaration on the Question of Macau on the transfer of the sovereignty of Macau to the PRC.

June 4–21. Zhao Ziyang makes a major tour of Eastern Europe, arriving in Poland on June 4, East Germany on June 8, Czechoslovakia on June 11, Hungary on June 14 and Bulgaria on June 18.

October 6. The US Senate unanimously condemns China's actions in Tibet. The vote follows the appearance of Tibet's Dalai Lama before two US Congressional bodies on September 21, during which he called for the designation of Tibet as a 'zone of peace' and denounced Chinese policies and actions there.

October 8. The Chinese NPC Foreign Affairs Committee responds to the US Senate vote of October 6 and other US Congressional moves on Tibet by demanding strongly that the US

Congress stop all its interference in China's internal affairs.

B Domestic Political Events

January 1. A *People's Daily* editorial attacks bourgeois liberalization and demands that the 'four cardinal principles' be upheld (see **B**. May 30, 1979).

January 6. A *People's Daily* editorial states that the recent student demonstrations have now subsided and that they show the need to oppose bourgeois liberalization and uphold the 'four cardinal principles'.

September 27. Demonstrations, mainly by monks, begin in Lhasa in favour of Tibetan independence; some demonstrators are arrested.

October 1. Demonstrations by some 2000 monks and others in Lhasa in favour of Tibetan independence lead to clashes with authorities and the death of at least six people, with NCNA claiming (on October 10) that at least 50 foreigners were directly involved.

October 6. Some 80 monks from three of Tibet's main monasteries march through Lhasa calling for independence for Tibet.

October 25. In his keynote speech to the Thirteenth Congress of the CCP (held October 25–November 1), Zhao Ziyang states that China is now in the 'primary stage of socialism', which began in the 1950s and would last at least a century 'to the time when socialist modernization will have been in the main accomplished'.

November 24. The NPC Standing Committee adopts the *Organic Law of the Village Committees of the PRC*, defining the character, functions and tasks of the village committees. Village committees are to be established as self-managing mass organizations throughout rural China.

C Economic Events

March 25. In his report on the work of the government to the NPC, Zhao Ziyang criticizes the failure of total supply to meet social demand, and excessive price rises.

December 1. Rationing of pork and sugar is reintroduced in Beijing, a move followed quickly by the administrations of Shanghai, Tianjin and other major cities.

December 28. A ceremony marks the formal opening of the new Shanghai Railway Station.

D Appointments, Dismissals, etc.

January 13. Writer Wang Ruofang is expelled from the CCP for advocating bourgeois liberalization and opposing the 'four cardinal principles'.

January 16. Hu Yaobang resigns as general secretary of the CCP in favour of Zhao Ziyang. (He was in effect dismissed by Deng Xiaoping for supporting the student movement of late 1986.)

January 17. Fang Lizhi is expelled from the CCP for the same reasons as Wang Ruofang four days earlier (see also December 5, 1986).

January 24. It is announced that *People's Daily* reporter Liu Binyan has been expelled from the CCP for advocating bourgeois liberalization and opposing the 'four cardinal principles'.

June 6. Yang Zhong is dismissed as minister of Forestry because of the catastrophic forest fires in the northeast (see **G**. below).

November 2. The First Plenum of the Thirteenth CCPCC confirms Zhao Ziyang as CCP general secretary. In addition, it appoints Li Peng, Qiao Shi, Hu Qili and Yao Yilin to the Politburo Standing Committee. Chen Yun is elected chairman of the Central Advisory Commission and Deng Xiaoping chairman of the CCPCC's Military Commission.

November 24. The NPC Standing Committee approves Zhao Ziyang's resignation as premier and his replacement by Li Peng as acting premier.

E Cultural and Social Events

July 3. *People's Daily* reports that any CCP member who takes bribes, however small, will be expelled. It notes the view of the CCP Central Discipline Inspection Commission that the practice of taking and asking for bribes has become rampant in some areas.

September 1. China's first Institute of Tibetan Buddhism officially opens in Beijing.

September 5–25. The first China Art Festival takes place in Beijing, featuring over 40 performances of all kinds, as well as fine art exhibitions and mass cultural activities.

F Births and Deaths

December 27. Rewi Alley, long-time China resident from New Zealand, dies.

G Natural Disasters

May 6. A gigantic forest fire breaks out in Heilongjiang Province; it later spreads to Inner Mongolia. The fire is extinguished on May 26, but revives two days later. Rain and firefighters finally extinguish it on June 2. It kills some 200 people, leaves more than 50 000 homeless, and burns an area of over one million hectares, causing incalculable damage to the environment.

May 20. Torrential rains begin in Guangdong, causing severe flooding over the following days. About 100 people are later reported killed and many thousands of houses destroyed, as well as 158 000 hectares of farmland swamped.

1988

A Foreign Affairs Events

March 14. A naval clash between China and Vietnam in the Spratly (Nansha) Islands leaves three Vietnamese sailors dead and 74 missing, according to Vietnamese accounts. Both countries claim the islands as within their territory.

April 15. Through a Foreign Ministry spokesman, China welcomes the Geneva Agreement on Afghanistan, signed the day before, which stipulates the withdrawal of all Soviet forces by February 15, 1989.

July 1. The Foreign Ministry issues a four-point statement on Kampuchea, including a freeze on all Kampuchean forces, after a Vietnamese withdrawal and the establishment of a provisional quadripartite government 'so that the Kampuchean people may conduct a free election without outside interference and threat of force'.

September 17–October 2. China takes part in the Twenty-fourth Olympic Games, held in Seoul, Republic of Korea.

October 17. In Beijing, Deng Xiaoping tells visiting Romanian President Nicolae Ceausescu that a Sino-Soviet summit might take place in 1989.

November 10–24. Li Peng makes his first overseas trip as premier, visiting Thailand, Australia and New Zealand.

December 1–3. Qian Qichen visits the Soviet Union, the first time a Chinese Foreign minister has done so since Zhou Enlai in 1956, and holds intensive talks with his Soviet counterpart Eduard Shevardnadze.

December 19–23. Rajiv Gandhi visits China, the first Indian prime minister to do so for 34 years, meeting Deng Xiaoping on December 21.

B Domestic Political Events

January 14. The CCPCC sends a message of condolence to the Guomindang Central Committee on the death of Jiang Jingguo.

March 5. Lamas and others demonstrate in Lhasa for independence on the last day of the traditional Tibetan Grand Summons Ceremony.

April 12. The NPC approves changes to the State Constitution, allowing the private sector of the economy to exist and develop, and permitting the buying and selling of land or the transfer of the right to the use of land.

April 13. The NPC adopts a resolution formally upgrading Hainan to the status of a province, and also making it a special economic zone, at this point China's largest.

June 15. At the European Parliament in Strasbourg, the Dalai Lama proposes that Tibet should become a self-governing political entity in association with China.

December 10. Lamas and others demonstrate in Lhasa for Tibetan independence. At least one person is killed by police.

C Economic Events

January 22. NCNA releases Zhao Ziyang's outline of a strategy for economic growth based on speeding up the development of urban coastal areas to become centres of export-oriented industries.

July 3. Li Peng signs regulations designed to encourage investment on the mainland from Taiwan.

August 15–17. A Politburo meeting in Beidaihe decides to allow prices for most commodities to be regulated by the market. The decision results in panic buying in the second half of August, creating accelerated inflation.

August 30. The State Council issues an urgent directive in an effort to control serious inflation.

December 21. The Datong Locomotive Plant in Shanxi turns out its last steam locomotive, marking the end of China's history of steam engine production.

D Appointments, Dismissals, etc.

March 5. The Railways Minister Ding Guan'gen resigns because of the air crash of January 18 and rail disaster of January 24 (see G. below) and other disasters.

April 8. The NPC elects Yang Shangkun as PRC president (replacing Li Xiannian) and Wang Zhen as vice-president (replacing Ulanfu); Wan Li is elected chairman of the Standing Committee of the NPC (replacing Peng Zhen); and Deng Xiaoping is reelected chairman of the Central Military Commission.

April 9. The NPC confirms Li Peng as premier of the State Council.

April 12. In the new State Council, elected on this day by the NPC, Wu Xueqian becomes a vice-premier and Qian Qichen replaces him as minister of Foreign Affairs.

E Cultural and Social Events

March 10. The Chinese mainland's first test-tube baby is born in Beijing.

March 17. The Ministry of Public Security announces the seizure of 4.5 kg of heroin in Shanghai from March 9 to 13.

June 3. Students demonstrate in protest against the murder of Chai Qingfeng (see F. below); in the next few days wall posters put forward such demands as press freedom, higher priority for education, and a better legal system.

July 1. The journal *Seeking Truth from Facts* (*Qiushi*) replaces *Red Flag* (*Hongqi*).

July 21. Li Peng promulgates a nineteen-article set of labour regulations for the protection of female workers, adopted by the State Council on June 28 and due to be put into effect on September 1.

October 22–28. The Eleventh National Congress of the All-China Federation of Trade Unions is held in Beijing, representing 93 365 000 trade union members.

November 8. The NPC Standing Committee adopts a law on the protection of wildlife, to take effect on March 1, 1989. At the Fifth Conference of the China Federation of Literary and Art Circles, Hu Qili gives a major speech on literature and art policies. He calls for the application of the 'four cardinal principles' and for freedom both of literary creation and criticism.

December 22. China's first exhibition of nude paintings opens in Beijing (closing on January 8, 1989).

December 24. A clash erupts between African students and Chinese college employees at the Hehai University in Nanjing. Trouble continues in the following days, with the Africans denouncing the Chinese as racist.

F Births and Deaths

January 13. Taiwan's President Jiang Jingguo dies.

February 16. Educator, writer, publisher and social activist Ye Shengtao dies in Beijing.

May 10. Writer Shen Congwen dies.

June 2. Postgraduate student Chai Qingfeng is murdered near Beijing University.

June 22. Writer Xiao Jun dies.

October 3. Long-time China resident, naturalized Chinese and the first originally foreign person to join the CCP, George Hatem, dies in Beijing.

December 8. Inner Mongolian CCP leader Ulanfu dies.

G Natural Disasters, Accidents

January 18. A passenger airliner crashes near Chongqing, Sichuan Province, killing all 98 passengers and ten crew.

January 24. The Kunming–Shanghai express is derailed and overturned nearly 350 km from Kunming, killing at least 90 people and injuring others.

July 29–30. Zhejiang suffers its worst floods in four decades. Over 200 people are killed and nearly 500 reported missing, with enormous destruction to property.

August 8. A typhoon strikes Hangzhou and other parts of Zhejiang Province; it eventually results in the deaths of 110 people, injuries to well over 1000, and massive destruction to property and crops.

November 6. Severe earthquakes shake the southwest of Yunnan Province; deaths total some 730 and about 3500 people are seriously injured, with over 400 000 houses destroyed and another 700 000 damaged.

1989 THE BEIJING MASSACRE (JUNE 4 INCIDENT)

A Foreign Affairs Events

February 1–4. Eduard Shevardnadze visits China, the first Soviet Foreign minister to do so since 1959.

February 11–13. Pakistani Prime Minister Benazir Bhutto visits China.

February 25–26. George Bush makes his first trip to China as US President.

May 15–18. Mikhail Gorbachev makes the first visit of a Soviet leader to China since 1959.

May 16. Gorbachev and Deng Xiaoping hold a meeting in the Great Hall of the People, after which Deng Xiaoping announces that Sino-Soviet relations are 'normalized'.

May 18. The Sino-Soviet Joint Communiqué is issued in Beijing. The two sides agree that 'the Sino-Soviet high level meeting symbolized the normalization of relations between the two countries' but that this normalization is not directed at any third country. On Kampuchea the two sides agree that, with the withdrawal of Vietnamese troops, 'the countries concerned should gradually reduce and eventually stop all their military aid to any of the parties in Kampuchea'.

June 5. In protest against the Beijing massacre of June 3–4, US President Bush announces suspension of all government-to-government sales and commercial export of weapons, and of all visits between senior American and Chinese military officials.

June 7. A Chinese Foreign Ministry announcement denounces President Bush's statement of June 5 as unacceptable pressure on the Chinese government. An official statement describes the United States sanctuary given to dissident Fang Lizhi on June 5 as 'interference in China's internal affairs'.

June 22. Ji Pengfei, Director of the Hong Kong and Macau Affairs Office, declares on China Central Television that the Chinese government will persist in its policies on Hong Kong and Macau, including adherence to the Sino-British and Sino-Portuguese Joint Declarations (see respectively **A**. December 19, 1984 and April 13, 1987) and the concept of 'one country, two systems'.

June 26. The World Bank announces that it will defer consideration of seven new development loans to China worth US$780.2 million because of the massacre and continuing repression.

July 15. Leaders of the seven major industrial capitalist nations—the United States, Japan, France, West Germany, Britain, Italy and Canada—issue a declaration in Paris that includes condemnation of China for its suppression of the pro-democracy movement. However, no new measures or economic sanctions are announced.

July 17. A *People's Daily* editorial rejects the Paris declaration of July 15 as unfair, since it was necessary for China to suppress the counter-revolutionary rebellion.

November 6. Deng Xiaoping holds talks with DPRK President Kim Il Sung during a three-day unofficial visit to China by Kim (November 5–7).

November 14–21. Li Peng undertakes his first overseas trip since the June 4 incident: to Pakistan (November 14–18), Bangladesh and Nepal.

December 10. During a 25-hour visit to China, Brent Scowcroft, the National Security Adviser to the US President, meets Deng Xiaoping and tells him that President Bush still regards him as a friend.

December 11. China formally protests to the Norwegian government over its participation in the December 10 ceremony to award the Dalai Lama the 1989 Nobel Peace Prize.

December 26. The Chinese Foreign Ministry announces that China will 'continue to maintain and develop its friendly relations with Romania', where the day before the previous president and vice-president, Nicolae and Elena Ceausescu, had been executed.

B Domestic Political Events

March 5–7. Anti-Chinese demonstrations take place in Lhasa; serious violence erupts between police and demonstrators, with looting of Han Chinese houses and shops, making the scale of trouble the worst since 1959. The State Council declares martial law on March 7, to take effect from midnight the same day.

April 22. Official mourning is held in central Beijing for Hu Yaobang. Many thousands of students demonstrate in Tiananmen Square to mourn him, and also to demand his rehabilitation as well as democratic reforms. This demonstration forms a climax to a series of such demonstrations for democracy sparked off by the death of Hu Yaobang a week before. (See **D**. Appointments, Dismissals, etc., January 16, 1987.)

April 26. An editorial in *People's Daily*, following the line laid down in a speech by Deng Xiaoping the preceding day, criticizes the student demonstrations and declares the situation to be 'a grave political struggle facing the whole Party and Chinese citizens of all nationalities'.

April 27. An enormous demonstration, with well over 100 000 student and other participants, takes place in Beijing in direct defiance of a government ban. The demands of the students include press freedom, government accountability and a crackdown on Party corruption.

May 4. Another enormous demonstration takes place in Beijing, with much smaller ones in several other cities, in commemoration of the May Fourth Movement of 1919 (China's first modern large-scale student movement). The demonstrations also put forward several demands, including democracy and press freedom. No violence or arrests result.

May 13. A large-scale rally for democracy and freedom converges on Tiananmen Square in the heart of Beijing. Students declare they will remain in occupation of the square until their pro-democracy demands are met, and about 1000 students begin a hunger strike.

May 18. Li Peng holds a televised meeting with representatives of the striking students at the Great Hall of the People, including the Uygur Wuerkaixi from Beijing Teachers' University and Wang Dan from Beijing University.

May 19. Early in the morning Zhao Ziyang appears in Tiananmen Square to express sympathy with hunger-striking demonstrators, his last public appearance before the Beijing massacre of June 3–4.

May 20. The State Council declares martial law in parts of Beijing to take effect from 10 a.m. the same day. Mass demonstrations continue in Beijing, with opposition to the imposition of martial law and demands for the overthrow of Li Peng being central issues. The army refuses to take action against the crowds, while people erect barricades to prevent its advance towards Tiananmen Square.

May 25. A pro-democracy demonstration of some 100 000 workers and intellectuals takes place in Beijing demanding the resignation of the premier, Li Peng, who appears on television announcing that his government is in full control of the situation and will press ahead with reform.

June 3. Crowds of people, especially students, again prevent mainly unarmed soldiers from entering Tiananmen Square by erecting barricades and other means. According to the government, leaders of the student movement incite the mobs to kill soldiers; this, together with other actions, marks the beginning of a 'counter-revolutionary rebellion'.

June 3–4. The Beijing massacre. Troops of the 27th Army of the PLA and the People's Armed Police move along the Chang'an Boulevard in Beijing to Tiananmen Square to clear the square of demonstrators. Violence erupts at about 10 p.m. on June 3 and continues at intervals throughout the night and following morning. Troops force their way through barricades set up by ordinary people, many casualties resulting. By midday on June 4, troops have sealed off Tiananmen Square.

June 4. In Chengdu, PLA troops advance into the square at the centre of the city to clear it of student protesters.

June 5. The CCPCC and the State Council claim initial victory against a counter-revolutionary riot instigated by a handful of people aimed at 'negating the leadership of the CCP, destroying the socialist system and overthrowing the People's Republic'.

June 6. In Shanghai, eight people are killed when an express train runs into a human barricade trying to prevent soldiers from entering the city. About 30 others sustain fatal injuries.

June 9. Deng Xiaoping, Yang Shangkun, Li Peng, Qiao Shi, Wan Li, Yao Yilin, Wang Zhen, Peng Zhen and other leaders appear at a televised meeting in central Beijing to praise the military action of June 3–4. Deng Xiaoping's speech commends the troops for suppressing 'counter-revolutionaries trying to overthrow the CCP' and for putting down 'the counter-revolutionary rebellion'. He also pledges continuation of the reform and open-door policies adopted at the end of 1978.

June 10. Chinese official media announce that 'martial law troops' have arrested over 400 people in Beijing, Hebei, Tianjin and Shanghai 'in order to protect Beijing'. This is the start of an extensive series of arrests.

June 16. In a speech to the new Politburo Standing Committee, Deng Xiaoping refers to three generations of the Chinese leadership core: Mao Zedong heading the first one, himself the second and Jiang Zemin the third. He also makes reference to attacking corruption to strengthen the country, among other tasks.

June 24. The Fourth Plenum of the Thirteenth CCPCC adopts a communiqué reaffirming the policies of reform adopted by and since the Third Plenum of the Eleventh CCPCC (December 1978).

June 30. Mayor of Beijing Chen Xitong gives a 'report on checking the turmoil and quelling the counter-revolutionary rebellion', in which he includes a detailed statement in defence of the government's account of the events of April, May and June. Its essence is that the government was forced to put down a counter-revolutionary rebellion.

December 29. Jiang Zemin makes a speech at a seminar on Party construction in which he warns of the danger posed by the 'strategy of "peaceful evolution"'. He claims 'hostile international forces' are trying to implement this to undermine the socialist system in China.

C Economic Events

March 20. In his opening speech to the Second Session of the Seventh NPC, Premier Li Peng sharply criticizes his own government for allowing the economy to become overheated.

July 11. An air route opens linking Ürümqi, in the Xinjiang Uygur Autonomous Region, and Alma-Ata, capital of the Soviet Union's Kazakh Soviet Socialist Republic.

October 1. A railway linking Shangqiu (Henan Province) with Fuyang (Anhui) opens to traffic.

November 9. The Thirteenth CCPCC's Fifth Plenum issues a communiqué that places emphasis on the economy. It expresses satisfaction over successes achieved in the cooling of the country's overheated economy in the past year, but points to several priority targets, the first being to slow down inflation and bring down the national rate of retail price rises to under 10 per cent.

D Appointments, Dismissals, etc.

June 24. The Fourth Plenum of the Thirteenth CCPCC dismisses Zhao Ziyang from all leading posts in the Party and elects Jiang Zemin to replace him as general secretary.

September 4. The Standing Committee of the NPC accepts Wang Meng's resignation as minister of Culture and appoints He Jingzhi to replace him, in an acting capacity.

September 14. The Ministry of Supervision announces the dismissal of the governor of Hainan Province, Liang Xiang, for the abuse of power for personal gain.

November 9. The Fifth Plenum endorses Deng Xiaoping's request to resign the chairmanship of the CCPCC's Military Commission. It appoints Jiang Zemin to replace him as chairman and appoints Yang Shangkun as first vice-chairman, Liu Huaqing as vice-chairman, and Yang Baibing as secretary. It appoints Yang Baibing as a new member of the CCPCC's Secretariat.

E Cultural and Social Events

Early March. The People's Press and the Central Documents Press publish the *Biography of Zhou Enlai* (*Zhou Enlai zhuan*) as the first in a series of major political biographies of the main communist leaders.

May 5. Some 2000 Muslims in Lanzhou, capital of Gansu, demonstrate against *Xing fengsu (Sexual Customs)*, published in Shanghai earlier in the year. They argue that the book is insulting to Islam, and demand punishment for the book's authors.

May 12. Some 2000 Muslim students in Beijing demonstrate against *Sexual Customs*, as 'full of slander against the Muslims'.

May 18. Several thousand fundamentalist Muslims from the Ürümqi Koranic Studies Institute and supporters demonstrate in Ürümqi, demanding the suppression of *Sexual Customs*.

May 30. Students erect the statue of the *Goddess of Democracy (Minzhu nüshen)*, modelled on the Statue of Liberty, in Tiananmen Square.

July 21. A State Education Commission spokesman announces the Chinese government's intention to cut the 1989 student intakes into colleges and universities by 5 per cent—from an originally planned 640 000 to about 610 000.

August 4. NCNA reports that the Xi'an Muslim Cultural Training University, designed for students from the Islamic minority nationalities, has begun to enrol students.

August 24. A *People's Daily* editorial promises to punish according to law only those students who took the lead in organizing the recent demonstrations. In a national teleconference, Li Ruihuan calls for the campaign against pornography to be combined with efforts to reinvigorate literature and art and liven up the people's cultural and recreational life, and for reactionary publications advocating bourgeois liberalization to be curbed.

November 14. China publishes a statement attacking the International Labour Organization for allegations of the suppression of the independent trade union movement and mass arrests and repression of workers. The statement claims the allegations are unfounded and represent an interference in China's internal affairs.

F Births and Deaths

January 28. The Tenth Bainqen (Panchen) Lama dies in Xigaze, Tibet.

February 28. International affairs expert Huan Xiang dies.

April 15. Former CCP General Secretary Hu Yaobang dies of a heart attack in Beijing.

June 21. Xu Guoming and two other men are executed in Shanghai for setting fire to the train which on June 6 had run into a human barricade trying to prevent soldiers from entering the city (see **B.** above).

July 31. Zhou Yang, former president of the China Federation of Literature and Art Circles, dies in Beijing.

August 27. Former Uygur Xinjiang leader Burhan Shahidi dies in Beijing.

September 20. Cultural Revolution leader Chen Boda dies, aged 85.

December 6. Painter Li Keran dies in Beijing, aged 82.

G Natural Disasters

July 7. Heavy, continuous and torrential rains begin falling in Sichuan Province, resulting in very serious flooding in twenty counties and prefectures in the province. Hundreds of people are killed, large areas of farmland are damaged or destroyed, and millions of people are affected by the ensuing floods. Other provinces seriously affected by flooding from early to mid-July include Anhui, Hubei, Jiangsu and Zhejiang. In the last province, 2.62 million people are affected, more than 300 villages are ruined and 10 000 houses are destroyed.

August 16. *People's Daily* quotes a report by the Ministry of Water Resources as saying that vast areas of China have experienced irregular rainfall and over ten million hectares have been hit by severe drought since July. Worst affected is Shandong Province, in which four million people have had problems finding drinking water.

1990

A Foreign Affairs Events

January 25. The US Senate votes to uphold a veto by President Bush on a bill that would have barred deportation of Chinese students once their American visas expired.

April 15. Fijian Prime Minister Sir Kamisese Mara arrives in China for a six-day official visit.

April 23–26. Li Peng pays an official visit to the Soviet Union, the first by a top Chinese leader for 26 years.

April 23–27. The Fourteenth World Law Conference takes place in Beijing attended by about 1500 jurists from 65 countries.

May 4. Mongolian People's Great Hural Presidium Chairman Punsalmaagiyn Ochirbat begins a three-day goodwill visit to China, meeting Jiang Zemin May 5. In a joint communiqué issued on May 7 at the end of the visit, Mongolian and Chinese leaders 'expressed their gratification at the normalization of the relations between the two countries'.

May 11. Egyptian President Husni Mubarak arrives for a three-day goodwill visit to China. In a meeting with Jiang Zemin on May 12 he welcomed China's domestic stability.

May 13–30. President Yang Shangkun visits Mexico, Brazil, Uruguay, Argentina and Chile, the first by a Chinese president to Latin America.

July 11. Meeting in Houston (July 9–11), the Group of Seven major industrialized countries decide to maintain the sanctions imposed on China due to the Beijing massacre, but allow some World Bank loans for environmental purposes. Japan announced it will resume lending money to China.

August 2. At the United Nations, Chinese Ambassador Li Daoyu urges Iraq to withdraw from Kuwait, condemning the invasion of the same day.

August 6–11. Premier Li Peng visits Indonesia, the first senior Chinese leader to do so for 25 years.

August 11–13. Li Peng pays a goodwill visit to Singapore. At the welcoming banquet on August 11, both he and Singapore's Prime Minister Lee Kuan Yew express the wish to establish diplomatic relations.

August 28. In his report to the Standing Committee of the NPC, Li Peng states that the problem between Iraq and Kuwait should be settled peacefully and within the Arab countries, but using United Nations mediation.

September 18. A senior Japanese economic delegation meets with Li Peng and confirms that Japan has decided to go ahead with a loan package of ¥810 billion over the years 1990–95, frozen due to the Beijing massacre, expressing the hope that the projects can be specified as soon as possible.

September 19. Vice-Chairman Vo Nguyen Giap of the Vietnamese Council of Ministers arrives in Beijing to attend the opening ceremony of the Asian Games. The significance of this visit is that it was the first visit by a senior Vietnamese for well over a decade and thus represented a thaw in the extremely strained relations between China and Vietnam.

September 22–October 7. The Asian Games take place in Beijing with delegations from 37 countries and regions, including both North and South Korea, Taiwan (called 'Chinese Taipei') and Kuwait, but not Iraq. China won by far the largest number of medals (341 gold, silver and bronze of a total of 976).

October 16. Lee Kuan Yew arrives in China for a nine-day visit, meeting with Jiang Zemin on October 17. This was his last visit as prime minister, since he stepped down the following month.

October 20. China and South Korea agree to establish trade offices in each other's capitals, with immediate effect.

October 22. The foreign ministers of the twelve-nation European Community decide to lift sanctions imposed on China as a result of the June 1989 crackdown on the student movement. The next day China expresses appreciation for this action.

October 27. In a meeting with the Japanese Ambassador, Chinese Vice-minister of Foreign Affairs Qi Huaiyuan criticizes Japan for doing nothing against the very recent installation of navigational lights by some Japanese right-wing organizations on the Diaoyu Islands, which China claims as its own territory.

October 31. NCNA reports a German Federal Assembly decision to reinstate aid to China, suspended since mid–1989, and provide new export credit guarantees. Germany had just reunited (ceremony held October 3) after 45 years of division, Chinese leaders sending messages of congratulation.

November 2. China and Japan exchange documents on a Japanese loan of ¥36.5 billion, finalizing the first stage in the 1990–95 loan package.

November 16. Jiang Zemin meets with Indonesian President Suharto, the first Indonesian leader to visit China for over 25 years.

November 29. The UN Security Council adopts Resolution 678 by 12 to 2, with one abstention (China), that, if Iraq has failed unconditionally to withdraw its troops from Kuwait before January 15, 1991, it would use 'all necessary means' to resolve the crisis.

November 29. The ADB formally grants a fifteen-year loan of US$50 million to the Agricultural Bank of China, the first ADB loan to China to be announced since the June 4 incident of 1989.

December 10–19. Li Peng makes a diplomatic tour to Malaysia, the Philippines, Laos and Sri Lanka.

December 26–28. Kuwaiti Emir Jaber al-Ahmed al-Sabah makes the first visit of a Kuwaiti Emir to China; he meets President Yang Shangkun on December 26, who expresses China's sympathy for the Kuwaiti people who were under Iraq's occupation.

B Domestic Political Events

January 10. Li Peng announces the State Council's decision to lift martial law in Beijing as from January 11.

February 7. A CCPCC document on relations between the eight democratic parties and the CCP is made public, having been issued on December 30, 1989. It declares that the democratic parties should take part in state power under the leadership of the CCP.

March 20. In his opening speech at the Third Session of the Seventh NPC, Li Peng emphasizes stability and adhering to the socialist road.

April 4. President Yang Shangkun promulgates the Basic Law of the Hong Kong Special Administrative Region of the People's Republic of China, adopted by the Seventh NPC on the same day and scheduled to take effect as of July 1, 1997.

April 5–6. Disturbances described in a local official television broadcast as an 'armed counter-revolutionary rebellion', and attributed to the Islamic Party of East Turkestan, occur in Akto County in the Kizilsu Kirghiz Autonomous Prefecture, Xinjiang. According to the broadcast, the disturbances are aimed at establishing a separatist Islamic republic but are suppressed by the People's Armed Police, resulting in at least 22 deaths, including that of the leader of the rebellion.

April 30. Premier Li Peng signs an order lifting martial law in Lhasa, Tibet, to take effect the following day.

June 12. The Central Commission for Discipline Inspection issues a circular urging stricter measures for combating corruption and cites several cases of officials punished for corrupt behaviour.

July 1. The fourth national census begins, being completed on July 10. The main data from it are announced on October 10 (see also Chapter 7).

July 20–30. Jiang Zemin makes an 'inspection tour' of Tibet, urging the need for acceleration of economic development there.

August 22–September 1. Jiang Zemin makes an 'inspection tour of Xinjiang, urging national unity and economic development.

October 1. The *Administrative Procedure Law* comes into effect; it is aimed at stopping any power from exercising illegal or arbitrary power and gives ordinary citizens the right to sue government officials.

C Economic Events

February 2. The US Export–Import Bank grants a loan of US$10 million to China's National Offshore Oil Corporation.

April 7. In Xichang, Sichuan, a Chinese carrier rocket launches Asia's first regional communications satellite, American-made Asiasat 1.

April 18. Premier Li Peng announces in Shanghai that China will open Pudong in Shanghai to foreign business.

May 7. During a meeting with a former Japanese prime minister, Li Peng declares that China has effectively curbed inflation.

September 1. China's first motorway, linking Shenyang and Dalian, a distance of 375 kilometres, opens to traffic. A ceremony, attended by Jiang Zemin, marks the opening of the newly constructed railway linking the Xinjiang capital Ürümqi with the Alataw Pass on the border with Kazakhstan in the Soviet Union. The completion, on September 12, of the short railway link with the Soviet rail system opened a complete Eurasian 'rail bridge' from Lianyungang on China's eastern coast to Rotterdam.

September 10. The Shanghai Municipality government holds a press conference at which the Shanghai Mayor Zhu Rongji and others announced nine laws and regulations regarding the development and opening up of the Pudong Development Zone.

September 12. The Beijing–Tianjin Expressway, the first inter-provincial motorway in China, comes into service.

September 13. Automatic direct-dial services begin operation in Tibet, enabling telephone calls to about 500 Chinese cities and 100 overseas countries without operator assistance.

November 10. The State Council issues a circular urging all localities to remove market barriers between them.

November 17. China announces a currency devaluation of 9.57 per cent: from 5.209 yuan to the US dollar to 4.71 yuan.

December 19. The Shanghai Securities Exchange is inaugurated. It is a major step forward in financial reform, being the first securities exchange on the Chinese mainland since 1949.

December 30. At the end of the Seventh Plenary Session of its Thirteenth Central Committee the CCP Central Committee adopts the Ten-Year Program (1991–2000) and the Eighth Five-Year Plan (1991–95). These programs envisage a rise in the gross national product of about 6 per cent per year over the following decade and suggest that the standard of living will rise significantly.

D Appointments, Dismissals, etc.

February 13. NCNA announces that on February 1 the State Council and the CCP's Central Military Commission appointed PLA Major-General Zhou Yushu as commander of the People's Armed Police in place of Li Lianxiu. The move is one of several representing a reorganization of the top echelons of the People's Armed Police.

March 21. The NPC endorses Deng Xiaoping's request to resign the chairmanship of the State Military Commission, replacing him with Jiang Zemin.

December 28. Tao Siju is appointed minister of Public Security in place of Wang Fang. Li Lanqing is appointed minister of Foreign Economic Relations and Trade, in place of Zheng Tuobin.

E Cultural and Social Events

January 10. In a speech at a national seminar on cultural affairs, Li Ruihuan emphasizes China's cultural and historical heritage and attacks 'wholesale Westernization'.

January 17. At a working conference of the State Education Commission, Jiang Zemin calls for the strengthening of the teaching of patriotism, national integrity and Chinese history.

January 18. A Ministry of Public Security spokesman announces the release of 573 law-breakers from the student movement of April–June 1989 because of their willingness to confess and reform.

March 5. A documentary film is released on the life of Zhou Enlai.

May 4. In a speech on intellectuals, Jiang Zemin reaffirmed their crucial role in the modernization process but warned against the influence of Western bourgeois values and 'national nihilism'.

May 29–June 4. A festival of children's films produced by the China Children's Film Studio takes place in Beijing.

August 6. The results of China's first survey on sexual education are announced in the overseas edition of *Liaowang* (*Outlook Weekly*).

September 1–October 7. A gala festival of Chinese and foreign performing arts, including regional Chinese theatre, plays and song and dance, takes place in Beijing.

September 10. Seven Catholic nuns graduate in Beijing, representative of about 1000 students in schools and eleven theological colleges preparing to be nuns throughout China.

October 18. Speaking at an anti-narcotics conference of countries and regions in the Asia-Pacific, Li Peng commits his government to stricter measures against drug trafficking and abuse and narcotics-related crime, which had increased dramatically in China in recent years.

November 1. An international symposium takes place in Fujian Province to mark the 840th birth date of the famous Neo-Confucian scholar Zhu Xi (1130–1200).

November 23. The Standing Committee of the State Council determines to set up the National Narcotics Control Commission in order to strengthen the fight against drug-peddling and drug-taking.

December 5. On the first day of a conference on religious affairs, Li Peng reiterates the government's policy in favour of religious freedom but also says he warns against any attempt to use religion to disrupt social stability. He favours religious exchanges with foreign countries but firmly opposes any attempt by 'hostile foreign forces' to use religion to carry out infiltration.

December 10. The twenty-day Second Chinese Theatre Festival ends in Beijing, having featured 44 programs by troupes from 22 provinces representing eighteen styles of local Chinese theatre. Of the 44 programs, fourteen were on contemporary themes.

F Births and Deaths

August 5. Peasant author Zhou Keqin dies at the age of 53.

September 11. Cai Chang, veteran revolutionary and leader of the women's movement, dies in Beijing at the age of 90.

September 21. Xu Xiangqian, one of the founders of the PLA, dies at the age of 88.

G Natural Disasters, Accidents

October 2. A hijacked aircraft from Xiamen attempts to land at Guangzhou's Baiyun Airport overshoots the main runway and crashes into two other planes, killing 127 people.

1991

A Foreign Affairs Events

January 15. Romanian President Ion Iliescu completes a three-day visit to China, with China announcing loans to Romania in the form of agricultural and industrial supplies.

January 17. China expresses 'deep anxiety and concern' at the outbreak of war in the Gulf the same day and urges maximum restraint in order to find a peaceful solution.

January 28. Gombojaryn Ochirbat becomes the first leader of the Mongolian People's Revolutionary Party to visit China in over three decades, holding talks with Jiang Zemin.

February 1. The general trading company Sunkyong Ltd opens a branch office in Beijing, being the first South Korean firm to establish a branch office in the PRC.

February 7. China Foreign Ministry spokesman Li Zhaoxing condemns as 'entirely unacceptable' the Human Rights Report issued by the US State Department on February 1. He is particularly scathing at the suggestion that China's population policy,

contributions by the public to the Asian Games projects and the building of water conservation works should be regarded as human rights violations.

February 26. Australian Foreign Minister Gareth Evans announces the removal of all economic and political restrictions imposed on China in July 1989. In a speech in Spain, Foreign Minister Qian Qichen proposes four principles for the establishment of a new international order: seeking common ground while playing down differences; mutual respect; non-interference in other nations' internal affairs; and equality and mutual benefit.

February 28. China welcomes the suspension of American combat operations in the Gulf against Iraq, and Yang Shangkun sends a message of congratulations to the Emir of Kuwait on the restoration of his country's independence and territorial sovereignty.

March 14. China advances a five-point peace plan for the Middle East, the first point being resolution through political channels and avoidance of force.

April 9. Peruvian President Alberto Fujimori arrives in Beijing, the first time for a Peruvian president to visit China, holding talks with Jiang Zemin the next day.

April 25. Tunisian President Zine el Abidine Ben Ali begins a three-day state visit to China, the first such visit by a Tunisian head of state.

April 29. The French Foreign Minister Roland Dumas arrives in Beijing for an official visit, China regarding the visit as signalling the normalization of relations with France following the June 4 Incident.

May 15–19. Jiang Zemin makes an official visit to the Soviet Union, the most senior Chinese leader to visit that country since 1957.

May 16. Chinese and Soviet representatives sign the Agreement on the Eastern

Section of the Boundary between the People's Republic of China and the USSR.

June 5–10. President Yang Shangkun makes an official visit to Indonesia, beginning an official visit to Thailand on the 10th.

July 2–14. Li Peng, Qian Qichen and other senior officials make a visit to Egypt, Jordan, Iran, Saudi Arabia, Syria and Kuwait.

August 10–13. Japanese Prime Minister Toshiki Kaifu visits China, being the first head of government of an industrialized democracy to make such a visit since the crisis of mid–1989.

August 10. China and Vietnam both issue statements announcing they intend to normalize relations, the end of a long period of hostility.

September 3. Li Peng and visiting British Prime Minister John Major sign the Memorandum of Understanding Concerning the Construction of the New Airport in Hong Kong and Related Questions. According to the Memorandum, already initialled July 4, China will support the construction of the multi-billion-dollar project, while Britain will consult with China on major matters relating to it.

September 15. British reporter Andrew Higgins, *Independent* correspondent, is expelled from China for possessing confidential information about an alleged crackdown on Inner Mongolian nationalists. Italian Prime Minister Giulio Andreotti arrives in China for a week's visit.

October 23. China hails the signing, the same day, of the agreements on a comprehensive political settlement of the conflict in Kampuchea, marking the end of thirteen years of fighting.

October 29. Xie Jun wins the World Women's Chess Championship in Manila, ending 41 years of Soviet dominance of women's chess.

November 5–9. Vietnamese Communist Party General Secretary Do Muoi visits China, leading to the normalization of relations between the two countries after a long period of hostility.

December 11–16. Li Peng, Qian Qichen and Minister of Foreign Economic Relations and Trade Li Lanqing visit India, Li Peng being the first Chinese premier to visit India since April 1960. On December 13, the two sides sign agreements on consular matters, trade and economic relations and cooperation in space and science and technology.

B Domestic Political Events

January 7. The Beijing Higher People's Court sentences Xu Tun to death with a two-year reprieve for embezzlement and bribery. Xu had been a director of the Transportation Bureau of the Ministry of Railways.

January 26. The Beijing Municipal Intermediate People's Court sentences Wang Dan to four years' imprisonment for his part in the 'turmoil' of 1989 (see B. May 18, 1989). Several other offenders are sentenced to varying terms of imprisonment or released.

February 12. The Beijing Municipal Intermediate People's Court sentences Chen Ziming and Wang Juntao to thirteen years in prison for their part in the disturbances of 1989, including 'wantonly inciting others to subvert the people's government and the socialist system'.

March 13. In a speech to a national conference on personnel management, Li Peng calls for government organizations to be streamlined in accordance with the principle of integrating planned economy and market regulation and separating governmental and business functions.

April 9. The NPC adopts the *Income Tax Law for Enterprises with Foreign Investment and Foreign Enterprises* and the *Civil Procedure Law of the PRC*.

May 31. NCNA reports the admission of 2 441 000 CCP members over the previous two years, bringing the total to 50 320 000.

October 9. A grand rally marks the eightieth anniversary of the 1911 Revolution. In a speech, President Yang Shangkun describes Sun Yatsen, leader of that revolution, as 'an outstanding representative of China's bourgeois revolutionaries'.

December 16. The Association for Relations Across the Taiwan Straits (ARATS) is founded in Beijing to promote contacts with Taiwan and eventual reunification.

C Economic Events

March 13. The State Statistical Bureau announces that, in the Seventh Five-Year Plan (1986–90), China's gross national product has grown by an average of 7.8 per cent, against a target of 7.5 per cent.

March 23. The Ministry of Agriculture issues an urgent circular urging great development of the township enterprises in the countryside in order to prevent further redundant labourers pouring into the coastal regions, where they were causing serious social strains.

March 25. In his report to the Fourth Session of the Seventh NPC, Li Peng urges further reform efforts to quadruple the 1980 gross national product by the end of the century, as well as expanding the role of market forces and lifting price controls.

September 23. Li Peng tells a working conference that China's large and medium state-owned enterprises are the pillars of the national economy, but that quite a few of them are operating badly and need reform. The conference closes September 27, with adoption of twelve measures aimed at invigorating them.

October 12. A ceremony marks the opening of a new airport in Shenzhen Special Economic Zone.

October 13. In a television speech Li Peng emphasizes the importance of economizing on grain, the key link in China's agricultural economy. The same day, *People's Daily* reveals that several dozen million tons of grain, or about 15 per cent of the nation's output, are wasted annually in harvesting, storing and processing, as well as from the dinner tables.

November 19. The Nanpu Bridge, over the Huangpu River in urban Shanghai, China's largest suspension bridge, opens for traffic.

November 29. The Eighth Plenum of the Thirteenth Central Committee adopts the Decision of the CCP Central Committee on Further Strengthening Agriculture and Work in Rural Areas, which, premised on the importance of agriculture, called for further improvements in the living standards of the peasants, the deepening of reform and the adoption of measures aimed at enhancing agricultural modernization.

D Appointments, Dismissals, etc.

January 22. Vice-Chairman Han Fucai of the Standing Committee of the Qinghai Provincial People's Congress is arrested for accepting large sums in bribes.

February 19. The Guangdong Provincial People's Congress announces the dismissal of Xu Jiatun, formerly director of the Hong Kong Branch of NCNA, for going to the United States without authorization (April 30, 1990) and refusing to return.

March 2. The NPC Standing Committee confirms the dismissal of Qian Yongchang as minister of Communications and of Lin Hanxiong as minister of Construction, respectively for abusing power for personal gain and violating state discipline.

April 8. The NPC appoints Mayor of Shanghai Zhu Rongji and Minister of the State Planning Commission Zou Jiahua as vice-premiers; Minister of Foreign Affairs Qian Qichen as a state councillor; and head of NCNA's Hong Kong Branch Zhou Nan to the Standing Committee of the NPC.

E Cultural and Social Events

January 1. The Soviet opera *The Taming of the Shrew*, composed by V. Shebalin in the 1950s, is premiered in China at the Central Opera Theatre, being the PRC's first Shakespearean performance in Western operatic style.

January 15–19. The All-China Journalists Association's Fourth Council meets and adopts a professional code of ethics for Chinese journalists which emphasizes the importance of truthful reporting and condemns all forms of falsehood.

January 30. During a meeting with five major leaders of different religious groups, Jiang Zemin reaffirms the CCP's belief in religious freedom and respect for citizens' rights of religious belief and normal religious activities, but asks in return that they support the leadership of the CCP and socialism and carry on their activities within state law.

February 9. At a meeting of artists and writers Li Ruihuan states that cultural workers must 'serve the people and socialism' and economic construction.

June 30. China's first copyright law goes into effect.

March 8. A spokesman for the Chinese Olympic Committee announces that China has decided to apply to hold the 2000 Olympic Games in Beijing.

June 10. A survey of China's spoken languages shows that among the country's Han people, 70 per cent speak the northern dialect, 8.4 per cent Shanghai dialect, 5 per cent each Hunanese and Cantonese, 4 per cent Hakka and 3 per cent Southern Fujian, with the remainder speaking Jiangxi and other dialects.

June 30. The National Tourism Administration and the Civil Aviation Administration of China announce plans for a large-scale campaign to attract tourists in 1992 to be called 'Visit China in 1992'.

September 4. China promulgates the *Law on the Protection of Minors*.

October 12–19. The First World Martial Arts Championships are held in Beijing, China winning fifteen of the 24 gold medals.

November 1. The State Council's Information Office releases the document 'Human Rights in China'.

December 1. Minister of Public Health Chen Minzhang announces that, of 300 000 people examined in 1991, 122 were found to be HIV positive and three to have contracted AIDS. Chen said that eight AIDS patients had been reported since 1985, among whom the first death was in July 1991.

F Births and Deaths

May 14. Jiang Qing, Mao Zedong's widow, commits suicide in prison.

G Natural Disasters, Accidents

April 21. In a coalmine in Shanxi, a huge gas and coal dust explosion kills all 147 miners, the worst coalmining accident in China in three decades.

August 21. An official announcement states that massive floods, especially in eastern and southeastern China and in June and July, have inundated 20 million hectares of cropland and affected some 206 million people, causing billions of dollars of damage to Chinese agriculture.

1992 DENG XIAOPING'S SOUTHERN VISIT MARKS REVITALIZATION OF REFORM

A Foreign Affairs Events

January 7–14. President Yang Shangkun visits Singapore and Malaysia.

January 17. China and the United States reach consensus on settling a potentially major dispute concerning American intellectual property rights, with China agreeing to adopt a series of measures aimed at greater protection of these rights and the United States agreeing to cease investigation of China under particular provisions of the US Trade Act.

January 31. Li Peng, having interrupted his visit to Western Europe (January 27–February 6) and flown from Switzerland to New York, makes a speech at the Summit Meeting of the UN Security Council and holds a meeting with Russian President Boris Yeltsin.

January 22–6. Israeli Foreign Minister David Levine visits China, the first Israeli government minister ever to visit China in an official capacity.

February 11–16. Qian Qichen visits Cambodia and Vietnam, the first Chinese Foreign minister to go to the former country since 1978 and the first ever to the latter.

February 21. The United States announces that it is lifting the ban on high-technology exports to China.

February 24–8. Kazakhstan Premier Tere Scenko visits China.

March 11. China formally accedes to the Treaty on the Non-Proliferation of Nuclear Weapons.

April 6–10. Jiang Zemin visits Japan.

April 14–17. UN Secretary-General Boutros Boutros-Ghali visits Beijing, for the first time as United Nations head.

May 18–23. Indian President Ramaswamy Venkataraman visits China.

June 12. Li Peng addresses the Summit Meeting of the UN Conference on Environment and Development (or 'Earth Summit') in Rio de Janeiro; he emphasizes the need for complementarity between economic development and environmental protection, but proposes that developed countries bear a greater responsibility for protecting the environment than those less developed.

July 30. China officially joins the Universal Copyright Convention in Paris.

September 9. Iranian President Hashemi Ali Akbar Rafsanjani arrives in Beijing for a three-day official visit. The next day China announces that it will build a nuclear power-plant in Iran.

September 17. Qian Qichen arrives in Tel Aviv for a three-day visit to Israel, the first ever made by a Chinese Foreign minister to that country.

September 28. President Roh Tae Woo arrives in Beijing for the first visit of a South Korean president to China.

October 4–10. Nelson Mandela, president of the African National Congress, makes his first visit to China.

October 10. A Sino-American Memorandum of Understanding, which follows five days of heated debate, marks agreement on United States access to Chinese markets.

October 21. Chinese UN Ambassador Hou Zhitong addresses the Forty-seventh Session of the UN General Assembly on the subject of nuclear disarmament.

October 23–9. Japanese Emperor Akihito and Empress Michiko visit Beijing, Xi'an and Shanghai, the first ever visit to China by a Japanese imperial couple. At the welcoming banquet, the Emperor noted 'the great sufferings' that his country 'inflicted on the people of China' during the 1930s and 1940s, adding 'I deeply deplore this'.

October 29–November 3. President Leonid Kravchuk of Ukraine visits China.

November 26. China lodges a strong protest with France for signing a contract with Taiwan to sell 60 Mirage 2000–5 fighters.

November 30–December 4. Li Peng visits Vietnam, the first Chinese premier to do so since 1971. On November 30, Li holds talks with his Vietnamese counterpart Vo Van Khiet, discussing such matters as the dispute over the Spratly Islands and agreeing that the two sides should seek a negotiated settlement.

December 17–20. Russian President Boris Yeltsin makes an official visit to China, signing 24 agreements with Chinese leaders. The joint declaration of December 18 states that the two countries will regard each other as friends.

December 24–30. Israeli President Hayim Herzog visits China, the first Israeli head of state ever to do so.

B Domestic Political Events

January 14. Jiang Zemin opens the First Central Nationalities Work Conference with a speech stressing national unity, the retention of the policies of autonomy, and improved economic development and social welfare for the minorities.

January 18–February 12. Deng Xiaoping makes a visit to southern China, including Wuhan, Guangzhou, Shenzhen, Zhuhai (January 19–23 in Shenzhen and Zhuhai) and Shanghai. This tour forms the basis of a reinvigorated reform process following the June 4 Incident.

February 25. The NPC Standing Committee adopts *The Law of the PRC on its Territorial Waters and Contiguous Areas*.

April 4. A ceremony marks the establishment of the China Tibet Development Foundation, a non-government body that aims at the social, economic and cultural development of Tibet.

July 23. In response to the most serious train robbery in PRC history, 45 train robbers, all peasants from Sichuan Province, are sentenced to death, given suspended death sentences, or sentenced to imprisonment of varying lengths.

October 4. A Foreign Ministry spokesman confirms that China has recently conducted an underground nuclear test (probably on September 25).

October 5–9. The Ninth Plenum of the Thirteenth Central Committee decides to maintain the verdict on Zhao Ziyang, former general secretary of the CCP (see **D.** June 24, 1989).

October 12. In his speech opening the Fourteenth CCP Congress, Jiang Zemin emphasizes the need to establish the 'socialist market economy', showing his adherence to the line advocated by Deng Xiaoping earlier in the year.

October 28. Routine talks open in Hong Kong between representatives of the PRC's ARATS and Taiwan's Straits Exchange Foundation (SEF), with very little progress being made on PRC–Taiwan relations.

C Economic Events

February 12. Jiang Zemin presides over a meeting of the CCP Central Committee's Politburo which discussed Deng Xiaoping's ideas of recent weeks. It decides to adopt these ideas: that absolute top priority should go to economic development, with new measures taken to speed up reform.

March 2. In a speech to the State Council, Li Peng urges all government departments to step up reform to promote national development.

April 3. The NPC votes in favour of the Three Gorges Project (1767 in favour, 177 against, with 664 abstentions).

June 29. Vice-Premier Tian Jiyun states that the emphasis in agriculture has changed from increasing farm output to raising both output and quality as well as economic efficiency.

August 10. A new-generation satellite is successfully launched from the Jiuquan Launch Centre in Gansu. It is designed to perform scientific surveys and technical experiments.

August 11. Riots break out in Shenzhen when would-be punters, after waiting in queues a long time, are denied the opportunity to buy shares on its new stock exchange.

September 25. The State Council decides to diversify and restructure agricultural production and proposes further marketizing agriculture, including deregulating grain purchase and market prices, one of the aims of this last measure being that it would ease the state's fiscal burden by cutting out the high subsidies given for grain purchases.

November 22. After five years of development, a new Chinese supercomputer goes on line.

December 21. For the first time, Shanghai sells land use rights to a domestic firm.

D Appointments, Dismissals, etc.

October 19. The First Plenum of the Fourteenth Central Committee chooses a new Standing Committee of the Politburo (see Chapter 2) including three new members, Zhu Rongji, Liu Huaqing and Hu Jintao, who replace Yao Yilin and Song Ping. Other than Yao and Song, Yang Shangkun, Wan Li, Qin Jiwei and Wu Xueqian resign their Politburo membership. Other than the seven members of the Standing Committee, those whom the Plenum chose for the Politburo include Ding Guan'gen, Tian Jiyun, Li Lanqing, Li Tieying, Yang Baibing, Wu Bangguo, Zou Jiahua, Chen Xitong, Jiang Chunyun, Qian Qichen and Wei Jianxing. The Plenum also chooses the following Central Military Commission: Chairman, Jiang Zemin, Vice-Chairmen, Liu Huaqing and Zhang Zhen, members, Chi Haotian, Zhang Wannian, Yu Yongbo and Fu Quanyou.

E Cultural and Social Events

February 28. The State Statistical Bureau reports that over 33 million children of school age (about one in five) are still not attending school, most of them in the countryside, where most children still leave school at the age of 13 or 14 in order to take up paid work. Attendance rates are highest in Jiangsu, and lowest in Guizhou, Yunnan and Qinghai.

April 3. The NPC adopts the *PRC Law Protecting Women's Rights and Interests*, and the *Trade Union Law*.

April 7. The Science and Technology Development Commission discloses the State Council's 'State Medium and Long-Term Science and Technology Development Programme', which sets down the general aim of reaching, by the year 2020, the level of technology reached by the developed countries by the turn of the century.

June 6. Six leading PRC scientists leave Beijing for Taiwan, the first of their kind since 1949.

July 26. In the women's 100 m freestyle swimming race Zhuang Yong wins China's first gold medal, also setting a new Olympic record for the event at 15.64 seconds.

September 27. O'kying Chilai is enthroned as the Seventeenth Incarnate Buddha of Karmapa and as the leader of the White Sect of Tibetan Buddhism.

F Births and Deaths

March 16. Wang Renzhong, former director of propaganda in the CCP, dies.

May 14. Marshal Nie Rongzhen, the last of the ten marshals of the PRC, dies in Beijing, aged 93.

June 21. Former President Li Xiannian dies in Beijing at the age of 83.

July 11. Zhou Enlai's widow Deng Yingchao dies in Beijing aged 88.

August 3. Former 'gang of four' member Wang Hongwen dies of a disease of the liver.

September 28. Marxist theorist Hu Qiaomu dies aged 81.

G Natural Disasters, Accidents

Summer. The middle and lower reaches of the Yellow River suffer serious drought, affecting 5.1 million hectares of farmland in Henan Province alone.

Late June to early July. A week's torrential rain in Fujian Province causes the most serious flooding since 1949 along the Min River, including in the capital Fuzhou.

July 31. An airliner crashes after take-off from Nanjing airport, killing at least 106 people on board.

August 8–13. Floods and landslides in Shaanxi Province kill at least 86 people and destroy three million hectares of farmland and 2000 houses. Worst hit is Lüeyang County in the far southwest of the province, where a landslide brings down rock and mud, killing 49 people.

November 24. A flight from Guangzhou to Guilin in Guangxi crashes near its destination, killing all 141 people on board.

1993

A Foreign Affairs Events

February 10. Spanish Prime Minister Felipe Gonzalez arrives in China for a four-day visit.

May 7. Zimbabwe Prime Minister Robert Mugabe arrives in Beijing for a five-day state visit to China.

May 15. New Zealand Prime Minister Bolger arrives in China for an official visit.

May 29. A Chinese Foreign Ministry spokesman condemns the statement made the previous day by US President Bill Clinton concerning conditions he plans to impose on the renewal of China's most-favoured-nation (MFN) trading status.

April 26. Philippines President Fidel Ramos arrives in Beijing for a five-day official visit, the first Philippines head of state to pay a state visit to China.

June 2. Georgian head of state Eduard Shevardnadze begins a visit to China.

June 15. At the World Conference on Human Rights in Vienna, Vice-Premier Liu Huaqiu gives a speech arguing that the main criterion for human rights in a developing country should be whether its policies assist in promoting economic and social progress.

June 23. Australian Prime Minister Paul Keating arrives for an official five-day visit to China.

July 27. The Chinese Olympic Committee strongly condemns the American House of Representatives, which the preceding day had adopted a resolution urging that Beijing not be allowed to host the 2000 Summer Olympic Games on human rights grounds.

September 6–9. Indian Prime Minister P. V. Narasimha Rao visits China, holding talks with Li Peng and Jiang Zemin on September 7. Four documents are signed the same day, one concerning the maintenance of border peace along the lines of actual control in part by reducing troops along the common borders, one on environmental cooperation and one on expanded border trade.

September 13. The Korean news agency reports that South Korea had reached agreement with China to cooperate in the development of Chinese nuclear power plants.

September 14. China joins the World Intellectual Property Organization.

September 23. By a narrow vote, the International Olympic Committee decides against Beijing and in favour of Sydney as the site for the 2000 Summer Olympic Games.

October 10–14. Yitzhaq Rabin makes the first visit of an Israeli prime minister to China.

October 19. In Hanoi China and Vietnam sign an agreement 'on the basic principles for the settlement of border territory disputes'.

November 9. During a week-long visit to China, Vietnamese President Le Duc Anh meets with Jiang Zemin. As the first Vietnamese president to visit China since 1955, this represents an improvement of relations between the two neighbours.

November 15. German Chancellor Helmut Kohl arrives in Beijing for a six-day visit to China, leading a delegation of some forty German business executives.

November 19. While in Seattle, Washington, for meetings of the Asia-Pacific Economic Cooperation (APEC) Forum, Jiang Zemin meets with Bill Clinton; and on this and the following day with the prime ministers of Australia, Canada, Japan and other countries.

November 21. Jiang Zemin arrives in Cuba for a short visit.

November 22–28. Jiang Zemin visits Brazil. After leaving Brazil, he makes a brief stopover in Lisbon on his way home.

B Domestic Political Events

March 16. Armed militiamen, called out to suppress a protest, shoot a dozen or so peasants dead in the town of Shengli, Heilongjiang.

March 22. The NPC approves the restructuring of the ministries and commissions under the State Council by cutting their number from 86 to 59 and the number of their employees by a fifth.

March 29. The First Session of the Eighth NPC amends the Constitution, among other points to declare China 'at the primary stage of socialism', to eliminate reference to rural people's communes in the list of rural social formations, and to enshrine the 'socialist market economy'.

March 31. The NPC approves *The Basic Law of the Macau Special Administrative Region*.

April 27–29. Chairman Wang Daohan of the PRC's ARATS and Chairman Koo Chen-fu of Taiwan's SEF meet in Singapore for the first high-level talks between the PRC and Taiwan since 1949. On April 29 they sign agreements on cooperation in a range of matters, such as direct shipping, flights, postal and telecommunications links.

May 3. The Thirteenth National Congress of the CCYL opens in Beijing, electing a new Central Committee on May 9.

May 8. *People's Daily* reveals that the CCP Central Committee and State Council General Office have prohibited all CCP and government institutions or their staff from accepting gifts of money or securities, with the aim of preventing corruption.

May 24. Large-scale demonstrations in Lhasa on behalf of independence and much smaller ones the following day result in up to nine deaths.

June 7. Order is restored in Renshou County, Sichuan, where, since November 1992, mass protests have occurred against increasing taxes and exactions aimed at building a road; the protests have climaxed in attacks on property and violent clashes between villagers and government officials. Provincial authorities have taken action against corrupt officials by sending in armed police and a work team.

June 17. A separatist group explodes two bombs in the Oasis Hotel in Kaxgar, Xinjiang, seriously damaging the building and killing three people.

August 23. Vice-minister for the State Physical Culture and Sports Commission He Zhenliang, arrives in Taipei, the most senior official to travel to Taiwan from the PRC since 1949.

August 31. The State Council issues a White Paper on Taiwan, entitled 'The Taiwan Question and the Reunification of China', which argues in favour of Taiwan's peaceful reunification with the mainland.

September 15. Wei Jingsheng, serving a fifteen-year prison term since 1979, is released one year early on probation.

October 5. China confirms that it has just conducted an underground nuclear test in Lop Nor, Xinjiang.

October 7. Muslim riots in Xining, which had begun over the publication of a book considered offensive but resulted in attacks on local Party and government offices and damage to other property, are suppressed by public security bodies and order is restored.

October 8. In a move aimed at tightening control over information, Li Peng signs an order banning individuals and businesses from using or setting up satellite dishes; it is due to go into effect on November 1.

December 26. A meeting in Beijing, attended by Jiang Zemin and Li Peng, marks the centenary of Mao Zedong's birth.

C Economic Events

February 22. The China Land Development Association is established in Beijing to serve real estate business, the first of its kind in China.

March 15. In his speech opening the First Session of the Eighth NPC, Li Peng places emphasis on the economy, giving a basically optimistic picture but also drawing attention to problems.

April 1. In a major speech on the economy, Jiang Zemin calls for accelerated development and deepening reform, with agriculture given priority, but warns against illegal exactions on peasants, and against widening inequalities between the east and west of the country and between the rich and the poor. He also warns against accelerating inflation and calls for clean and honest government.

April 21. The State Planning Commission announces an enormous investment scheme designed to promote the development of the Yangzi Valley.

May 27. The National Environmental Protection Agency announces the names of 3000 Chinese enterprises held responsible for about 60 per cent of annual industrial pollutants discharged in the country.

June 20. The State Council announces the abolition of 37 fees and taxes on peasants.

September 15. The world's largest cable-stayed bridge, the 7658 m Yangpu spanning the Huangpu River in Shanghai, is completed, opening to traffic on October 23.

October 18. Jiang Zemin criticizes the weak performance of agriculture but declares that its position as the 'foundation of the national economy' must be upheld.

November 14. The Third Plenary Session of the Fourteenth Central Committee adopts its decision 'concerning the establishment of a socialist market economic structure', which outlines economic policy in considerable detail. It affirms the need to change the traditional concepts of the planned economy and declares that 'economic development and social stability promote one another and form a single entity'. Among its many major ideas are that the market should be allowed to play a basic role in allocating resources; and that the government should manage the national economy by economic, legal and necessary administrative means but not interfere directly in the production and management of enterprises. It also pushes for better yields in agriculture and emphasizes the role of science and technology in economic development.

December 15. The first China–Japan underwater fibre-optic cable goes into operation.

D Appointments, Dismissals, etc.

March 26. Li Ruihuan is elected to chair the CCPCC.

March 27. The NPC appoints Jiang Zemin as state president (replacing Yang Shangkun) and Rong Yiren as state vice-president (replacing the late Wang Zhen; see below F. March 12). It also mandates Jiang Zemin as chairman of the State Central Military Commission and thus commander-in-chief of the PLA. The NPC appoints Qiao Shi as chairman of the NPC Standing Committee.

March 28. The NPC chooses Liu Huaqing and Zhang Zhen as vice-chairmen of the State Central Military Commission.

March 29. The NPC reappoints Zhu Rongji and Zou Jiahua as vice-premiers and, as new appointments, Qian Qichen and Li Lanqing.

July 2. Zhu Rongji is appointed governor of the People's Bank of China, replacing Li Guixian.

September 26. Fan Jinyi replaces Shao Huaze as editor-in-chief of *Renmin ribao* (*People's Daily*).

E Cultural and Social Events

February 25. NCNA publishes the 'Programme for China's Educational Reform and Development'.

April 20. China publishes its first Blue Book on the country's society and social situation.

May 9–18. The First East Asian Games take place in Shanghai, with China winning two-thirds of the available gold medals.

June 12. A Chinese Foreign Ministry spokesman announces a series of measures to curb illegal emigration.

June 29. The State Council adopts regulations for the resettlement of over one million people to be displaced by the Three Gorges Dam Project.

September 1. At the opening of the six-day Seventh National Congress of Chinese Women, Hu Jintao gives a speech, emphasizing that women should play a greater role in China's economic and social life and in the professions. According to the Congress, there are 56 million female workers in China, or 38 per cent of the labour force, of whom 175 000 have senior professional titles.

September 2–12. The '93 Beijing Ancient Capital Cultural Relics Fair takes place in Beijing, the largest of its kind ever held there.

October 7–14. The First Shanghai International Film Festival takes place, with 161 films from 30 countries and regions being screened.

October 23. The China Tibetan Buddhism Symposium opens in Beijing, the largest of its kind since 1949, attended by incarnate lamas and eminent monks from all over China.

November 2. The People's Press publishes Volume 3 of *Deng Xiaoping wenxuan* (*The Selected Works of Deng Xiaoping*).

November 7. At a meeting with participants in a national conference on united front work (held November 3–7) Jiang Zemin calls for the strengthening of this work. In particular, he urges respect for religious beliefs and cultural differences among the minorities.

December 1. China marks the Sixth World AIDS Day by setting up the China Venereal Disease and AIDS Prevention Association in Beijing, aimed at mobilizing action to control the spread of these diseases.

F Births and Deaths

March 7. In Guangxi, eighteen criminals are executed for abducting and selling women and children and for rape.

March 12. Vice-President Wang Zhen dies, aged 85, in Guangzhou.

June 27. About 100 drug traffickers are executed in Yunnan Province.

July 13. Twelve people are executed in Guangdong Province for kidnapping women and forcing them into prostitution.

September 27. The Supreme People's Court sentences eight officials to death for grafting enormous sums of government bank savings.

October 29. Three high-ranking officials are executed for embezzlement and accepting bribes.

November 27. Five people are executed in Beijing for embezzlement.

G Natural Disasters, Accidents

March 8. Heavy snows in Qinghai cause enormous destruction of livestock.

April 2. A mine explosion in Shenyang kills 22 people.

July 23. A plane crash on takeoff at Yinchuan, Ningxia, kills some 60 people.

1994

A Foreign Affairs Events

January 11. *People's Daily* condemns the unilateral decision of the United States (January 6) to cut textile imports from China.

February 28. The Chinese Ministry of Foreign Affairs issues a lengthy attack on Britain for publishing the 1993 Sino-British negotiations over elections in Hong Kong.

February 20. Slovak Prime Minister Vladimir Mediar arrives in China for his first official visit there since his country split from the Czech Republic.

March 17. China and the United States sign a memorandum of agreement concerning bilateral textile trade.

March 19. Japanese Prime Minister Morihiro Hosokawa begins a three-day visit to China.

May 3. Kenyan President Daniel T. Arap Moi arrives in Kunming for a five-day state visit to China.

May 10. Japanese Prime Minister Tsutomu Hata notifies Chinese Premier Li Peng of his regret for a statement which his minister of Finance, Shigeto Nagano, had made a few days earlier which underplayed the severity of Japanese aggression against China in the 1930s and 1940s and, in particular, cast doubt on whether the Nanjing Massacre beginning in December 1937 had taken place.

May 26. US President Bill Clinton announces the extension of China's MFN trading status; it includes expectations concerning China's performance on human rights, but no preconditions.

May 27. China's Foreign Ministry welcomes President Clinton's announcement of the preceding day.

July 5. China's leaders send a message of condolence on the death of North Korean President Kim Il Sung, who died the previous day.

July 22. Chinese UN Ambassador Li Zhaoxing meets with UN Secretary-General Boutros Boutros-Ghali, and strongly opposes a move by Nicaragua and other countries to open discussion on Taiwan's representation in the United Nations.

July 28. China and Latvia agree to normalize their relations. China undertook to reopen its embassy in Riga, the Latvian capital, the Taiwanese consulate having in the meantime been closed.

September 2–13. Jiang Zemin arrives in Moscow for a five-day visit to Russia, going on to Ukraine and arriving in Kiev on September 6, and France, arriving September 8.

September 3. Chinese and Russian foreign ministers sign the Agreement on the Western Section of the Boundary Between the People's Republic of China and the Russian Federation.

September 14–18. Hungarian President Goncz Arpad visits China.

September 23–4. The Ministerial Conference on Space Applications for Development in Asia and the Pacific, organized by the Economic and Social Commission for Asia and the Pacific (ESCAP) and the PRC government, takes place in Beijing. The Conference issues a declaration that asserts, among other points, 'that all members of ESCAP have the right to carry out the exploration and peaceful use of outer space and to the use of space technologies for their natural resources and environmental management and sustainable development planning'.

October 14–20. At a meeting in Moscow, delegates from Russia, China and Mongolia agree on a protocol defining their mutual borders.

October 31. Li Peng arrives in Seoul for a five-day visit to South Korea, the first ever made by a Chinese prime minister there, meeting with President Kim Young-sam the same day.

November 6. Canadian Prime Minster Jean Chrétien arrives in Beijing for a six-day official visit to China.

November 8–22. Jiang Zemin visits Singapore, Malaysia, Indonesia and Vietnam. In Bogor, Indonesia, Jiang attends and makes speeches to the APEC conference and meets with various world leaders, notably (on November 14) President Clinton. On November 22, China and Vietnam sign a joint communiqué that includes a pledge to 'try and solve the issues of demarcation of their land border and in the Beibu Bay area as soon as possible'.

B Domestic Political Events

March 7. Jiang Zemin gives a speech at a national Party school work conference in which he emphasizes the still crucial importance of theoretical study.

March 30. Dissidents in Shanghai present a petition to the NPC asking for freedom of the press and a multi-party system.

March 31. The deaths of 24 Taiwanese tourists in a pleasure boat on Qiandao Lake, Zhejiang, lead on to complications in relations between the PRC and Taiwan in the following months.

June 10. NCNA reports that China has held an underground nuclear test.

September 28. The Fourth Plenary Session of the Fourteenth Central Committee of the CCP adopts a document on Party building, which aims to improve Party leadership in the context of accelerating reform and modernization.

October 7. A Chinese Foreign Ministry spokesman confirms that China has conducted another underground nuclear test.

October 8. Czech Prime Minister Václav Klaus arrives in China for visit.

November 4. Following over two years of negotiations, China and Britain sign an agreement on financing a new airport at Chek Lap Kok in Hong Kong.

C Economic Events

February 6. Li Peng attends a ceremony marking the beginning of operations of the Daya Bay Nuclear Power Plant near Hong Kong.

March 10. Li Peng's report to the Second Session of the Eighth NPC gives an account of good performance but expresses concern over some aspects, especially excessive investment in fixed assets and inflation.

March 22. The NPC adopts China's first *Budget Law*, which, among many provisions, forbids regional governments to incur a budget deficit.

July 21. China successfully launches its Asia-Pacific No. 1 satellite at Xichang in Sichuan.

August 28. The Chinese carrier Long March–2E blasts off at Xichang, Sichuan Province, sending into orbit the American-made, Australian-owned Optus-B3 satellite.

D Appointments, Dismissals, etc.

November 1. NCNA announces the appointment of Zhang Quanjing as director of the CCP Central Committee's Organizational Department, replacing Lu Feng.

E Cultural and Social Events

February 14. An official report claims that smoking has become one of the major causes of death in China.

June 12. Jiang Zemin addresses a national education conference, urging greater priority to education and educational reforms.

June 19. *Gongren ribao* (*Workers' Daily*) claims that in 1992 about half a million teachers left their profession due to low salaries and poor social status.

October 5. At an international conference to honour Confucius and Confucianism, Li Ruihuan praises Confucian theory as still holding some validity and worthy of study, especially if combined with modern practices.

October 10. China publishes a government report on women entitled 'The Report of the PRC on the Implementation of the Nairobi Forward-Looking Strategies for the Advancement of Women'.

November 3. A new edition of the first two volumes of *Deng Xiaoping wenxuan* (*The Selected Works of Deng Xiaoping*) appears in the bookshops, a CCP circular the same day describing these volumes as 'the groundwork of the theory of building socialism with Chinese characteristics'.

F Births and Deaths

January 18. Tibetan chamois preservation activist Galsang Soinam Targyai is fatally shot in a gun battle with nineteen armed hunters of the animal.

February 27. Aisin Giorro Pujie, the brother of the last emperor, Puyi, dies at the age of 87.

June 12. A court in Hangzhou sentences three men to death for robbing and murdering 24 tourists from Taiwan and eight crew members on a pleasure boat on Qiandao Lake, Zhejiang Province, on March 31, the three being executed a week later.

June 24–5. Numerous drug traffickers are executed or sentenced to death in a dozen or so cities in Guangdong, Fujian, Sichuan, Shaanxi and other provinces, indicating a major crackdown on narcotics and drug abuse.

December 11. Former Politburo Standing Committee member Yao Yilin dies, aged 77.

December 23. *China Daily* reports that five people have been sentenced to death in Yunnan for hunting elephants.

G Natural Disasters, Accidents

June 6. A China Northwest Airlines aircraft crashes near Xi'an, killing all 160 people on board.

June 8–18. An enormous typhoon series sweeps Guangdong, Fujian, Hunan, Jiangxi and Guangxi, killing at least 300 people and causing torrential rains and serious flooding, which destroy large areas of crops. By the end of the month some 20 million people have been affected by the floods.

Summer. High temperatures and drought affect the provinces of Anhui, Jiangsu, Hubei, Sichuan, Henan and Shaanxi. In the case of Anhui and Jiangsu, the drought is the worst since 1934.

August 4. The Disaster Relief Section of the Ministry of Civil Affairs reports that storms and flooding in Guangdong, Guangxi, Hunan and Fujian Provinces have resulted in 7523 casualties, the destruction of over half a million houses and of over 1.5 million hectares of farmland.

August 11. *China Daily* reports that floods killed 1019 people and caused economic loss to the value of ¥540 million in the first half of 1994.

1995

A Foreign Affairs Events

January 15. Chinese and French officials sign a Memorandum of Understanding on the construction of the Daya Bay Second Nuclear Power Station in Guangdong.

January 20. Following ten months of talks, agreement is reached on Chinese textile exports to the European Union.

February 8. The Philippines issues a protest against Chinese-built structures on Mischief Reef near the Philippines island of Palawan, the Chinese arguing that they are for sheltering fishermen.

February 26. After about two months' extremely acrimonious discussion between Chinese and American representatives, as well as American threats and Chinese counter-threats, American action and Chinese reaction, a letter of exchange is signed by which China guarantees to protect American intellectual property rights. This agreement forestalls a major trade war between the two countries.

March 11. Mickey Kantor and Wu Yi, the relevant Trade ministers, sign the 'Agreement on Intellectual Property Rights' in Beijing.

March 22. Sino-Philippines talks over Mischief Reef end in deadlock, after which the Philippines navy begins blowing up Chinese perimeter markers in its claimed territorial waters.

March 28. King Juan Carlos and Queen Dona Sofia of Spain arrive in China for a state visit, meeting with Jiang Zemin the next day.

May 7. Jiang Zemin arrives in Moscow to attend the celebrations for the fiftieth anniversary of the victory in the war against Germany, meeting with President Boris Yeltsin the next day.

May 23. Foreign Minister Qian Qichen lodges a strong protest with the American Ambassador to China, Stapleton Roy, against the decision of the previous day to grant Lee Teng-hui a visa to visit the United States to attend the commencement ceremony at Cornell University, his alma mater.

June 8. US President Bill Clinton meets Chinese Ambassador Li Daoyu at the White House, reaffirming his commitment to a one-China policy and attempting to persuade him that Lee Teng-hui's visit to the United States (June 7–12) was totally unofficial and private.

June 25–28. Li Peng visits Russia, following visits to Belarus and Ukraine.

July 5–15. Jiang Zemin visits Finland, Hungary and Germany.

July 8. Naturalized American Harry Wu (Wu Hongda) is arrested in Wuhan for criminal activities, such as obtaining state secrets. The United States protests, taking the bilateral Sino-American relationship to a new low.

August 24. Russia and China sign an agreement on cooperation in border guard issues. The Wuhan People's Intermediate Court convicts Harry Wu of espionage and sentences him to a long term in prison, but he is immediately released and expelled from China.

September 4–15. The UN Fourth World Conference on Women takes place in Beijing, adopting the Beijing Declaration and Platform for Action on the last day.

September 11. Jiang Zemin and visiting Kazakhstan President Nursultan Nazarbayev sign a joint declaration concerning a range of bilateral ties, including reduction in the border forces.

October 24. While in New York to attend the fiftieth anniversary commemorations of the United Nations, Jiang Zemin holds a summit meeting with US President Bill Clinton at the Lincoln Center, the third since 1993. Clinton calls for constructive partnership with China and an early solution to China's membership of the World Trade Organization (WTO). He also states that the United States opposes Taiwan's independence as well as its admission into the United Nations.

November 12. German Chancellor Helmut Kohl arrives in China for a five-day official visit.

November 13. Jiang Zemin arrives in Seoul to begin a five-day state visit to South Korea, the first Chinese head of state ever to make such a visit. The following day he delivers a speech to the National Assembly of the Republic of Korea in which, among other points, he dismisses as totally groundless the theory that China has the potential to pose a threat to other countries.

November 19. Jiang Zemin addresses the APEC forum in Osaka, Japan. Among many other points, Jiang announces that China will shortly implement a sharp reduction in its general level of import tariffs.

B Domestic Political Events

January 30. Jiang Zemin gives a speech on Taiwan. He advocated reunification of

Taiwan with the mainland on the basis of Deng Xiaoping's theory of 'one country, two systems'.

May 15. China conducts an underground nuclear test.

May 16. The *Interim Regulations on Selection and Appointment of Party and Government Leading Cadres*, formulated February 9, 1995, are published.

August 17. China conducts an underground nuclear test.

September 3. Jiang Zemin makes a speech at a mass rally held in Beijing to mark the fiftieth anniversary of the victory over Japan.

December 13. The Beijing No. 1 Intermediate People's Court sentences Wei Jingsheng to prison for fourteen years, his appeal against the sentence being rejected December 28.

C Economic Events

March 18. The NPC adopts *The Law on the People's Bank of China*, China's first banking law. It aims to help China stabilize its currency, strengthen banking management, improve government economic control, and ensure smooth progress in banking system reform.

April 25. *Liberation Army Daily* reports the first successful trial flight of a supersonic unmanned plane.

June 27. NCNA publishes new regulations on foreign investment, which encourage moving foreign investment towards the central and western regions, and show commitment to agriculture, energy, communications, and other sectors.

September 28. At the conclusion of the Fifth Plenary Session of the Fourteenth CCP Central Committee, the CCP confirms that the Plenum has adopted the 'CCP Central Committee's Proposal Concerning the Formulation of the Ninth Five-Year Plan (1996–2000) for the National Economic and Social Development and the Long-Term

Target for the Year 2010'. Among numerous other points, this very important document declares that China must hold its population to 1.3 billion by the year 2000 and 1.4 billion by 2010.

November 16. A ceremony marks the completion of work on the 2536 km Beijing–Kowloon railway.

November 28. The Satellite Launching Center at Xichang, southwest Sichuan, successfully launches a commercial satellite.

D Appointments, Dismissals, etc.

March 17. The NPC appoints two new vice-premiers: Wu Bangguo and Jiang Chunyun. Most unusually, both have votes recorded against their appointment, especially Jiang.

April 27. Beijing CCP Municipal Secretary Chen Xitong resigns (see also Chapter 2), being replaced by Wei Jianxing.

May 14. The Dalai Lama names the 6-year-old Tibetan boy Gehun Choekyi Nyima as the Eleventh Panchen Lama, to the subsequent fury of the Chinese.

December 8. The 6-year-old Tibetan Gyaincain Norbu is formally enthroned as the Eleventh Panchen Lama at the Tashilhunbo Monastery in Xigaze, Tibet. This follows the drawing of lots from a gold urn on November 29, which yielded his name.

E Cultural and Social Events

January 17. Workers at the Japanese-owned Panasonic Motor Factory in Zhuhai end a one-day strike after management agrees to open negotiations over wages.

February 15. According to official estimates, China's population reaches 1.2 billion.

September 1. *The Education Law of the PRC*, adopted by the NPC in March, goes into effect.

November 17–24. The First China Peking Opera Arts Festival takes place in Tianjin.

December 13–January 21. A major festival of modern regional operas takes place in

Beijing, featuring 38 items of twenty regional styles from eighteen provinces and municipalities.

December 27. NCNA issues a white paper entitled 'The Progress of Human Rights in China'.

F Births and Deaths

March 30. NCNA reports the death of Gong Laifa in his Guizhou home town at the age of 147: China's oldest man.

April 4. Vice-Mayor of Beijing Wang Baosen commits suicide.

April 10. Chen Yun, highly influential economic CCP leader, dies in Beijing, aged 90.

November 29. Businesswomen Deng Bin and Yao Jingyi are executed for massive embezzlement, bribery and illegal profit-making.

G Natural Disasters

July 7. A flood peak reaches the city of Wuhan, a climax in calamitous floods which hit the lower and middle reaches of the Yangzi River and the Dongting and Poyang lake valleys in June and early July, causing the deaths of 1179 people and direct economic losses of ¥36.6 billion, and displacing about 1.2 million people, mostly in Hunan Province.

October 24. An earthquake measuring 6.5 on the Richter scale hits Yunnan Province, with the epicentre about 150 km northwest of Kunming; 44 people are killed and about 240 seriously injured.

1996

A Foreign Affairs Events

January 7–13. The head of state of Myanmar, General Than Shwe, visits China.

March 13. In response to China's military exercises in the Taiwan Straits (see below, B.) planes from the USS Independence, located about 320 km off the east coast of Taiwan, carry out a show of American support for Taiwan.

The American Administration intends to send also the USS Nimitz to join it.

March 20. A meeting of American and Taiwan officials discuss the American defence of Taiwan. The United States agrees to sell Stinger surface-to-air missiles and other military equipment to Taiwan, but refuses Taiwan's request for six submarines.

March 25–28. UN Secretary-General Boutros Boutros-Ghali visits China.

April 17. A Chinese Foreign Ministry spokesman condemns the decision by Vietnam to grant oil companies the right to undertake oil exploration in the sea area of the Nansha Islands.

April 18–19. In Beijing, representatives of the countries of Northeast Asia hold a meeting to discuss the development of the Tumen River Zone on the border between China and North Korea.

April 24–26. Russian President Boris Yeltsin visits China.

April 26. The presidents of China, Russia, Kazakhstan, Kyrgyzstan and Tajikistan meet in Shanghai and sign an agreement on military confidence-building in the border areas. Military forces along the borders undertake not to attack each other or to carry out hostile military exercises.

May 8–22. Jiang Zemin visits Kenya, Ethiopia, Egypt, Mali, Namibia and Zimbabwe. On May 13 he addresses the Organization of African Unity, criticizing the persistence of 'hegemonism' and bemoaning the weak economic conditions that many African countries have inherited from colonialism.

May 15. The United States announces a list of retaliatory measures against China for alleged intellectual property rights infringements.

June 13. A Chinese Foreign Ministry spokesman announces that China has decided to close the China office of the German Friedrich Naumann Foundation, because of its plans to hold an international conference of groups favouring independence for Tibet.

June 13–17. Chinese and American representatives hold talks, eventually reaching consensus on the last day that they will cancel trade sanctions against each other.

June 23–July 6. Jiang Zemin visits Spain, Norway, Romania, Uzbekistan, Kyrgyzstan and Kazakhstan, signing an agreement on the borders between China and Kyrgyzstan on July 4.

June 27–28. Li Peng heads a CCP delegation to Hanoi to take part in the Eighth National Congress of the Communist Party of Vietnam.

July 18. A Chinese Foreign Ministry spokesman criticizes Japan for encroaching on its territory in the Diaoyu Islands, where some Japanese had set up facilities on one of the islands.

July 19–August 4. China takes part in the Olympic Games in the American city of Atlanta, taking fourth place in terms of medals.

July 22–25. Chinese Foreign Minister Qian Qichen visits Indonesia, for the first time taking part in the deliberations of the Association of Southeast Asian Nations (ASEAN) as a full dialogue partner. On July 23 he addresses the third meeting of the ASEAN Regional Forum.

July 29. Chinese Foreign Ministry Spokesman Cui Tiankai sharply criticizes Japanese Prime Minister Ryutaro Hashimoto for making a 'private visit' to the Yasukuni Shrine to honour Japanese war dead (Hashimoto subsequently cancelling a further visit planned for September).

August 24–27. Malaysian Prime Minister Mahathir Mohamad visits China.

September 12–16. Bangladeshi Prime Minister Mrs Sheikh Hasina visits China.

September 24. China signs the Comprehensive Nuclear Test Ban Treaty in New York.

September 25. Chinese and Japanese Foreign Ministers Qian Qichen and Yukihiko Ikeda agree to ease tension over the Diaoyu Islands, with Ikeda agreeing not to recognize the status of a lighthouse that a 'rightist group' had erected there.

October 9–11. Jean-Pascal Delamuraz makes the first visit to China by a president of the Swiss Confederation.

November 6. At the United Nations, Chinese representative Wang Xuexian denounces Western countries, especially the United States, for practising power politics in the mass media on the pretext of 'freedom of information', for instance by establishing any 'freedom radio' to stir up trouble in countries like China.

November 6–18. Li Peng visits Chile, Brazil, Venezuela and Italy, delivering a speech to the World Food Summit in Rome (held November 13–17).

November 25. Jiang Zemin makes a speech to the APEC Forum, meeting in Subic Bay in the Philippines, criticizing the view that economic and technical cooperation among nations should be subordinate to trade and investment liberalization.

November 26–December 5. Jiang Zemin makes state visits to the Philippines, India, Pakistan and Nepal, addressing the Pakistani Senate on December 2.

December 26–28. Li Peng visits Russia, the two sides agreeing, on December 27, to the joint construction of a nuclear power plant in Lianyungang, Jiangsu Province.

B Domestic Political Events

January 15. The Japanese newsagency Kyodo reports that Chinese CCP and government officials have agreed to cut the size of the PLA by 500 000 to 2.5 million.

February 19. The CCP Central Committee and the State Council publish their decision on 'Strengthening Comprehensive Management of Public Order'.

March 8–15. China sends four M9 surface-to-surface missiles towards Taiwan.

March 12–20. China holds further naval and air force exercises, with live ammunition, in the Taiwan Straits.

March 17. The Fourth Session of the Eighth NPC adopts the *Law on Administrative Punishment* (due to take effect on October 1, 1996) and the *Criminal Procedure Law* (due to take effect on January 1, 1997).

March 19–25. China holds joint ground, naval and air operations in the Taiwan Straits, as Taiwan holds its first general elections (March 23).

May 19. In his inaugural speech as Taiwan's president, Lee Teng-hui states that he would be prepared to make a 'journey of peace' to the Chinese mainland to talk to the leaders there.

June 8. A Chinese Foreign Ministry spokesman announces that China has carried out a nuclear test the same day, the announcement provoking strong international protest, especially from Japan.

June 21. In a speech to a meeting to celebrate the CCP's seventy-fifth anniversary, Jiang Zemin draws attention to the changing cadre profile since 1949. He criticizes some younger cadres for poor ideological style and a lack of organization and discipline.

June 25. *People's Daily* urges cadres to integrate Confucian ethics with Marxism, taking the notion of 'self-accomplishment' as a way of improving ethical standards.

July 29. China announces that it has conducted an underground nuclear test the same day, but that a Chinese moratorium on all nuclear tests will go into effect the next day.

August 29. In a meeting with a visiting business delegation from Taiwan, Jiang Zemin calls for greater economic cooperation, despite political differences.

September 14. NCNA announces that the State Council has decided to extend the powers of provinces and autonomous regions in China's interior, with a view to attracting foreign investment and narrowing their economic gap with the regions of the eastern seaboard.

October 4. NCNA issues an article strongly criticizing the Taiwan government for trying to obstruct cross-Straits trade, in particular for the adoption of two sets of rules, dated August 20 and August 21, which cover, respectively, shipping and cargo transportation services across the Taiwan Straits.

October 10. The CCP Fourteenth Central Committee's Sixth Plenum adopts resolutions 'Regarding Important Questions on Promoting Socialist Ethical and Cultural Progress'.

C Economic Events

January 6. The Daliuta coalmine in Shaanxi Province, the largest of all modern coal mines in China, formally goes into production.

January 10. A ceremony in Beijing marks the formal opening of the Yacheng 13–1 natural gasfield in the South China Sea, a large project involving China, the United States and Kuwait.

January 12. A ceremony marks the inauguration of the China Mingsheng Banking Corporation, the first one in the PRC sponsored by non-state enterprises.

January 21. A ceremony marks the opening of the new West Beijing Railway Station, the largest and most technically advanced in China.

January 26. The 947 km double-track railway from Hangzhou, capital of Zhejiang, to Zhuzhou in Hunan opens to traffic.

April 1. A reduction of the general level of import tariffs by 35 per cent to 23 per cent comes into effect; many Western commentators interpret this move as an attempt to advance China's entry into the WTO.

May 6. The CCP Central Committee and State Council issue a circular urging CCP committees and governments at all levels to lighten the burdens on farmers.

June 25. The 144 km expressway linking Taiyuan to Pingding County in Shanxi Province opens to traffic.

July 11. NCNA reports the signing of an oil agreement between the China National Offshore Oil Corporation and Taiwan's China Petroleum Corporation, claiming it as the first of its kind between China and Taiwan and hailing it as a major breakthrough in economic cooperation across the Straits.

July 24. The People's Insurance Company (Group) of China is formally founded.

September 1. The 2552 km Beijing–Kowloon railway formally opens to traffic.

September 16. The Jilin Chemical Industry Group formally goes into production, this large ethylene unit being a key project of the Eighth Five-Year Plan (1991–95).

September 17. A large water diversion project on the upper reaches of the Yellow River is completed after eight years of work.

September 19. The 133 km Changchun–Siping expressway opens to traffic.

September 23–25. A central work conference is held in Beijing aimed at aiding underdeveloped regions of China in economic development.

October. The State Council issues a document called 'The Grain Issue in China', which argues, among many other points, that agriculture is the basis of China's economy and that China is, and can continue to be, basically self-sufficient in grain.

October 1. The Lianjiang International Airport of Guilin, Guangxi, opens to traffic.

November 21–24. A central economic work conference calls for greater reform of state-owned enterprises (SOEs) and a higher priority for agriculture, among other points.

D Appointments, Dismissals, etc.

January 26. The Preparatory Committee of the Hong Kong Special Administrative Region (HKSAR) is formally established in Beijing, one of its tasks being to select the first chief executive for the Region.

February 8. Tie Ying, a very senior female legislative official in Beijing, is dismissed from various posts for accepting bribes.

December 11. In Hong Kong, the specially appointed Selection Committee for the First Government of the HKSAR selects Tung Chee Hwa as the first chief executive of the HKSAR, to take effect with the withdrawal of the British at 24:00 on June 30, 1997.

December 12. In Shenzhen, the Preparatory Committee of the HKSAR endorses the selection of Tung Chee Hwa as first chief executive of the HKSAR.

December 16. In Beijing, the State Council ratifies the appointment of Tung Chee Hwa as first chief executive of the HKSAR.

December 21. The Selection Committee for the First Government of the HKSAR selects 60 members of the Provisional Legislative Council of the HKSAR.

December 26. The CCP Central Commission for Discipline Inspection decides to expel senior Beijing official Huang Jisheng from the CCP for bribery.

E Cultural and Social Events

January 24. In a speech to the heads of provincial CCP committee propaganda departments, Jiang Zemin declares that 'the media must remain firmly in the hands of our Party'.

March 14. In Liaoning Province, scientists discover a bird fossil from the Jurassic period.

April 3. NCNA publishes the document 'The Situation of Children in China'.

April 4. Some 50 000 people gather in Huangling County, Shaanxi Province, for commemorative rites in honour of the Yellow Emperor, the mythical ancestor of the Chinese people.

April 10. The State Education Commission issues the Ninth Five-Year Plan (1996–2000) and Longterm Development Plan for Education to 2010.

April 16. The Beijing Observatory announces the discovery of a supernova 65 million light years away from earth, the first supernova ever discovered by Chinese scientists in the external galaxy.

May. The Chinese Industrial and Commercial Combined Press publishes *Zhongguo keyi shuo bu* (*China Can Say No*) by Song Qiang, Zhang Zangzang and Qiao Bian.

May 3–6. The Xinjiang CCP holds a work conference to discuss issues related to the Autonomous Region's stability.

May 10–15. The Fourth National Games for the Disabled take place in Dalian, Liaoning Province, breaking 40 world records.

May 15. A ban against smoking in indoor public places in Beijing comes into effect.

August 6. The Institute of Modern Physics of the Chinese Academy of Sciences announces the world's first synthesis and identification of the new nuclide americium (Am)–235, indicating that Chinese scientists had begun working in the neutron-deficient region of hyperuranium.

August 21. In Beijing, China publishes its first official report on state foreign affairs activities.

September 24. *People's Daily* reports that the State Environmental Protection Bureau has issued an urgent notice demanding the shutdown of small enterprises in fifteen industries which had been causing excessive pollution.

September 26. Jiang Zemin makes an inspection of the *People's Daily* office, stressing the need for journalists and news organizations to follow the correct political direction and to serve national economic construction.

October. The New World Press in Beijing publishes *Zhongguo weishenmo shuo bu* (*Why Does China Say No?*) by Peng Qian, Yang Mingjie and Xu Deren; the Chinese Literature and Arts Federation Publishing Company in Beijing publishes *Zhongguo haishi neng shuo bu* (*China Can Still Say No*) by Song Qiang and others.

October 18. Beijing Observatory reports discovery of a new superstar outside the galaxy.

November 4. A Chinese satellite launched (on October 20) for the purposes of scientific exploration and technological experiment successfully returns to earth.

December. The Chinese Social Sciences Press in Beijing publishes *Yaomohua Zhongguo de beihou* (*Behind the Demonization of China*) by Li Xiguang and others.

December 28. *People's Daily* reports the unearthing of tens of thousands of inscribed bamboo and wooden strips, dating back some 1700 years, in a central area of Changsha, the capital of Hunan Province.

F Births and Deaths

January 7. Former NPC Standing Committee vice-chairman Zhu Xuefen dies in Beijing, aged 91.

February 2. NPC Standing Committee vice-chairman Li Peiyao is murdered in Beijing, aged 63.

March 14. Chinese folk song composer Wang Luobin dies of cancer in Xinjiang, at the age of 83.

May 5. Poet and painter Ai Qing dies.

July 12. Four former officials of Taian Municipality in Shandong Province are condemned to death, three with two-year reprieves, for taking bribes.

September 26. David Chan Yuk-cheung from Hong Kong is drowned while protesting against the erection of Japanese signs and facilities in the Diaoyu Islands. He has jumped into the sea in protest against the obstruction of his protest boat by those of Japanese patrollers.

December 12. Noted writer Xu Chi dies in Wuhan, aged 82.

December 13. China's most important twentieth-century playwright, Cao Yu, dies in Beijing, at the age of 86.

G Natural Disasters, Accidents

February 3. An earthquake strikes Lijiang in Yunnan Province and surrounding areas, killing 245 people.

February 15. An accident at the Xichang Satellite Launching Center, when a Chinese carrier rocket fails to send an 'International 708' communications satellite into orbit, kills eight people and injures 57.

March 13 and 19. Two earthquakes strike Xinjiang, respectively in Altay in the north and Artux in the southwest, and measuring 6.1 and 6.9 on the Richter scale. The latter earthquake kills at least 24 people and over 7000 livestock.

May 1. Forest and grassland fires, originating in Mongolia and spreading to the Hulunbuir and two other leagues (equivalent to counties) on April 23, are eventually extinguished, having swept over 300 000 hectares of land, including 46 000 hectares of forests.

May 3. An earthquake measuring 6.4 on the Richter scale strikes Inner Mongolia, killing sixteen people and injuring about 300.

June 22. A Chinese-made Y-12 plane crashes on Dachangshan Island, Liaoning Province, killing two of the twelve passengers and injuring the other ten.

July 17. A fire at the Duanxi Hotel in Shenzhen kills 29 people and injures thirteen.

1997 DENG XIAOPING DIES; HONG KONG REVERTS TO CHINA

A Foreign Affairs Events

January 28–February 2. Sino-American talks, which the Chinese describe as 'tough but fruitful', yield an agreement on textiles.

February 12. On his way back from Japan, Hwang Chang-yop, Secretary of the (North) Korean Workers' Party, goes to the South Korean Embassy in Beijing to seek political asylum. Chinese and other diplomacy results in his arrival in a third country (the Philippines) on March 18.

February 23–March 2. Portuguese President Jorge Sampãio visits China, meeting with Jiang Zemin on February 24.

March 6–8. The ASEAN Regional Form holds a meeting in Beijing, with representatives from 21 countries.

March 22–27. The Dalai Lama pays a visit to Taiwan, his first to the island, meeting with Taiwan President Lee Teng-hui on March 27. The Chinese government issues several condemnatory statements in response, in particular denouncing the meeting with Lee as a 'collusion of splitists'.

March 24–28. US Vice-President Al Gore visits China, holding talks with Premier Li Peng on March 25.

March 26–30. Bolivian President Gonzalo Sanchez de Lozada visits China.

March 28–April 2. Australian Prime Minister John Howard visits China.

April 2–5. Thai Prime Minister Chavalit Yongchaiyudh visits China, holding talks with Li Peng and signing six documents on trade, scientific and agricultural cooperation, among other matters, on April 2.

April 22–26. Jiang Zemin visits Russia. On April 23, Jiang and Russian President Boris Yeltsin sign a joint statement on the multipolarization of the world and the new international order, and emphasizing partnership between the two countries.

April 24. The presidents of China, Russia, Tajikistan, Kyrgyzstan and Kazakhstan sign an agreement in Moscow, the terms including troop and armament reductions and limitations along mutual borders.

April 27–May 3. Singaporean Prime Minister Goh Chok Tong visits China.

April 29–30. Pakistan President Farooq Ahmad Khan Leghari visits China and holds talks with Jiang Zemin and Li Peng.

May 5–14. Premier Li Peng visits six African countries: Zambia, Mozambique, Gabon, Cameroon, Nigeria and Tanzania.

May 7–11. UN Secretary-General Kofi Annan visits China.

May 15–18. French President Jacques Chirac makes a state visit to China, the first French president to do so for fourteen years. On May 16, Chirac and Chinese counterpart Jiang Zemin sign a joint declaration pledging to seek a comprehensive partnership.

June 5–6. Italian Prime Minister Romano Prodi visits China.

June 9–13. Macedonian President Kiro Gligorov visits China.

June 30–July 1. In the presence of various international dignitaries, notably Prince Charles, Prince of Wales, representing the Queen of England, British Prime Minister Tony Blair and Foreign Secretary Robin Cook, US Secretary of State Madeleine Albright, and Chinese President Jiang Zemin and Premier Li Peng, a ceremony takes place in Hong Kong marking the end of British rule and the formal return of Hong Kong's sovereignty to China at midnight.

July 14–18. Vietnamese Communist Party General Secretary Do Muoi visits China.

August 13. In Beidaihe, Hebei, Premier Li Peng tells a high-level delegation from Cambodia, led by acting Head of State Chea Sim and Prime Ministers Ung Huot and Hun Sen, that China has no intention of interfering in Cambodia's internal affairs. Hun Sen had recently carried out a *coup d'état*.

August 14. Governor of the People's Bank of China Dai Xianglong announces that China has decided to lend US$1 billion to help Thailand overcome the serious economic crisis that had struck first Thailand and then other countries in the middle of the year.

August 21–26. Premier Li Peng visits Malaysia (21–24) and Singapore, delivering a speech on China's relations with ASEAN on August 22.

September 4–7. Japanese Prime Minister Ryutaro Hashimoto visits China. Li Peng, meeting with him on September 4, tells him that China 'can never accept any activity directly proposing or hinting obliquely at including Taiwan in the scope of Japan–United States security cooperation'.

September 24–25. Li Peng visits Kazakhstan, China and Kazakhstan signing a boundary and other agreements on the first day.

October 26–November 3. President Jiang Zemin visits the United States, the first visit by a Chinese president in twelve years. On October 29, he and US President Bill Clinton hold their fifth summit meeting and issue a joint statement in which they declare that they are 'determined to build toward a constructive strategic partnership between China and the United States'. On November 1, Jiang Zemin gives a speech at Harvard University.

October 27. At the United Nations headquarters in New York, China signs the International Covenant on Economic, Social and Cultural Rights.

November 9–11. Russian President Boris Yeltsin makes his third state visit to China. He and Jiang Zemin sign a joint declaration on November 10, declaring that demarcation and surveying of the 4200 km eastern section of their mutual border has been completed according to agreement (see **A.** May 16, 1991); demarcation along the western section of the border (about 55 km) will be completed within the agreed time.

November 11–16. Premier Li Peng visits Japan. In a speech in Tokyo on November 12, Li outlines five principles for guiding the bilateral relationship, including mutual respect and non-interference in each other's affairs; seeking common ground while reserving differences; and handling the differences properly. Bilateral agreements on fisheries and environmental protection were reached during the visit, but tension persisted over the Diaoyu Islands and China's strongly stated opposition to including the Taiwan Strait in United States–Japan defence cooperation.

November 13–16. Yugoslav President Slobodan Milosevic visits China, signing a joint statement with President Jiang Zemin on November 13.

November 16–21. Polish President Aleksander Kwasniewski visits China, the first such visit for 38 years, signing a joint communiqué with President Jiang Zemin on November 17.

November 23–December 3. President Jiang Zemin visits Canada and Mexico. He attends the fifth summit of APEC (held November 24–25) and addresses it on November 25. On December 2 he addresses the Mexican Senate, calling for developing countries to enjoy equality and non-discrimination in decision-making in the international economic relationships they developed.

December 15. Jiang Zemin makes a speech at the Thirtieth Anniversary Summit of ASEAN, held in Kuala Lumpur.

B Domestic Political Events

February 5–6. Disturbances erupt in Yining, Xinjiang, with significant numbers of Uygurs attacking and smashing Han Chinese shops and many shouting Uygur independence slogans. Authorities quickly suppress the disturbances, some bloodshed resulting.

February 25. Three bombs planted on buses in Ürümqi, the Xinjiang capital, explode, killing at least nine people; they are apparently the work of Uygur separatists aiming to show disrespect to the memory of Deng Xiaoping, whose memorial service occurs the same day (see **F.** below).

March 7. A bomb blast occurs in a bus in Beijing, injuring a dozen passengers and probably exploded by Uygur separatists.

March 10. A Taiwanese civilian plane is hijacked to Xiamen. The hijacker Liu Shanzhong is arrested but returned to Taiwan for trial on May 14.

March 14. The NPC resolves to establish Chongqing as a provincial-level municipality under central government authority; it also adopts the National Defence Law and the amended Criminal Law.

April 28. Xinjiang television announces the launch of an intensive campaign to improve public order and crack down on terrorism in Xinjiang.

July 1. At midnight, the Hong Kong Special Administrative Region is inaugurated.

September 12. Among many other points in his report at the opening session of the Fifteenth CCP Congress, Jiang Zemin suggests establishing Deng Xiaoping Theory as the CCP's 'guiding ideology' and corporatizing the SOEs. He also announces that China's army will be reduced by 500 000 persons by the year 2000.

September 18. At the closing session of the CCP's Fifteenth Congress, the CCP's Constitution is amended to take 'Marxism-Leninism, Mao Zedong Thought and Deng Xiaoping Theory as its guide to action'.

November 16. A Chinese Ministry of Justice spokesman announces the release of dissident Wei Jingsheng, who immediately goes to Detroit for medical treatment.

C Economic Events

January 16. The State Power Corporation is inaugurated, authorized to manage the nationwide power network and inter-regional power transmission.

May 1. Guangxi's first expressway, nearly 140 km from Guilin to Liuzhou, opens to traffic.

May 12. After a first failed launch, the East-is-Red 3 communication satellite is successfully launched at the Xichang Satellite Launch Centre.

May 18. NCNA announces a circular issued by the CCP Central Committee and State Council enhancing land management and protecting cultivated land. It prohibits the allocation of cultivated land for non-agricultural projects for one year, unless specifically investigated and approved by the State Council.

June 5. The People's Bank issues a circular prohibiting the unauthorized flow of bank capital to the stock market, the reason being that, since bank capital is public property, it ought not to be used for speculative purposes.

June 9. The 4.7 km Humen Bridge formally opens to traffic, linking the Guangzhou–Shenzhen and Guangzhou–Zhuhai expressways.

June 29. Nanjing's new Lukou Airport, opens to traffic, with a 29 km expressway leading to it opening to traffic the day before.

July 8. Inner Mongolia's first expressway, linking Hohhot with Baotou, opens to traffic.

August 26. The State Council Press Office announces that all China's cities at county level or above had entered the age of program telephone communication, with more than 100 million program-controlled telephone lines; China's was thus the second largest telephone network in the world after the United States.

September 1. The Chinese-made rocket carrier Long March–2C successfully sends two American simulation iridium satellites into a preordained orbit.

September 10. The 860 km Shaanxi–Beijing natural gas pipeline, a key project in China's Ninth Five-Year Plan (1996–2000), is completed and goes into use, supplying natural gas produced by the Changqing Oilfield to Beijing.

September 14. The State Council announces a reduction in important export tariff rates from 23 to 17 per cent, to come into effect on October 1, 1997.

September 19. The Yamzho Yumco Hydropower Station, the largest in Tibet, goes into full operation.

October 13. *People's Daily* reports the discovery, by the China National Offshore Oil Corporation, of a giant oil well in the East China Sea.

October 28. The Yellow River is successfully dammed at Xiaolangdi.

November 8. The Yangzi River's main stream is successfully dammed. Part of the Three Gorges Project, this damming signals the construction of two parallel earth-and-stone coffer dams, to be completed over a six-year period.

December 2. A ceremony marks the inauguration of the 900 km electrified single-track Nanning–Kunming railway.

D Appointments, Dismissals, etc.

January 25. At the first meeting of the Provisional Legislative Council of the Hong Kong Special Administrative Region held in Shenzhen, Rita Fan is elected Council president.

August 26. NCNA announces the appointment of Jia Qinglin as secretary of the Beijing Municipal CCP Committee, replacing Wei Jianxing.

September 9. The Central Commission for Discipline Inspection of the CCP announces its decision to expel former Beijing Municipal CCP Committee Secretary Chen Xitong from the CCP for corruption (see **D**. April 27, 1995 and Chapter 2).

September 18. NCNA publishes the full list of the new (Fifteenth) CCP Central Committee. Prominent absences include Qiao Shi, Liu Huaqing, Yang Baibing, Zou Jiahua and Zhang Zhen.

September 19. The First Plenum of the Fifteenth CCP Central Committee reappoints Jiang Zemin as general secretary of the CCP Central Committee and the Standing Committee of the Politburo (see Chapter 2), among many other appointments. On the Central Military Commission, Zhang Wannian and Chi Haotian replace Zhang Zhen and Liu Huaqing.

E Cultural and Social Events

January 20. Chinese astronomers at the Beijing Observatory find a minor planet orbiting close to earth: the first such close-to-earth planet discovered by China.

March 9. A total solar eclipse occurs in Mohe, Heilongjiang.

April 12. In Shanghai, plastic surgeon Cao Yilin succeeds in replicating a human ear from the body of an animal by adopting extrinsic cell reproduction: a world first.

May 1. The deadline is reached for implementation of a 1995 circular on working hours which laid down a limit of 40 hours and five days per week.

June 20. Some 400 demonstrators, representing about 2000 victims of a fraud, protest outside the seat of government against a developer whose machinations had left them homeless. No violence is reported.

June 30. China's first successful liver transplant operation is carried out in Xi'an, Shaanxi, one-third of a father's liver being transplanted to his 10-year-old daughter.

July 17. The State Council resolves to establish a unified staff old-age basic insurance scheme. Local government must integrate this scheme into their socioeconomic planning to guarantee basic living needs for the aged.

August 22. *People's Daily* announces that, in Huantai County, Shandong, archaeologists have discovered what they believe to be the oldest Chinese characters ever written on oracle bones and the oldest inscriptions on bronzeware.

November 13. *People's Daily* reports that the government has decided to allocate 130 million yuan to spread compulsory education in poverty-stricken and minority areas.

F Births and Deaths

January 21. Film cameraman Huang Shaofen dies.

February 2. Long March veteran and former state councillor Qin Jiwei dies in Beijing, aged 82.

February 19. Deng Xiaoping dies in Beijing at the age of 93.

February 28. Journalist and diplomat Zeng Tao dies, aged 83.

March 12. Writer Liu Shaotang dies, aged 58.

March 25. Film star Zhao Ziyue dies in Beijing at the age of 88.

April 9. Wu Zuoren, well known in the field of fine arts education, dies in Beijing at the age of 89.

April 23. Fine arts master Liang Huangzhou dies in Guangzhou at the age of 72.

April 26. Peng Zhen dies in Beijing aged 95.

May 16. Famous writer Wang Zengqi dies in Beijing aged 77.

May 27. Famous Peking Opera actor Zhang Junqiu dies in Beijing aged 77.

June 1. Painter Xie Zhiliu dies in Shanghai at the age of 87.

June 2. Astronautics pioneer Zhang Jun dies at the age of 78.

June 7. Noted playwright Yu Ling dies in Shanghai, aged 90.

June 21. Painter Dong Shouping dies in Beijing, aged 93.

June 26. Scientist Jin Shanbao dies.

June 27. Noted Catholic Bishop Zong Huaide dies in Beijing at the age of 80.

July 3. Chinese Daoist Association president Fu Yuantian dies on Mount Qingcheng, Sichuan, at the age of 73.

July 20. Ai Zhisheng, former minister of Radio, Film and Television, dies of illness.

July 21. Economist and Beijing University Professor Chen Daisun dies of illness.

September 20. Jing Puchun, wife of Liao Chengzhi, dies in Beijing, aged 80.

October 17. Former Politburo member and vice-premier, Fang Yi, dies of illness.

November 6. Chinese judge Li Haopei, dies in The Hague, at the age of 91.

November 9. Former deputy-chief of the General Staff of the PLA and diplomat Wu Xiuquan dies, aged 89.

G Natural Disasters, Accidents

January 21. An earthquake in Kaxgar, Xinjiang, kills twelve people.

January 29. A fire in the Yanshan Hotel in Changsha, Hunan, kills more than 30 people and injures about 40.

March 4. An explosion at a coalmine in Lushan County, Henan, leaves 89 people dead.

April 6, 11 and 16. Earthquakes shake Jiashi County, Xinjiang, killing nine people and injuring many others.

April 29. A train accident in Yueyang County, northern Hunan, on the Beijing–Guangzhou Railway kills 58 passengers and injures over 90.

May 8. A China Southern Airlines Boeing 737 crash lands at Shenzhen airport, killing some 35 people.

June 4–6. A large fire breaks out on the *Daqing 243* oil tanker, anchored in Nanjing. Of the 48 people on board, 39 are rescued, the others being reported missing.

November 28. An emergency circular, published December 2, claims that during 1997, down to November 27, there were twelve serious accidents in key national coalmines, each killing at least ten people, and two killing more than 50.

1998

A Foreign Affairs Events

March 31–April 5. Premier Zhu Rongji makes a visit to Great Britain, attending the two-day Second Asia–Europe Meeting in London (April 3–4).

April 5. Zhu Rongji begins a three-day visit to France.

April 19. Portuguese Prime Minister Antonio Guterres begins a five-day official visit to China, mainly aimed at discussing the Macau handover.

May 14. The Chinese Foreign Ministry condemns India's nuclear tests of May 11 and 13, describing as 'utterly groundless' India's contention that China poses a nuclear threat to India.

May 25. Israeli Prime Minister Benjamin Netanyahu arrives in China for a four-day official visit, meeting with Jiang Zemin and Zhu Rongji May 26.

June 3. Jiang Zemin declares in Beijing that China opposes all nuclear tests and will not resume such tests itself.

June 9. During a meeting with visiting Italian President Oscar Luigi Scalfaro, Jiang Zemin calls for long-term stable relations with Italy.

June 25–July 3. US President Bill Clinton visits China. On June 27 Clinton holds official talks with Jiang Zemin, followed by a joint live news conference on Chinese television, during which the two expressed different views on human rights and Tibet.

June 30. In Shanghai, Clinton states that he does not support independence for Taiwan, or two Chinas, or one Taiwan, one China, and does not believe that Taiwan should be a member in any organization for which statehood is a requirement (the 'three noes').

July 3. The presidents of China, Russia, Kazakhstan, Tajikistan and Kyrgyzstan meet in Alma-Ata and issue a joint statement.

August 3. Foreign Minister Tang Jiaxuan expresses grave concern and indignation over the suffering of ethnic Chinese in Indonesia, following riots, ransacking and burning of shops and rape of Chinese women in May.

October 5. China signs the International Covenant on Civil and Political Rights.

October 6–10. British Prime Minister Tony Blair visits Beijing, Shanghai and Hong Kong.

November 11–15. South Korean President Kim Dae Jung visits China, holding talks with Jiang Zemin on November 12.

November 18. Jiang Zemin addresses the Sixth APEC Meeting, held in Kuala Lumpur, calling for the establishment of a 'fair and reasonable new international economic order'.

November 22–25. Jiang Zemin visits Russia, meeting Boris Yeltsin (in hospital) on November 23.

November 25–30. Jiang Zemin visits Japan, the first Chinese head of state ever to do so. He meets Japanese Prime Minister Keizo Obuchi on November 26, the two issuing a joint statement. This statement includes Japan's 'retrospection' over its occupation of China during World War II and reaffirms its one-China policy, but includes no written 'apology' for the war nor any reference to the 'three noes' (see above, June 30).

December 17–19. Vice-President Hu Jintao visits Vietnam, meeting with Vietnamese Communist Party General Secretary Le Kha Phieu on December 18.

December 20. The Asian Games end in Bangkok; China turns out the leading Asian sporting power, winning more medals than any other country.

B Domestic Political Events

May 11. Aiming to put judges under public supervision, the Supreme People's Court of China sets up a reporting centre to handle telephone calls and letters of complaint about the improper or corrupt actions of judges in the supreme court, provincial higher people's courts and intermediate people's courts.

July 13–15. A national anti-smuggling conference takes place in Beijing, at which Jiang Zemin announces that a national police force will be established to suppress smuggling.

October 14–19. Taiwan's SEF Chairman Koo Chen-fu (Gu Zhenfu) visits Shanghai and Beijing (the latter for the first time in 55 years). In Shanghai he meets with ARATS chairman Wang Daohan (October 14 and 15), the two agreeing to engage in further dialogue and step up exchanges, and Koo inviting Wang to visit Taiwan. On October 18, Koo meets with Jiang Zemin in Beijing.

November 30. Following a Politburo decision earlier in the month, large numbers of liberal political activists are arrested all over the country, signalling the end of a period of comparatively liberal politics.

December 18. At a meeting to mark the twentieth anniversary of the opening of the Third Plenum of the Eleventh Central Committee, which inaugurated the reform policies, Jiang Zemin lauds the policies as 'entirely correct' as well as the achievements China has made under them. He demands adherence to the political system, arguing that China 'cannot follow Western models'.

December 21. A Beijing court sentences Xu Wenli, 55, one of the founders of the China Democracy Party, to thirteen years' imprisonment for subversion. A Hangzhou court sentences another key organizer of the China Democracy Party, Wang Youcai, to a prison term of eleven years for trying to overthrow the state.

December 22. In Wuhan, China Democracy Party activist Qin Yongmin is sentenced to twelve years' imprisonment for harming state security.

December 29. Dissident Wei Jingsheng meets with Taiwan President Lee Teng-hui in Taiwan, provoking strong opposition from the PRC, a spokesman for which said 'we oppose any person and any party using Wei Jingsheng for political purposes'.

December 31. In the eleven villages of Buyun township, Sichuan Province, 6236 voters cast secret ballots to vote directly for their head. Up to this point only villages had voted directly for their head, with township leaders appointed by local people's congresses.

C Economic Events

March 24. China's first large foreign trade group, China General Technology (Group) Holding Ltd, is inaugurated in Beijing.

April 28. Jiang Zemin receives the UN Food and Agricultural Organization's medal, which honours state leaders who have made outstanding contributions to the world's agricultural development. It is the first time that a Chinese president has won the medal.

June 15–17. A national work conference on housing reform in urban areas determines to abolish the welfare housing distribution system from the second half of 1998, replacing it with a market-oriented housing system.

October 14. The CCP Central Committee adopts the 'Resolution of the CCP Central Committee on Several Major Issues Concerning Agriculture and Rural Work', which calls for the raising of farmers' incomes and boosting the vitality of the rural economy.

December 21. A ceremony marks the completion of Gulong New Model Village in Xinzhou County, Hubei Province, built specifically to house homeless victims of the summer 1998 floods (see G. below).

D Appointments, Dismissals, etc.

March 16. NCNA reports the election or reelection of the following: Jiang Zemin, president of the PRC; Li Peng, chairman of the Ninth NPC Standing Committee; and Hu Jintao, vice-president of the PRC.

March 17. Jiang Zemin formally appoints Zhu Rongji premier of the State Council in succession to Li Peng.

March 18. Li Lanqing, Qian Qichen, Wu Bangguo and Wen Jiabao are appointed vice-premiers.

May 5. The 100-member Preparatory Committee for the Macau Special Administrative Region is established in Beijing.

July 16. The Beijing Municipal Higher People's Court sentences former Beijing Mayor Chen Xitong to sixteen years' imprisonment for corruption and dereliction of duty .

December 29. The expulsion of former vice-governor of Hubei Meng Qingping from the CCP for corruption and serious violation of CCP discipline and laws is announced.

E Cultural and Social Events

April 15. Supreme People's Court President Xiao Yang calls for the introduction of live television and radio broadcasts of trials as a step towards an open legal system.

May 14. Jiang Zemin calls for guarantees of a basic living standard and job creation for laid-off workers from state-owned enterprises.

September. Puccini's opera *Turandot* is given numerous performances in Beijing's Imperial Palaces, directed by famous Chinese film director Zhang Yimou, conducted by renowned Indian conductor Zubin Mehta and with American soprano Sharon Sweet in the title role.

November 30. The magazine *Nature Genetics* announces the cloning of neural deafness genes by Professor Xia Jiahui of the Hunan Medical Sciences University, the first successful human disease cloning in China.

December 1. To mark World AIDS Day, the Chinese Ministry of Health releases China's latest epidemic report on the prevalence of the disease: HIV-infected people are found in all China's province-level units, with the total number rising from zero in the mid–1980s to 300 000 in 1998. By September 30, 1998, there had been 11 170 confirmed HIV cases, leading to AIDS in 338 people, with 184 deaths.

December 17. The Beijing Municipal Government adopts nineteen emergency anti-air-pollution measures in an effort to improve the city's deteriorating air quality.

F Births and Deaths

September 14. Former President Yang Shangkun dies in Beijing, aged 92.

November 16. Pirates posing as police hijack the cargo ship *Changsheng*, bludgeoning 23 of the crew to death.

November 24. Shanghai's first test-tube twins, a boy and a girl, are born.

December 19. Writer and comparative literature scholar Qian Zhongshu dies in Beijing, aged 88.

G Natural Disasters

January 10. An earthquake 200 km northwest of Beijing kills 47 people.

May 22. A fire lasting nine days in the Greater Xing'an Mountains Range in Inner Mongolia is finally extinguished.

Mid-June–August. Regions along the Yangzi River experience their worst flooding since 1954. In August Heilongjiang Province experiences its worst flooding in recorded history. Official figures claim that some 240 million people were affected by the floods, 13.4 million had to be relocated, with a total

death toll of 3004. Over 5.5 million houses were destroyed and an additional 12 million damaged, resulting in widespread homelessness. The casualty figures and losses are said to be reduced by the mobilization of some 4.3 million members of the PLA and armed police, who assist in flood prevention and relief work.

August 7–12. A breach in a Yangzi River embankment near Jiujiang, Jiangxi Province threatens the city with inundation, but prompt measures taken by the government and PLA succeed in reducing damage through a 105 m bank and a large dyke.

August 14. An earthquake strikes Jiashi in Xinjiang.

August 21–22. After several earlier flood crests, torrential rains cause a major crest at Harbin, capital of Heilongjiang Province, which though well above safety level results in serious inundation. Prompt government, military and police action reduce casualties and losses by erecting a temporary but adequate 1000 m embankment with 108 000 sandbags.

August 26. Vice-Premier Wen Jiabao reports that almost 14 per cent of China's total sown area has been damaged in the summer floods, with 8.5 per cent suffering a total crop loss.

1999 NATO BOMBS THE CHINESE EMBASSY IN BELGRADE

A Foreign Affairs Events

January 1. China begins accepting the Euro, the new European Union currency coming into use the same day.

January 20. In his State of the Union address, US President Bill Clinton states that 'The more we bring China into the world, the more the world will bring change and freedom to China'. He also cautions China against suppressing dissidents: 'In China last year, I said to the leaders and the people what I'd like to say again tonight: Stability can no longer be bought at the expense of liberty.'

February 25. Visiting Vietnamese Communist Party General Secretary Le Kha Phieu meets with his Chinese counterpart Jiang Zemin in Beijing during a six-day visit to China.

March 20–30. President Jiang Zemin visits Italy, Switzerland (March 25–27) and Austria, being the first Chinese president ever to visit the last two countries. On March 26 he addresses the Conference on Disarmament in Geneva, calling for a new security concept based on mutual trust, mutual benefit, equality and cooperation.

March 25. The Chinese Foreign Ministry condemns NATO, and especially the United States, for bombing Yugoslavia and demands immediate cessation. The bombing, begun on March 24, was in response to Yugoslav President Slobodan Milosevic's refusal to sign a NATO settlement that aimed to solve the Kosovo problem.

April 5. During a five-day visit to China, Egyptian President Hosni Mubarak signs a joint communiqué with President Jiang Zemin, one point being a call for reform of the UN Security Council to allow more regional balance and greater say for developing countries.

April 6–20. Premier Zhu Rongji visits the United States (until April 14) and Canada.

April 7. In Washington US President Bill Clinton makes a major speech on relations with China. He argues strongly against containing China or allowing a 'cold war with China' to develop. He denounces any policy which 'isolates China from the global forces that have begun to empower the Chinese people to change their society and build a better future'.

April 17. At the end of a visit to Greece, Turkey, Syria, Pakistan, Bangladesh

and Thailand, NPC Standing Committee chairman Li Peng gives a wide-ranging press conference in Bangkok. Among many other issues he calls for the UN Security Council to bring an end to the NATO air strikes against Yugoslavia.

May 7. In its bombing campaign in Yugoslavia, three NATO missiles strike the Chinese Embassy in Belgrade shortly before midnight, setting the building on fire, killing three people and injuring at least six others. At the United Nations, Chinese Ambassador Qin Huasun condemns the act as that of a barbarian, while the United States apologizes, claiming it would never target an embassy and denying the strike was deliberate.

May 8. China issues a strongly worded statement in protest against the NATO bombing of its Belgrade Embassy, expressing its 'utmost indignation and severe condemnation of this barbaric act'. NATO military spokesman Major-General Walter Jertz acknowledges that the Embassy was targeted but contests that this was through a mistaken belief that the building was a Yugoslav government building. President Clinton apologizes to China for the bombing, claiming it as a tragic accident.

May 9. In the first of a series of very strongly worded articles on this and following days, *People's Daily* claims that the bombing of the Embassy exposes the NATO aggressors' 'evil intentions'.

May 10. Chinese Foreign Minister Tang Jiaxuan makes several demands on the US Ambassador to China James Sasser, including an open and official policy and severe punishment for those responsible for the attack.

May 12. German Chancellor Gerhard Schroeder arrives in Beijing for a visit.

May 23. A Philippines navy patrol vessel sinks a Chinese fishing vessel near a small island in an area claimed by both countries, resulting in the capture of three Chinese fishermen. Philippines President Joseph Estrada later offers his regrets to the Chinese Ambassador Fu Ying, and Philippines authorities release the three fishermen instead of detaining them for illegal poaching.

May 24. Foreign Ministry spokesman Zhu Bangzao denounces the decision of the Japanese House of Councillors to confirm the Special Defense Policy which strengthened joint Japanese–United States defence, China seeing this development as threatening.

May 25. In Washington, Republican Congressman Christopher Cox, head of an eleven-month inquiry, releases the resultant lengthy report, which accuses China of having stolen nuclear secrets from the United States since the 1970s. The same day a Chinese Foreign Ministry statement denounces the results of the inquiry as absurd and baseless.

June 1. The European Union instructs its member countries immediately to adopt new quarantine standards against wood-packaging of Chinese exports, except those from Hong Kong. China later attacks this decision as having been taken unilaterally and against China's interests, threatening retaliatory action.

June 1–3. Russian Foreign Minister Igor Ivanov pays an official visit to China.

June 9. To protect consumers from the threat of a cancer-causing dioxin, China bans the imports and suspends the sales of food products from Belgium, France, Germany and the Netherlands produced after January 15, the dioxin already having caused a scare in Europe.

June 10. In the UN Security Council, China abstains on the resolution that ends the Kosovo crisis.

June 16. US President Bill Clinton's representative Thomas Pickering presents an apology in Beijing for the American bombing of the Chinese Embassy. Chinese Foreign Minister Tang Jiaxuan describes the apology as unconvincing.

June 17. NCNA publishes an account of Pickering's apology, but describes it as unconvincing.

June 28–9. Pakistan Prime Minister Nawaz Sharif visits Beijing, meeting with Premier Zhu Rongji on June 28, Zhu telling him that China wants a peaceful settlement to the Kashmir conflict.

July 8–10. Japanese Prime Minister Keizo Obuchi visits China, meeting with President Jiang Zemin and other major leaders on July 9. The visit results in bilateral agreement that China would enter the WTO, Japan becoming the first major industrialized nation to officially approve China's membership.

July 15–17. President Jiang Zemin pays a state visit to Mongolia.

July 31. The United States agrees to pay US$4.5 million to the Chinese government as compensation for the three killed and twenty injured by the NATO bombing of the Chinese Embassy on May 7.

August 25. President Jiang Zemin and the presidents of Russia, Kazakhstan, Kyrgyzstan and Tajikistan issue a joint communiqué at the end of a meeting in the capital of Kyrgyzstan Bishkek, held to discuss mutual issues of security and cooperation.

September 1–12. The UN Educational, Scientific and Cultural Organization (UNESCO) and the Information Office of the Chinese State Council hold a China Culture Week in Paris, the largest exhibition of Chinese culture in Europe for half a century.

September 4. The Chinese Foreign Ministry issues a statement pledging to respect the will of the East Timorese people, who voted 78 per cent for independence from Indonesia at a referendum held on August 30.

September 2–16. President Jiang Zemin visits Thailand (making a major speech at the National Cultural Center in Bangkok on September 3), Australia (6–11) and New Zealand (11–16), meeting leaders such as US President Bill Clinton (11) and taking part in the APEC meeting in Auckland (12–13), and returning to Beijing September 16.

October 18–November 4. President Jiang Zemin makes a visit to six European and Arab countries: Britain (18–22), France (22–25), Portugal (26–27), Morocco (27–30), Algeria (30–31) and Saudi Arabia (31–November 3).

November 15. In Beijing, Chinese and American representatives Shi Guangsheng and Charlene Barshefsky sign an agreement under which the United States agrees to China's membership of the WTO.

November 19. Chinese Foreign Ministry spokesman Sun Yuxi expresses China's 'strong resentment' and opposition towards a US House of Representatives resolution condemning China for imprisoning Falungong practitioners and demanding their release.

December 1. Newly elected Indonesian President Abdurrahman Wahid meets with Jiang Zemin on the first day of his first official visit to China as president.

December 9–10. Russian President Boris Yeltsin makes a 30-hour visit to China, his last as president, the two sides signing a joint statement advocating a multipolar world and the strengthening of the United Nations role in international affairs.

December 10. China protests to the US Government over President Clinton's signing motions supporting Taiwan's entry into the World Health Organization.

December 16. China and the United States agree that the latter will pay US$28 million as compensation for the property losses caused by the American bombing of the Chinese Embassy in Belgrade (see above, May 7).

December 19–20. In the presence of various international dignitaries, notably Portuguese President Jorge Sampãio, East Timorese leader Xanana Gusmao and Chinese President Jiang Zemin, a ceremony takes place in Macau marking the end of some 440 years of Portuguese rule and the formal return of Macau's sovereignty to China at midnight. Jiang Zemin's speech, made early on December 20, emphasizes Chinese determination for reunification and the applicability of the 'one country, two systems' to Taiwan.

B Domestic Political Events

January 5. The CCP Central Committee and State Council formally establish a 6000-strong anti-smuggling police force.

January 8. About 5000 farmers demonstrate in Daolin township, some 40 km from Changsha, the Hunan capital, in protest against government corruption, excessive taxes and police attempts to disband the Society for Reducing Taxes and Saving the Nation. One farmer is killed and about 100 injured. This is one of a series of similar events in Hunan at about this time, caused by corruption, high unemployment resulting from the corporatization of the state-owned enterprises, and the effects of the summer floods of 1998.

January 29. In Hong Kong the Court of Final Appeal interprets the Basic Law to give right of abode in Hong Kong to children born of a Hong Kong permanent resident, regardless of whether the parent became a permanent resident before or after the child's birth; and gives children born out of wedlock the right of abode in Hong Kong deriving either from their natural father or natural mother. A man-made nail bomb explosion in a market square in Hunan Province kills nine people and injures 65.

March 6. For the first time in PRC history, an elected village head is voted out in an election: Dong Shouyong in Jili, near Harbin, the Heilongjiang capital.

March 15. On its final day, the Second Session of the Ninth NPC adopts three major changes to the Constitution: adding Deng Xiaoping Theory to the Constitution; replacing the responsibility system in rural areas with a 'dual-operation system characterized by the combination of centralized and decentralized operation based on households working under a contract'; and replacing a proscription against 'counter-revolutionary activities' with one against 'criminal activities that endanger State security'. The vote shows 2811 in favour of the changes, 21 against with 24 abstentions. The NPC also adopts the *Contract Law of the PRC*, which goes into effect on October 1.

May 8. Many thousands of students and others demonstrate in Beijing at the American and British embassies, in protest against the NATO bombing of the Chinese Embassy in Belgrade. For the same reason, hundreds of students demonstrate in front of the American consulates in Shanghai, Guangzhou and Chengdu, burning American flags.

May 9. Demonstrations against American and British embassies and consulates grow in Beijing and several other major cities in China. In Beijing, crowds besiege the American Embassy, making it impossible for members to leave. The American consulate in Chengdu is set on fire. In a television statement Vice-President Hu Jintao condemns the bombing of the Belgrade Chinese Embassy as a 'criminal act' and expresses support for the demonstrations as patriotic reflections of justified indignation, but warns that 'we must prevent over-reaction, and ensure social stability by guarding against some people making use of the opportunities to disrupt the normal public order'.

May 13. In a speech welcoming back Chinese workers in Yugoslavia, Jiang Zemin mourns the three journalists killed in the bombing raid on the Chinese Embassy and calls them revolutionary martyrs, who died for peace, justice and the motherland.

May 18. The Executive Council of the HKSAR decides to appeal to the NPC Standing Committee for a ruling on the Basic Law regarding the right of abode (see January 29 above).

June 4. The tenth anniversary of the Beijing massacre passes without serious incident or, except for a Hong Kong vigil of some 70 000 people, significant demonstrations.

June 26. In Beijing the NPC Standing Committee votes to restrict the Hong Kong Court of Final Appeal's ruling of January 29. Under the NPC Standing Committee's interpretation, only children with one or both parents already qualified as permanent residents of Hong Kong under the Basic Law have the right of abode in Hong Kong, greatly limiting the number of people eligible to move to Hong Kong.

June 28. Officials of ARATS and SEF meet in Beijing and agree that the ARATS president Wang Daohan will visit Taiwan later in 1999. Beijing's Tiananmen Square reopens to the public after eight months' renovation.

July 13. The State Council and CCP Central Committee issue a joint statement condemning Taiwan President Lee Teng-hui as a separatist for a reference, on July 9 in an interview with German *Radio Deutsche Welle*, that the cross-straits relationship should operate on a 'state-to-state' basis or at least be considered as 'special state-to-state relations'. (On July 12, Su Chi, chairman of Taiwan's Mainland Affairs Council, announced that Taiwan would drop the term 'one China' and, in

English, stated that Taiwan regarded its ties with the mainland as a 'state-to-state' relationship, but not as a 'country-to-country' one.)

August 20. Foreign Ministry spokesman Zhu Bangzao condemns President Lee Teng-hui's comment of August 18 defending the inclusion of Taiwan in the Theater Missile Defense (TMD) system and claiming that it accords with the long-term interests of the country.

September 9. In Guangzhou, the Guangdong Provincial People's Congress holds a legislative hearing open to the public, who are able to speak on and oppose proposed legislation, an unprecedented move in the PRC. Provincial Congress chairman Zhu Senlin, in his opening speech, observes that the move will play 'a significant role in promoting the country's legislative democratization'.

October 1. A large-scale parade, including military, economic and cultural displays, is held in the centre of Beijing to mark the fiftieth anniversary of the establishment of the PRC, the first for many years.

November 20. At about 6:30 a.m. China launches from the Jiuquan Satellite Launch Centre in Gansu Province a Chinese-made spacecraft called Shenzhou, which is unmanned but capable of being manned. It returns to earth in Inner Mongolia in the morning of November 21 about 21 hours later, after making fourteen complete orbits of the earth.

December 3. The Court of Final Appeal in Hong Kong reverses its own decision of January 29, 1999, and describes Beijing's interpretation (see above, June 26) as valid and binding.

C Economic Events

January 5. At the opening ceremony of a training course on finance, Hu Jintao urges Chinese officials to learn more about finance in order to improve their competency in handling economic matters.

January 10. The Guangdong provincial government announces that the Guangdong International Trust and Investment Corp. (GITIC) is to seek bankruptcy, the first firm to declare bankruptcy since 1949. GITIC's assets stand at RMB¥21.47 billion, its debt load at RMB¥36.17 billion.

February 4. Minister of the Information Industry Wu Jichuan announces that China Telecom will be restructured into four companies: China Telecom Group Corp. (mainly handling fixed lines), Chinese Mobile Telecom Group Corp., China Paging Telecom Group Corp., and China Satellite Telcom Group Corp.

April 24. The State Environmental Protection Administration announces that China will invest RMB¥66.7 billion in 836 key projects to clean up the Haihe and Liaohe rivers.

May 6. The 975 km Korle–Kaxgar section of the South Xinjiang railway is completed, linking Turpan to Kaxgar by rail and marking the completion of the 1451 km South Xinjiang railway project (see also C. August 7, 1984).

May 10. The Chinese-made Fengyun–1C metereological satellite is launched on a Long March–4B rocket, tested from June 24 to July 13, and shortly thereafter handed over to the China Meteorological Administration for use.

June 12. Wei 12–1 oilfield of South China Sea (West) Oil Corporation, the largest oilfield in the western part of the South China Sea, begins operations.

June 24. The World Bank Board of Executive Directors approves US$160 million towards the Chinese Western Poverty Reduction Project, worth US$311 million, but lays down the condition that the Board reviews an inspection study of the Qinghai component of the project. The reason for the condition, which also led the United States and Germany to vote against the funding, is the fear that the resettlement program involved in the Qinghai component would harm the interests of local Tibetans in the host area and damage the environment.

June 25. In order to support technological innovation among small and medium-sized enterprises, the government launches the State Council-approved Technological Innovation Fund for Technology-Based Small and Medium-Sized Enterprises with a preliminary allocation of ¥1 billion.

June 28. A formal ceremony marks the opening of Metro Line 1, Guangzhou's first underground railway line.

September 22. The CCPCC adopts its 'Decision on Major Issues Concerning the Reform and Development of State-owned Enterprises', which calls for the continuing reform of the SOEs but also the need for the government to retain its dominant control over important industries.

September 27–29. The Fortune Global Forum takes place in Shanghai on China over the next half-century, gathering chief executives from over 300 multinational corporations, and other luminaries. Jiang Zemin addresses the Forum, promising that China will continue the policy of reform.

October 5–10. The First China International Hi-Tech Results Fair is held in Shenzhen, the first to focus on the trade of international technologies and the export of high-technology products.

October 31. The Ji'nan–Taian expressway goes into service, completing the linking of Beijing by expressway with both Shanghai and Fuzhou, and bringing the total length of China's expressways to over 10 300 km.

December 4. The Ertan Power Station on the Yalong River in Sichuan goes into

operation. It is China's second largest hydropower project after the Three Gorges.

December 6. A ceremony at Kaxgar's newly built railway station marks the opening to traffic of the entire South Xinjiang railway (see above, May 6), Li Peng making the main speech.

D Appointments, Dismissals, etc.

May 15. The Selection Committee for the first Government of the Macau SAR elects Edmund Ho Hau Wah as chief executive of the future Macau SAR (by 163 of the 199 votes cast), the State Council confirming the appointment on May 20.

May 24. At Liaodong village in Zhejiang Province, a corrupt village chief elected three years earlier is defeated at an election as a result of embezzlement, one of many similar cases at about this time.

June 15. HKSAR Chief Executive Tung Chee Hwa appoints Leung Chung-ying as Executive Council convenor, replacing Chung Sze-yuen whose term ends June 30, 1999.

September 22. The CCPCC announces the appointment Hu Jintao as vice-chairman of the Central Military Commission, and Guo Baoxiong and Xu Caihou as members.

September 22. The CCPCC announces the expulsion from the CCPCC of Xu Yunhong, alternate member of the CCPCC, secretary of Ningbo Municipality CCP Committee and CCP Zhejiang Provincial Standing Committee member, for massive corruption, especially for abusing his power to obtain benefits for his family members.

December 20. Edmund Ho Hau Wah is inaugurated as chief executive of the Macau Special Administrative Region, together with a team led by Secretary for Administration and Justice Florinda da Rosa Silva Chan.

E Cultural and Social Events

January 5. A 6000-strong anti-smuggling police force is formally established.

January 6. The general session of the Chinese Olympic Committee approves Beijing's bid application for the 2008 Olympic Games; it is submitted to the International Olympic Committee the next month.

January 17. An explosion in a Changsha bus injures 37 people, four seriously. A police spokesman comments that 'the explosion on the bus was a criminal action and not an accident'. The explosion is one of several occurring in China at about the same time.

January 20. In a judgment important for electronic communications in China, a Shanghai court sentences Lin Hai to two years in prison for 'inciting to subvert state power' through the Internet.

January 29. The Hong Kong Court of Final Appeal rules that mainland children born to Hong Kong permanent residents have the right of abode in the territory, no matter whether their parents were married or were residents at the time the children were born. The ruling sparks intense controversy over the potential for increased population pressures.

March 8–16. An exhibition of Tibetan history, culture and social and cultural achievements since 1959, entitled Shining Pearl of the Snowlands: China Tibetan Culture Exhibition, takes place in Beijing.

April 1. The amended Adoption Law, which among other matters relaxes stipulations on the requirements for adoption and facilitates the adoption of children, goes into effect.

April 25. A demonstration of Falungong followers, reaching well over 10 000 people at its height, takes place outside Zhongnanhai, the leadership's compound, in central Beijing.

May 1–October 31. The '99 International Horticultural Exposition is held in Kunming, capital of Yunnan, the first time in China, with 95 participating countries and international organizations, an Expo Garden of 218 hectares, and a total of over 9.4 visitors.

June. Encyclopaedia Britannica Inc. and the Chinese Encyclopaedia Press publish the Chinese edition of the *Encyclopaedia Britannica International* in twenty volumes.

June 21. Scientists from the Chinese Academy of Sciences announce that, using clone technology, they have developed an embryo of a giant panda, a breakthrough they claim to have the potential to save the endangered species.

June 25. *Qomolangma*, a Tibetan-style gala music and dance performance, celebrating Tibetan history, culture and religion, is premiered in Beijing.

June 26. At awards given in Budapest, the International Sporting Press Association includes former world gymnastics champion Li Ning among the 25 best athletes of the century, the only Chinese to win such an award.

July 1. The *Xuelong* icebreaker leaves Shanghai for the North Pole: the first navigation to the Arctic Ocean by a Chinese scientific research vessel. Among other matters, the 50 scientists on board aim to learn about the interaction of the sea, ice and atmosphere and their impact on climate. The ship turns home on August 25, after completing its mission.

July 19. The CCP Central Committee issues a notice forbidding members of the CCP to belong to the Falungong.

July 22. The government and the CCP Central Committee declare the Falungong to be an illegal organization.

September 20. A large exhibition showcasing the PRC's accomplishments formally opens in the Beijing

Exhibition Centre, Zhu Rongji making the main speech.

September 24. A performance of Chinese poems of the Tang and Song dynasties premieres in the Beijing Concert Hall to honour traditional Chinese culture and mark the fiftieth anniversary of the PRC's founding.

September 25. A ceremony marks the launching of the large-scale *Zhongguo zhengqu dadian* (*Compendium of China's Political Regions*), compiled by the Ministry of Civil Affairs and published by the Zhejiang People's Press.

September 28. The large-scale performance *In Praise of the Motherland* (*Zuguo song*), celebrating the 50 years of the PRC's achievements, is held in the Great Hall of the People in Beijing, attended by Jiang Zemin, Zhu Rongji, Li Peng and other leaders.

October 5. The Tibet Museum in Lhasa is officially opened.

November. The China Social Science Press publishes *Quanqiuhua yinxingxia de Zhongguo zhi lu* (*China's Path Under the Shadow of Globalization*), by Fang Ning and others.

November 16. On the authority of the CCPCC and State Council, the News Publications Bureau bans government and party organizations from publishing newspapers; existing ones are barred from receiving public money and those with a circulation under 30 000 must be closed. The ban, which aims to save the large amounts of public money spent on compulsory subscriptions to official newspapers and subsidies, comes into force on January 1, 2000.

October 1. Shanghai's first English-language newspaper under the PRC, *Shanghai Daily*, begins publication.

October 30. The NPC Standing Committee adopts its Decision on Banning Heretical Cult Organizations, and Preventing and Punishing Cult Activities.

December 4. *China Daily* reports that some 60 000 schools throughout the country have courses using computers, but that, beginning from 2001, the government will increasingly mandate computer-aided teaching courses to help students to move into the information age.

December 26. A Beijing court sentences four Falungong organizers to prison terms ranging from seven to eighteen years for using the sect to cause deaths, obtain state secrets, and other illegal activities.

December 30. To mark the introduction of the new millennium, a major performance of traditional and modern Beijing operas takes place in the leadership compound Zhongnanhai in the presence of Jiang Zemin, Zhu Rongji, Li Ruihuan, Hu Jintao and nearly 1000 other guests.

F Births and Deaths

February 3. Yu Qiuli, leader in the petroleum industry, dies in Beijing.

February 28. Famous female writer Bing Xin (born Xie Wangying) dies in Beijing at the age of 98.

April 3. A Chongqing court hands down the death sentence on Lin Shiyuan, former deputy secretary of Qijiang County CCP Committee, for taking bribes and dereliction of duty leading to the Rainbow Bridge disaster (see **G**. January 4, 1999).

April 18. Ye Fei, former vice-chairman of the NPC and member of the Red Army who joined the CCP in March 1932, dies in Beijing at the age of 85.

April 28. He Luting, composer, lyricist and former president of the Shanghai Conservatorium, dies in Shanghai at the age of 96.

May 8. Female NCNA journalist Shao Yunhuan, and *Guangming Daily* journalists Xu Xinghu and his wife Zhu Ying are killed by NATO bombs on China's Belgrade Embassy, aged respectively 48, 31 and 28.

June 7. Six men, ringleaders in a group involved in China's largest ever smuggling case, are executed in Guangdong. They included two former very senior customs officials: Cao Xiukang and Zhu Xiangcheng.

June 10. Former vice-premier Chen Xilian dies in Beijing after a long illness, aged 85.

June 24. At the order of Beijing No. 1 Intermediate People's Court, Ma Wenhua, Ma Wenquan and Ma Zhongcai are executed for drug trafficking, having been caught selling more than 6000 grams of heroin in 1997. They are among many executed for drug-related offences throughout China.

September 13. Reuters reports the court-martial and execution of Major-General Liu Liankun (retired) and Senior Colonel Shao Zhengzhong, aged respectively 58 and 56, the previous month for having sold military secrets to Taiwan since 1994. Liu had been a department director in the PLA's General Logistics Department.

October 3. Yu Zuomin dies of a heart attack. In the mid–1980s Yu had been declared a 'model' peasant for creating China's richest village, but was later imprisoned for leading his village against a siege by armed police.

October 27. Politburo member and former Guangdong Party secretary Xie Fei dies of leukemia in Guangzhou, aged 67.

November 9. Former Supreme People's Procuratorate head Huang Huoqing dies in Beijing, aged 99.

November 18. Gladys Yang, Beijing-born long-term British resident of China and famous as a translator of Chinese literature into English, dies in Beijing, aged 80.

December 22. Thirteen pirates (twelve Chinese, one Indonesian) are sentenced to death for the hijacking of the *Changsheng* (see **F**. November 16, 1998).

December 24. Former Supreme People's Court president Jiang Hua dies in Hangzhou of illness, aged 93.

G Natural Disasters, Accidents

January 4. The Rainbow Bridge in Qijiang County, 100 km from Chongqing Municipality, collapses, killing 40 people, injuring fourteen, and causing enormous economic loss.

February 24. An aircraft explodes just before landing at Wenzhou, Zhejiang, killing all 61 people on board.

March 11. An earthquake in Zhangbei County, Hebei Province, destroys hundreds of houses.

April 7. *China Daily* cites a report by the State Forestry Administration to the effect that, due to drought in North and Northeast China, forest fires had risen by 270 per cent over the preceding year, while the damage caused by them was up by 850 per cent.

April 15. A Korean Air cargo aircraft crashes after takeoff from Shanghai, killing three crew and six local residents.

June 29. From late April to this day, floods in Sichuan Province hit 23 counties, killing 49 people and affecting 830 000 people in terms of economic losses and damage to homes and farms, according to statistics from the Sichuan flood-control office.

July 5–6. A disastrous rainstorm in Xuanhan County of Chongqing Municipality results in eight deaths and damage to the economy valued at about ¥50 million (US$6 million).

July 23. Flooding along the Yangzi breaks through the dyke of Yiyang Municipality, Hunan, causing the evacuation of some 120 000 people from three nearby townships, destroying numerous buildings and over 3300 hectares of cropland.

August 18. *China Daily* reports the Yangzi River has dropped to safe levels after an extended period of damage and threat. Severe flooding has been caused in many provinces along the river and states of emergency have been declared in Hubei, Anhui and Hunan Provinces. The total death toll was less than 1000.

November 24. The 9000 tonne ferry *Dashun* sinks after catching fire in very stormy weather in the Yellow Sea about three hours out of Yantai, Shandong Province, on its way to Dalian, Liaoning Province. The death toll includes all but 22 of the 302 people on board, the worst maritime disaster in the PRC's history.

December 26. A fire breaks out in the bathhouse of the Hawaii Grand Hotel in Changchun, capital of Jilin, killing twenty people and injuring 31 others.

2000

A Foreign Affairs Events

January 23. Chinese Foreign Ministry spokesman Zhu Bangzao condemns Japan for a right-wing demonstration held the same day in Osaka, one of several recent developments aimed at playing down or negating the Nanjing Massacre, which began on December 13, 1937.

January 24–27. East Timor leader Xanana Gusmao visits China, receiving a promise of ¥50 million aid on the first day.

January 26. Foreign Minister Tang Jiaxuan demands that the Japanese government curb attempts to whitewash past Japanese aggression, especially its role in the Nanjing Massacre. The following day Japan's Chief Cabinet Secretary Mikio Aoki declares that there is no denying the Nanjing Massacre.

February 27. Foreign Ministry spokesman Zhu Bangzao condemns the US State Department's human rights report for 1999 for its attacks on China's human rights and condemns the United States for its own poor and deteriorating human rights situation.

March 6. In Beijing Chinese and Indian representatives hold their first security dialogue.

March 9. The Chinese Embassy in Washington protests against an American Defense Department decision (reported to Congress March 7) to sell defence missiles and an anti-aircraft radar system to Taiwan.

March 27. Jiang Zemin telephones Vladimir Putin, who had been elected Russian president the day before.

April 10. China rejects as an inadequate explanation a report handed to it by the US government on April 8 on how the United States could mistakenly have bombed the Chinese Embassy in Belgrade (see **A.** May 7, 1999).

April 12–27. Jiang Zemin undertakes a visit to Israel (12–17), including Palestine (15–16), Egypt (17–18), Turkey (18–21), Greece (21–4) and South Africa (24–7), signing the Declaration on Partnership between China and South Africa on April 25 and arriving back in Beijing April 28.

April 18. Foreign policy spokesman Sun Yuxi thanks supporters for defeating an American-sponsored motion condemning China for human rights abuses, the Commission deciding the same day to take no action on the motion.

May 25. China welcomes the US House of Representatives vote granting China permanent normal trading relations (NTR), as MFN had been renamed, but declares the establishment of a commission to scrutinize China's human rights unacceptable.

May 29. During a visit of Indian President Kocheril Raman Narayanan to China, he and Jiang Zemin agree to work towards a settlement of mutual border problems.

May 29–31. DPRK leader Kim Jong Il visits China, discussing, among other matters, the Republic of Korea President Kim Dae Jung's forthcoming visit to the DPRK capital Pyongyang.

June 22. Commenting on the death of 58 illegal immigrants in Europe (see **F.** below), Foreign Ministry spokesman

Zhu Bangzao condemns illegal immigration traffickers who sacrifice human lives for profit and urges the international community to take more effective measures to stamp out the trafficking of human beings.

July 5. President Jiang Zemin and the presidents of Russia, Kazakhstan, Kyrgyzstan and Tajikistan meet in the capital of Tajikistan, Dushanbe, to discuss mutual issues of security and cooperation. They set up a joint anti-terrorist centre to combat incursions by Muslim extremists and drug traffickers and issue the 'Dushanbe Declaration'.

July 18. In Beijing, Russian President Vladimir Putin and Jiang Zemin issue a joint statement, which includes strengthening security relations and opposition to the United States proposal for a National Missile Defence (NMD) system.

August 4. In response to a move by Senegal for Taiwan's representation in the United Nations, Chinese UN representative Wang Yingfan writes to UN Secretary-General Kofi Annan reaffirming China's view that there is but one China, that Taiwan is part of its territory and that the government of the PRC is the sole legal government representing all China.

B Domestic Political Events

January 7. The minister of the State Environmental Protection Administration, Xie Zhenhua, announces his view that 'the pollution situation on the national scale has stopped worsening for the first time in recent decades'.

February 21. A State Council policy white paper declares that China would be forced to use 'drastic measures, including military force' should Taiwan indefinitely delay negotiations aimed at reunification with the mainland.

March 15. The NPC approves the *Legislative Law*, which aims to correct overlapping and contradictory laws.

March 16. At a news conference in Beijing, Premier Zhu Rongji warns that 'if the Taiwan independence forces come into power it could trigger a war between the two sides of the strait'.

March 18. In a response to the victory of the Democratic Progressive Party's Chen Shui-bian in the Taiwan presidential elections the same day, NCNA reiterates China's insistence on a one-China policy, with Taiwan being part of China. It states that China will talk to anybody who believes in the one-China policy. On Chen Shui-bian specifically, it says: 'We should listen to what the new leader in Taiwan says and watch what he does.'

March 20. Commenting on Chen Shui-bian's victory in the Taiwan elections, Jiang Zemin states: 'No matter who is in power in Taiwan we shall welcome him to the mainland, and we may go to Taiwan. But dialogue and negotiations need a basis, which is that he must acknowledge (*chengren*) the principle of one China. On this precondition, anything can be discussed.'

May 4. Tsai Ing-wen, chair-designate of Chen Shui-bian's Mainland Affairs Council in Taiwan asserts that there should be no future mention of the 'state-to-state relationship' notion advocated by Lee Teng-hui (see B. July 13, 1999).

May 20. In his speech at the ceremony inaugurating him as president of Taiwan, Chen Shui-bian pledges not to declare the independence of Taiwan during his term in office 'as long as the CCP regime has no intention to use military force against Taiwan', and affirms his belief that the leaders on both sides of the Taiwan Strait 'possess enough wisdom and creativity to jointly deal with the question of a future "one China"'. China responds the same day, agreeing to hold dialogue if Taiwan accepted that it could not negotiate as a sovereign state and if it agreed to a 1992 compromise formula on the 'one China' principle by which both sides agreed to accept the principle but without defining its precise meaning.

May 24. China's state media announce that, from June 1, Beijing's 5000 neighbourhood committees will be chosen by direct popular election.

June 27. Chen Shui-bian tells a visiting American delegation that he accepts 'one China', but according to the 1992 formula by which each side adopts its own interpretation.

November 1. The fifth national census begins.

C Economic Events

January 26. A Long March 3-A rocket at the Xichang Satellite Launch Centre in Sichuan sends a 2300 kg telecommunications satellite into orbit; designed to stay in space for eight years, the satellite is to be used mainly for ground-based telecommunications.

March 12. China's first passenger aircraft, the MA–60, manufactured by the Xi'an Aeroplane Group, gives its inaugural flight performance in Beijing.

April 25. The People's Bank of China announces that the Renminbi Administrative Regulations will come into effect on May 1. For the first time, the regulations put comprehensive legal regulations in place and standardize policies governing the Chinese currency, defining its legal status, unit, design, printing and circulation.

May 19. China and the European Union sign an agreement for China to join the WTO.

July 10. China's Ministry of Finance rejects conditions the World Bank Board of Executive Directors lays down for China's Western Poverty Reduction Project (see **C.** June 24, 1999), conditions tantamount to rejection on human rights and environmental

grounds; it declares China's intention to proceed with the project anyway.

July 21. China announces that it will merge ten of its airlines into its three largest groups: Air China, China Eastern and China Southern.

D Appointments, Dismissals, etc.

January 6. Bishop Liu Yuanren, president of the Chinese Catholic Bishops College, consecrates five new Catholic bishops in Beijing, the move being opposed by the Vatican.

January 16. Two-year-old Soinam Puncog is ordained as Tibet's Seventh Reting Lama.

February 20. Hong Yongshi resigns as mayor of Xiamen, after admitting tardy knowledge of a major smuggling racket.

April 20. The Central Commission for Discipline Inspection announces the expulsion of Cheng Kejie, vice-chairman of the NPC Standing Committee, from the CCP for serious corruption. His dismissal from the NPC Standing Committee is announced on April 25.

May 20. Chen Shui-bian is inaugurated as the president of Taiwan.

June 30. Bai Kemian replaces Shao Huaze as director of the *People's Daily*, and Tian Congming becomes president of NCNA, both appointments part of a shakeup of publicity organs ordered by Jiang Zemin.

E Cultural and Social Events

January 6. A Chinese court condemns retired Lieutenant-General Yu Changxin to seventeen years' imprisonment for strong involvement with the Falungong.

February 5. In central Beijing, police break up a Falungong demonstration gathered to mark the Chinese New Year and the Year of the Dragon, beating and detaining some demonstrators.

February 14. A Ministry of Education document urges educators throughout the country to include courses on patriotism, culture, collectivism and socialism; and on parents to focus more on bringing up well-adjusted people and less on exerting pressure on their children to do well in examinations.

February 17. The State Council's Information Office releases its white paper *Zhongguo renquan fazhan 50 nian* (*Fifty Years of Progress in China's Human Rights*); NCNA announces the 'recent' publication by the Science Press of *Mao Zedong Deng Xiaoping Jiang Zemin lun sixiang zhengzhi gongzuo* (*Mao Zedong, Deng Xiaoping and Jiang Zemin on Ideological and Political Work*), edited by the Central Propaganda Department.

February 29. The Public Security Bureau issues a notice ordering the end of rioting by about 20 000 workers of a molybdenum mine in Yangjiazhangzi near Huludao, coastal Liaoning Province, and signalling military suppression of the rioting. The workers had been rioting for many days because the mine had been declared bankrupt and the workers dismissed with inadequate compensation. Police failed to restore order, but troops regained control peacefully at the end of February, remaining on guard in the town until March 31. This was one of a number of similar incidents caused by China's preparations to join the WTO.

March 2. A CCP Central Committee and State Council document announces China's intention to limit population growth to 1.5 per cent annually, declaring the next decade a vital period for sustaining a low birth rate.

March 16. Police shut down a brick factory in Kunming, which had imprisoned eighteen slave workers, forcing them to work under inhuman conditions. The police arrest four factory supervisors, but the owner escapes.

April 12. Deputy Director Wang Fengchao of the Chinese government's Liaison Office in Hong Kong issues a state declaring that the Hong Kong media have 'a responsibility and a duty to uphold the country's reunification and territorial integrity', and should neither disseminate nor advocate Taiwan independence views.

April 13. Police suppress a Falungong protest in Tiananmen Square, Beijing, detaining some 200 members.

April 22. The Declaration on Green Lifestyles for Earth Day 2000 China is issued in Beijing. The Ministry of Land and Resources publicizes a report on China's geological environment, reporting that over half China's geological disasters were largely man-made.

April 25. Police suppress a series of coordinated protests in Tiananmen Square by the Falungong, marking the anniversary of the major demonstrations outside Zhongnanhai in 1999 which marked the beginning of such activities of this body.

May 23–4. At Beijing University well over 1000 students hold an orderly and apolitical midnight march and candlelight vigil to protest against the lax security that led to the murder of Qiu Qingfeng (see F. May 19, 2000) and against the University's suppression of the news; campus guards make no attempt to prevent the action. Within a day, University President Xu Zhihong responds by thanking the students for their criticisms and declaring that the University would organize a mourning ceremony for Qiu Qingfeng, informing students of the time and place.

May 25. An officially sanctioned memorial service for Qiu Qingfeng (see preceding entry) draws thousands of people.

July 11. A ceremony marks the merging of nine local colleges into a new Guangzhou University.

July 15. A riot erupts in Xi'an, the capital of Shaanxi, when the home team loses a promotional soccer match against a visiting team from Chengdu.

F Births and Deaths

February 10. Ji Pengfei, former minister of Foreign Affairs and director of the State Council's Hong Kong and Macau Affairs Office, dies in Beijing, aged 91.

February 15. Li Xiangshan, whom police claim as a farmer and mental patient from Hubei, sets off a bomb explosion in Tiananmen Square, Beijing, killing himself and injuring a South Korean tourist.

February 21. Falungong practitioner Chen Zixiu, who had taken part in the April 25, 1999 demonstrations in Beijing, dies in prison in Weifang, central Shandong, after suffering serious police brutality.

February 28. Huang Faxiang, the central figure in a corruption scandal involving the Three Gorges Dam project, is executed for large-scale embezzlement.

March 8. Former Jiangxi Vice-Governor Hu Changqing is executed in Nanchang for serious bribery and corruption.

March 10 and 11. Public trials in the Aksu region of Xinjiang lead to the execution of eleven Uygurs on charges that include murder and separatism.

March 21. Eminent Hui historian Bai Shouyi of the Beijing Normal University dies in Beijing, aged 91; *Zhongguo tongshi (Complete History of China)*, of which he was chief editor, had been published the previous year in 22 volumes.

April 2. In Nanjing, four thieves break into the home of Juergen Pfrang, a German working for Sino-German bus-manufacturing company Yaxing-Benz, killing him, his wife and two children.

April 7. Chen Dequ is executed in Fujian for leading the abduction and trading of women, part of a major nationwide crackdown on this crime.

May 10. Li Fuxiang, director of the State Administration of Foreign Exchange and a key economic reformer, dies after falling from the seventh storey of a Beijing hospital.

May 19. The murdered and raped body of female Beijing University student Qiu Qingfeng is found near the University's rural branch campus.

May 21. Chinese Buddhist Association President Zhao Puchu dies, aged 92.

June 15. NCNA President Guo Chaoren dies of illness.

June 18–19. Fifty-eight Chinese illegal immigrants die of suffocation in a turned-off air-tight refrigeration container during ferry passage from Zeebrugge, Belgium, to Dover, England.

July 31. Cheng Kejie, former Guangxi governor and former vice-chairman of the NPC Standing Committee, is sentenced to death for massive corruption, the most senior person ever to be so sentenced under the PRC. The execution takes place on September 14.

G Natural Disasters, Accidents

January 15. Two earthquakes strike Yunnan Province, killing five people, injuring 1500 and causing extensive property damage.

March 29. Fire in a cinema in Jiaozuo, Henan, kills over 70 people.

June 22. A ferry boat accident in Hejiang County, Sichuan, kills at least seventeen people. In Wuhan, a passenger aircraft explodes in mid-air on descent due to lightning, with about 50 people killed.

June 28. The government decides to allocate ¥400 million to build emergency water supply projects to counter ongoing serious drought in north China.

June 30. An explosion in a fireworks factory in Jiangmen, Guangdong, kills 36 people and injures over 160.

August 2. An explosion occurs at a firecracker factory in Shangli County, Jiangxi Province, killing 27 people, including factory owner Huang Lexing and Huang's daughter, and destroying the five-storey factory building.

THE PARTY

There are nine political parties in China, the Chinese Communist Party and eight 'democratic parties' (*minzhu dangpai*). Among these, only the CCP holds any real power.

The CCP is the leading organ in society. It sees itself as the vanguard of the proletariat and its role is to lay down policy, which the state then implements. The CCP structure is in evidence everywhere in China, with branches right down to the lowest level. The province-level structures follow the central structure closely, but on a smaller scale. County-level CCP structures are also similar. Deng Xiaoping's 'four cardinal principles' (see Chapter 1, **B**. March 30, 1979) emphasized the leadership of the CCP, and the continual insistence on these principles showed very clearly that the CCP had no intention of allowing itself to be overthrown.

The eight 'democratic parties' are the Revolutionary Committee of the Chinese Nationalist Party (*Zhongguo guomin dang geming weiyuanhui*), the China Democratic League (*Zhongguo minzhu tongmeng*), the China Democratic National Construction Association (*Zhongguo minzhu jianguo hui*), the China Association for Promoting Democracy (*Zhongguo minzhu cujin hui*), the Chinese Peasants' and Workers' Democratic Party (*Zhongguo nonggong minzhu dang*), the China Zhi Gong Dang (*Zhongguo zhigong dang*), the September Third Society (*Jiu san xuehui*), and the Taiwan Democratic Self-Government League (*Taiwan minzhu zizhi tongmeng*)

The 'democratic parties' are in no sense opposition parties and they take part in a united front: on May 5, 1948 they responded to the CCP's invitation to hold the CPPCC (Chinese People's Political Consultative Conference), the meeting which in September 1949 decided to establish the People's Republic of China. In theory the CCP still promises to consult with the democratic parties and accept political supervision from them. It is possible for members of these to achieve high office, an example being Duanmu Zheng, member of the China Democratic League Standing Committee, who became vice-president of the Supreme People's Court in September 1990. However, these democratic parties really have no choice but to accept the CCP's leadership. The reality is that they survive on sufferance from the CCP and could be immediately crushed if they refused to do the CCP's bidding.

The National CCP Congress

The highest body of the Party is the National CCP Congress. There have been fifteen of these in the history of the Party, as listed in Table 2.1.

The CCP Congress may adopt a new CCP Constitution or amend the existing one. The Fifteenth Congress, which took place later in the same year Deng Xiaoping died, amended the CCP Constitution to incorporate Deng Xiaoping Theory as 'a crystallization of the collective wisdom' of the CCP which 'is guiding China's socialist modernization drive forward'. It defined Deng Xiaoping Theory as 'a product of the integration of the fundamental tenets of Marxism-Leninism with the practice in present-day China and the fea-

tures of the times' and 'a continuation and development of Mao Zedong Thought under the new historical conditions'.

The CPP's Central Committee and Plenums

Each Congress elects its own Central Committee, which meets in full session from time to time. These plenary sessions, or Plenums as they are usually termed, often reach decisions of crucial importance for the PRC. The Fifteenth Party Congress elected a Central Committee of 193 full members and 151 alternate members. The number of each Central Committee is that of the National Party Congress which selected its members.

Table 2.1 The National Congresses of the CCP

National CCP Congress	Opening and closing dates	Place held
First	July 23–August 1, 1921	Shanghai and (on August 1) Jiaxing, Zhejiang
Second	July 16–23, 1922	Shanghai
Third	June 10–20, 1923	Guangzhou
Fourth	January 11–22, 1925	Shanghai
Fifth	April 27–May 10, 1927	Hankou
Sixth	June 18–July 11, 1928	Moscow
Seventh	April 23–June 11, 1945	Yan'an
Eighth (First Session)	September 15–27, 1956	Beijing
Eighth (Second Session)	May 5–23, 1958	Beijing
Ninth	April 1–24, 1969	Beijing
Tenth	August 24–28, 1973	Beijing
Eleventh	August 12–18, 1977	Beijing
Twelfth	September 1–11, 1982	Beijing
Thirteenth	October 25–November 1, 1987	Beijing
Fourteenth	October 12–18, 1992	Beijing
Fifteenth	September 12–18, 1997	Beijing

Table 2.2 Plenary Sessions of the Central Committee of the CCP

Central Committee	Plenum	Dates	Place held
First	–	–	–
Second	–	–	–
Third	–	–	–
Fourth	–	–	–
	Emergency Conference of the CCPCC	August 7, 1927	Hankou
Fifth	–	–	–
Sixth	No first plenum	–	–
	Second	Six days late in June (probably 25–30) 1929, the resolution being issued on July 9, 1929	Shanghai
	Third	September 24–28, 1930	Shanghai
	Fourth	January 7–13, 1931	Shanghai
	Fifth	January 18–26, 1934	Ruijin, Jiangxi
	Sixth	September 29–November 6, 1938	Yan'an
	Seventh	May 21, 1944–April 20, 1945	Yan'an
Seventh	First	June 19, 1945	Yan'an
	Second	March 5–13, 1949	Pingshan, Hebei
	Third	June 6–9, 1950	Beijing
	Fourth	February 6–10, 1954	Beijing
	Fifth	October 4–11, 1955	Beijing
Eighth	First	September 28, 1956	Beijing
	Second	November 10–15, 1956	Beijing
	Third	September 20–October 9, 1957	Beijing
	Fourth	May 3, 1958	Beijing
	Fifth	May 25, 1958	Beijing
	Sixth	November 28–December 10, 1958	Wuchang
	Seventh	April 2–5, 1959	Shanghai
	Eighth	August 2–16, 1959	Lushan, Jiangxi
	Ninth	January 14–18, 1961	Beijing
	Tenth	September 24–27, 1962	Beijing
	Eleventh	August 1–12, 1966	Beijing
	Twelfth	October 13–31, 1968	Beijing

Table 2.2 (cont.)

Central Committee	Plenum	Dates	Place held
Ninth	First	April 28, 1969	Beijing
	Second	August 23–September 6, 1970	Lushan
Tenth	First	August 30, 1973	Beijing
	Second	January 8–10, 1975	Beijing
	Third	July 16–21, 1977	Beijing
Eleventh	First	August 19, 1977	Beijing
	Second	February 18–23, 1978	Beijing
	Third	December 18–22, 1978	Beijing
	Fourth	September 25–28, 1979	Beijing
	Fifth	February 23–29, 1980	Beijing
	Sixth	June 27–29, 1981	Beijing
Twelfth	First	September 12–13, 1982	Beijing
	Second	October 11–12, 1983	Beijing
	Third	October 20, 1984	Beijing
	Fourth	September 16, 1985	Beijing
	Fifth	September 24, 1985	Beijing
	Sixth	September 28, 1986	Beijing
Thirteenth	First	November 2, 1987	Beijing
	Second	March 15–19, 1988	Beijing
	Third	September 26–30, 1988	Beijing
	Fourth	June 23–24, 1989	Beijing
	Fifth	November 6–9, 1989	Beijing
	Sixth	March 9–12, 1990	Beijing
	Seventh	December 25–30, 1990	Beijing
	Eighth	November 25–9, 1991	Beijing
	Ninth	October 5–9, 1992	Beijing
Fourteenth	First	October 19, 1992	Beijing
	Second	March 5–7, 1992	Beijing
	Third	November 11–14, 1993	Beijing
	Fourth	September 25–28, 1994	Beijing
	Fifth	September 25–28, 1995	Beijing
	Sixth	October 7–10, 1996	Beijing
	Seventh	September 6–9, 1997	Beijing
Fifteenth	First	September 19, 1997	Beijing
	Second	February 25–26, 1998	Beijing
	Third	October 12–14, 1998	Beijing
	Fourth	September 19–22, 1999	Beijing
	Fifth	October 9–11, 2000	Beijing

The Politburo and its Standing Committee

The First Plenum of the Central Committee is held immediately after its election by the retiring Party Congress. This meeting elects the Political Bureau, or Politburo, which carries on the work of the Central Committee when the latter body is not in session. The First Plenum of the Fifteenth Central Committee elected 22 full members to the Politburo: (listed in alphabetical order) Chi Haotian, Ding Guan'gen, Hu Jintao, Huang Ju, Jia Qinglin, Jiang Chunyun, Jiang Zemin, Li Changchun, Li Lanqing, Li Peng, Li Rui-huan, Li Tieying, Luo Gan, Qian Qichen, Tian Jiyun, Wei Jianxing, Wen Jiabao, Wu Bangguo, Wu Guangzhen, Xie Fei, Zhang Wannian and Zhu Rongji; and two alternate members: Wu Yi (female) and Zeng Qing-hong. More information on almost all these leaders is given in Chapter 3.

Even more select than the Politburo is the Standing Committee of the Politburo, also elected by the Central Committee. In theory, and also largely in practice, this small body contains the most influential and powerful people in China. The composition of the Politburo Standing Committees elected by the First Plenums of the Central Committees since the Eighth Central Committee in 1956, that being the first after the CCP came to power, has been as follows:

- *Eighth:* Mao Zedong, Liu Shaoqi, Zhou Enlai, Zhu De, Chen Yun and Deng Xiaoping
- *Ninth:* Mao Zedong, Lin Biao, Zhou Enlai, Chen Boda and Kang Sheng
- *Tenth:* Mao Zedong, Zhou Enlai, Wang Hongwen, Kang Sheng, Ye Jianying, Li Desheng, Zhang Chunqiao, Zhu De and Dong Biwu
- *Eleventh:* Hua Guofeng, Ye Jianying, Deng Xiaoping, Li Xiannian and Wang Dongxing
- *Twelfth:* Hu Yaobang, Ye Jianying, Deng Xiaoping, Li Xiannian, Chen Yun and Zhao Ziyang
- *Thirteenth:* Zhao Ziyang, Li Peng, Hu Qili, Qiao Shi and Yao Yilin.
- *Fourteenth:* Jiang Zemin, Li Peng, Qiao Shi, Li Ruihuan, Zhu Rongji, Liu Huaqing and Hu Jintao.
- *Fifteenth:* Jiang Zemin, Li Peng, Zhu Rongji, Li Ruihuan, Hu Jintao, Wei Jianxing and Li Lanqing

Political disturbances have sometimes brought about changes in the composition of the Standing Committee of the Politburo, even between National Party Congresses. For example, on June 24, 1989 the Fourth Plenum of the Thirteenth Central Committee dismissed Zhao Ziyang and Hu Qili and replaced them with Jiang Zemin, Song Ping and Li Ruihuan.

Mao Zedong was elected chairman at a meeting of the Politburo in March 1943 and from that time until his death on September

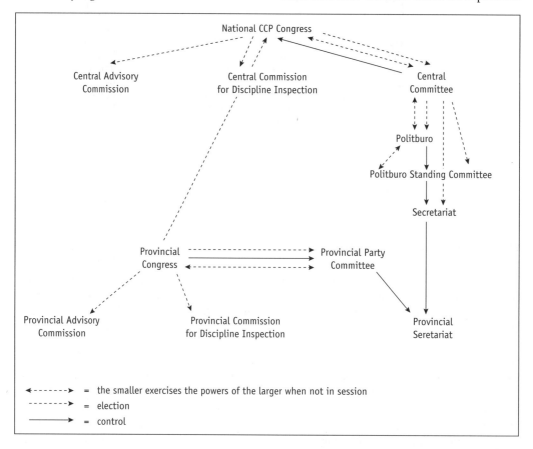

Figure 2.1 CCP structure

9, 1976 was regarded as chairman both of the Central Committee and of the whole CCP. His deputy, Hua Guofeng, became acting chairman and, on October 7, 1976, following the arrest and fall of the 'gang of four' the preceding day, he was appointed as chairman to succeed Mao Zedong. This was confirmed by the Third Plenum of the Tenth Central Committee and the First Plenum of the Eleventh. On June 29, 1981 the Sixth Plenum of the Eleventh Central Committee replaced Hua Guofeng with Hu Yaobang as chairman, but the post was abolished by the Twelfth CCP Congress in September 1982, formally making the general secretary the highest position within the CCP. General secretaries since the Twelfth Congress have been:

- Hu Yaobang, dismissed on January 16, 1987
- Zhao Ziyang, appointed by the Politburo on January 16, 1987 and confirmed by the First Plenum of the Thirteenth Congress in November 1987 but in effect dismissed in May 1989
- Jiang Zemin, appointed by the Fourth Plenum of the Thirteenth Central Committee on June 24, 1989 and confirmed at the Fourteenth and Fifteenth CCP Congresses.

Other CCP Bodies, Deng Xiaoping

A crucially important body is the Central Military Commission (CMC) of the Central Committee (CCPCP), which supervises the organizational links between the Party and the army. The First Plenum of the Thirteenth Congress appointed Deng Xiaoping as its chairman, and it was mainly this position that enabled Deng to carry out the suppression of student demonstrators which led to the Beijing massacre of June 3–4, 1989. On September 4, 1989, Deng Xiaoping wrote to the Central Committee requesting permission to resign from this position, and on November 9, 1989, the Fifth Plenum endorsed his request. It appointed Jiang Zemin to replace him as chairman. (The CCPCC's CMC should not be confused with its much less powerful state counterpart, on which see below.)

Another central Party body to have assumed great importance in the 1980s was the Central Advisory Commission, set up by the Twelfth Congress in 1982 'to act as political assistant and consultant to the Central Committee', as the Constitution adopted by the Twelfth Congress put it. The Commission functioned as a council of elders. Initially Deng Xiaoping was its chairman, but he retired from the post in favour of Chen Yun at the First Plenum of the Thirteenth Congress. This body was abolished at the Fourteenth Congress in October 1992.

Unlike Mao Zedong, Deng Xiaoping never achieved the position of CCP chairman or, after the abolition of that post in 1982, that of general secretary. From 1987 on, he was not even a member of the Central Committee. Yet he was called 'China's patriarch' and was rightly regarded as the architect and leader of reform in China, remaining a man of immense influence and power until well after he retired from his position as chairman of the CMC. The reasons why he was able to wield such power included his personal authority, his ability to persuade others to his way of thinking, his connections within the military and other major power organs both inside and outside China, and his vast revolutionary experience. (See Chapter 3 for a biography of Deng.)

Membership of the CCP

Table 2.3 shows CCP membership figures since 1921.

Table 2.4 shows the proportions of the CCP occupied by certain groups of society.

Democratic Centralism

The central idea of the CCP's operation is in theory democratic centralism, which means that Party members may contribute to debates before the central leadership decides on its view, after which all must toe the line. In practice, under Mao Zedong, it was usually he that decided the line and, although there was debate at the highest level, he could be very arbitrary in his behaviour towards colleagues, and anybody who disagreed with or even appeared to be opposing him could find himself in serious trouble. The 'mass line' of the Cultural Revolution proved even more dictatorial in practice, with Mao becoming increasingly paranoid about opposition.

Under reform, democratic centralism continued to be the theory. However, it was subject to Deng Xiaoping's 'four cardinal principles', one of which was the maintenance of the CCP's leadership. In other words, at no time did Deng envisage the possibility of the CCP's sharing power, let alone resigning it. The opposite of upholding these 'four cardinal principles' was 'bourgeois liberalization', which was opposed strongly, especially in the second half of 1986 and first half of 1987 and in the period following the suppression of the 1989 student movement. On July 15, 1990, *People's Daily* ran an editorial which again

Table 2.3 Figures of membership of the CCP

Year	Number of members	Year	Number of members
1921	57	1952 (end)	6 001 698
1922 (July)	123	1953 (mid)	6 000 000
1923 (June)	432	1953 (end)	6 612 254
1925 (early)	950	1954 (early)	6 500 000
1927 (April)	57 967	1954 (end)	7 859 473
1927 (later)	10 000	1955 (end)	9 393 394
1928	40 000	1956 (September)	10 734 384
1930	122 318	1957 (mid)	12 720 000
1933	300 000	1959 (mid)	13 960 000
1934	300 000	1961 (mid)	17 000 000
1937	40 000	1966	20 000 000
1940	800 000	1969	22 000 000
1941	763 447	1973 (August)	28 000 000
1942	736 151	1977 (August)	35 000 000+
1944	853 420	1982 (September)	39 650 000
1945 (April)	1 211 128	1984 (July)	40 000 000
1946	1 348 320	1986 (end)	46 011 951
1947 (Jan.)	2 200 000	1989 (early)	47 755 000
1947 (end)	2 759 456	1989 (August)	48 000 000
1948 (mid)	3 000 000	1991 (May)	50 320 000
1948 (end)	3 065 533	1992 (October)	over 51 000 000
1949 (Oct.)	4 488 080	1992 (end)	52 000 000
1949 (end)	4 500 000	1995	55 000 000
1950 (mid)	5 000 000	1996	57 000 000
1950 (end)	5 821 604	1997	58 000 000
1951 (mid)	5 800 000	1998 (end)	61 000 000
1951 (end)	5 762 293	1999 (end)	63 000 000

Sources: Figures for 1921 to 1961 are from Franz Schurmann, *Ideology and Organization in Communist China* (University of California Press, Berkeley, Los Angeles, London, 2nd enlarged edn 1968), p. 129. Most of the later figures were released in connection with major Party meetings, in particular Party Congresses. They are recorded in *Peking Review* and its successor *Beijing Review* XVI, 35 and 36 (September 7, 1973), p. 18; XX, 35 (August 26, 1977), p. 6; XXV, 37 (September 13, 1982), p. 5; XXVII, 29 (July 16, 1984), p. 7; XXX, 44 (November 2–8, 1987), p. 5; XXXII, 23 (June 5–11, 1989), p. 26; XXXII, 36 (September 4–10, 1989), p. 5; and XXXIV, 24 (June 17–23, 1991), p. 4; and in 'Quarterly Chronicle and Documentation', *China Quarterly* 144 (December 1995), p. 1245, *China Quarterly* 148 (December 1996), p. 1405 and *China Quarterly* 152 (December 1997), p. 913. See also *Beijing Review* XLI, 8 (February 23–March 1, 1998), p. 22 and Reuters, June 28, 1999, quoting NCNA.

Table 2.4 Some details of CCP membership (%)

Category	1989	1995	1997	1998	1999
Women	14.2	15.3	20.1	16.6	17
Minority nationalities	5.5	5.8	n/a	6.2	6.2
Aged 35 or less	27	21.1	22.4	n/a	22.5
Graduated senior secondary school or higher	28.5	n/a	43.4	47	n/a

denounced bourgeois liberalization, attacking as one of its views that democracy meant the style followed in the West, a view apparently widespread even within the CCP. The editorial argued instead that it was necessary to uphold democratic centralism, which meant that the CCP must 'implement centralism on the basis of democracy and democracy under centralized guidance'.

The Fourth Plenum of the Fourteenth Central Committee, meeting in September 1994, aimed for a blueprint for 'Party building' and placed a great deal of emphasis on democratic centralism. It defined the term as follows:

> The democracy in democratic centralism means a full expression of the will and ideas of Party members, giving full play to their enthusiasm and creativeness; the centralism in democratic centralism means the concentration of the whole Party's will and wisdom and its unified action. Implementation of the system is aimed at striving for a lively political situation in which there are both centralism and democracy, both discipline and freedom, both unity of will and personal ease of mind and liveliness.

The Plenum claimed that current implementation was generally good, but declared that there were 'still many problems', the first being that 'some localities and departments have not put sufficient strength into implementing certain decisions of the central authorities, and some orders are not carried out, and even ignored'.

Over the following months, the official press and the CCP gave a good deal of attention to trying to overcome these problems. It emphasized the role the CCP should play at grassroots level in order to retain healthy links with the masses, and it stressed the need for all cadres to be honest and hard-working; in other words it acknowledged that corruption posed a continuing problem for the Party and its popular support. One point to be stressed was that the reform of the economy and the new social situation it created should not allow any deviance from Party leadership within society, nor did it absolve the Party itself from taking the means necessary to implement that leadership properly.

Factions

Although the Party aims at unity, there have in fact been factions within it at almost all times since it began. During the Cultural Revolution, Mao Zedong's obsession with class struggle led to more open and intense attempts to humiliate proponents of any views alternative to his own. The slogan was 'unity—struggle—unity', but the reality was acrimony and open fighting among supporters and opponents of Mao's line. At the height of the Cultural Revolution the Party found great difficulty even in carrying on day-to-day business.

Factions were much less intense in the period of reform than during the Cultural Revolution. Although Deng Xiaoping gradually got rid of, or eased out, those who were directly hostile to his notion of reform, that did not mean that there was unanimity on the speed and extent of reform. Many in the Party, including leaders such as Chen Yun, were afraid that the ultimate implication of the kind of reform that Deng and strongly reformist supporters like Zhao Ziyang were trying to implement was the overthrow of the CCP. They urged greater caution than Deng and Zhao favoured.

The student movements of the 1980s, and especially that of 1989, appeared to prove them right. Deng came down heavily on the side of the cautious line, arguing that what had happened (see Chapter 1, **B**. June 3–4, June 9, 1989) was in fact the quelling of a counter-revolutionary rebellion that aimed to overthrow the CCP, and Zhao was ousted. Yet there remained Party members who wished not only for openness but even to make public the factions within the senior echelons of the Party. On July 23, 1990, *People's Daily* attacked this view strongly, arguing that the CCP was a 'concentrated and united' Party which did not tolerate factions.

Deng Xiaoping's visit to the south in early 1992 reinvigorated the reform policies, but again not without opposition. Chen Yun was the leader of the faction that urged a more cautious approach. It is reported that in remarks to the Central Advisory Commission and senior members of the State Council he made early in March 1992, he attacked Deng's policies of as 'a grave tendency' which would 'certainly create chaos, affect the entire national economy and lead to social turmoil'.[1] Although these words showed the strength of Chen's feelings, it was Deng's line that won out and dominated the 1990s.

Attempting to Revive CCP Power and Spirit

Despite the rhetoric about CCP leadership, the 1980s and especially the 1990s tended to see a decline in the power of the CCP. The Hong Kong newspaper *Lianhe bao* stated on July 18, 1995 that the influence of the CCP had been declining for some time in the countryside, and that in China's central and western regions 'traditional clans, religious organizations and sects' were taking over the former authority of the Party. In other regions, capable people with financial status were usurping the Party's influence.[2] Moreover, belief in the CCP's ideology has been declining markedly since the mid–1970s.

The Sixth Plenum of the Fourteenth Central Committee (see Chapter 1, **B**. October 10, 1996) focused on ethics and culture as a component part of 'socialism with Chinese characteristics'. It summed up the problems that needed to be handled and solved in the process of socialist modernization as follows:

How to complement and coordinate the development of material progress and ethical and cultural progress and avoid emphasizing the former while neglecting the latter under the premise of centring on economic development; how to foster common aspirations, values and moral standards to the interests of the socialist modernization drive and prevent and curb decadent ideas and social evils from spreading under the condition of deepening reform and building a socialist market

economy; and how to absorb outstanding achievements in foreign civilizations, carry forward the cream of our traditional culture, prevent and eliminate the spread of cultural garbage, resist the conspiracy by hostile forces to Westernize and split our country as we widen the opening and face a new world scientific and technological revolution.[3]

The document also argues strongly in favour of a hard-working and pioneering spirit and patriotism. The Twelfth Congress had stressed the importance of the spiritual civilization, but this had tended to recede into the background as people competed to get rich as quickly as they could and corruption became more serious. The attempt to change emphasis at the Sixth Plenum of the Fourteenth Central Committee by upgrading the importance of the ethical and cultural sides of life can be seen as important in this context. The specific observation that 'hostile forces' were conspiring to westernize and split China is also striking and suggests that the Chinese leadership were distinctly unhappy with American policies towards their country at the time (see Chapter 5).

At the end of 1998, Jiang Zemin and his main supporters in the leadership launched another nationwide campaign based on 'three emphases': on the study of the CCP's official ideology; on politics; and on healthy tendencies or stamping out corruption. Aimed at promoting cohesiveness and fighting spirit within the senior ranks of the CCP, the campaign was piloted in three provinces, three ministries and the CCYL, and was taken up in the remaining provinces and departments in June and July 1999. Lasting three months in most workplaces, it required senior cadres to attend all-day work sessions on ideology and the other 'emphases'.

In July 1999 the campaign on the 'three emphases' merged with one against a quasi-religious body called the Falungong (see Chapter 1, **C**. April 25, July 19 and 22, 1999) in the sense that it gave Jiang Zemin and his leadership supporters added incentive for attempting a purification of the senior levels of the CCP, because many CCP members were found to belong to this organization. Led by Li Hongzhi, a Chinese living in New York, the Falungong was formally banned on July 22, 1999, and a CCP-sponsored media campaign against it followed, persisting for many months. On July 23, 1999, *People's Daily* ran a front-page editorial justifying the ban, declaring it 'very timely and entirely correct'. The editorial stated the need 'to see clearly the "Falungong" organization's political essence and serious harm' and it charged the Falungong with jeopardizing social stability. Of particular concern was the Falungong's attempts, through Li Hongzhi's false doctrines, to 'develop a nationwide organizational structure'. This was trying 'to take over the masses, and even gain entry into some of our Party and government organizations and crucial departments, thus attempting to become a political force which can compete with our Party and government'. Quite a few CCP members were charged with membership of this outlawed organization and imprisoned. There is no doubt that the CCP saw the Falungong as not only an ideological threat to itself but a political one as well.

Corruption within the CCP and among Officials

Corruption has become a very pressing problem within the CCP and among officials. Corruption has been more or less endemic to the Chinese bureaucracy for thousands of years. The CCP did manage to curb it successfully in the early years of its rule, but the Cultural Revolution saw many cases of corruption, and the economic reforms begun in the late 1970s helped open the way for a major expansion of corruption because they enabled power-holders to use their influence to gain money, jobs for their relatives, and various privileges for themselves and their families. Nepotism, bribery, graft and embezzlement have thus once again become very common indeed. Between 1983 and 1986 some 40 000 members of the Party were

expelled for corrupt practices, and in 1987 alone the figure was 109 000. Quite a few people have been prosecuted and condemned by the law courts, including some of very high rank. According to the president of the Supreme People's Court, Ren Jianxin, reporting to the National People's Congress on March 29, 1989, the Supreme People's Court in 1988 sentenced 111 embezzlers and bribetakers to death or life imprisonment and 5642 to prison terms. Of these 5642, 3754 (66.54 per cent) were members of the CCP. In his report to the National People's Congress on March 10, 1999, Han Zhubin, procurator-general of the Supreme People's Procuratorate, reported that, the preceding year, legal proceedings had been taken against 26 834 people involved in 22 700 cases of abuse of power, including embezzlement, bribery and dereliction of duty. Although the 1988 and 1998 figures are admittedly not exactly comparable, they appear to indicate that corruption by power-holders had become considerably worse over the decade.

In the aftermath of the mid–1989 crisis there was a series of campaigns attempting to curb corruption. One of the most vigorous of them was launched in August 1993, when Jiang Zemin expressed alarm at the scale and type of corruption, including such general trends as worship of money, bribery, lavish banqueting and even illegal sex. The Central Discipline Inspection Commission, a CCP body with the primary aim of curbing corruption, bemoaned low morale in the CCP and attacked lawless and undisciplined members whose corruption was eating away at the prestige and vigour of the Party and its ideals. Towards the end of October 1993, the CCP Central Committee and State Council announced a series of regulations aimed at combating corruption, including one document calling for strict control over government-funded trips abroad. At the same time publicity was given to a few executions of corrupt officials (see Chapter 1, **F.** various dates). The campaign brought some success, but corruption continued to plague the CCP. At a meeting of the CCP's Central Commission for Discipline held from February 25 to March 2, 1994, Commission General Secretary Wei Jianxing reported that the number of important graft and bribery cases involving funds of over RMB¥10 000 had increased 3.1 times over the 1992 period. Wei argued that such facts denoted 'breakthroughs in prosecuting important corruption cases', but made no attempt to deny the gravity of the situation.[4] At the same meeting Jiang Zemin acknowledged the corrosive impact of corruption on the CCP and government, declaring that, if not resolved, the problem could eventually eat away at the CCP's authority and public support.

The *Interim Regulations on Selection and Appointment of Party and Government Leading Cadres*, formulated on February 19, 1995 and released three months later (see Chapter 1, **B. May 16, 1995**), set out the criteria for people who were to be appointed to senior positions and the mechanism by which they should be appointed. The 'general provisions' spoke 'of developing a personnel recruitment mechanism that is full of vitality; of bringing about a contingent of cadres that is more revolutionary, younger in average age, better educated and professionally more competent; and of ensuring the full implementation of the party's basic line and the small progress of the building of the cause of socialism with Chinese characteristics'. Among the following basic conditions that leading cadres of the Party and government should possess are that they 'work hard and live a plain life, . . . voluntarily accept criticism and supervision from the party and masses, oppose bureaucratism and oppose any abuse of power and the unhealthy tendency of seeking personal gain'. This suggests that combating corruption was among the factors involved in formulating the regulations. The regulations also make clear the importance of combating nepotism by specifying, in the section on 'job avoidance', a list of categories of people whom leading cadres should *not* appoint: spouses, lineal relatives by blood, collateral relatives by blood within three generations, and close relatives by marriage. The regulations state that 'People of aforesaid relations shall not hold jobs under the same superior in an organization or jobs of superior–subordinate relationship; nor shall they hold organization, personnel, discipline inspection, supervisory, auditing or financial jobs in an organization of which one of them holds the leading post'.[5]

The issue of corruption was highlighted also in April 1995 because of the suicide that month of Beijing Vice-Mayor Wang Baosen, who faced imminent investigation into embezzlement and other forms of economic corruption and crime. The Municipal Secretary Chen Xitong took the blame and resigned, but was implicated and stripped of his party positions later in the year, being sentenced to sixteen years' imprisonment on July 16, 1998. The man who replaced Chen was Wei Jianxing, who had been a member of the Politburo and secretary of the Central Commission for Discipline Inspection since 1992 and a crucial figure for handling corruption; the choice was almost certainly not accidental.

Corruption remained a problem as the twentieth century drew to its end. Jiang Zemin was among those who continued to attack it. The Central Discipline Inspection Commission meeting of January 29, 1997 heard Jiang Zemin condemn ostentation and extravagance among cadres and issued a communiqué highlighting the duties of leading cadres to observe clean practices and refrain from seizing privileges, especially in such areas as housing. On May 26, 1997, the Spiritual Civilization Construction Guiding Committee held its first plenary session. This body, set up under the CCP Central Committee, aims to accomplish the implementation of central directives and policies concerning spiritual civilization and to coordinate solutions to problems connected with it, especially of ethics and culture. On July 11, the CCP Central Committee and State Council published 'Some Regulations about Enforcing Thrifty Practices and Prohibiting Extravagance and Waste in Party and Government Agencies'. This document, although evaluating the overall situation highly, condemned extravagance and squandering of public money. It called for strict controls over building and renovating offices, holding meetings, festivities and travelling at government expense. It also condemned the holding of unnecessary lavish banquets.

These measures may have done some good. But they came nowhere near solving the problem, which continued to worsen. In January 2000 Auditor-General Li Jinhua exposed that corrupt officials had extorted money to the value of many billions of dollars. In particular, he charged that fourteen officials involved in the resettlement project for the Three Gorges Dam Project had diverted RMB¥500 million (about US$60.4 million), or 12 per cent of RMB¥4 billion resettlement funds, in order to set up companies, build houses and trade stocks. The same month the PRC's largest contraband scandal broke, with confirmation of the news that nearly 200 people were being held on suspicion of having accepted bribes from the local Xiamen magnate Lai Changxin in order to allow him and his company, the Yuanhuan Group, to evade tariffs on imports valued at nearly US$10 billion. At the same time, the government increased its suppression of corruption, a good illustrative example being that in mid-February 2000 the Nanchang People's Intermediate Court actually sentenced former Jiangxi vice-governor Hu Changqing to death for taking bribes.

THE GOVERNMENT

The structure of the Chinese government mirrors that of the Party in many respects. For example, both Party and government have national congresses at their highest levels, with inner elite bodies representing them when they are not in session; both have province-level congresses and congresses at lower regional levels. There are also differences. Unlike the Party, the government includes ministries in charge of particular areas of work, such as foreign affairs, finance, education, or culture. However, it is important to note that the government, like everything else in China, must follow the leadership of the CCP, which means that in fact it holds very much less power. It must

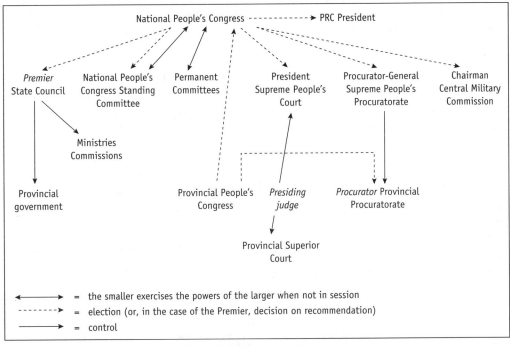

Figure 2.2 PRC state structure

implement Party policy in the particular area of its specialization and competence.

The National People's Congress

The most important government body is the NPC (National People's Congress), which is like a parliament. In theory, the NPC is elected for a term of five years, and is supposed to meet every year. However, during the Cultural Revolution years, from 1966 to 1976, there was only one meeting of the NPC, in January 1975. Since the reforms of the late 1970s, the NPC has again met every year. The NPC has its own Standing Committee, a permanent body that carries out NPC work when it is not in session.

The following shows all the occasions on which the NPC has met.

First NPC
First Session, September 15–28, 1954
Second Session, July 5–30, 1955
Third Session, June 15–30, 1956
Fourth Session, June 26–July 15, 1957
Fifth Session, February 1–24, 1958

Second NPC
First Session, April 18–28, 1959
Second Session, March 30–April 10, 1960
Third Session, March 27–April 16, 1962
Fourth Session, November 17–December 3, 1963

Third NPC
First Session, December 21, 1964–January 4, 1965

Fourth NPC
First Session, January 13–17, 1975

Fifth NPC
First Session, February 26–March 5, 1978
Second Session, June 18–July 1, 1979
Third Session, August 30–September 10, 1980
Fourth Session, November 30–December 13, 1981
Fifth Session, November 26–December 10, 1982

Sixth NPC
First Session, June 6–21, 1983
Second Session, May 15–31, 1984
Third Session, March 27–April 10, 1985
Fourth Session, March 25–April 12, 1986
Fifth Session, March 25–April 11, 1987

Seventh NPC
First Session, March 25–April 13, 1988
Second Session, March 20–April 4, 1989
Third Session, March 20–April 4, 1990
Fourth Session, March 25–April 9, 1991
Fifth Session, March 20–April 3, 1992

Eighth NPC
First Session, March 15–31, 1993
Second Session, March 1–22, 1994
Third Session, March 5–18, 1995
Fourth Session, March 5–17, 1996
Fifth Session, March 1–14, 1997

Ninth NPC
First Session, March 5–19, 1998
Second Session, March 5–15, 1999
Third Session, March 5–15, 2000

Further figures on the composition of the Ninth NPC show that 563 members, or 18.89 per cent, were workers or farmers; 628 members, or 21.07 per cent, were intellectuals;

Table 2.5 Numbers of deputies to the NPC

	1st NPC	2nd NPC	3rd NPC	4th NPC	5th NPC	6th NPC	7th NPC	8th NPC	9th NPC
Female	147	150	542	653	742	632	634	627	650
Percentage	12.0	12.2	17.8	22.6	21.2	21.2	21.3	21.03	21.81
From minority nationalities	178	179	372	270	381	403	445	439	428
Percentage	14.5	14.6	12.2	9.4	10.9	13.5	15	14.75	14.37
Total	1226	1226	3040	2885	3497	2978	2970	2978	2979

Sources: Figures from the Chinese Academy of Social Sciences, edited for Pergamon Press by C. V. James, *Information China, The Comprehensive and Authoritative Reference Source of New China,* vol. 1 (Pergamon Press, Oxford, New York, 1989), p. 392; *Beijing Review* XXXI, 13 (March 28–April 3, 1989), p. 7; and Information Office of the State Council of the People's Republic of China, 'China's Policy on National Minorities and Its Practice', *Beijing Review* XLII, 42 (October 18, 1999), p. 19.

988, or 33.16 per cent, were cadres; 268, or 8.99 per cent, belonged to the PLA; and 460, or 15.44 per cent, belonged to one of the eight democratic parties or had no party affiliation, the remainder being members of the CCP.

NPC Functions and Powers

One of the tasks of the NPC is to adopt the PRC Constitution. There have been four of these since 1949, adopted respectively on September 20, 1954, January 17, 1975, March 5, 1978 and December 4, 1982. However, significant amendments were made on April 12, 1988, March 29, 1993, and March 15, 1999 (see under these dates in Chapter 1, **B**).

Among other powers given to the NPC are those enabling it to enact or amend laws, to examine and approve the state budget, to approve, change or negate decisions of its Standing Committee, to decide on the establishment of provinces, autonomous regions, municipalities and special administrative regions, and to decide on questions of war and peace.

The NPC has the power to elect the chairman of the state CMC (as opposed to the CCP's CMC), the president of the Supreme Court, and the procurator-general of the Supreme People's Procuratorate. (See also the two following sections.)

The President of the PRC

The NPC also elects the president of the PRC. The following have held the office of president of the PRC (or president of the Central People's Government before the adoption of the 1954 Constitution). The date shown is the date of election to that post by the NPC.

- Mao Zedong, September 27, 1954 (Chairman of the Central People's Government from September 30, 1949)
- Liu Shaoqi, April 27, 1959
- Li Xiannian, June 18, 1983
- Yang Shangkun, April 8, 1988
- Jiang Zemin, March 27, 1993.

Liu Shaoqi became Mao's chief rival and opponent at the time of the Cultural Revolution. This led Mao not only to arrange for Liu's dismissal and humiliation—he was dismissed from all posts by the Twelfth Plenum of the

Eighth Central Committee in October 1968—but also to abolish the post itself. The decision to abolish the post was taken at the Second Plenum of the Ninth Central Committee, and there is no mention of it in the 1975 Constitution. Liu was posthumously rehabilitated in February 1980, and the post of PRC president was restored in the 1982 Constitution.

The State Council and the Premier

The State Council, also called the Central People's Government (CPG; or Government Administrative Council before the adoption of the 1954 Constitution), is the highest organ of state administration. It is headed by the premier, and consists also of vice-premiers, state councillors, ministers in charge of ministries, and others. It generally meets once a month and its Standing Committee, comprising the premier, vice-premiers, secretary-general and state councillors, holds a meeting twice a week.

The office of premier is normally more powerful for the government than that of president of the PRC. The premier's position is equivalent to that of the prime minister in the Westminster system. It is the premier who carries out the day-to-day work of the government.

The NPC chooses the premier, but the nomination and final act of appointment is made by the president of the PRC. The NPC also chooses the vice-premiers, state councillors and ministers of the government, on the nomination of the premier. The following have occupied the position of premier (shown with the date of appointment):

- Zhou Enlai, September 27, 1954, premier of the Government Administrative Council from October 1, 1949;
- Hua Guofeng, March 5, 1978. Hua became acting premier on February 3, 1976 following the death of Zhou Enlai the preceding month, and was confirmed in the position by the Politburo on April 7, 1976;
- Zhao Ziyang, September 10, 1980;
- Li Peng, April 9, 1988. On November 24, 1987, the National People's Congress Standing Committee approved Zhao

Ziyang's resignation as premier after he became Party general secretary, together with his replacement by Li Peng as acting premier;

- Zhu Rongji, March 17, 1998.

The First Session of the Ninth NPC of 1998 reduced the number of government ministries and ministry-level state commissions from 40 to 29. Other than the Premier, it appointed vice-premiers and state councillors as follows:

- Vice-Premiers Li Lanqing, Qian Qichen, Wu Bangguo and Wen Jiabao;
- State Councillors Chi Haotian, Luo Gan, Wu Yi (female), Ismail Amat (Uygur nationality) and Wang Zhongyu (concurrently secretary-general).

The First Session of the Ninth NPC also determined the following ministries (or state commissions), with ministers placed in parentheses.

- Ministry of Foreign Affairs (Tang Jiaxuan)
- Ministry of National Defence (Chi Haotian)
- State Development Planning Commission (Zeng Peiyan)
- State Economic and Trade Commission (Sheng Huaren)
- Ministry of Education (Chen Zhili, female)
- Ministry of Science and Technology (Zhu Lilan, female)
- Commission of Science, Technology and Industry for National Defence (Liu Jibin)
- State Ethnic Affairs Commission (Li Dezhu, Korean nationality)
- Ministry of Public Security (Jia Chunwang)
- Ministry of State Security (Xu Yongyue)
- Ministry of Supervision (He Yong)
- Ministry of Civil Affairs (Dorje Cering, Tibetan nationality)
- Ministry of Justice (Gao Changli)
- Ministry of Finance (Xiang Huaicheng)
- Ministry of Personnel (Song Defu)
- Ministry of Labour and Social Security (Zhang Zuoji)
- Ministry of Land and Natural Resources (Zhou Yongkang)
- Ministry of Construction (Yu Zhengsheng)
- Ministry of Railways (Fu Zhihuan)

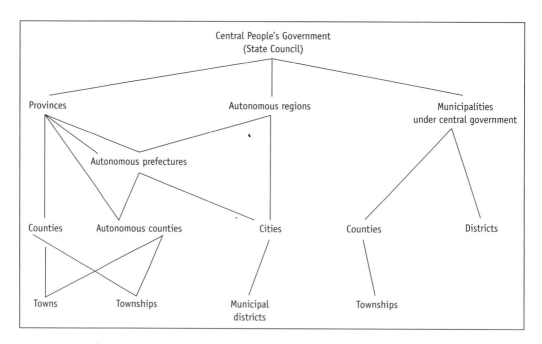

Figure 2.3 Levels of government under the Central People's Government

- Ministry of Communications (Huang Zhendong)
- Ministry of Information Industry (Wu Jichuan)
- Ministry of Water Resources (Niu Maosheng, Manchu nationality)
- Ministry of Agriculture (Chen Yaobang)
- Ministry of Foreign Trade and Economic Cooperation (Shi Guangsheng)
- Ministry of Culture (Sun Jiazheng)
- Ministry of Public Health (Zhang Wenkang);
- State Family Planning Commission (Zhang Weiqing)
- People's Bank of China (Dai Xianglong)
- National Audit Office (Li Jinhua).

The Chinese People's Political Consultative Conference

The formal decision to establish the PRC was taken by the first meeting of the Chinese People's Political Consultative Conference in September 1949. This body continued to play a united front role in politics until the Cultural Revolution, which abolished it. It resumed this role when its Fifth National Committee met for its First Session in Beijing from February 24 to March 8, 1978. The CPPCC's 1978 Constitution specifies it as 'an organization of the revolutionary united front under the leadership of the CCP'. By the end of the twentieth century there had been nine CPPCC National Committees, the Ninth holding its First session in March 1998. The CPPCC contains members of the eight 'democratic parties', as well as a few CCP members. It is mainly a prestige body and does not exercise any real power.

Regional Government

Under the 1982 Constitution, the types of administrative unit below provincial level are autonomous prefectures, counties, autonomous counties, cities, municipal districts, townships, nationality townships and towns. The townships replace the people's communes specified in the 1975 and 1978 Constitutions. The autonomous prefectures and autonomous counties are self-governing according to policy.

At the end of the twentieth century there were in the People's Republic of China 22 provinces (not including Taiwan), five autonomous regions, four municipalities under the central government, and two special administrative regions (Hong Kong and Macau). At the end of 1998, there were in the 31 province-level units (not including Hong and Macau), a total of 331 prefectures (including 227 cities at prefectural level) and 2126 counties (including 437 cities at county level). The number of cities at all levels was 664.[6]

Government exists at the regional levels as well as centrally. The highest regional level is the province. There are three kinds of area at provincial level: the provinces, the autonomous regions, and the municipalities directly under the central government. The autonomous regions are established for the minority nationalities, and reflect the formal policy, though not necessarily the reality, that the minority nationalities should enjoy autonomy (see Chapter 9). The four municipalities directly under the central government are Beijing, Shanghai, Tianjin and Chongqing. There are also government structures at lower levels, right down to the village level.

On July 1, 1979, the NPC adopted the *Organic Law of the Local People's Congresses and Local People's Governments*, which came into effect on January 1, 1980. The structures introduced by this law replaced those of the Cultural Revolution. For example, the revolutionary committees that were emphasized during the Cultural Revolution were abolished. The local government structure reflects the central structure closely, with units having their own people's congress and corresponding standing committee. The provincial people's congresses are empowered to pass their own local legislation, provided it does not conflict with central legislation. Their term of office is five years.

Under the 1982 Constitution, the government head of all autonomous regions, autonomous prefectures and autonomous counties must be a citizen of one of the nationalities represented, or of the nationality exercising regional autonomy. In the people's congresses of these autonomous regions, prefectures and counties, the nationalities inhabiting the area are by law entitled to appropriate representation. (See Chapter 9 for a listing of these autonomous regions, prefectures and counties.)

Elections

The members of the NPC are elected according to the *Electoral Law* of 1979. However, there are no general elections in China; instead, small-scale elections take place at various levels, and at different times. These elect representatives for their particular level, and it is the representatives who make the choices for the higher levels, going up to the NPC. Thus, though all citizens have the right to vote, they do not decide and may not necessarily influence who becomes a member of the NPC. Under the 1979 *Electoral Law*, which was adopted by the NPC on July 1, 1979, direct elections are possible at the county level. More than one person can stand for election, and surprise candidates with no backing from the CCP have occasionally won. On the whole, however, the CCP candidates have a very much better chance of success than any others, and elections that could result in the ousting of CCP power remained impossible at the beginning of the twenty-first century.

In November 1987, the NPC adopted the *Organic Law on Villagers' Committees of the PRC*, which allowed for the direct election of the directors, deputy directors and members of village committees and did not require that village heads or members of village committees be members of the CCP. On November 4, 1998 the NPC Standing Committee adopted the *PRC Village Committee Organization Law*, thereby changing the rules to the nomination process and allowing for a primary election at which voters would write in the names of favoured candidates on a blank ballot. The effect was to widen nominations and make the elections 'significantly more free', according to observers from the Atlanta-based Carter Center who observed a primary in

Hebei province on January 7, 2000.[7] By the end of the twentieth century, over one million village elections had taken place throughout China. About 60 per cent of these resulted in victories for CCP members as village heads, but about 20 per cent of them saw CCP incumbents removed from office. According to some observers, 'giving peasants the right to remove corrupt or abusive officials is a part of Beijing's strategy to maintain stability in rural areas'.[8]

At the end of 1998, a new development occurred when the eleven villages of Buyun Township in Sichuan cast secret ballots to elect their head. Under the Constitution, it is the local people's congress that appoints the township heads. This election was held secretly by local CCP cadres, and there were suggestions that it was strongly contrary to the wishes of the central leadership. However, on February 26, 1999 China Central Television ran extended coverage of the election, including the fact that open debates had taken place during the campaign leading up to the vote. Early in 2000, twenty cities began elections for neighbourhood committees, and from June 1, 2000, open elections were introduced for all neighbourhood committee posts in Beijing. The election process points towards greater democracy in China but is unlikely to lead to nationwide general elections in the short term.

THE LEGAL SYSTEM

The Chinese legal system has three arms: the public security organs, the people's procuratorate, and the people's courts. The public security arm is responsible for investigating crime and detaining suspects, the procuratorate for approval of arrests and establishing an *a priori* case against suspects, and for initiating and sustaining prosecutions, and the courts for the passing of judgments. The vast majority of those who appear before the courts are convicted, and the role of their defence lawyers is more to get the punishment reduced than to establish their innocence. As an example to illustrate the point, on March 10, 1998, Supreme People's

Court president Ren Jianxin reported that, over the preceding five years, only 0.43 per cent of criminal cases had yielded a not-guilty verdict.

The Supreme People's Court and Supreme People's Procuratorate are responsible to the National People's Congress and its Standing Committee. Both people's courts and procuratorates exist at various levels. Apart from the Supreme People's Court, the hierarchy of the courts moves down through the higher, intermediate, basic and special people's courts.

The formal law system suffered almost to the point of total destruction during the Cultural Revolution. However, the Third Plenum of the Eleventh Central Committee in 1978 called for the re-establishment of a formal law system. By the end of the twentieth century, the Chinese state had consolidated a basic framework for a legal order which covered virtually all aspects of social life, including not only criminal matters but also a wide variety of civil matters, such as debts, housing and land real estate law, and family law, especially divorce. The policy of openness to the outside world has resulted in many economic disputes arising from such areas as contracts, foreign trade, joint ventures, maritime transportation, collision of ships, capital construction, insurance, patent rights, trademarks and copyright. Public confidence in the legal processes appeared to strengthen in the late 1980s. Although this confidence suffered in some quarters as a result of the 1989 crisis, it revived to a large extent as the twentieth century drew to its close.

The following table shows the number of first trial cases of economic disputes settled by the courts. As can be seen, most are over contracts. The large number of 'others' includes economic rights, water transport and aviation transport. It is striking that the Chinese statistical yearbooks did not include these figures until 1997, which explains the lack of earlier years in this table.

Article 78 of the 1954 Constitution states: 'The people's courts administer justice independently and are subject only to law.' Article 126 of the 1982 Constitution states: 'The people's courts shall, in accordance with the law, exercise judicial power independently and are not subject to interference by administrative organs, public organizations, or individuals.' Neither the 1975 nor the 1978 Constitution makes any mention of the independence of the law system.

The Anti-Rightist Campaign of 1957 saw the greater subordination of the law system to the Party, and during the Cultural Revolution period from 1966 to 1976 there was a complete withdrawal of all vestiges of legal independence. Since the 1980s, the trend has generally been towards reviving and recognizing the principle that the law should be independent of the Party or state.

In January 1995 the *State Compensation Law* came into effect. In theory this protects and demands compensation for those whose legal rights have been violated by government

Table 2.6 Economic legal cases by type

Dispute type	Cases settled 1997	% of total	Cases settled 1998	% of total
Economic contracts	1 368 808	92.6	1 332 932	91.5
Compensation for damages	3 801	2.5	4 000	2.7
Bankruptcy	5 697	3.9	6 206	4.3
Railway transport	1 214	0.8	1 293	0.9
Road transport	4 884	3.3	4 549	3.1
Maritime affairs	4 364	3.0	4 735	3.3
Others	89 371	6.0	102 532	7.0

Sources: State Statistical Bureau (comp.), *Zhongguo tongji nianjian 1998* (*China Statistical Yearbook 1998*) (Statistical Press of China, Beijing, 1998), p. 791 and State Statistical Bureau (comp.), *Zhongguo tongji nianjian 1999* (*China Statistical Yearbook 1999*) (Statistical Press of China, Beijing, 1999), p. 759.

authorities. If a government official unjustly defames an individual or group, the law provides for indemnity and a public apology. In cases where such violation of rights is specifically in line with government policy, this law would no doubt be rendered ineffective. Still, the very idea of suing a government official is new and radical in the context of the PRC.

In March 1996 the National People's Congress adopted the amended *Criminal Procedure Law* (see Chapter 1, **B.** March 17, 1996), which increased defendants' rights and the independence of law. Its provisions included the following:

- judges were to be independent adjudicators, not simply part of the prosecution;
- the practice whereby the public security organs could detain a suspect for investigation indefinitely was terminated;
- no one should be regarded as guilty until convicted by a court; and
- defendants were guaranteed access to lawyers while under detention.

These provisions strengthened the rights of defendants before the state, at least in the realm of criminal law.

On December 1, 1998, Beijing had its first open trial. This meant that any citizen aged 18 or over could enter any court to listen to cases, provided they produced their identification card. One implication was that journalists could observe and report on cases, a step in the direction of accountability.

In the realm of property ownership the trend has been similar. An illustrative case is that of Zhang Xiaojing, who set up a factory in Dalian in 1978 and registered it in the name of a collectively owned plant but then transferred the factory's property and debts to his newly established private firm in 1995. He was accused of embezzlement of public property and in 1998 sentenced to three years' imprisonment, with a five-year reprieve. Zhang appealed, forcing the Dalian Intermediate Court to a lengthy investigation which reached the conclusion that Zhang's firm was indeed privately owned. As a result, the court upheld Zhang's appeal on February 11, 1999, quashing the first verdict against him.[9]

When they perceive the state to be under threat, however, both the state and individual leaders still use the law system to crack down on perceived enemies or dissidents and to promote the Party's, the state's or their own political power. Two examples illustrate the point. The period following the Beijing massacre saw blatant use of the legal system to

Table 2.7 Mediated cases by type

Category	1985	1990	1994	1998
Marriage	1 072 116	1 222 214	1 191 925	952 317
Percentage	16.93	16.50	19.46	18.08
Housing, residences	1 035 618	894 349	659 980	544 742
Percentage	16.35	12.07	10.78	10.34
Inheritance	206 943	284 979	296 227	274 689
Family provision, alimony, etc.	347 377	445 963	440 621	388 352
Percentage	5.49	6.02	7.20	7.37
Debts	254 669	498 564	462 539	453 866
Percentage	4.02	6.73	7.55	8.62
Business	900 093	751 651	611 555	539 614
Neighbourhood disputes	n/a	989 827	899 226	794 588
Percentage	n/a	13.36	14.68	15.09
Damage compensation	570 595	528 148	492 325	386 595
Percentage	9.01	7.13	8.04	7.34
Others	1 945 501	1 793 525	1 069 331	998 795
Percentage	30.72	24.21	17.46	17.70

Sources: State Statistical Bureau (comp.), *Zhongguo tongji nianjian 1986* (*China Statistical Yearbook 1986*) (Statistical Press of China, Beijing, 1986), p. 803; later Statistical Yearbooks of China, including *Zhongguo tongji nianjian 1999*, p. 747.

buttress the political power of the Party and government leadership. In 1999 and 2000 the CCP used the law system to assist its crackdown on the Falungong. China has come under criticism from international human rights bodies for deficiencies in its legal system, an issue considered briefly below.

There are certain implications for the power of the CCP in allowing the law system to be too independent of the government. The main one is that this poses a threat to the power of the CCP, because, as shown in Western countries, an independent legal system frequently reaches judgments strongly inimical to government officials and can bring down governments and political parties. Under these circumstances, what is striking is how much progress the Chinese law system has made in matters where politics is more or less irrelevant.

The Legal Profession

The nature of the legal system in the People's Republic has meant that the legal profession has always been small and relatively powerless, with a correspondingly low social status and salary. In the period of reform, the numbers of lawyers has risen dramatically, while more and more have moved into private legal business, where they can make far more money than in the state-run law firms. However, the number of lawyers is still far too small and their social status far too low to approach anywhere near making China a law-based society.

In 1957 there were about 2100 lawyers in the whole country, a figure which rose to about 3000 by 1960. During the Cultural Revolution, the legal profession was all but destroyed, but the legal reforms of the late 1970s brought about its revival. By late 1980 there were 380 legal advisory offices in China, with some 3000 lawyers. The preference for mediation noted above is very evident in the figures below, as is the changing balance between mediation and formal law at the end of the twentieth century.

Crime and Punishment

The PRC's first *Criminal Law* was adopted in 1979 (see Chapter 1, **B.** July 1, 1979), going into effect on January 1 the following year. This law lays down types of crime and appropriate penalties. However, some of the categories are very vague and can be all-encompassing, for example 'crimes of counter-revolution'. There is a category of crimes of infringing upon the rights of the person and the democratic rights of citizens, which include rape and sexual relations with a girl under the age of 14, which is deemed to be rape.

The criminal process is designed more to suppress crime than to protect the rights of the individual. Although China's history shows the logic of an emphasis on public order, the law is extremely harsh against suspected criminals—many would argue excessively so. The amended 1996 *Criminal Procedure Law* took a positive step by reducing the maximum time police could detain suspects without trial from two months to 30 days. This still gives them considerable powers, which could be considered excessive. The People's Armed Police, which was transferred from the PLA to public security in 1983, has shown itself capable of behaving very sav-

Table 2.8 Legal personnel

	1985	1989	1993	1995	1998
Legal offices	3 131	3 646	5 129	7 263	8 946
Lawyers	13 403	43 715	68 834	96 602	101 220
Full-time	6 830	23 606	30 401	45 094	51 008
Notary offices	2 674	2 914	3 066	3 148	3 179
Public notaries	3 205	9 408	10 371	10 663	13 006
Mediators	4 739 000	5 937 000	9 767 000	10 259 000	9 175 000

Sources: State Statistical Bureau (comp.), *Zhongguo tongji nianjian 1987* (*China Statistical Yearbook 1987*) (Statistical Press of China, Beijing, 1987), p. 836; later *Statistical Yearbooks of China*, especially *Zhongguo tongji nianjian 1999*, p. 745.

agely when it perceives public order to be under threat, for instance in suppressing independence demonstrations in Tibet.

Although crime rates are still quite low by world standards, they appear to have increased greatly in the 1980s and 1990s. In the 1990s rural crime also assumed particular importance. A report in the *Fazhi ribao* (*Legal System Daily*) condemned the fact that law and order had deteriorated seriously in the countryside over the previous years. It blamed local 'tyrants' for lording it over villages and said that train robbers and highwaymen were common in some districts. Other types of people to come under condemnation were 'people from other localities', meaning that many crimes were not committed by locals but by outsiders and 'rural patriarchal clans', suggesting that violent clan warfare had reemerged in the countryside. The article also blamed rural cadres, CCP networks and the police for being unable, or unwilling, to do anything to combat these shocking tendencies. Indeed, a figure from early 1995 claimed that 'lax and paralyzed Party organizations' were about 8 per cent of

all village-level Party branches. Population pressures did not help in solving the many problems. For example, there was far too much surplus rural labour, with many people turning to crime and even flooding the cities, becoming there a '"reserve force" for urban crime'.[10]

Statistical information on crime—as on more or less everything else—has improved enormously since the 1980s. The presidents of the Supreme People's Court and Supreme People's Procuratorate make regular published reports to the NPC, which contain a wealth of detail of many kinds, including statistics. However, there are still many lacunae, with much important information never consolidated into national statistics. Moreover, it is often unclear precisely what the statistics mean or what they include, and the categories are frequently vague.

The following table shows some types of crime cases as they were registered with the public security organs in the 1990s. They do not necessarily imply that the case was handled or solved, let alone taken to court. However, it was reported that in 1996, the

Table 2.9 Criminal cases registered in the public security organs

Type of crime	1995	1996	1997	1998
Homicide	27 356	25 411	26 070	27 670
Percentage	1.69	1.59	1.62	1.39
Personal injury	72 259	68 992	69 071	80 862
Percentage	4.46	4.31	4.28	4.07
Robbery	164 478	151 147	141 514	175 116
Percentage	10.15	9.44	8.77	8.82
Rape	41 823	42 820	40 699	40 967
Percentage	2.58	2.68	2.52	2.06
Kidnap and sale of people	10 670	8 290	6 425	6 513
Percentage	0.66	0.52	0.40	0.33
Larceny	1 132 789	1 043 982	1 058 110	1 296 988
Percentage	69.88	65.22	65.57	65.30
Fraud	64 047	69 688	78 284	83 080
Percentage	3.95	4.35	4.85	4.18
Smuggling	1 119	1 147	1 133	2 301
Percentage	0.07	0.07	0.07	0.12
Counterfeit and sale of banknotes	5 237	5 128	5 422	6 654
Percentage	0.37	0.32	0.34	0.34
Others	101 225	184 111	186 901	265 901
Total	1 621 003	1 600 716	1 613 629	1 986 068

Sources: State Statistical Bureau (comp.); *Zhongguo tongji nianjian 1997* (*China Statistical Yearbook 1997*) (Statistical Press of China, Beijing, 1997), p. 752; *Zhongguo tongji nianjian 1999*, p. 750.

public security organs solved 1 279 091 criminal cases in 1996, with a rate of 79.9 per cent of those cases registered. In 1998, the figure for criminal cases solved by the public security organs was 1 264 635, the rate being 63.7 per cent. The number of criminal cases has thus risen, but the solution rate had fallen.

Just after the suppression of the 1989 student movement, the government began a campaign against what it termed 'six evils' (*liuhai*): narcotics, prostitution, pornography, gambling, superstition and the buying and selling of women. Among these the last was the most serious. The women bought or sold were to become wives, maids and concubines, with the crime arising, at least in part, from the shortage of women in the countryside. In Table 2.10 (p. 106) the crime of kidnapping and selling people refers mainly to this development. Clearly, the campaign begun in 1989 did not succeed in stamping out this crime. In 2000 the government undertook a major crackdown. Spokespersons acknowledged that some gangs regarded the abduction and trade of women and children as an occupation and set up businesses equipped with vehicles, mobile phones and other means of communication to make profits from this criminal behaviour. They even conceded that the crime had spread from the remote rural areas to the cities and throughout the country.[11] On April 12, 2000, Hong Kong's *South China Morning Post* reported that thousands of women and children had been rescued from abduction and human trafficking in various parts of China. Two days before the Guangdong police had announced that they had arrested 484 suspects working for 54 trafficking syndicates, thus saving over 1000 women and 500 children from slavery. Similar police actions had taken place in Fujian, Anhui and Sichuan.

Statistics are also available on offences against public order which are handled by the public security organs. Table 2.10 shows certain categories of crimes, and the numbers that the public security organs accepted for investigation and handling. The proportions of those that were in fact handled were 90.23 per cent (1995), 93.06 per cent (1997) and 92.64 per cent (1998). This list also gives an insight into what are considered crimes against public order in China. Unreported crimes are of course not included in these figures, nor do they show the numbers of crimes which came before the courts.

One category of 'crime' included under 'disturbing public order' or 'others' is unauthorized demonstrations. Under the *Law of Assembly, Procession and Demonstration of the People's Republic of China* (1989) and the Regulations for the Implementation of the same law (promulgated June 1992), it is regarded as a criminal offence to hold demonstrations without the permission of the relevant authorities. This law has been used against such bodies as the Falungong in 1999 and 2000.

In descending order of severity, the types of punishment meted out in the Chinese legal system are death sentence (by shooting), death sentence with reprieve, life imprisonment, imprisonment for varying periods, and supervision. Accessory penalties include fines, deprivation of political rights and forfeiture of property. The most famous case of 'death sentence with reprieve' is that of Jiang Qing and Zhang Chunqiao, members of the 'gang of four'. They were given death sentences with two-year reprieves which were then commuted to life imprisonment (see Chapter 1, **B**. January 25, 1981 and January 25, 1983). A consistent policy has been 'leniency for those who confess, severity for those who remain obdurate'.

Imprisonment is combined with reform through labour and 'ideological education' or indoctrination. To detain a criminal, a written judgment or warrant is in theory necessary. Prison authorities are armed and may use their arms if criminals rebel or attempt escape. Female prisoners are controlled by female warders. They are not allowed to keep their children in prison, but all criminals may receive their relatives twice a month. If a female criminal is unable to find anybody to look after her children, the state takes responsibility for finding appropriate residences, orphanages or kindergartens.

Minor criminals who are judged to be exempt from responsibility are subjected to 'rehabilitation through labour', usually for periods of one to three years. Political education and productive labour are features of this form of punishment. People are instructed in a job and payment is given for their work, either to the prisoner or to relations.

Those sentenced to 'supervision' are placed under the supervision of the public security or the people at their place of work for a specified period. Although this form of punishment does not involve imprisonment, it is considered a humiliation both by those affected and by their relations.

Work-study schools are semi-coercive organizations which educate and reform juvenile delinquents who have committed minor offences. Most inmates are teenagers under 15 years of age whom their parents, teachers or unit-leaders are unable to handle. Like other Chinese corrective institutions, they combine labour with education or indoctrination. Since they are semi-coercive only, the parents pay tuition and living expenses.

The Chinese and Human Rights

The Chinese legal and penal system has been the target of serious criticism by foreign and international human rights organizations. Bodies such as Amnesty International, Asia Watch (renamed Human Rights Watch/Asia) and the US State Department issue annual reports about China's human rights record

Table 2.10 Crimes against public order

Type of crime	1995	1997	1998
Disturbing work or public order	332 120	330 886	300 201
Percentage	10.10	10.25	9.29
Gang or other serious fighting	84 588	90 233	99 050
Percentage	2.57	2.80	3.06
Sexual crimes against women	63 220	53 976	41 294
Percentage	1.92	1.67	1.28
Obstructing government workers from their duty	45 999	45 998	45 971
Percentage	1.40	1.43	1.42
Violating firearms regulations	23 070	35 461	26 234
Percentage	0.70	1.10	0.81
Violating explosives regulations	26 883	35 114	34 912
Percentage	0.82	1.09	1.08
Inflicting bodily harm	503 283	537 455	568 438
Percentage	15.30	16.65	17.59
Robbery	735 528	520 080	533 677
Percentage	22.36	16.11	16.51
Fraud, extortion and racketeering	93 471	78 257	86 537
Percentage	2.84	2.42	2.68
Damaging property	48 737	49 779	53 033
Percentage	1.48	1.54	1.64
Forgery and sales of bills or notes	43 318	29 700	26 119
Percentage	1.32	0.92	0.81
Preying on superstitions for deceit, theft or fraud	13 061	10 945	9 000
Percentage	0.40	0.34	0.28
Prostitution	186 661	210 390	189 972
Percentage	5.67	6.52	5.88
Gambling	433 831	417 784	365 221
Percentage	13.19	12.94	11.30
Violation of residence or identity card regulations	197 808	217 676	268 537
Percentage	6.01	6.74	8.29
Others	458 182	563 935	583 917
Percentage	13.93	17.47	18.07
Total	3 289 760	3 227 669	3 232 113

Sources: Zhongguo tongji nianjian 1997, p. 752; Zhongguo tongji nianjian 1999, p. 750.

and, although improvements are occasionally acknowledged, virtually all reports are condemnatory. Even before the crisis of 1989, Amnesty International charged that China had hundreds of thousands of political prisoners. It was among a number of international and non-Chinese organizations that claimed a very serious worsening of the legal and human rights situation following the Beijing massacre of June 1989. In particular, it made allegations about and denounced punishments inflicted for no other 'crime' than disagreeing with the ideas of the government. The US State Department's 'Human Rights Report of 1989', issued on February 21, 1990, had a great deal to say about a wide range of violations of human rights in China, especially in connection with the suppression of the pro-democracy movement from early June and with the situation in Tibet.

An example of a later report is that issued by Amnesty International concerning the 'strike hard' (yanda) anti-crime campaign, alleging that from April 28 to June 27, 1996, 1014 death sentences had been carried out. A report which Amnesty International issued at the beginning of February 2000 claimed that in 1998 China had executed nearly 1800 people, and probably somewhat more, including political prisoners and those involved in non-violent crimes. It added that China accounted for more than half the total executions carried out throughout the world in 1998. Amnesty International also accused Beijing of executing political prisoners in Xinjiang; these were people who had been engaged in the secessionist activities that were common there at the turn of the century (see Chapter 9). It charged Beijing with holding show trials for which the verdicts had been predetermined, with confessions often extracted through torture.[12] Human rights bodies have also attacked the *Law of Assembly, Procession and Demonstration* mentioned above, and its application to sentence to prison terms such people as the Falungong leaders and other practitioners.

Chinese authorities have taken two general approaches towards international criticism of China's human rights record. One is to argue that the foremost human right is 'the right to subsistence', in which China has done very well. The other is to charge that criticism of human rights is interference in their domestic affairs and a contravention of their national sovereignty. Spokespersons have generally denied or placed a different slant on foreign reports of human rights violations, especially those concerning purely political prisoners. In the case of the Amnesty report of February 2000, Foreign Ministry spokesman Zhu Bangzao defended China's legal record and in particular denied that the separatists in Xinjiang were political prisoners; instead he condemned them as terrorists.

On the other hand, Chinese sources have themselves conceded serious abuses of power and personal rights by police and other authorities. The Cultural Revolution period of 1966 to 1976 is regularly castigated as a period of savage oppression. The special court trying the 'gang of four' and six others in 1980 (see Chapter 1, **B.** October 20–December 29) revealed that in the cases mentioned in the indictment alone, 729 511 people had been 'framed and persecuted' and 34 800 had been 'persecuted to death'.

These cases concern a period that is now totally discredited in the official version of history. However, serious abuses have also been acknowledged in 'positive' periods. In September 1986, a Chinese English-language newspaper reported several cases of abuse of police power, including one in which two university professors had been detained by police for no other reason than the wish to take revenge.[13] In his report of March 1999 to the NPC, Procurator-General of the Supreme People's Procuratorate Han Zhubin acknowledged that in 1998 procuratorial organs at various levels had handled '1467 cases involving government employees who committed the offenses of illegal custody, extorting confessions by torture, taking revenge and making false charges'.[14] It has become quite standard to acknowledge such shortcomings in the Chinese system. Where Han is at odds with many Western journalists is in his implication that the Chinese legal system is attempting to solve such problems, not contribute to them.

Serious cases of abuse through 'turning a blind eye' to major crime rackets have also been recorded. Late in 1988, a Chinese-language newspaper in Shanghai reported on rings of people who traded in women; the most expensive were slightly mentally retarded, because they worked hard but did what they were told without complaining or trying to run away. One man in Hebei province had been imprisoned for trading in women, but used his connections with authorities to secure an early release and simply re-established his former trade.[15] As noted above, figures on the 'kidnap and sale of people' have been regularly announced in the *China Statistical Yearbooks* since the mid–1990s (see Table 2.9).

3 EMINENT CONTEMPORARY FIGURES

The following is a highly selective sample of biographies of those Chinese who are, or have recently been, eminent or influential in the PRC in the political, economic, cultural and other fields, especially since 1990.[1] For reasons of space and the immensity of the subject, it excludes all politicians who were rendered politically inoperable before 1990 (e.g. Mao Zedong, Zhao Ziyang, or the 'gang of four'), and the emphasis is strongly on people living at the time the book was completed, with exceptions granted for only a very limited number of people, e.g. Deng Xiaoping. It also excludes those who did not live on the Chinese mainland when the book was written. Some of those prominent politically during the 1980s, but with much less influence in the 1990s, can be found in the first edition of the present work. Except for most minority nationality members, the names given in parentheses immediately after each heading are the names of the biographees in the Wade–Giles romanization.

Ba Jin (Pa Chin)—b. Li Yaotang, November 25, 1904, Chengdu, Sichuan. Attended Chengdu Foreign Languages School, graduating 1923. Studied in France, 1927–28. First novel *Destruction* (*Miewang*), published October 1929 in Shanghai. His masterpiece, which is also one of the landmarks of modern Chinese literature, is *Family* (*Jia*), which was published in a daily in 1931, but as a book in 1933. Before the war he lived mainly in Shanghai, although he lived in Japan 1934–35, and during the war travelled in various places in China, including Shanghai, Guilin, Guangzhou and Chongqing. In the 1950s and early 1960s he was vice-chairman, and sometimes acting chairman, both of the All-China Federation of Literary and Art Circles and the Chinese Writers' Association, but was a victim of the Cultural Revolution. In the late 1970s he was rehabilitated and during most of the 1980s and 1990s was again vice-chairman of the All-China Federation of Literary and Art Circles and chairman of the Chinese Writers' Association. Elected vice-chairman of the Ninth NPC (1998). Has won several international honours, including Italian International Dante Prize 1982, and is a Fellow of the American Academy of Arts and Letters. Apart from those mentioned above, his publications include: *Trilogy of Love* (*Aiqing sanbuqu*) 1933–35; *Spring* (*Chun*) 1937; *Autumn* (*Qiu*) 1940; *Fire: A Trilogy* (*Huo*) 1938–43; *Ba Jin's Collected Works* (*Ba Jin wenji*, 14 volumes) 1958–62. Ba Jin is (as of 2000) China's foremost living literary figure.

Bo Xilai (Po Hsi-lai)—b. July 1949, Dingxiang, Shanxi Province, son of Bo Yibo. Mayor of Dalian. Spent five years in prison during the Cultural Revolution, because of Red Guard persecution of his father. Joined CCP 1980. Graduated from Graduate School, Chinese Academy of Social Sciences, 1982. Various appointments in the CCP Central Committee's offices. In Dalian, became propaganda head 1988, achieving senior positions in the Dalian municipal government and CCP, and being appointed Mayor of Dalian 1993 and secretary of the Dalian CCP Committee September 1999. Influential as a modern-minded official, willing to take questions directly from viewers on television. Adopted very pro-environment policy in Dalian, enforcing strict anti-pollution laws there. Under his leadership, Dalian holds an annual fashion fair.

Bo Yibo (Po I-po)—b. 1908 Dingxiang, Shanxi Province. While studying at Beijing University in 1925, joined CCP and was imprisoned for over three years. During Sino-Japanese War 1937–45 built up pro-Communist anti-Japanese guerrilla force in native province. Appointed member, Central People's Government Council and Government Administrative Council, and vice-chairman, Financial and Economic

Affairs Committee, 1949 and Minister of Finance 1949–53. Served in State Planning Commission 1952–59, becoming chairman 1956. Appointed alternate Politburo member and vice-premier 1956. Early victim of Cultural Revolution, probably due to relationships with Liu Shaoqi. Vice-premier, member, State Financial and Economic Commission, and member of Eleventh Central Committee 1979–82; then vice-chairman, Central Advisory Commission 1982–92. Minister, State Machine Building Industry Commission 1979–82; state councillor 1982–83 and vice-minister, State Commission for Restructuring the Economic System 1982–88. Played major role in CCP rectification 1983–87 and presided over early 1987 meeting which deposed CCP General Secretary Hu Yaobang. Also played a key role in the writing of CCP history into the 1990s. A highly influential figure throughout the history of the PRC, especially in economic matters, and has played a moderating role.

Cao Gangchuan (Ts'ao Kang-ch'uan)—b. December 1935, Wugang, Henan. Senior PLA general. Joined PLA 1954, and CCP 1956. Graduated from Advanced Military Engineering School, Soviet Artillery Corps, 1963. In December 1996 appointed director of the Commission of Science, Technology, and Industry for National Defence, a high-level PLA organization which plays an important role in China's weapon programs. This post gives him the rank equivalent to a government minister and he also has a military rank equivalent to a lieutenant general. He is thus very influential in the supply of weaponry to the PLA, and he believes that the West, especially the United States, does not wish to see China prosper.

Chen Muhua (Ch'en Mu-hua)—b. June 1921 Qingtian, Zhejiang. Joined CCP 1938 and was active with the CCP in Yan'an against the Japanese, then serving in the CCP's military and in other ways against the Guomindang from 1945. Studied building construction at Jiaotong University in Shanghai. Later she held leadership positions in the Ministry of Railways and the State Planning Commission and from 1961 was deputy bureau director of the Foreign Economic Liaison Commission; when the commission was upgraded to a ministry, she was vice-minister and then minister. Vice-premier 1978–82; minister of the State Family Planning Commission 1981–82; minister, Foreign Trade and Economic Relations, 1982–85, and state councillor 1982–87. Served on Presidium Standing Committee, Twelfth (1982) and Thirteenth (1987) Party Congress. Member of Tenth to Fourteenth Central Committees, 1973–97. President, People's Bank of China (under State Council), 1985–88. Chair of the China Women's Federation 1988–98. Has led countless government, economic and trade delegations to over 30 nations. Among the most senior women in the CCP and government over a very long period, especially in the economy, banking, and economic relations with foreign countries.

Chen Xitong (Ch'en Hsi-t'ung)—b. June 1930, Anyue, Sichuan. Studied Chinese language, Beijing University. Joined CCP 1949. Served in various minor posts at municipal and county level prior to 1979. Served in Beijing as vice-mayor from 1979 and mayor from 1987; also deputy secretary Beijing CCP Committee 1987–92 and secretary 1992–95. Appointed chairman, 1990 Asian Games Organizing Committee. Central Committee member, Twelfth Party Congress, 1982–95, and Presidium member, Thirteenth Party Congress, 1987; promoted to Politburo at Fourteenth CCP Congress, 1992. State councillor 1988–95. Author of a detailed official report, dated June 30, 1989, defending military action of June 3–4, 1989. In 1995 involved in a major scandal in Beijing (see Chapter 1, **D.** April 27, 1995). In 1997 expelled from CCP for corruption (see Chapter 1, **D.** September 9, 1997). On July 31, 1998, Beijing People's High Court sentenced Chen to sixteen years' imprisonment for corruption and dereliction of duty because 'he violated regulations, accepted expensive gifts and kept them illegally'. Chen appealed against the sentence, but on August 19, 1998, China's Supreme People's Court dismissed his appeal. At the time, he was the highest-ranking official in the history of the PRC to be sentenced by the courts.

Chen Yaobang (Ch'en Yao-pang)—b. December 1935, from Panyu, Guangdong. Graduated from Central China Agricultural College 1957. Joined CCP 1982. After interruption due to the Cultural Revolution, gained increasingly senior positions, especially in the Ministry of Agriculture, being vice-minister of Agriculture 1986–93. Appointed vice-minister of the State Planning Commission 1993, minister of Forestry 1997 and then minister of Agriculture March 1998. Became member of Fifteenth CCP Central Committee, September 1997.

Chen Yun (Ch'en Yün)—b. as Liao Chengyun, near Shanghai in 1905, d. in Beijing 1995. Became active in trade union movement about 1921. Joined CCP 1925 and together with Liu Shaoqi was leading initiator of May Thirtieth Movement that year. Played very active role in the CCP, against the Japanese and against the Guomindang, before 1949. Appointed vice-premier, Government Administrative Council; Minister of Heavy Industry; and chairman, government's Financial and Economic Affairs Committee, 1949. Member, State Planning Commission, 1952–54. Elected to Politburo Standing Committee and vice-chairman, Eighth Central Committee, 1956. Mao had him dismissed in 1962 as a rightist, and for the next fifteen years Chen Yun played a minimal role. From 1977 he pushed for the rehabilitation of Deng Xiaoping. Again appointed to Politburo Standing Committee, and as first secretary to Central Committee Commission for Inspecting Discipline at Eleventh Party Congress, 1978; confirmed at Twelfth Party Congress, 1982. Vice-chairman, Fourth NPC, 1975; confirmed at Fifth NPC, 1978. Again vice-premier 1979–80, and chairman, State Financial and Economic Commission, 1979–81. In 1987 elected chairman, Central Advisory Commission. Historically, one of

the most influential of CCP leaders, especially in the field of economics, who generally adopted a policy of party discipline, even under very difficult circumstances.

Chen Zhili (Ch'en Chih-li)—b. November 1942, Xianyou, Fujian. China's first female minister of education, appointed March 1998. Joined CCP 1961. Graduated from Fudan University, Shanghai, 1964 and Shanghai Silicate Institute of Chinese Academy of Sciences 1968. Deputy secretary of Shanghai CCP Committee 1989–97. Deputy minister of State Education Commission 1997–98. Alternate member of Thirteenth and Fourteenth CCP Central Committees (1987–97). Made full member of Fifteenth CCP Central Committee 1997. Lays emphasis on the eradication of illiteracy in China.

Chi Haotian (Ch'ih Hao-t'ien)—b. July 1929 in Zhaoyuan, Shandong. Served against both the Japanese and Guomindang before 1949 and joined the CCP October 1946. Graduated from PLA Military College 1960. Held increasingly senior military positions from 1950s to 1970s. Also served as leading official in *Liberation Army Daily* and as deputy editor-in-chief of *People's Daily* in the 1970s. Became deputy chief, PLA General Staff, 1977, and was chief, 1987–92. Achieved rank of general 1988. Appointed member of Central Military Commission 1992, and became vice-chairman 1995. Appointed state councillor and minister of National Defence 1993, reappointed to both positions 1998. By-elected to CCP's Twelfth Central Committee 1985; confirmed Thirteenth to Fifteenth CCP Central Committees (1987, 1992 and 1997); promoted to Politburo 1997.

Cui Jian (Ts'ui Chien)—b. 1961 Beijing, belongs to Korean minority. China's foremost performer of pop music, especially rock and roll. Has a distinct style incorporating classic rock, jazz, rap and, later, punk and heavy metal. Not encouraged by authorities because of his independent themes, which are sometimes anti-government, but very popular with youth.

Dai Xianglong (Tai Hsiang-lung)—b. October 1944, Yizheng, Jiangsu. Banker. Graduated from Central Institute of Finance and Banking, Beijing, 1967. Joined CCP 1973. Appointed vice-governor, 1993 and governor, 1995, of People's Bank of China. Alternate member of Fourteenth CCP Central Committee, 1992–97, and became full member of Fifteenth, 1997. Strongly reformist economically and in banking. In the three years leading up to October 1999, he cut bank interest rates seven times with the aim of stimulating domestic consumer spending and was exceedingly influential in preventing devaluation of the Chinese currency during the Asian financial crisis of the late 1990s.

Deng Xiaoping (Teng Hsiao-p'ing)—b. 1904 Guang'an, Sichuan, d. 1997 Beijing. Among group of returned students from France who gained great prominence in CCP; joined CCP 1924. Active in Jiangxi Soviet 1931–34 and took part in the Long March 1934–35, being an active supporter of Mao Zedong at the time. Active on behalf of the CCP against the Japanese and the Guomindang. Transferred to Beijing and became vice-premier under Zhou Enlai 1952. Played prominent role as Zhou's general secretary, and as the only person to serve on all three committees set up under the CCP's most important leaders (Mao, Liu Shaoqi and Zhou) to establish a national legislative committee, 1953–54. Minister of Finance 1953–54. Briefly removed from office; then apparently victor of a power struggle, subsequently identified as secretary-general, CCP's Central Committee, and elevated to Politburo 1955 (re-elected at Eighth Party Congress 1956). Also reappointed vice-premier under Zhou and vice-chairman, Mao's National Defence Council: confirmed 1959 and 1965. Appointed to uniquely powerful position of first secretary of the CCP's Secretariat and member, Politburo Standing Committee, 1956. Maintained high public profile until Cultural Revolution, when accused of collaborating with Liu Shaoqi, and purged. Restored to vice-premiership 1973–76 and Politburo Standing Committee 1975–76, and again purged 1976–77, then restored to all prior posts. Chief, PLA General Staff and vice-premier 1977–80. Chairman, PRC and CCP's Central Military Commissions, 1981–90 and 1983–89 respectively. Reelected to Politburo Standing Committee, Twelfth Party Congress, 1982–87. Was chiefly responsible for suppression of student movement on June 3–4, 1989, but retired soon after from all major posts. During the 1990s he remained influential, and his 'southern visit' early in 1992 was regarded as a major reinvigoration of reform policies following the crisis of 1989. Deng is given the credit as the chief architect of reform in China since the end of 1978.

Ding Guan'gen (Ting Kuan-ken)—b. September 1929, from Wuxi, Jiangsu. Graduated from Jiaotong University, Shanghai, 1951; joined CCP 1956. Minister for Railways 1985–88 and appointed vice-minister, State Planning Commission, 1988. Head of United Front Work Department of CCP Central Committee 1990. Member of Twelfth, Thirteenth, Fourteenth and Fifteenth Central Committees (1982, 1987, 1992, and 1997); promoted to membership of the Politburo 1992, confirmed 1997.

Ding Guangxun (Ting Kuang-hsün)—b. September 1915, native of Shanghai. Graduated from College of Theology, St John's University, Shanghai 1942, and in late 1940s obtained MA from Columbia University and New York Union Theology College, returning to PRC 1951. President, Nanjing Union Theological Seminary, 1952; vice-chairman of Council of Self-Administration of Protestant Church by 1962, and bishop and director, Institute of Protestant Theology, Nanjing, by 1964. Disappeared 1967–72 due to Cultural Revolution. Appointed vice-president of Nanjing University 1979; president, Christian Council of China, and chairman, Three-Self Patriotic Movement Committee of Protestant Churches in China, 1980; vice-president, Association for Peace and Disarmament, 1985. Elected vice-chairman of CPPCC Seventh, Eighth and Ninth National Committees 1988 to present (as of 2000). Influential as among China's most senior and government-sponsored Christians.

Dorje Cering—b. 1938, from Xiahe, Gansu. Tibetan. Moved to Tibet in 1959 to help with its development, spending over 30 years there. Physically harmed during Cultural Revolution, two ribs being broken. In 1980s achieved various positions in Tibet, including deputy secretary of CCP Tibet Committee and vice-chairman of Tibet Regional Government. Appointed vice-minister of Civil Affairs, 1990, and minister of Civil Affairs March 1993, the first Tibetan to become a Chinese national minister in Chinese history. Reappointed to same post March 1998. Member of CCP Thirteenth, Fourteenth and Fifteenth Central Committees (1987, 1992, and 1997). Lays emphasis on social security.

Fei Xiaotong (Fei Hsiao-t'ung)—b. November 1910 Wujiang County, Jiangsu Province. Graduated from Graduate School, Beijing's Qinghua University 1935, received PhD from London University, 1938. Professor, Southwest Associated University 1938–45. Joined China Democratic League 1944. Attended first plenum of CPPCC 1949. In 1957–58 associated with Hundred Flowers Movement and subsequently forced to engage in self-criticism and repent past errors. Professor of Central Institute for Nationalities 1957–87, although work severely disrupted during Cultural Revolution, especially 1967–72. Professor of Sociology at Peking University from 1979. Vice-chairman of Central Committee of China Democratic League 1979–87 and then elected chairman. President, Society of Sociology, 1979–90. Special court judge for trial of Lin Biao and Jiang Qing and 'gang of four' 1980. Has received many international awards and honours, including the Malinowski Award, Society of Applied Anthropology Institute, London, 1981 and the Ramon Magsaysay Award for Community Leadership, 1994. His many works include several books in English, such as *Peasant Life in China* (London, 1939), *Earthbound China* (Chicago, 1945), *Toward a People's Anthropol-*ogy (Beijing, 1982), and *Rural Development in China* (Chicago, 1989). Fei Xiaotong is noted as China's best known, most distinguished and most influential ethnologist and social anthropologist. He is reported to have developed his own methodology for incorporating China's traditional culture and regional diversities.

Han Zhubin (Han Chu-pin)—b. February 1932, from Harbin. Joined CCP April 1950. Worked in railways in Liuzhou, Guangxi, 1950–83, and then as director and secretary of CCP Committee of Shanghai Railway Bureau, 1983–90. Became minister of Railways 1992. Also became member of Fourteenth and Fifteenth CCP Central Committees 1992 and 1997, and was elected deputy secretary of CCP's Central Commission for Discipline Inspection 1997.

He Jingzhi (Ho Ching-chih)—b. November 1924, Zaozhuang, Shandong. Attended primary and middle school. Began publishing poetry in Chongqing newspaper in 1939. Went to Yan'an 1940. Joined CCP 1941. Graduated in literature, Yan'an Lu Xun Art and Literature Academy, 1942, and worked in the Art Troupe of the same academy 1943–45. Wrote libretto for *The White-Haired Girl* (*Baimao nü*) with Ding Yi. A pioneering example of the form 'song-opera' (*geju*), this opera is a landmark in the history of CCP revolutionary theatre and remains very popular despite its age. Based on a folk tale, it was premiered in Yan'an in April 1945 and awarded the Stalin Prize for Literature in 1951. Worked in various literary and theatre jobs, including deputy director of Arts Department of *People's Daily* 1964–66. Poems at the time carried propaganda content, including 'Return to Yan'an' ('*Hui Yan'an*'), 1956 and 'Song of Lei Feng' ('*Lei Feng zhi ge*'), 1963. Condemned as counter-revolutionary and disappeared during Cultural Revolution 1967–76. Identified as vice-minister of Culture 1978–82. Deputy director, CCP Central Committee's Propaganda Department 1980–87. Central Committee member, Twelfth and Thirteenth Party Congress, 1982 to present. Acting Minister of Culture, September 1989 to 1992, having replaced Wang Meng (q.v.) who had fallen out of favour due to the mid–1989 crisis. Influential as a pro-CCP poet and dramatist.

He Kang (Ho K'ang)—b. March 1923, Fuzhou, Fujian. Joined CCP 1939. Graduated in agriculture, Guangxi University, 1946. Held various jobs in agriculture, especially in Guangdong, but was severely affected by Cultural Revolution. Became vice-minister of Agriculture and Forestry 1978 and vice-minister of Agriculture, Animal Husbandry and Fisheries 1982. Vice-minister of State Planning Commission, 1982–85. Minister of Agriculture, Animal Husbandry and Fisheries 1983–88 and minister of Agriculture 1988–93. Served on various central health campaign committees and State Council agricultural committees and commissions (e.g. elected vice-chairman, National Agricultural Zoning Committee, 1983). Led many agricultural delegations outside China. Awarded World Food Prize 1993. Extremely influential in revival of Chinese agriculture after Cultural Revolution. The statement that accompanied his winning the World Food Prize in 1993 claimed that he had 'provided the leadership that enabled China, in little more than a decade, to become self-sufficient in basic food for the first time in modern history. This is a major accomplishment when one considers that China, with over one billion people, has twenty-two per cent of the world's population that hold only seven per cent of its arable land'.[2]

Hu Jintao (Hu Chin-t'ao)—b. December 1942 in Shanghai. Graduated from Qinghua University, July 1965. Lived and worked in Gansu 1968–82, becoming very active in the CCYL in his later years there. In November 1984 became first secretary of CCYL's Central Committee's Secretariat, thus becoming the most powerful person in China's largest youth organization. Secretary of CCP's Guizhou Provincial Committee 1985–88, the youngest person to occupy a provincial CCP secretary's position at that time, and was very

active in eliminating poverty in that province. Secretary of the CCP's Tibet Autonomous Region Committee 1988–92; gained reputation for contributing to economic growth and stability. Became a member of CCP Central Committee's Politburo Standing Committee, October 1992, at the time the youngest person ever to be a member of that body, the most powerful in China. In 1993 became president of CCP Central Committee's Party School, the CCP's main training ground for future leaders. Vice-president of PRC, March 1998. His meteoric rise makes him the first in the younger generation of leaders.

He Xuntian (Ho Hsün-t'ien)—b. May 15, 1953, Suining, Sichuan; musical composer and theorist, whose works are claimed to have marked the emergence of China's own school of music. BA, Sichuan Conservatorium of Music, 1982. Appointments in composition at Sichuan Conservatorium of Music 1982–97; appointed professor of composition at Shanghai Conservatorium of Music 1996. Various musical awards in China and overseas, such as Outstanding Musical Achievement Awards, USA, 1989–90. Composer of symphonies, such as *Four Dreams* (1986); chamber music, such as *The Pattern of Sound Suite* (1997); and song albums, such as *Sister Drum* (1994), and *Voice from the Sky* (1996). His music has been published, performed and broadcast in more than 65 countries and territories, including Austria, Germany, China, Britain and the United States; *Sister Drum* is said to be the first Chinese-language album in the international music industry.

Hu Qili (Hu Ch'i-li)—b. October 1929, Yulin, Shaanxi Province. Joined CCP 1948. Graduated from Peking University 1951. Prominent in All-China Students' Federation: chairman 1956–65 and 1979–80; and also in CCYL and All-China Youth Federation. Dismissed from CCYL posts 1966, and attacked as follower of Liu Shaoqi and purged by Red Guards 1967; sent to labour camp in Ningxia. Identified in several CCP posts at county and regional level in Ningxia 1972–78. Tianjin CCP secretary and mayor 1980–82. Appointed director, CCP Central Committee's General Office, 1982. In 1985 became member of CCPCC's Politburo and at Thirteenth Congress rose to be a member of Politburo Standing Committee. However, was dismissed at time of 1989 crisis and was unemployed for a period. In May 1991 returned as vice-minister of Machine-Building and Electronics Industry, and served as minister of Electronics Industry 1993–98. Was elected vice-chairman of Ninth CPPCC National Committee in March 1998.

Huang Ju (Huang Chü)—b. September 1938, from Jiashan, Zhejiang. Graduated from Qinghua University 1963. Technician Shanghai's Artificial Board-Making Machinery Plan 1963–67. Joined CCP 1966. Various appointments in Shanghai, deputy secretary of Shanghai CCP Committee 1985, CCP Secretary 1994, Shanghai deputy mayor 1986, mayor of Shanghai 1991, member of Twelfth Politburo 1994 and of Thirteenth Politburo 1997. As CCP secretary and mayor of Shanghai particularly influential and with great potential in China's power structure.

Huang Kun (Huang K'un)—b. September 1919, Jiaxing, Zhejiang. Graduated from Yenching University Physics Department 1941 and received doctorate from Bristol University 1947, continuing research at Edinburgh and Liverpool Universities, returning to China 1951. Appointed member, Academy of Sciences' Department of Mathematics, Physics and Chemistry 1955. Identified as physics professor, Peking University, 1959. Joined CCP 1959. Elected foreign member, Swedish Royal Academy, 1980. Elected Fellow, Third World Academy of Sciences, Trieste, 1985, and president, Physics Society, 1987. Huang has developed physics theories which bear his name, such as 'Huang's diffuse scattering', and has written widely on physics, especially (jointly with Nobel Laureate Max Born) *The Dynamical Theory of Crystal Lattices* (Clarendon Press, Oxford, first published 1954), which is a standard work on its subject. Influential as one of China's most

distinguished physicists, especially in the field of solid state physics.

Huang Zhendong (Huang Chen-tung)—b. December 1940, from Dafeng, Jiangsu. Graduated from Nanjing School of Shipping Engineering, 1962. Joined CCP 1981. Deputy minister of Communications in charge of the construction of coastal ports, 1985–88, and general manager of State Communications Investment Corp. 1988–91, another body with concern with transport and port facilities. Appointed minister of Communications 1991, and later as president of China Merchants' Steam Navigation Group. Reappointed minister of Communications March 1998. Member of Fourteenth and Fifteenth Central Committees, 1992 and 1997. Huang has played a vital role in developing China's transport system, especially its port facilities.

Ismail Amat (Simayi Aimaiti)—b. September 1935 in Uygur community, Qira County, Hotan Prefecture, Xinjiang. Joined CCP 1953. Active in people's commune movement up to 1960. Gained many significant positions in Xinjiang, including during Cultural Revolution, rising to be either CCP Xinjiang secretary and/or chairman of Xinjiang Uygur Autonomous Regional People's Government 1972–86. Minister, State Nationalities Affairs Commission, 1986–88. Appointed state councillor 1993 and 1998. Member of Tenth (1973) to Fifteenth (1997) Central Committees. He is among the most senior of the members of the minority nationalities in the Chinese leadership.

Jia Chunwang (Chia Ch'un-wang)—b. May 1938, from Beijing. Joined CCP 1962. Graduated from Qinghua University, 1964. Active in CYL affairs at Qinghua University down to 1982; deputy secretary and then secretary, Beijing CYL 1982–83, being a member in the same years of the Beijing Municipal CCP Committee; deputy secretary Beijing CCP Committee 1984–85. Minister of State Security 1985–98 and appointed minister of Public Security in March 1998. Member of Twelfth (1982) to Fifteenth (1998) Central

Committees. Given highest police rank, commissioner-general, December 1992. Noted as the country's most senior police authority.

Jia Qinglin (Chia Ch'ing-lin)—b. March 1940, from Botou, Hebei. Joined CCP 1959. Graduated from Hebei Engineering College 1962. Series of major appointments in Fujian, including secretary of Fujian CCP Committee. Member of Eleventh to Fifteenth Central Committees, Member of Fifteenth Politburo, summoned to Beijing 1996 shortly becoming mayor and CCP secretary following the disgrace of Chen Xitong (see Chapter 1, **D.** August 26, 1997). He has given priority to serious environmental, pollution, traffic control and unemployment problems in the capital, as well as to solving problems posed by the Falungong.

Jiang Chunyun (Chiang Ch'un-yün)—b. April 1930, from Laixi, Shandong. Joined CCP February 1947. Achieved many and increasingly powerful positions in Shandong Province, becoming both provincial governor and CCP provincial secretary in 1988, but not remaining long in the former post. Became vice-premier of State Council in March 1995 and vice-chairman of NPC Standing Committee March 1998. Member of Thirteenth (1987) to Fifteenth (1997) Central Committees, including the Fourteenth (1992) and Fifteenth (1997) Politburos. Noted for his Shandong connections and for the fact that when elected vice-premier in March 1995, over a third of the NPC either abstained or voted against him, a vote without precedent in the NPC leadership elections.

Jiang Wen (Chiang Wen)—b. January 5, 1963, Beijing. The best known and highest paid actor living on the Chinese mainland. Also directs films. First made reputation for lead role in *Red Sorghum* (*Hong Gaoliang*), 1987, directed by Zhang Yimou. Has acted in films like *In the Heat of the Sun* (*Yangguang canlan de rizi*), 1995, based on a novel by Wang Shuo, and *The Emperor's Shadow* (*Qin song*), 1996, set in the Qin dynasty. Other films include *The Song Sisters* (*Songjia*

huangchao), 1997, and *Keep Cool* (*Youhua haohao shuo*), 1997. Jiang is often at odds with authorities over his films, and in mid–2000 was banned from working in China because one of his films was screened at the Cannes Film Festival without official permission, but he has an enormous popular following in China.

Jiang Zemin (Chiang Tse-min)—b. August 17, 1926, in Yangzhou, Jiangsu. Joined CCP April 1946. Graduated from Shanghai Jiaotong University 1947, majoring in electrical engineering. After 1949 served as engineer and went to Soviet Union as trainee in 1955–56, then served as director of factories and research institutes in Changchun, Shanghai and Wuhan. Deputy minister of Electronics Industry 1982–83 and minister 1983. Elected to Twelfth Central Committee 1982, and Thirteenth Party Congress's Presidium and Politburo 1987. Mayor of Shanghai 1985–88; deputy secretary, Shanghai CCP Committee, 1985–87 and secretary 1987–89; Replaced Zhao Ziyang as Party secretary general June 1989, following suppression of student movement of April to June that year, and retains that position (2001). Also became chairman of the State and CCP Central Military Commissions in November 1989 and March 1990 respectively. Appointed President of China in March 1993, a position he retains. Deng Xiaoping dubbed Jiang Zemin as 'the core of leadership of the third generation', Mao Zedong being that of the first and Deng of the second. As China's leader, Jiang has shown himself very much in favour of economic but less of political reform, and is absolutely determined to keep the CCP in power in China as long as possible. He has used many opportunities to place his own ideological stamp on the CCP by lengthy speeches at well chosen forums. His foreign policy is very pro-Russian and also determined to maintain good relations with the United States, especially in the economic field. As China's president, he has made many trips abroad.

Li Changchun (Li Ch'ang-ch'un)—b. February 1944, Jilin. Joined CCP 1965. Graduated from Harbin Industrial University 1966. Series of appointments in northeast, notably mayor and CCP secretary of Shenyang Municipality in 1983 and governor of Liaoning Province in 1986. Moved to Henan, with a series of appointments there, culminating in CCP secretary in 1992. Moved to Guangdong as CCP secretary 1997. Member of Thirteenth (1987), Fourteenth (1992) and Fifteenth (1997) Central Committees. In 1997 he became the youngest ever person to be selected to the Politburo. Noted for anti-corruption drives and for hostility to nepotism and cronyism, and for insistence on family planning in Guangdong, including harsh penalties for those who break the one-child-per-couple rule.

Li Desheng (Li Te-sheng)—b. 1916 from Xinxian, Henan. Joined Red Army 1930 and CCP 1932. Took part in Long March 1934–35. In newly reorganized 8th Route Army became detachment commander 1937, battalion commander 1940 and regimental commander 1943. Forces integrated into Central Plains Field Army 1948, and became commander, 2nd Field Army's 35th Division 1949. Division joined Chinese People's Volunteers in Korea in 1951, where appointed chief of staff, 12th Army 1952. Trained at PLA Military Academy, Nanjing,1954. Promoted to major-general 1955, and identified as commander, 12th Army, 1958. In response to Lin Biao's call for military commanders to return to basic service, served for some time as private in 1960. Moderating role and sense of restraint during Cultural Revolution led to appointment as commander, Anhui Military District, 1967. Served in Anhui as chairman, Revolutionary Committee, 1968–74 and first secretary, new CP Secretariat, 1971–74. Elected to Ninth Central Committee and alternate Politburo membership 1969; elevated to Politburo Standing Committee 1973–75. Director, PLA's Political Department, 1970–74. Commander, Shenyang Military Region, 1974–85, and first secretary of its CCP 1977–85. Resigned from Politburo and Central Committee posts and elected to

Standing Committee, Central Advisory Commission, 1985–92. Elected to Presidium, Thirteenth (1987) and Fourteenth (1992) Party Congress.

Li Dezhu (Li Te-chu)—b. November 1943, from Wangqing, Jilin, of Korean ethnicity. Graduated from Yanbian University in Yanji, Jilin 1967. Held increasingly powerful positions in Jilin, including secretary of CCP Committee and government head of Yanbian Korean Autonomous Prefecture in Jilin. Became deputy governor of Jilin Province in 1988 and vice-minister of State Ethnic Affairs Commission 1990–92, being appointed minister of State Ethnic Affairs Commission 1998. Alternate member of Twelfth CCP Central Committee (1982) and full member of Thirteenth (1987) to Fifteenth (1997) CCP Central Committee. He is among the most senior members of an ethnic minority in the Chinese leadership.

Li Lanqing (Li Lan-ch'ing)—b. May 1932, from Zhenjiang, Jiangsu. Graduated from Fudan University 1952. Joined CCP September 1952. Served in various economic posts, especially those connected with automobile industry, being trained in two automobile factories in Moscow in 1956 and 1957. Deputy mayor of Tianjin 1983–86. Vice-minister of Foreign Economic Relations and Trade 1986–90, and minister 1990–92. Appointed vice-premier 1993 and confirmed in the post 1998. Alternate member of Thirteenth Central Committee (1987), but promoted to the Politburo of the Fourteenth (1992) and Fifteenth (1997) Central Committees. Noted for his moves to encourage foreign investment and for his very rapid promotion to full membership of the Politburo after being only an alternate member of the Central Committee.

Li Peng (Li P'eng)—b. October 20, 1928 in Chengdu, Sichuan. Reputed to have been adopted by Zhou Enlai. Joined CCP November 1945. Sent to study at Moscow Power Institute 1948, graduating in 1954 and returning to China the next year. Prior to

1980 held various posts related to electricity and power. Throughout Cultural Revolution, 1966–76, worked in various jobs in Beijing connected with power. Deputy minister, then minister of Power Industry 1979–82; vice-minister, newly established Ministry of Water Conservation and Power, 1982–83. Appointed vice-premier 1983, being concurrently minister, State Education Commission, from 1985. Then in 1987 became acting premier and in 1988 premier of State Council, a position he held until replaced by Zhu Rongji in 1998. Between 1988 and 1990 served concurrently as minister of State Commission for Economic Restructuring. In 1998 became chairman of NPC Standing Committee. CCP Central Committee member, Twelfth Party Congress 1982. Served on Presidium Standing Committee and elevated to Politburo Standing Committee, Thirteenth Party Congress 1987, and remains on that most powerful of bodies. Since the 1980s, Li Peng has made many diplomatic trips abroad, including a high-profile visit to Rio de Janeiro in June 1992 for the Earth Summit. He followed Deng Xiaoping's line very closely during the crisis of 1989, and declared martial law in Beijing on May 20, 1989, refusing dialogue with the student protestors. He also strongly supported the suppression of the student movement early in June, a fact that has attracted odium from many quarters, especially overseas. He suffered a heart attack in 1993 and tended to lose ground after that to Vice-Premier Zhu Rongji, who advocated faster and more intense economic reform.

Li Ruihuan (Li Jui-huan)—b. September 1934, from Tianjin. Joined CCP September 1959. Studied at Beijing Spare-time Architectural Engineering Institute 1958–63. Served as carpenter and also gained experience in trade unions and CYL. Director-general of work site for the Mao Zedong Memorial Hall 1977. Named national model worker 1979. Mayor of Tianjin 1982–89 and secretary of the Tianjin CCP Committee 1987–89. Elected to Twelfth Central Committee 1982. Elevated to Politburo, and served on Presid-

ium, Thirteenth Party Congress, 1987, and to Politburo Standing Committee June 1989, being one of the three men (along with Jiang Zemin and Song Ping) to replace the fallen Zhao Ziyang and Hu Qili at the time of the crisis of 1989. He remains on the Politburo Standing Committee. In March 1993 elected chairman of the Eighth Chinese People's Political Consultative Conference National Committee, holding the position for the Ninth in 1998. Li Ruihuan has been concerned with ideological and cultural matters. For example he has taken a lead in trying to revive the old art of Peking Opera, and in November 1995 he attended and gave a speech at the opening gala performance of the week-long First Peking Opera Art Festival held in Tianjin.

Li Tieying (Li T'ieh-ying)—b. September 1936, Yan'an, Shaanxi, son of Li Weihan, one of the earliest CCP Central Committee members. Joined CCP 1955. Graduated in solid physics, Mathematics Department, Charles University, Czechoslovakia, 1961. Then worked in three Shenyang research institutes and was elected labour hero 1978. Identified as secretary, Shenyang CP 1981, and elected secretary, Liaoning Province CP 1983–85. Elected alternate member, Twelfth Central Committee 1982 and promoted to the Politburo just after the Thirteenth CCP Congress (1987), remaining in that position with the Fourteenth (1992) and Fifteenth (1997) Central Committees. Appointed minister of Electronics Industry 1985, minister of State Commission for Restructuring the Economy 1987, minister of State Education Commission 1988, minister of State Commission for Economic Restructuring 1993; and state councillor 1988–98.

Li Ximing (Li Hsi-ming)—b. February 1926, Shulu, Hebei. Joined CCP 1948. Studied civil engineering and architecture at Qinghua University and served as director and secretary CCP Committee, Beijing Shijingshan Power Plant, 1956–75. Deputy minister of Water Conservancy and Electric Power 1975–80; minister of Urban and Rural Construction and Environmental Protection 1982–84. Elected vice-chairman, State Council's Central Greening Committee and Central Patriotic Public Health Campaign Committee 1983; chairman, Urban Science Society, 1984–88. Secretary of Beijing CCP Committee 1984–92. Member Twelfth (1982) and Thirteenth (1987) Central Committees. Elevated to Politburo 1987–92. Elected vice-chairman of Eighth NPC 1993–98.

Li Yinhe (Li Yin-ho)—b. 1952. Graduated from Shanxi University and gained PhD at the University of Pittsburgh (United States). Fellow and professor at Sociology Institute of Chinese Academy of Social Sciences, she is probably China's foremost sexologist. Ardent opponent of Confucian values in sexual matters, but supporter of moderation and gradual but firm, as opposed to rapid, change. Author of many books, such as *Sex and Love of Chinese Women*, *The Counter-Culture of Homosexuality* and *The Counter-Culture of Sadomasochism*.

Li Yining (Li I-ning)—b. 1930, from Yizheng, Jiangsu. Well-known economist. Graduated from Beijing University 1955, later joining staff of same university and in 1983 becoming dean of Department of Economic Management there. Joined CCP 1984. Member of NPC Standing Committee 1988, 1993 and 1998 and in great demand as economic adviser to government, including drafting of economic laws. Believes that government should not interfere in the market and that workers should hold shares in the companies where they work. His works include books on economics, such as *On the System Economics of John Kenneth Galbraith* (*Lun Jiaerbuleisi de zhidu jingji xueshuo*), *Concise Introduction to Modern Western Economics* (*Xiandai xifang jingjixue gailun*), and *Socialist Political Economy* (*Shehuizhuyi zhengzhi jingjixue*), as well as a book of poems published in 1999.

Liang Xiaosheng (Liang Hsiao-sheng)—b. September 1949 Harbin. Well-known writer. Graduated in literature from Fudan University, Shanghai, 1977. Works include an anthology of short stories and one of

medium-length novels, as well as two novels and an analysis of the strata of Chinese society, most of his works being adapted as films or television plays. He is known for siding with the downtrodden, including those thrown out of work by restructuring, and believes that urban impoverishment caused by such factors as the large-scale dismissal of workers from state-owned factories will remain a major factor in Chinese society and economy into the twenty-first century.

Lin Zhaohua (Lin Chao-hua)—b. July 1936, Tianjin. Graduated from Central Theatre Academy 1961. Director of Beijing People's Art Theatre 1984-present; member, Standing Committee of the China Theatre Association, 1984 to present. Lin is regarded as one of the best and most innovative directors of Chinese spoken theatre, and the Beijing People's Art Theatre as among the best and most adventurous companies of that genre. Among Lin's productions are *Red Heart* (*Danxin pu*), 1978; *Warning Signal* (*Juedui xinhao*), 1982; *Bus Stop* (*Chezhan*), 1983; *Wild Men* (*Yeren*), 1985; *Doggy Father's Nirvana* (*Gouerye niepan*), 1985; Shakespeare's *Hamlet*, 1990; Friedrich Durrenmatt's *Romulus the Great*, 1992; *Bird Men* (*Niaoren*), 1993; Goethe's *Faust*, 1994; *Ruan Lingyu*, 1994; and *Three Sisters Waiting for Godot* (adapted from Chekhov's *Three Sisters* and Beckett's *Waiting for Godot*), 1998. He has also written extensively on his experiences in theatre directing, including editing a book, published in 1985, on directing *Warning Signal*.

Liu Danzhai (Liu Tan-chai)—b. March 1931, Wenzhou, Zhejiang. Also known by other names, including Liu Xiaosu and Hai Yun Sheng. A painter in the traditional style, known especially for his figure paintings (*renwu hua*). Worked as a painter in various Shanghai publishing houses from 1951 to 1983, working concurrently as an artist in the Shanghai Academy of Chinese Arts from 1956. Appointed professor at Shanghai Teachers' University and a visiting professor at Wenzhou University 1985, and head of Faculty of Fine Arts at Shanghai Teachers

University in 1987. Has held many exhibitions in Wenzhou, Shanghai, Hangzhou and Hong Kong, and also overseas, including in Taiwan in 1996, and a travelling exhibition the same year in Paris, Rome, Amsterdam and Heidelberg. His paintings are kept in Beijing and in many overseas private collections and he has published albums of paintings.

Liu Hong (Liu Hung)—b. 1963, Shanxi. Graduated in law from Beijing University, entering 1978 and gaining a PhD. Gained research fellowships at overseas universities, Harvard, Stanford and Oxford. Held job in law in New York but returned home 1995, shortly becoming general counsel for the China Securities Regulatory Commission, the youngest person ever to hold a senior position in that body. Has contributed greatly to development of stock market law in China, in particular helping to get landmark Securities Law adopted in December 1998, which imposes heavy penalties for insider trading.

Liu Huaqing (Liu Hua-ch'ing)—b. October 1916 Dawu, Hubei. Joined CCP guerrilla unit 1932, which became 15th Red Army Corps 1935. Took part in Long March and joined CCP 1935. Held many major military positions both before and after 1949. Transferred to Navy 1950 and became vice-president of First Naval Academy 1952–53 and its deputy political commissar 1953–54. Awarded Order of Liberation, first class, 1955. Studied naval affairs Soviet Union and graduated from Leningrad's Voroshilov Naval Academy, returning to China 1958. Several senior military, naval and government posts followed. Appointed member of PLA Cultural Revolutionary Group 1967 but attacked as revisionist the following year. Was deputy chief of staff of the PLA Navy 1970–75. Deputy chief of staff, PLA 1980–88. Commander PLA Navy 1982–88. Won rank of general 1988. Elected to Twelfth Central Committee 1982; resigned 1985 and served on Central Advisory Commission 1985–92. Member of Politburo Standing Committee 1992–97, the only military member, but retired even from the Central Committee, and

naturally its Politburo Standing Committee, at the Fifteenth Congress (1997). Deputy secretary-general, CCP Central Military Commission 1987–89 and, following the 1989 crisis, appointed vice-chairman November 1989, holding that position until the Fifteenth CCP Congress of September 1997. Liu is often regarded as the father of the Chinese navy for his work in that area. He has taken a lead in getting CCP policy accepted within the PLA. *People's Daily* quoted him early in 1996 as urging his soldiers to continue 'resisting the temptations to worship money and hedonism'.

Luo Gan (Lo Kan)—b. July 1935, Ji'nan, Shandong. In the mid–1950s studied German in Leipzig, East Germany, did field work in the Leipzig Iron and Steel Plant and Metal Casting Plant and then studied for six years at the Freiburg Institute of Mining and Metallurgy, southwestern Germany, graduating in 1962. Joined CCP 1960. Held many positions in engineering matters, especially metallurgy and machine-building. Vice-governor of Henan Province and secretary of Henan CCP Provincial Committee 1981–83. Vice-president of All-China Federation of Trade Unions 1983–88. Appointed minister of Labour and secretary-general of State Council 1988; in 1993 became state councillor and retains positions of state councillor and secretary-general of State Council. In March 1998 Luo put forward a plan to restructure State Council, calling it an institutional revolution designed to create a 'highly efficient, well coordinated and standardized administrative system with Chinese characteristics'. Member of the Thirteenth (1987) to Fifteenth (1997) Central Committee, being promoted to the Politburo in 1997.

Ma Hong (Ma Hung)—b. May 1920, from Dingxiang, Shanxi. Joined CCP 1937. Member and secretary-general of State Planning Commission and leader of Policy Research Office of State Economic Commission 1956–65. Various kinds of economic research work during Cultural Revolution. Vice-president, Academy of Social Sciences,

1979–82, and president, 1982–85. Director-general, State Council's Economic, Technological and Social Development Research Centre, 1985, reappointed 1990 and again, on an honorary basis, 1993. Has also held various other senior advisory positions relevant to the economy. Has written widely on China's economic system and its restructuring since late 1970s, and is editor-in-chief of Contemporary China Series. Influential as a senior economist who is closely associated with the CCP and the government.

Ngapoi Ngawang Jigme (Apei Awang Jinmei)—b. February 1910 in present-day Qinghai Province as son of Tibetan aristocrat, governor of Qamdo and commander Tibetan armed forces. Studied in Britain, and upon return in 1932, joined Tibetan Army. As cabinet member under Dalai Lama, advocated reform. While serving as governor of Qamdo 1950, captured by occupying communist forces, but subsequently released and returned to Lhasa. Headed Tibetan delegation to Beijing which resulted in the agreement of 1951 by which Tibet was part of the PRC (see Chapter 1, **B.** May 23, 1951) and signed on behalf of the Tibetan local government. Deputy commander Tibet Military Region 1952–77 and member National Defence Council 1954–64. Appointed lieutenant-general and awarded Order of Liberation first class 1955. Tibetan deputy to first seven NPCs 1954–92. Key figure in Preparatory Committee for establishment of Tibetan Autonomous Region 1956–65, as variously secretary-general, vice-chairman and acting chairman, and accompanied Bainqen Lama on several trips to Beijing. Elected chairman, First People's Congress of Tibet, and Presidium executive chairman, first session 1965. Vice-chairman, Tibet's Revolutionary Committee 1968–79. In marked contrast to many other leading figures, made numerous public appearances as NPC representative 1969–74. Elected chairman, Tibetan Autonomous Region People's Government, 1981. Elected vice-chairman, CPPCC, March 1998. As a Tibetan aristocrat who had been a member of the former regime but sided with China, he has played an influential role, and is an object of scorn and hatred by Tibetan nationalists. Although retired, he continued to play an active propaganda role on behalf of China in the 1990s.

Ni Zhifu (Ni Chih-fu)—b. May 1933, Shanghai, joined CCP 1958. Held technical jobs mainly at Yongding Machinery Plant in Beijing 1953–74. Having done very well through the Cultural Revolution, he took on positions in Beijing and Shanghai Municipal Revolutionary Committees and CCP Committees at that time. Chairman, Council of All-China Federation of Trade Unions, 1993–97. Member of Politburos of Eleventh (1977) and Twelfth (1982) Central Committees.

Pagbalha Geleg Namgyai (Pabala Zhoulie Langjie)—b. February 1940 Litang, Sichuan. Member, Qamdo Tibetan Monastery, and confirmed 1942 as eleventh incarnation of Pagbalha Hutugtu. Vice-chairman, Qamdo Liberation Committee, 1951–59, and served on Preparatory Committee for Tibet Autonomous Region 1956–59, becoming its vice-chairman 1960–65. Also served as chairman, Religious Affairs Committee, 1956–65, accompanying Bainqen Lama on several trips to Beijing during this period. Elected vice-president, Buddhist Association, 1980. Deputy to Second (1959), Third (1964–65), Fourth (1975) and Fifth (1978) NPC, and became vice-chairman of the Eighth NPC Standing Committee (1998). Notable as a Tibetan incarnate lama willing to work with the Chinese government from boyhood onwards, with the notable exception of the Cultural Revolution years.

Peng Peiyun (P'eng P'ei-yün)—b. December 1929, Liuyang, Hunan. Joined CCP 1946. Studied and worked for CCP at Qinghua University, both before and after 1949, and graduated there. Deputy secretary of CCP Beijing University Committee 1964–66. Served as vice-minister of Education 1982–85 and of State Education Commission 1985–88. Minister in charge of State Family Planning

Commission from 1988–98, state councillor since 1993. Elected vice-chair of NPC Standing Committee 1998. Elected member of CCP's Central Commission for Discipline Inspection 1987, member of Fourteenth (1992) and Fifteenth (1997) Central Committees. Peng is among the most senior women in the Chinese government and her job in the area of family planning, which is described as 'a basic policy of China' but has excited great controversy both in China and abroad, has made her role particularly sensitive.

Qian Qichen (Ch'ien Ch'i-ch'en)—b. November 1928, from Shanghai. Joined CCP 1942. Active in student politics in Shanghai before 1949 and in CYL after 1949, also in Shanghai. In 1954 studied in Moscow in CCYL School, then worked in Chinese Embassy in Moscow. Returning home in 1963, worked in Ministry of Higher Education as section chief in charge of Chinese students studying abroad and then in Department of External Relations. From 1972 to 1974, worked in Chinese Embassy in Moscow and then became Ambassador to Guinea-Bissau and to Guinea (1974–76). Moved to Ministry of Foreign Affairs in 1977 and became vice-minister of Foreign Affairs 1982–88, and minister of Foreign Affairs 1988–98. State councillor 1991 to present (as of 2000), vice-premier from 1993 to present. Elected alternate Central Committee member Twelfth Party Congress 1982, full member from 1987 to present, promoted to Politburo of Fourteenth (1992) and Fifteenth (1997) Central Committees. Appointed dean, Peking University's School of International Studies, September 1999.

Qian Weichang (Ch'ien Wei-ch'ang)—b. October 1912, from Wuxi, Jiangsu. Graduated from Qinghua University 1935, PhD Toronto University, Canada, 1942. Nuclear physicist, apparently assistant to Qian Xuesen, California Institute of Technology, before returning to China 1946. Professor of Physics and Applied Mathematics, Qinghua University, Beijing, 1946–83; vice-president there 1956–58. Elected to All-China Demo-cratic Youth League and Federation of Scientific Societies Standing Committees 1949–58 and 1950–58 respectively. Member of Academia Sinica 1954–58 and from 1980 on. Jiangsu deputy, First NPC 1954–58 and Fourth NPC 1975–78. Member, Academy of Sciences' newly formed Mathematics, Physics and Chemistry (later, Mathematics and Physics) Department from 1955 on and awarded Academy's second prize 1957. Awarded title of Academician by Polish Academy of Sciences 1956. Member, State Council Scientific Planning Commission, 1956–58. Due to views expressed in Hundred Flowers Movement, labelled as rightist 1958. By-elected Standing Committee member, Fifth CPPCC, 1980 and vice-chairman, Sixth to Ninth CPPCC, 1987 to present (as of 2000). Became president, Society for Chinese Language Information Processing, 1980; developed new method of encoding Chinese characters 1984. Appointed president of Shanghai University of Technology 1982, and director of Shanghai Institute of Applied Mathematics and Mechanics 1984. Vice-chairman, Democratic League, 1983–97, then became honorary chairman. Member, Committee for Drafting Hong Kong SAR Basic Law, 1986–91; vice-chairman, Committee for Drafting Basic Law Macao SAR, 1988–93. Prolific author of many books and scientific papers, including *Selected Scientific Papers of Qian Weichang* (*Qian Weichang kexue lunwen xuanji*), 1989.

Qian Xinzhong (Ch'ien Hsin-chung)—b. 1911, Baoshan, Shanghai, and studied German in his youth. Studied medicine, Tongji University, Shanghai, and after graduating worked as physician. Later served as director, 25th Red Army Hospital, and director, Public Health Department, Eighth Route Army's 129th Division and, subsequently, Second Field Army: 2nd Field Army representative, First CPPCC, 1949. Director, Health Department, Southwest China Military Region, Military and Administrative Council, and Administrative Council at various times from 1950 to 1954. Identified in Ministry of Public

Health, as Medical Research Committee member 1955 and vice-minister 1957–66. Identified as member, State Council's Scientific Planning Commission, 1957–58, Scientific and Technical Association 1958, Sino-Soviet Committee for Scientific and Technical Co-operation, 1959, and Red Cross Society Executive Council, 1961; elected chairman 1965. Jiangsu deputy, Third NPC 1964. Purged 1966–72. Reconfirmed as vice-minister, Public Health 1973; minister 1979–82; and advisor 1982. Identified as deputy head, two Central Committee leading groups, 1978 and 1979; president, Medical Association, 1978–80, and Red Cross Society, 1978–85. Shanghai deputy and Standing Committee member, Fifth and Sixth NPC, 1978 and 1983. Minister, State Family Planning Commission, 1982–88. Qian was joint winner (along with India's Indira Gandhi) of the UN Population Award 1983 (see Chapter 1, **A**. March 18, 1983), an official of the award committee stating that he had facilitated China's family planning policy through research and education and made contraceptives easily available in China. Member, Central Advisory Commission, 1988–92.

Qian Xuesen (Ch'ien Hsüeh-sen)—b. December 1911, from Hangzhou, Zhejiang, and graduated from Shanghai's Jiaotong University 1934, majoring in railway mechanical engineering. Scholarship student in United States: Master's degree in aeronautics and aerodynamics, MIT, 1935–36 and doctorate in supersonic jet propulsion, California Institute of Technology, from 1936, graduating 1939. Became assistant professor, Laboratory for Supersonic Research. Worked as director, Rocket Section, US National Defense Scientific Advisory Board in World War II, with rank of colonel from 1945. At 34, MIT's youngest professor in 1946. Returned briefly to Shanghai and married Jiang Ying, daughter of General Jiang Baili, 1947. Professor, Californian Institute of Technology 1947–49 and director, Guggenheim Jet Propulsion Laboratory 1949–55. Then returned home

and became key figure in establishment of Academy of Sciences' Institute of Mechanics. Appointed director 1956 and became permanent member, of Academy's Mathematics, Physics and Chemistry (later, Mathematics and Physics) Department from 1957; awarded Academy's Science Award first prize for dissertation written in United States, *Engineering Cybernetics*, 1957. Elected to Second CPPCC 1956, and appointed member, State Council Scientific Planning Commission, 1956–58. Elected chairman, Dynamics Society, and Executive Council member, International Federation of Automatic Control, 1957. In 1959 joined CCP; elected to newly founded Scientific and Technical Association, and key figure in setting up Automation Society, in which he served as chairman 1961. Deputy to NPC 1958–78. Appointed director, Mathematics Department, University of Science and Technology, 1959. Appointed editor of monthly journal *Zhongguo Kexue* (*Scientia Sinica*) 1961. Remained in favour during Cultural Revolution for his scientific prominence. Transferred to Commission of Science, Technology and Industry of National Defence 1970, became its vice-chairman 1978–88 and advisor 1988. Alternate CCP Central Committee member 1969–82. Vice-chairman of CPPCC 1986–98. Leader of many scientific commissions and associations. Won many scientific honours and on October 16, 1991, State Council and Central Military Commission awarded him the title 'state scientist of outstanding contributions'. Chapter 4 of the Cox report (see Chapter 1, **A**. May 25, 1999), which concerns PRC missile and space forces, includes a section on 'the role of Qian Xuesen in the development of the PRC's ballistic missile and space programs'. Author of *The Engineering Control Theory*, 1955, and many other scientific books and papers. Qian Xuesen is China's most distinguished living (as of 2000) scientist, so influential that he remained immune even from the Cultural Revolution and has been favoured at all periods. On December 8, 1999, President Jiang Zemin called on him at his home, using the occasion to promote the importance of science in China's development.

Qiao Shi (Ch'iao Shih)—b. December 1924, from Dinghai, Zhejiang. Joined CCP 1940 and undertook extensive CCP work in Shanghai to 1949. In 1950–63 served successively as secretary, Hangzhou CCP Youth Committee; under Youth Committee, Central Committee's East China Bureau; and then in various positions in the iron and steel industry. Served under CCP Central Committee as deputy bureau chief, bureau chief, deputy director and director, International Liaison Department 1963–83. Took on several very important posts 1982 to 1986, such as head of CCP's Organization Department and vice-premier of State Council. Elected CCP Central Committee member and alternate Politburo member, Twelfth Party Congress, 1982, and full Politburo member 1985; rose to Politburo Standing Committee membership at Thirteenth CCP Congress (1987), remained there at Fourteenth CCP Congress (1992), but not at Fifteenth (1997). Appointed president of Central CCP School 1989. Chairman of NPC Standing Committee 1993–98. Qiao's meteoric rise from early 1980s and into the 1990s made many tout him as a possible future CCP and government head, but he was in effect dismissed in 1997, due to rivalry and differing views with Jiang Zemin.

Qu Geping (Ch'ü Ke-p'ing)—b. June 1930, from Feicheng, Shandong. Graduated from Shandong University 1952. Later distinguished himself in field of environmental protection, both in academic and political fields. His first book, *There is Only One Earth*, was on the environment, in 1972, at a time when official policy was very sceptical of the importance of such issues in socialist China. The book reached its third edition in 1998, by which time nobody needed persuading of the importance of the issue. Qu has drafted environmental policy and written numerous books and articles on environmental protection.

Ren Jianxin (Jen Chien-hsin)—b. August 1925, Xiangfen, Shanxi. Joined CCP 1948. Held several legal posts in early years of PRC, including as secretary in Legislative Affairs Bureau, State Council, 1954–59. From 1959 to 1983 worked in China Council for Promotion of International Trade, becoming vice-chairman 1981. Travelled widely in 1960s and 1970s: deputy secretary-general and head, economic exhibitions to Japan and Syria, respectively; and head, international law observer groups, Madrid, Hamburg and Bordeaux. Vice-president, Supreme People's Court, 1983–88 and president, 1988–98. Member, Thirteenth and Fourteenth CCP Central Committees (1987–97). Elected vice-chairman, CPPCC, March 1998. Has played leading role in numerous Chinese and international legal associations and bodies and has taken a leadership role in creating a Chinese legal system in the aftermath of the Cultural Revolution.

Rong Yiren (Jung I-jen)—b. May 1916, Wuxi, Jiangsu. Graduated from St John's University, Shanghai 1937. Comes from a family that was already famous as capitalists by 1949, known as 'cotton tycoons' and 'flour kings'. Served in Wuxi as assistant manager and then manager, Maoxin Flour Mill, 1937–49. When the PRC was founded in 1949, served in leading positions of Shenxin Cotton Mills and Fuxin Flour Company, both Rong family concerns. Appointed member, Finance and Economic Affairs Committee, East China Military and Administrative Council (Administrative Council after 1952), 1950–54. Elected member, Shanghai People's Government Council (Shanghai People's Council after 1955), 1950. Elected vice-chairman, Shanghai Federation of Industry and Commerce, 1954. Shanghai deputy, First NPC 1954–Cultural Revolution; mayor of Shanghai 1957–59; vice-minister, Textile Industry, 1959–66. Vice-chairman, CPPCC, 1978–93; vice-chairman, NPC Standing Committee, 1983–93. Managing director, Bank of China 1979–88; chairman, CITIC (Group), the largest of China's state investment companies, 1979–93; vice-president of China 1993–98. Awarded honorary doctorate by Hofstra University, New York, 1986; and held many leading positions in Chinese associations. Rong Yiren is famous as China's most prominent 'red capitalist' and played a decisive role at a crucially important time when, in 1978, Deng Xiaoping had CITIC established and personally chose Rong to head it. A cover story, dated November 15, 1999 in *Forbes Magazine* (December 14, 1999) ranked Rong Yiren top among 'China's 50 Richest Businessmen'.

Seypidin Äzizi (Saifuding Aze)—b. March 1915, Artux, Xinjiang, of Uygur nationality. Studied political science, Central Asian University, Tashkent, graduating 1937, and later also joined Soviet Communist Party. Important role in founding East Turkestan Republic, 1944. Joined CCP 1949 and assumed senior military, government and CCP roles in Xinjiang. Was head of government of Xinjiang Uygur Autonomous Region (XUAR) from its foundation in 1955 until 1968. Vice-chairman 1968–73, then chairman 1973–78 of XUAR Revolutionary Committee, first secretary of XUAR CCP Committee 1973–78, and also first political commissar of Xinjiang Regional Command 1972–77. Full member of CCP Central Committee 1969–73 and 1985–92 and of Politburo 1973–82. Vice-chairman of NPC Standing Committee 1954–93; vice-chairman of CPPCC National Committee 1993–98. Vice-chairman, Sino-Soviet Friendship Association and Federation of Literature and Art Circles, and chancellor, Xinjiang University, 1954, 1960 and 1964, respectively. Elected honorary president, Minority Writers' Society, 1985, and Minority Literature Foundation, 1986. Seypidin has played an influential role as a senior Uygur in the CCP and Chinese government. However, due to the XUAR's fairly poor economic performance in the 1970s, he moved to Beijing and was given tasks there, his influence declining considerably after he left the Politburo in 1982.

Sheng Huaren (Sheng Hua-jen)—b. 1935, from Yancheng, Jiangsu. Joined CCP 1954. Very active and distinguished in field of petrochemicals. Worked for fifteen years in management of China Petrochemical Corporation, before becoming, in 1990, both general manager and CCP head of the company. China Petrochemical Corporation, or Sinopec, ranked as the largest company in China in *Asiaweek*'s 1000 largest companies, and the largest in Asia outside Japan.[3] Appointed minister in charge of the State Economic and Trade Commission March 1998, and member of the Fifteenth CCP Central Committee 1997. The Fifteenth Congress adopted a policy in favour of corporatizing the state-owned enterprises, a process in which Sheng has taken a leading role, demanding a leaner, meaner and more efficient state sector.

Song Defu (Sung Te-fu)—b. February 1946, from Yanshan, Hebei. Joined PLA Airforce and CCP 1965 and served as squadron leader, platoon leader, company political instructor and youth department head. CYL Standing Committee member since 1982, secretary 1983–85 and first secretary 1985–93. By-elected alternate Central Committee member, Twelfth Party Congress, 1985; full Central Committee member 1985 to present (as of 2000). Minister of Personnel 1993 to present.

Song Hongzhao (Sung Hung-chao)—b. August 1915, from Suzhou, Jiangsu. Graduated from Peiping Union Medical College 1943. Served as resident doctor there, becoming Associate Professor 1966–78 and full Professor (from 1978) of Obstetrics and Gynaecology, Chinese Union Medical University, and has held many other senior positions concerned with obstetrics. Joined Chinese Peasants and Workers Democratic Party 1984 and occupied senior posts within it. Has gained many Chinese and international honours, including State Scientific and Technological Progress Award, 1st Class, 1985 and Ho-Leung-Ho-Lee Foundation (Hong Kong) Prize for Promotion of Sciences and Technology, 1995. Elected Fellow *ad eundem* of the Royal College of Obstetricians and Gynaecologists (UK), 1995. Has researched chorioepithelioma and tropho-blastic tumours since the 1950s. Published widely on obstetrics and tumour treatment, including *Studies of Trophoblastic Diseases in China*, 1988, and *Basic Knowledge of Obstetrics and Gynaecology*, 1993, as well as some 160 papers in Chinese and foreign scientific journals. One of China's foremost medical researchers and gynaecologists.

Song Jian (Sung Chien)—b. December 1931 Rongcheng, Shandong. Joined Eighth Route Army 1946 and CCP 1947. Studied at Harbin Technical University 1951–53; studied mechanics and automatic control at Bauman Engineering Institute, Moscow, from 1953, receiving associate doctorate, returning to China in 1960. Held various major positions in research into cybernetics, space and guided missiles, including head of Cybernetics Laboratory, Institute of Mathematics, Academia Sinica 1960–70. Lectured at Harvard University, Washington University, MIT and Minnesota University 1980. Director, Institute of Information Processing and Control, 1980, and vice-minister, Seventh Ministry of Machine-building, 1981–82; vice-minister, Astronautics Industry, 1981–84; minister in charge of State Science and Technology Commission, 1984–98; state councillor 1986–98; vice-chairman, CPPCC National Committee, 1998 to present. Elected alternate Central Committee member, Twelfth Party Congress, 1982,and full member 1985 to present. Widely recognized internationally for science, being invited to join many foreign academies, for instance corresponding member of National Academy of Engineering of Mexico 1984, member of Russian Academy of Sciences 1994, and member of Royal Swedish Academy of Engineering Sciences 1994. Appointed lifelong honorary distinguished visiting professor, Washington University, USA. Won Chinese and international prizes and awards, including State Scientific and Technological Progress Award, 1st Class, 1987; and 'Albert Einstein' Award from International Association for Mathematical Modelling 1987. Also written very widely on demography, space

engineering and cybernetics, including *Engineering Cybernetics* (*Gongcheng kongzhi lun*, co-author), 1980, *China's Population: Problems and Prospects* (in English), 1981, and many other books and papers.

Song Ping (Sung P'ing)—b. 1917 Juxian, Shandong. Joined CCP December 1937. Between 1938 and 1947 he worked in Yan'an, in journalistic positions, such as in the Chongqing-based *Xinhua Daily*'s Editorial Department and in the Xinhua News Agency, and then served as political secretary to Zhou Enlai in Nanjing. In 1953 he became vice-minister of Labour and later vice-chairman of the State Planning Commission, among other positions. Disappeared during early years of Cultural Revolution, but reappeared in 1970. Secretary, Gansu CCP, 1972–77, and first secretary 1977–81; vice-chairman, Gansu Revolutionary Committee, 1972–77 and chairman 1977–79. First political commissar, Gansu Military District, and second political commissar, Lanzhou Military Region, 1977–81. Again vice-minister, State Planning Commission, 1981–83, and minister 1983–87. Elected to Academy of Sciences' Presidium 1981. Appointed deputy director, CCP's Leading Group for Co-ordinating National Scientific Work,1981, and state councillor 1983–88. Vice-chairman, Environmental Protection Committee, 1984–88; and head, Leading Group for Economic Information Management, 1986–88. Elected deputy secretary-general and Politburo member, Thirteenth Party Congress, and appointed head, Central Committee's Organization Department, 1987–90. Elevated to Politburo Standing Committee following 1989 Beijing 'pro-democracy' demonstrations; he was not confirmed on that body, or even on the Politburo, at the Fourteenth CCP Congress in 1992 but did remain on the Presidium. In the 1990s has filled leading positions in many associations, such as the China Family Planning Association from 1990, and also honorary positions, and he has exerted considerable influence over personnel matters through his relationships network.

Song Renqiong (Sung Jen-ch'iung)—b. 1909, Liuyang County, Hunan Province. Joined CCP 1926; later graduated from Whampoa Military Academy. Served in 4th Red Army 1927, and under Liu Bocheng 1932. Political commissar, Red Army Cadre Corps, Long March 1934–35, and political commissar, 129th Division, at start of Sino-Japanese War 1937. Lectured at CCP's Central Academy 1943. Alternate member, Seventh Central Committee, 1945. Key commander in Hebei during civil war (1946–49). Held posts in southwest China in CCP military and administrative hierarchies then recalled to Beijing and appointed member, National Defence Council, 1954. Promoted to rank of army general and awarded Orders of August 1st, Independence and Freedom, and Liberation, first class, 1955. Elected full Central Committee member and secretary-general, Eighth Party Congress, 1956; elevated to alternate Politburo membership 1966. Appointed minister, Third Ministry of Machine-building, mid–1950s, but became minister, Second Ministry of Machine-building when Third Ministry incorporated with Second Ministry in 1958. Political commissar, Shenyang Military Region, 1964 and first political commissar 1965. Disappeared 1968–74 due to Cultural Revolution. Central Committee member, Eleventh and Twelfth Party Congress, 1978 and 1982, and member of CCPCC's Politburo 1982–85. Director, Central Committee's Organization Department, 1979–83 and member, CCP Secretariat, 1980–82. Elected vice-chairman, Central Advisory Commission, 1985–92 and to Presidium of Thirteenth (1987) and Fourteenth (1992) Party Congresses.

Sun Jiazheng (Sun Chia-cheng)—b. March 1944, from Siyang, Jiangsu. Joined CCP 1966. Graduated from Faculty of Chinese Language, Nanjing University, 1968. Held various CCP and CYL positions in Jiangsu, becoming secretary-general of CCP Jiangsu Provincial Committee 1984. Served as minister of Radio, Film and Television 1994–98, and then became minister of Culture 1998.

Was alternate member of CCP Central Committee from 1982 and was promoted to being a full member in 1997.

Tang Aoqing (T'ang Ao-ch'ing)—b. November 1915, from Yixing, Jiangsu. Studied chemistry at Beijing University 1936–40, then taught at National South-west Associated University, Kunming; later did postgraduate studies at Columbia University, New York, returning to China 1950 as specialist in quantum chemistry and serving as professor at Peking University 1950–52. Jilin deputy, Second and Third NPC, 1958 and 1964. Professor at Jilin University from 1952, vice-president, Jilin University, 1956–78, and president 1978–86. Member, State Council's Natural Science Award Committee and National Academic Degrees Committee 1980; Presidium member, Academy of Science, 1981; and identified as member, Academy's Department of Chemistry, 1985; chairman, Natural Science Foundation Committee 1986–88. Vice-chairman, National Committee, Seventh CPPCC, 1988–93, and member National Committee, Eighth CPPCC, 1993–98. Won many honours and awards, including National Science Award, first class, 1982, 1987, and Chen Jiang Chemistry Award 1994. Published many books, including *Quantum Chemistry* (1982), *Statistical Theory on Polymeric Reactions* (1985), *Graph Theoretical Molecular Orbitals* (1986), and *Dynamics of Molecular Reactions* (1989), and over 300 articles and book chapters. Tang is one of China's leading chemistry specialists: a leading researcher in quantum chemistry and in the physical chemistry of macromolecules.

Tang Jiaxuan (T'ang Chia-hsüan)—b. January 1938, from Zhenjiang, Jiangsu. Graduated from Department of Oriental Languages, Peking University, 1962 and joined CCP 1973. Worked in Association for Friendship with Foreign Countries 1975–78 and in Chinese Embassy in Japan 1978–83 and 1988–91. Worked in Ministry of Foreign Affairs 1985–88. Assistant minister of Foreign Affairs 1991–93; vice-minister 1993–98, and minister of Foreign Affairs 1998 to present (2000).

Tian Jiyun (T'ien Chi-yün)—b. June 1929 Feicheng, Shandong. Member Eighth Route Army 1941, fighting actively against the Japanese, and joined CCP May 1945. Head, land reform work team 1948. Cadre, Guiyang Military Control Commission, and held a number of important financial positions in Guizhou Province before Cultural Revolution. After 1969 worked in Sichuan People's Government's Provincial Finance Bureau. State Council deputy secretary-general 1981–83 and secretary-general 1983–87. Elected Central Committee member, Twelfth Party Congress, 1982 to present (as of 2000), Politburo member 1985 to present; vice-premier, State Council, 1983–87. Vice-chairman of the NPC Standing Committee 1993 to present.

Tomur Dawamat (Tiemuer Dawamaiti)—b. June 1927, Toksun, Xinjiang, of Uygur nationality. Uygur farmhand until 1949. Became village chief 1950 and joined CCP 1952. Graduated from Beijing's Central Nationalities Institute 1957. First member of Xinjiang Uygur people to hold post of CCP secretary at county level, when appointed secretary of Toksun County 1956; vicechairman, XUAR, 1964–68. Elected to Xinjiang's new Revolutionary Committee 1968, but then disappeared 1968–76 due to the Cultural Revolution. Again key figure in Xinjiang by 1978; secretary of CCP XUAR Committee 1978–85. Vice-minister, State Nationalities Affairs Commission, 1979–82; chairman, XUAR People's Congress, 1979–85; and chairman, XUAR People's Government, 1985–94. Central Committee member, Twelfth Party Congress, 1982 to present (2000). Member of CCP Central Committee 1982–97. Vice-chairman of NPC Standing Committee 1993 to present.

Wan Li (Wan Li)—b. December 1916, Dongping, Shandong; studied in France during youth; also possibly involved with prominent Beijing youth leaders mid–1930s. Joined CCP 1936 and involved in communist liberation of Nanjing and Chongqing 1949–50, subsequently holding important financial posts in both cities. In Chongqing served under Southwest Military and Administrative Committee as member, Deng Xiaoping's Finance and Economics Committee and deputy director, Industry Department. Transferred to Beijing as vice-minister, new Ministry of Building, 1952–56 and concurrently appointed director, Urban Construction General Bureau, 1955–56; then, with redesignation of Bureau as Ministry, became minister until 1958. Identified as secretary, Beijing CCP Committee, and elected vice-mayor of Beijing 1958, posts in which he was subordinate to Peng Zhen. Beijing deputy, Second and Third NPC 1958 and 1964. Disappeared twice during Cultural Revolution decade, first from 1966 to 1971. Identified in successively higher posts in Beijing 1971–75, and as Minister of Railways 1975–76, in which positions he terminated several strikes; disappeared again 1976–77. Member of Eleventh Central Committee 1977, and became member of Politburo Twelfth (1982) and Thirteenth (1987) Central Committees. Appointed first secretary, Anhui CCP Committee and chairman, Anhui Revolutionary Committee, 1977–79; Anhui Military District first political commissar 1977–80, and first CCP secretary 1979–80. From these powerful positions in Anhui he helped pave the way for the abolition of the communes and the establishment of the agricultural responsibility system. Vice-premier 1980–88; briefly acting premier 1982 and 1983. Minister, State Agricultural Commission, 1980–82; chairman, NPC Standing Committee, 1988–93. Honorary president of China's Bridge Association and an excellent bridge player, winning Solomon Award, highest international bridge players' award, 1985. Has reputation for sympathy with democracy and, on a visit to the United States and Canada at the time, opposed martial law in May 1989 just before suppression of student movement. However, he changed his mind on return to China. He remains influential despite retirement from all major posts in 1993.

Wang Bingqian (Wang Ping-ch'ien)—b. June 1925, from Lixian, Hebei. Joined CCP 1940. Began work in finance and economy 1945. Served in various posts in Ministry of Finance 1949–62, and identified as director, Budget Department, 1963. Vice-minister of Finance 1973–80, and minister 1980–92. President, Accounting Society 1980–88, and honorary president, 1988 to present. Honorary chairman, China Investment Bank, since 1981 and Chinese governor, World Bank, since 1986. State councillor since 1983–93 and served under Council as chairman, Administrative Committee for Underdeveloped Regions Development Fund and Customs Tax Regulations Committee, 1986–88 and 1987–88 respectively. CCP Central Committee member 1982–92. Vice-chairman, NPC Standing Committee, 1993–98. Member, State Planning Commission, 1988–92.

Wang Daohan (Wang Tao-han)—b. March 1915, from Jiashan, Anhui. Studied at Jiaotong University. Joined CCP 1938. Before 1949, served in CCP's organizations in Anhui, and fought against both the Japanese and the Guomindang, forming a close association with Jiang Zemin. Had numerous senior appointments after 1949, including vice-minister for Foreign Economic Relations. In 1980 became deputy mayor of Shanghai, and later mayor of Shanghai, recommending Jiang Zemin to succeed him on retirement from the position in 1985. Became president of ARATS in 1991 and still (2000) occupies that position. In that capacity he has been the main negotiator for the PRC over the delicate and difficult issues involving Taiwan. A planned visit to Taiwan was called off indefinitely when Taiwan in effect declared itself a 'state' (see Chapter 1, **B**. June 29 and July 13, 1999). Remains on close relations with President Jiang Zemin, who is reported to regard him as one of his mentors.

Wang Ganchang (Wang Kan-ch'ang)—b. May 1907, from Changshu, Jiangsu. Studied physics at Qinghua University 1925–29 and at Berlin University 1930–34; awarded PhD in nuclear physics. Returned to China 1934, taking up research jobs in nuclear physics at Shandong and Zhejiang Universities 1934–50. Also did research at University of California 1948. Joined September Third Society 1951 and played a vital role in this non-communist 'democratic' political party (see Chapter 2), including being chairman of its Central Advisory Committee 1989–97. Deputy director, Academy of Science's Physics Institute, 1953–58. Organized research team at Joint Soviet Nuclear Research Centre, Dubna, Soviet Union, 1958; deputy director 1959–61 and head, joint Sino-Soviet scientific team responsible for discovering in 1960 anti-sigma negative hyperon, which in 1982 won First Class State Award for Natural Sciences. Put forward new concept of restriction of nuclear fusion through laser inertia 1964 and was one of the leading scientists responsible for the development of China's first atomic bomb in 1964 (see Chapter 1, **B**. October 16, 1964) and first hydrogen bomb 1967 (see Chapter 1, **B**. June 17, 1967). He was unscathed by Cultural Revolution as his work was of vital strategic importance. Deputy director, Academy of Science's Atomic Energy Institute, 1958–78; director 1978–86; and honorary director, 1986 to present. NPC Standing Committee member 1978–88; member, NPC Education, Science, Culture and Public Health Committee, 1983–88. Identified as vice-minister, Second Ministry of Machine Building, 1979–82; president, Society of Nuclear Physics, 1980–84 and honorary president 1984 to present (2000). Continues to play role in nuclear physics, although retired.

Wang Guangying (Wang Kuang-ying)—b. July 1919, family from Beijing. Studied Beijing Experimental Primary School; graduated Furen (Catholic) University, Beijing, 1942. Director, Tianjin Modern Chemical Plant, 1943–57; Manager, Tianjin Knitwear Factory, 1955–66. Imprisoned for eight years (1969–75) due to Cultural Revolution. Appointed director, China International Trust and Investment Corporation, and elected vice-chairman, China Democratic

National Construction Association, 1979. Vice-chairman, CPPCC National Committee, 1983–93 and NPC Standing Committee 1993 to present (as of 2000). Vice-mayor of Tianjin 1978–82; vice-chairman, All-China Federation of Industry and Commerce, 1982–93 and honorary chairman since then. Received honorary Doctorate of Law from University of Maryland, USA, 1986. Though retired, retains influence as a senior capitalist loyal to the Chinese government and as the elder brother of Wang Guangmei, a highly respected woman whose husband, Liu Shaoqi, was once the president of China and is still regarded as having played a very positive role in PRC history.

Wang Meng (Wang Meng)—b. October 1934, from Nanpi, Hebei. Joined CCP 1948. One of China's foremost literary figures, who has had an unstable relationship with the CCP, despite joining it very young and before it even came to power. His earliest novel was *Long Live Youth* (*Qingchun wansui*), 1953. His short novel *The Young Newcomer in the Organization Department* (*Zuzhi bu xinlai de nianqingren*), 1956, portrays the clash between young and idealistic revolutionaries and older and entrenched CCP bureaucrats. It won great attention but strong criticism from the CCP itself, with Wang being condemned as a rightist in 1957. In 1963 he was sent to labour at a farm in Yili, Xinjiang, staying there for seven years, during which time he learned to read, speak and write in Uygur. He was rehabilitated in 1978 and returned to Beijing in 1979, where he worked at the Municipal Association of Literary and Art Circles 1979, served as member of the Secretariat of the Chinese Writers Association 1985–86 and as Association vice-chairman 1985 to the present. He rose to be minister of Culture from 1986 to September 1989, but was a casualty of the crisis of 1989. During the 1980s he wrote many short stories and short novels, reportage, poems and literary criticism, establishing himself as among China's foremost literary figures. His short novel *The Butterfly* (*Hudie*) was published in 1980 in the literary journal *October* (*Shiyue*) (No. 4), winning first prize in the national awards for short novels. It is innovative for its impressionistic technique and represents a 'literature of questions', rather than one in which stories are paramount. Member of CCP Central Committee 1982–92. Chief editor *People's Literature* (*Renmin wenxue*) 1983–86. His *Selected Works of Wang Meng* appeared in English translation in 1989 in two volumes published by the Foreign Languages Press in Beijing, and Beijing's Huayi Press published *Wang Meng wenji* (*The Works of Wang Meng*) in ten volumes in 1993. He continued to write in the 1990s, but his most important work belongs to the 1980s. Noted for his acerbic and innovative style.

Wang Shuo (Wang Shuo)—b. 1958 in Nanjing. A novelist whose books were banned by the authorities in 1996, but who can claim to be one of the most popular writers in contemporary China. Fiercely satirical of life, especially in Beijing, his works have been described as *pizi wenxue* (punk literature). Encompassing people of many classes and strata, from dismissed factory workers to academics, Wang's novels show the underbelly of Beijing society. Late in 1999 became involved in a major literary controversy against the Hong Kong *kung fu* novelist Louis Cha. Frequently visits the United States. Wang Shuo's works were published in two volumes under the title *Wang Shuo wenji* (*Wang Shuo's Works*) in 1992 by Beijing's Huayi Press.

Wang Tianren (Wang T'ien-jen)—b. July 1939, Henan. Worked as designer and sculptor at the Shaanxi Exhibition Hall 1963–79, creating cultured works for at the Yan'an Revolutionary Memorial Hall 1968–71; took part in group sculptures for Chairman Mao Memorial Hall 1976–78; president of Xi'an's Shaanxi Sculpture Institute since 1995 (as of 2000). Has won several national prizes for his sculptures. Works include sculptures of human figures, for example Hou Ji (1980–81 and again 1996) and a group of Tang dynasty musicians 1983, animals, such as oxen, zebra, morning rooster and letter-carrier goose (the last 1983) and even events, such as the unification of China under the Qin dynasty, 1994.

Wang Zhongyu (Wang Chung-yü)—b. February 1933, in Changchun, Jilin. Joined the CCP May 1956. Held a series of posts in Jilin, being vice-governor, acting governor and finally governor, filling the last post from 1989 to 1992. He went to Beijing, where he occupied positions under State Council, notably minister in charge of the State Economic and Trade Commission (1993). Prime Minister Zhu Rongji finally nominated him to State Council in March 1998. Became member of Fourteenth (1992) and Fifteenth (1997) Central Committees. Reported to be close to Zhu Rongji and to share ideas with him on economic and other reform.

Wei Jianxing (Wei Chien-hsing)—b. January 1931, from Xinchang, Zhejiang. Joined CCP 1949. Graduated Dalian Institute of Engineering 1952. Studied industrial and business management in Soviet Union 1953–55 and served in industry until early 1980s, being stripped of all posts 1966–70 due to the Cultural Revolution. Trained at Central Party School 1980–81. Mayor of Harbin 1981–83. Deputy head and head of CCP Central Committee's Organization Department 1984–85. Vice-chairman, All-China Federation of Trade Unions, 1984 and chairman since 1993 (as of 2000). Appointed deputy head of CCP Central Committee's Organization Department, being head 1985–87. Served as minister of Supervision 1987–92. After the corruption scandal of 1995, Wei Jianxing replaced Chen Xitong (q.v.) as secretary of Beijing Municipal CCP Committee, holding the position until 1997. Alternate member of CCP Central Committee 1982 and full member since 1992, also taking over then as head of CCP's Central Commission for Discipline Inspection. Elected to CCP Central Committee Politburo Standing Committee 1997. Wei Jianxing has taken a very high profile in trying to eradicate the serious problem of corruption, through a combination of education (which he dubs the base), the legal system (the guarantee), and supervision (the key).

Wen Jiabao (Wen Chia-pao)—b. September 1942 in Tianjin. One of Zhu Rongji's successful nominees as vice-premier in March 1998. Joined CCP 1965 and graduated from Beijing Geology Institute in 1965, completing a postgraduate course there 1968. Became vice-minister of Geology and Mineral Resources, 1983. Member of the CCP's Central Committee since 1987. Appointed to the Politburo in 1997. In the 1980s Wen was a protégé of Zhao Ziyang and during the 1989 crisis was the main government negotiator with the students. He has followed a pro-market policy since the 1990s and taken the lead in dealing with the corporatization of the SOEs. In 1998 he was a major figure deciding to destroy dykes during the floods of that year, thus diverting water away from major cities and saving them. Formerly played bridge with Deng Xiaoping.

Wu Bangguo (Wu Pang-kuo)—b. July 1941, from Feidong, Anhui. Joined the CCP April 1964. Graduated from Qinghua University 1967, then moved to Shanghai, working there in industry. In 1983 he became a member of the Shanghai Municipal CCP Committee, then served as deputy secretary of the Committee 1985–91 and as secretary 1991–92. Transferred to Beijing 1994, becoming vice-premier 1995, but only against an unusually large number of opposing or abstaining votes. Member of the Politburo 1992 to present (as of 2000).

Wu Jieping (Wu Chieh-p'ing)—b. January 1917, from Changzhou, Jiangsu. Graduated from Peking Union Medical College 1942. Studied at University of Chicago, USA, 1947–48, returning to China 1948. Associate professor and professor at Beijing Medical Institute 1948–60 and vice-president and professor of Beijing No. 2 Medical Institute 1960–70. Treated Indonesian President Sukarno for kidney disease in Jakarta in 1962. Joined September Third Society 1952, taking an active role in this political party, including vice-chairman and chairman 1970 to present (as of 2000). Vice-president, Chinese Medical Association, 1978–84, president 1984–89; honorary president since 1989. President and honorary president, China Union Medical University, 1984 to present. Vice-chairman, NPC Standing Committee, 1993 to present. Has been admitted to various Chinese and overseas academies, such as Chinese Academy of Science 1981, American College of Physicians 1989, Royal College of Surgeons, Edinburgh, 1996. Has carried out original research in contralateral hydronephrosis in renal tuberculosis and adrenal medullary hyperplasia and contributed to instillation of a distal seminal tract during vasectomy to produce immediate sterilization. Author of books, including co-editing *Miniaowai kexue* (*The Science of Urology*), Shanghai, 1982, and many medical papers in Chinese, English or Russian. Among China's most eminent surgeons, especially urologists.

Wu Yi (Wu I)—b. November 1938, Wuhan. Joined CCP 1962. Graduated from Beijing Petroleum College 1962. After a series of technical jobs relevant to petroleum, served as deputy mayor of Beijing 1988–91; vice-minister and deputy CCP secretary of Ministry of Foreign Economic Relations and Trade, 1991–93; appointed minister and CCP secretary of the same ministry 1993. Became member of the Fourteenth CCP Central Committee (1992) and Fifteenth (1997; in the latter being promoted to alternate Politburo member). Became member of State Council March 1998. As China's top trade and investment negotiator, she has a reputation for both toughness and flexibility.

Wu Xueqian (Wu Hsüeh-ch'ien)—b. December 1921, from Shanghai. Joined CCP 1939. Worked for CCP in Shanghai before 1949, especially in student and youth affairs. Active in youth affairs, especially in CCYL during the 1950s. Also active in the Association for Cultural Relations with Foreign Countries, visiting many socialist and/or developing countries in Asia, Africa and Eastern Europe and attending peace conferences in Moscow

and Tokyo in the 1950s and 1960s. Disappeared due to the Cultural Revolution 1967–77. Reappeared in CCP's International Liaison Department 1978–82. Minister of Foreign Affairs 1982–88. State councillor 1983–88; vice-premier 1988–93. Elected to CCP Central Committee at Twelfth Congress 1982, being promoted to Politburo 1985–92. Vice-chairman, CPPCC, 1993–98. Also president of Association for the International Understanding of China since 1993.

Xiao Yang (Hsiao Yang)—b. August 1938, Heyuan, Guangdong. Joined CCP May 1966. Graduated from People's University, Department of Law, 1962. After graduation worked for a few years in Xinjiang as a teacher of politics and law and then went to Guangdong, working in legal and CCP affairs. Was deputy procurator-general of Guangdong Provincial People's Procuratorate 1983–86 and procurator-general 1986–90. In 1990 appointed deputy procurator-general of Supreme People's Procuratorate and then minister of Justice 1993–98. In September 1997 became a member of CCP's Central Committee. Appointed president of Supreme People's Court March 1998.

Xu Kuangdi (Hsü K'uang-ti)—December 1937, from Tongxiang Zhejiang. Graduated from Beijing Institute of Iron and Steel 1959; sent to the countryside during the Cultural Revolution; joined CCP 1983. Distinguished academic career in Shanghai in the field of metallurgy, then appointed as deputy director to Shanghai Municipal Education and Health Office and head of Shanghai Higher Education Office 1989. In 1991 became director of the Shanghai Municipal Planning Committee, then in 1992 deputy mayor of Shanghai and in February 1995 mayor of Shanghai. Much of the credit has been given to him for transformation of Pudong area in Shanghai into a major economic development zone, making it perhaps the most prosperous area of China at the turn of the century and home to many of China's main companies.

Xu Yongguang (Hsü Yung-kuang)—b. 1959, non-government promoter of education.

Main force behind establishment of China Youth Development Foundation in March 1989, which later the same year launched Project Hope (see Chapter 10). By the end of the century this project had raised enough money to construct some 7000 primary schools, giving many impoverished children the chance for an education.

Yang Baibing (Yang Pai-ping)—b. September 1920, Tongnan, Sichuan. Joined CCP 1938. Fought with CCP against the Japanese, including in 129th Division of Eighth Route Army, 1939–43. Entered Yan'an Party School 1943. Took part actively in civil war which CCP won against the Guomindang 1946–49. Worked as a senior officer in Southwest China Military Area Command 1950–55, and in PLA Chengdu Military Area Command 1955–79. Then moved to senior roles in PLA Beijing Military Area Command 1979–87. Granted rank of general 1988. Became member of PRC's powerful Central Military Commission April 1988 and the even more powerful CCP's Central Military Commission the next year, the same day being appointed also to CCP Central Committee's Secretariat (see Chapter 1, **D.** November 9, 1989). Along with his brother President Yang Shangkun, Yang Baibing had taken a very active role in suppressing the student movement in June, and both benefited politically from the outcome. However, he was not renominated for the CCP Central Military Commission in 1992. Member of Fourteenth CCP Committee's Politburo (1992), but failed to be renominated for Fifteenth (1997), showing that his influence was considerably weaker at the end of the decade than it had been at the beginning.

Yang Liqing (Yang Li-ch'ing)—b. April 30, 1942, composer of 'new music', educator and theorist. BA, Shenyang Conservatorium, 1970; MA, Shanghai Conservatorium, 1980; then diplomas Musikhochschule, Hanover, Germany. Various musical appointments, leading to dean of Department of Composition at Shanghai Conservatorium in 1991 and vice-president of the same unit in 1996. Vari-

ous overseas appointments, including Mozarteum Music Academy, Salzburg, Austria, 1990, and Cornell University, USA, 1995. Various musical awards and prizes in China, Germany and grants in USA. Compositions include 'Festive Overture' for orchestra, 1987 and a quintet for traditional Chinese instruments, 1997. His book *The Compositional Techniques of Olivier Messiaen* (1989) is said to be the first book by a Chinese on a Western avant-garde composer.

Yang Rudai (Yang Ju-tai)—b. December 1926, from Renshou, Sichuan. Joined CCP 1952. Did a great deal of CCP work in Sichuan, being secretary of Renshou County CCP Committee 1955–68. Moved to provincial work late 1970s, being vice-governor of Sichuan and then secretary of CCP Provincial Committee during the 1980s, as well as holding senior military posts in Sichuan, at that time China's most populous province. Member of Politburo 1987–92. Member of CPPCC since 1993, appointed vice-chairman of CPPCC March 1998.

Zeng Qinghong (Tseng Ch'ing-hung)—b. July 1939, from Ji'an, Jiangxi. Joined CCP 1960. Graduated from Beijing Engineering Institute 1963. Served in various posts relevant to petroleum, energy, economic planning and others. Deputy head and head of Organization Department of the CCP's Shanghai Municipal Committee, 1984–86, deputy secretary of CCP's Shanghai Municipal Committee 1986. Became deputy director of General Office of CCP Central Committee 1989, then director of the same office in 1993. Promoted to alternate member of Fifteenth Politburo 1997; appointed director of the CCP's Organization Department March 1999. Since working together in Shanghai in 1985, Zeng has been on very close terms with Jiang Zemin and helped him to defend his position as head of the CCP and the state and to overcome opposition.

Zhang Aiping (Chang Ai-p'ing)—b. 1910, Daxian, Sichuan. Joined CCP 1928 and Red Army 1929, serving under Peng Dehuai from

1927 to 1929 and fighting for CCP in various places before 1949. Senior military positions in East China 1948–54; deputy chief of PLA General Staff 1954–67; won rank of colonel-general 1955. Became alternate member of CCP Central Committee 1958. Condemned as revisionist during the Cultural Revolution. Reappeared as chairman, Science and Technology Commission for National Defence 1975–77. Elected to full membership of Central Committee 1977–85. Again identified as deputy chief of PLA General Staff 1977–82. Vice-premier 1980–82, state councillor 1982–88, minister of Defence 1982–88. Member, PRC Central Military Commission, 1983–88. Member, Standing Committee of the Central Advisory Committee, 1987–92.

Zhang Chaoyang (Chang Ch'ao-yang)—b. 1969. Graduated from Qinghua University, gained PhD from MIT. On return home he launched Information Technologies China in 1996 and the following year his computer search engine sohu.com, which is at the forefront of China's information sector.

Zhang Wannian (Chang Wan-nien)—b. August 1928 in Longkou, Shandong. Joined CCP August 1945. Took part in military action against the Japanese and the Guomindang in the 1940s, and rose through the ranks from 1950s to 1970s: division commander 1968–78, commander of Guangzhou Military Command 1987–90, commander of Ji'nan Military Command 1990–92. Appointed member of CCP's Central Military Commission and chief of PLA General Staff 1992. Became member of Politburo September 1997, vice-chairman of CCP Central Military Commission 1995, confirmed 1997, and vice-chairman of the state's Central Military Commission March 1998. Coordinated missile tests off Taiwan March 1996 and reported to be the armed forces' most senior advocate of military action against Taiwan, given the correct conditions. Favours partnership with Russia against American dominance. Strong advocate of measures to combat corruption in the military.

Zhang Wenkang (Chang Wen-k'ang)—b. February 1940, from Shanghai. Graduated from Shanghai First Medical College 1962. Joined CCP 1966. Worked at PLA Second Medical University 1962–90, rising to become vice-president, then became deputy director of Public Health Department in PLA General Logistics Department 1990–93. Vice-minister of Public Health and director of State Traditional Chinese Medicine Administration 1993–98; minister of Public Health March 1998; elected member of Fifteenth CCP Central Committee 1997.

Zhang Yimou (Chang I-mou)—b. 1951, Xi'an. Graduated Beijing Film Academy, China's internationally most famous film director and actor and foremost among the 'fifth generation' film-makers. First major directed film was *Red Sorghum* (*Hong Gaoliang*, 1987), about a village girl who becomes head of a brewery. Other films to gain international acclaim are *Raise the Red Lantern* (1991) and *The Story of Qiu Ju* (*Qiu Ju zhuan*, 1992). He was also director of the star-studded performance of *Turandot* (see Chapter 1, E. September 1998) in Beijing in 1998. Won Golden Lion award at Venice Film Festival in September 1999 for his film *Not One Less* (*Yige dou buneng shao*) about a young female substitute teacher whose determination brought fame and money to the education of the backward village where she taught. Won Silver Bear Award at 2000 Berlin International Film Festival for just released film *The Road Home* (*Wode fuqin muqin*). Zhang has won Oscar nominations and more international film awards than any other Chinese director but is less popular with authorities at home, who have often censored him for his reluctance to toe the official line.

Zhang Zhen (Chang Chen)—b. October 1914, from Pingjiang, Hunan. Joined the Red Army and CCP 1930; took part in the Long March; very active on behalf of the CCP in the war against Japan and in the civil war of 1946–49 which resulted in the establishment of the PRC. Took part in the Korean War

1953, serving as acting commander and political commissar of Chinese troops. Promoted to lieutenant-general 1955 and general 1988. Graduated from PLA Military Academy 1957. Served as vice-president and president of Nanjing Military Academy 1957–70. Deputy commander, PLA Wuhan Military Area Command, 1970–75. Deputy chief, PLA General Staff, 1980–85. Vice-chairman, CCP Central Military Commission, 1992–97 and PRC Central Military Commission, 1993–98. Alternate member, Eleventh Central Committee (1977), full member Twelfth (1982) and Fourteenth (1992) Central Committees; member Central Advisory Committee 1987–92.

Zhang Zuoji (Chang Tso-chi)—b. January 1945, from Bayan, Heilongjiang. Graduated Heilongjiang University 1966, joined CCP 1972. Worked in the government, especially the Ministries of Ordnance Industry and of Labour during the 1980s. Served as vice-minister of Labour 1993–94, then deputy secretary-general of State Council, elected member of CCP Central Commission for Discipline Inspection 1997. Appointed minister of Labour and Social Security March 1998. Has written several dozen papers on labour matters.

Zhu Lilan (Chu Li-lan)—b. August 1935, from Huzhou, Zhejiang. Joined CCP 1956. Graduated from Odessa University, USSR, 1961, returning to China the same year. Worked as researcher and finally director, Beijing Chemistry Institute of Chinese Academy of Sciences, 1961–86, but worked in Germany in field of high polymer chemistry 1979–80. Vice-minister in charge of State Science and Technology Commission 1986–98, then minister of Science and Technology since March 1998 (as of 2000). Alternate member of CCP Central Committee 1992–97, rising to full membership 1997. She has made major achievements in research and analysis of the structural characteristics of high polymer materials and written widely in the field of high polymer chemistry. Also the main editor of *Practical Comments: Dialogues with Experts on High Science and Technology*

(*Shiji zhijiao: yu gao keji zhuanjia duihua*), 1995.

Zhu Muzhi (Chu Mu-chih)—b. December 1916, Jiangyin, Jiangsu. Joined CCP 1938. Deputy director of Xinhua News Agency 1952–72, but disappeared during Cultural Revolution; director, Xinhua News Agency, 1972–77. Member of the Tenth (1973), Eleventh (1977), Twelfth (1982), and Thirteenth (1987) CCPCC, and appointed member of the Central Advisory Committee 1985. Minister of Culture 1982–86. Appointed director of Office of News under State Council 1991. President of Association for Cultural Exchanges with Foreign Countries since 1986 (as of 2000) and of Chinese Society for the Study of Human Rights since 1994. This society, founded in January 1993, carries out studies of human rights theories, establishes academic ties with overseas human rights organizations and scholars and works to promote understanding of China's view of human rights. As president, Zhu Muzhi has frequently defended China's human rights record against attack from overseas at a time when China is consistently under criticism from the West and elsewhere for its human rights abuses. Zhu led a delegation to Norway, Sweden, Italy and Spain in June 1997. Publications include *On News Reporting* (*Lun xinwen baodao*), 1987.

Zhu Rongji (Chu Jung-chi)—b. Changsha, Hunan, October 1928, rose to become premier of State Council. Joined CCP in 1949. Graduated in electrical engineering from Qinghua University. Worked in State Planning Commission 1952–69, but from 1970 to 1975 was sent for 're-education' to a May Seventh Cadre school, due to the Cultural Revolution. From 1987 to 1990 he was mayor of Shanghai, overseeing the opening up of the Pudong area there. In 1991 he became a vice-premier, moving to Beijing, and launched a drive to solve the problems created by the debt-ridden state-owned enterprises. From 1993 to 1995 he was concurrently a member of the CCP Politburo Standing Committee, vice-premier of the State Council and governor of the People's Bank of China, relinquishing the last position in favour of Dai Xianglong in 1995. He was confirmed on the CCP Politburo Standing Committee in 1997 and promoted to premier of the State Council in 1998. With a reputation for straight talking, getting things done, intolerance of bureaucracy and incorruptibility, Zhu is especially noted for economic management and has been dubbed China's 'economic tsar'. He was given primary credit for halting the threatening inflationary spiral of the early to mid–1990s. Deng Xiaoping is reported to have said of Zhu that he 'has his own views, dares to make decisions and knows economics'.

Zou Jiahua (Tsou Chia-hua)—b. October 1926, Shanghai. Joined CCP June 1945. Served in CCP's New Fourth Army 1944–46. Graduated from Moscow Engineering Institute 1955 in machine-making. Worked in senior management at Shenyang Second Machine Tool Plant 1958–60. Moved to Beijing and worked at First Ministry of Machine Building. Held various vice-ministerial and especially ministerial positions from the 1980s, including minister of Ordnance Industry 1985–86, minister in charge of State Machine-building Industry Commission 1986–88, minister of Machine-building and Electronics Industry 1988–93, and minister in charge of State Planning Commission 1988–93. State councillor 1988–91 and vice-premier 1991–98. Member of the Twelfth (1982) to Fourteenth (1992) CCPCCs, promoted to Fourteenth CCPCC's Politburo 1992–97 but not reelected to Fifteenth (1997). Vice-chairman, Standing Committee Ninth NPC 1998 to present (as of 2000). Main responsibilities have been in the areas of planning, basic investment policy and machine-building industries, but as of 2000 he has not so far fulfilled the promise of the 1980s and early 1990s.

The following classified and annotated bibliography makes no pretence at being comprehensive. There has been an explosion of writing on China in recent times and it has proven necessary to restrict the entries for the sake of manageability. Each of the items included has been chosen on the following grounds:

1 It is published in 1990 or afterwards. Second or later revised editions may be included. For a bibliography of earlier books see *The Cambridge Handbook of Contemporary China*, Cambridge University Press, Cambridge, 1991, pp. 120–45.
2 It is entirely or almost entirely in the English language.
3 It is a book of at least 100 pages.
4 It focuses mainly on the People's Republic of China or its foreign relations; comparative works about several countries, works mainly about Taiwan or Hong Kong or historical works dealing mainly with the period before 1949 are not included.
5 Its principal concern is those aspects of China which are focal to the present book. Topics such as philosophy, ideology, society, gender or the arts, although recognized as extremely important, are therefore not covered. Other than reference books, yearbooks, scholarly journals, newspapers and websites, the categories below follow the topics of the chapters of this handbook, and in the same order.
6 It is judged by the compiler to be substantial, valuable and interesting enough to warrant inclusion in a list such as this.
7 In the case of journals, only scholarly items are included. For newspapers or websites, items with news referring to the whole East Asian region or only to one part of China are omitted. For instance, websites exclusively about Tibet or Xinjiang, or newspapers focusing on one city only are not included.

A REFERENCE BOOKS, YEARBOOKS

Bartke, Wolfgang, *Who's Who in the People's Republic of China*, 3rd edn (K.G. Saur, Munich, New York, London, 1991). The first edition of this work was published by M. E. Sharpe, Armonk NY and Harvester Press, Sussex, in 1981. It consists mainly of biographies presented in alphabetical order. The biography of each individual is given, with posts held and a photograph where possible, followed by activities, appointments and identifications presented in chronological order.

China Briefing, edited by various scholars (Westview Press, Colorado, in cooperation with the China Council of the Asia Society, 1980–). A roughly annual rundown on China the year before publication. There is a chronology and suggestions for further reading, but although specific aspects of coverage vary from year to year they include such topics as the economy, politics, gender, popular culture, Tibet, law and foreign relations.

China Directory in Pinyin and Chinese (Radiopress, Tokyo, 1971–). This is an annual publication giving extremely detailed information on the administrative structure of China, including the most recent information about who occupies which position. It covers the CCP, the National People's Congress, the State Council and all its various ministries and other organs, academic, economic and mass organizations, and the military. It provides very detailed information about regional as well as central organs, together with a thorough name index.

China Review (Chinese University Press, Hong Kong, 1991–). An annual publication, this book is edited from Hong Kong. Although the topics are not the same every year, they cover such matters as domestic politics, foreign relations, human rights, the economy, and culture. The authors are chosen as specialists in their field.

Editorial Board of PRC Yearbook, *People's Republic of China Yearbook* (PRC Yearbook Ltd, Beijing; distributed by Economic Information & Agency, Hong Kong, 1981 and later years). This is an encyclopedia yearbook sponsored by the NCNA, focusing on developments in China for a particular year. Aspects include state structure, public security, foreign and military affairs, the economy, industry, population, religion, labour, people in the news, science and technology, and culture and the arts. Extremely detailed, this yearbook expresses the view of the Chinese government.

Mackerras, Colin, with Donald H. McMillen and Andrew Watson, *Dictionary of the Politics of the People's Republic of China* (Routledge, London and New York, 1998). Contains nine introductory essays and over 140 A–Z entries. The focus is politics, including major political processes and events, political personalities, foreign policy environment and regions of particular political importance. There is coverage also of such social matters as education, minorities, marriage and women, but again with a political perspective.

Scherer, John L. (ed.), *China: Facts and Figures Annual* (Academic International Press, Gulf Breeze, Florida). This is an annual work which began publication in 1978, although since the 1988 edition, a series of editors other than Scherer have worked on the *Annual*. It collects an enormous amount of information and a large number of statistics and dates of various sorts. The sections are not totally consistent from year to year, but generally include government, the CCP, the military, population, the economy, agriculture, trade and aid, communications, health, education and welfare.

B SCHOLARLY JOURNALS, NEWSPAPERS AND WEBSITES

china.com. This online English-language daily newspaper covers many aspects of China, including news, finance, business, community, travel, culture and everyday life. Website: english.china.com/cdc/en/.

China (JPRS), continuation of *China Report: Political Sociological and Military Affairs* (JPRS). The abbreviation refers to the Joint Publication Research Service, a sub-agency of the Central Intelligence Agency. JPRS translates enormous quantities of foreign-language materials from newspapers, journals, speeches and broadcasts from all over the world, including China.

China Daily. This is China's main English-language daily, coming out also on Sunday. Its coverage is broad, including news, culture, foreign affairs, sport, and other aspects of China's development. Although there is treatment of foreign news, much more than half the content is about China. Website: www.chinadaily.net/.

China in the World Press, issued by NCNA, or the Xinhua News Agency, which is the PRC's state-run media organization. Among other matters it covers news on politics, economy, industry, trade, agriculture, sports and culture, and Chinese views on international affairs. Website: www.xinhua.org.

China Information. A Journal on Contemporary China Studies. Put out by the Documentation and Research Center for Contemporary China, Leiden University, this journal focuses on recent developments in China but covers other Chinese societies. The disciplinary fields include politics, economics, law, ecology, culture and society, and much space is allocated to book reviews. Website: www.let.leidenuniv.nl/tcc/journal.

China Informed. A News Service Focused on China, Taiwan and Hong Kong was established in February 1997 and appears online four or five times a week. The aim is for balanced and accurate coverage and a rounded diet of political, social and less commonly reported news. Debate is encouraged, including through letters to the editor. Website: chinainformed.com/.

The China Journal. Formerly *The Australian Journal of Chinese Affairs*, this journal is put out by the Contemporary China Centre at the Australian National University, Canberra. Published twice annually, its focus is topics relating to China since 1949, in addition to studies of CCP history, plus book reviews. Website: www.anu.edu.au./RSPAS/ccc/journal.htm.

The China Quarterly is edited from the School of Oriental and African Studies, University of London. Its focus is on contemporary China, from all points of view, but it also has material on pre–1949 history, especially that of the CCP. It includes book reviews and also a regular and very useful 'Quarterly Chronicle and Documentation'. Website: www.oup.co.uk/chinaq.

China News Digest. This comes out several times a week on the Internet. It includes brief reports on all aspects of events in China, including those relating to foreign relations, and also more detailed commentaries. Website: www.cnd.org/.

ChinaSite.com: The Complete Reference to China/China-Related Web Sites. First created in 1994, this vast network of websites on China is put out by the Chinese Consulate-General in Chicago and is updated more or less daily. It contains an enormous amount of information on a great many aspects of China, both past and present, including 'Current Events', 'China's leaders', and others relevant to the present book. Its address is http://www.Chinasite.com/.

Journal of Contemporary China is edited in North America and published by Taylor & Francis. It publishes articles of theoretical and policy research and research notes on China, as well as book reviews. Its fields of interest include economics, political science, law, culture, history, international relations and sociology. It is included in Taylor & Francis's general website: www.tandf.co.uk/journals.

Xinhua News Bulletin contains the daily reports of China's state-run news agency from over 135 bureaux throughout the world on political, economic, cultural, educational and other issues relevant to China, and international issues affecting Asia and the Pacific Rim. Website: www/xinhua.org.

C HISTORY OR GENERAL

Bakken, Børge, *The Exemplary Society, Human Improvement, Social Control, and the Dangers of Modernity in China* (Oxford University Press, Oxford, 2000). The concern here is the modern 'disorders' and deviant behaviour in China, which are met by official attempts to create an 'exemplary society' of 'human quality' and model behaviour. It also considers how modern Chinese society resists being reduced to the exemplary discipline of its social engineers, and the routine strategies of resistance.

Barmé, Geremie, and Linda Jaivin (eds), *New Ghosts, Old Dreams, Chinese Rebel Voices* (Times Books, Random House, New York, 1992). With a brief Introduction to the whole book and very short ones to each passage, this book contains numerous 'rebel' documents concerning China's recent history. These include especially the 'Protest Movement' of 1989 and the restraints imposed on China by its history and culture, and by the Communist system. The translations generally use a highly colloquial style, chosen not to be representative of Chinese as a whole but to express opinion from the people, notably those hostile to the government.

Benewick, Robert and Paul Wingrove (eds), *China in the 1990s* (Macmillan, London, 1995, rev. edn 1999). This book is an attempt to understand the complex processes of 'change and the management of stability' (p. 3). There are 21 essays by different authors, on topics ranging from political structure and reform and change in the countryside and the urban economy to gender, family, population, literature and film, and foreign relations. The 1999 edition adds two chapters. The book is similar in structure to the same editors' *Reforming the Revolution, China in Transition* (Macmillan, London, 1988). However, Chapter 1 on 'The Tiananmen Crackdown and its Legacy' shows the different concerns of the 1990s.

Brahm, Laurence J., *China as No. 1, The New Superpower Takes Centre Stage* (Butterworth-Heinemann Asia, Singapore, 1996). With chapters on ideology, politics, humanism, macro-controls, structures, trade, enterprises and monetary policy, Hong Kong and Macau, Taiwan and red capital, this book presents a 'positive and hopeful look at many of the hard and difficult reforms which China has undertaken' (p. viii) and is particularly enthusiastic about China's economic progress in the 1990s.

Brugger, Bill, and Stephen Reglar, *Politics, Economy and Society in Contemporary China* (Macmillan, Houndmills and London, 1994). Part 1 is an overview history with chapters on China under and after Mao Zedong. Part 2 takes up six themes, including state and countryside, law and policing, intellectuals, family and gender relations, and minority nationalities. The book's authors try 'to marshal various conflicting arguments around controversial themes' chosen 'to highlight questions of general relevance' (p. 3).

Canyon, A.M. (ed.), *Assessment of China into the 21st Century* (Nova Science Publishers, New York, 1997). A collection of American Congressional Research Services reports and briefing papers, this book takes up themes such as China's global economic role, its politics and its security context. Several chapters consider issues relating to Sino-American relations. Although there is some historical background and predictions of the future, the focus is on the 1990s.

Cheek, Timothy, and Tony Saich (eds), *New Perspectives on State Socialism in China* (M.E. Sharpe, Armonk NY and London, 1997). The eight chapters, plus Introduction and Conclusion, focus mainly on the first eight years of the PRC, with one chapter on the Great Leap Forward and its aftermath. The book covers such aspects as the household registration system, the

Zhejiang provincial purges of 1957–58, and the Shanghai strike wave of 1957. It is based on a conference held in 1993 which tried, among other aims, to cast new light and interpretations on the early PRC period.

Cheng, Joseph Y.S. (ed.), *China in the Post-Deng Era* (Chinese University Press, Hong Kong, 1998) focuses on the late 1980s and first half of the 1990s. There is coverage of politics, leadership, ideology, and foreign policy. Topics of reform include rural, banking, administrative, and legal. The final chapter, by the editor, discusses the challenges faced by Deng Xiaoping's successors.

Christiansen, Flemming, and Rai, Shirin M., *Chinese Politics and Society: An Introduction* (Prentice Hall, Harvester Wheatsheaf, London and New York, 1996). Other than a theoretical Introduction on the 'approaches to the study of Chinese politics', this book has four parts: on history, politics, the economy, and society. Coverage includes all the PRC period. The conclusion summarizes the problems China faces and where the authors see the country going. They conclude that 'Political stability is the major issue before China today. Its programme of modernization depends on how successfully it resolves this issue' (p. 317).

Dietrich, Craig, *People's China, A Brief History*, 3rd edn (Oxford University Press, New York, Oxford, 1998). In this book, the first two editions of which came out in 1986 and 1994, the author hopes to provide 'a reasonably good idea of the general contours of historical events in China over the last several decades' (p. 9) and succeeds admirably. It is well documented with a good bibliography but makes no pretence at being original research. The author is critical but generally very positive about the Chinese revolution and, despite some serious caveats, remains quite optimistic about China's future.

Dutton, Michael, *Streetlife China* (Cambridge University Press, Cambridge, 1998). In this remarkable book, the author collects fascinating documents about contemporary China, mostly written in the 1980s or 1990s. The documents cover such subjects as human rights, the work unit, homosexuals in Beijing, peasant movements, beggars, prostitution, the body, the badge as biography, tattooing, and Chinese architecture as symbolic hierarchy. There are quite lengthy and highly perceptive introductions to the extracts, so that the book offers a most unusual view of contemporary China at street level.

Dwyer, Denis (ed.), *China: The Next Decades* (Longman Scientific and Technical, Harlow, 1994). This is a general survey of the PRC's policies and conditions in the economy and society, with the focus on the 1980s and 1990s. Topics covered include population, economic reform, urbanization, the environment, water resources and health care.

Goodman, David S.G., and Gerald Segal (eds), *China Deconstructs: Politics, Trade and Regionalism* (Routledge, London and New York, 1994). In twelve chapters, most of them dealing with specific and different parts of China, the authors take up the issue of regionalism in the late 1980s and early 1990s, especially against the background of political and economic reform and foreign trade. In the first chapter David Goodman discusses the possibility that China will split up and concludes that while 'there is considerable evidence of the many ways in which China is changing shape, there is much less to suggest political separatism' (p. 16).

Hudson, Christopher (ed.), *The China Handbook* (Fitzroy Dearborn Publishers, Chicago and London, 1997). With chapters written by different specialists, there are four sections: history, from 1949 to Deng Xiaoping's death early in 1997; regional context, such as relations between China and Taiwan, China in East Asia and China and Southeast Asia in the 1990s; political economy and development policy, including urban industry, financial reform, foreign trade reform, and mass

communications; and society, including population, education, social welfare, and minorities. The aim is to provide an overview of China's development path since 1949, with emphasis on the period since 1978. There is a brief chronology, a glossary of terms and one of people, and an analytical bibliography; each chapter also has a list of further reading.

Joseph, William A., Christine P.W. Wong and David Zweig (eds), *New Perspectives on the Cultural Revolution* (Harvard University Press, Cambridge, Mass., 1991). Based on a 1987 conference of mainly American scholars, this volume is among the few to look at the Cultural Revolution decade 1966–76 as a whole. It offers new interpretations of the decade in the political, economic and cultural realms.

Kristof, Nicholas D., and Sheryl WuDunn, *China Wakes: The Struggle for the Soul of a Rising Power* (Vintage Books, New York, 1995). An excellent journalistic account of the late 1980s and early 1990s by a married couple who worked for the *New York Times*. It covers a wide range of topics, such as the leaders, intellectuals, the economy, women, and population policy. Although harshly critical in many places, the couple left China believing, for all their misgivings and caveats, 'that China will flourish and evolve' (p. 453).

MacFarquhar, Roderick, *The Origins of the Cultural Revolution* vol. 3, *The Coming of the Cataclysm 1961–1966* (Columbia University Press, New York, 1997). This is the third volume of an extremely detailed, scholarly and illuminating study of Chinese politics in the period leading up to the Cultural Revolution. The books aim to explain the Cultural Revolution, but each volume is self-contained as well as part of the series, and each reaches its own conclusions on its period of focus. Among the many conclusions is that Mao Zedong, who 'always made the difference', was motivated by a desire to revitalize the revolution: 'The revolution was dead; long live the revolution!' (p. 469).

MacFarquar, Roderick, and John K. Fairbank (eds), *The Cambridge History of China* vol. 15, *The People's Republic,* Part 2: *Revolutions within the Chinese Revolution, 1966–1982* (Cambridge University Press, Cambridge, 1991). Itself nearly the last of the multi-volumed *Cambridge History of China*, this is the second of two volumes to deal with the PRC period. Its authors take up key issues involved in the history of the Cultural Revolution and the first years of reform and discuss developments in politics, economics, education, 'creativity and politics', foreign relations, everyday life, and literature. There is also a chapter on Taiwan and bibliographical essays. The Epilogue emphasizes the 'onus of unity' which all Chinese leaders have taken on. They conclude that this onus is becoming an incubus and that in the 1990s and beyond, 'unity will be preserved only by diversity' (p. 881).

Mackerras, Colin, Pradeep Taneja and Graham Young, *China Since 1978: Reform, Modernisation and 'Socialism with Chinese Characteristics'* (Longman, Melbourne, 1993, 2nd rev. edn 1998). This book covers China's political history from 1978, aspects of the economy, political institutions and reform, the law, the environment, education, health delivery and social welfare, population, and foreign relations. In addition, there is a select analytical bibliography of topics relevant to the book's content. The main themes are modernization and reform. The second edition updates the first but also has extensive revisions of several chapters.

McCormick, Barrett L., and Jonathan Unger (eds), *China After Socialism: In the Footsteps of Eastern Europe or East Asia?* (M.E. Sharpe, Armonk NY, 1996). Covering aspects such as politics, political dynamics, economic and financial reforms, corporatism and society, the editors and other authors ask the question whether, in the wake of the collapse of Marxist-Leninist parties in Eastern Europe, the CCP is more likely to follow them into collapse or to lead economic triumph, as in Japan and the small dragons. Various authors give different answers to this question.

Meisner, Maurice, *Mao's China and After: A History of the People's Republic* 3rd edn (Free Press, New York, 1999). The first two editions came out in 1977 and 1986. With a chronological framework, the author treats 'the revolutionary heritage' and then traces the PRC's history from 1949 to 1998. He is very impressed with the economic results of Deng's 'capitalism', but states that they have 'exacted a fearful social price' (p. 532).

Miles, James A. R., *The Legacy of Tiananmen: China in Disarray* (University of Michigan Press, Ann Arbor, 1996). This account of China from the late 1980s to the mid–1990s is both scholarly, with many notes and a bibliography of Chinese- and English-language works, and journalistic, being written by a professional reporter and based mainly on his observations. Its emphasis is on the problems spawned by the suppression of the student movement in 1989 and it is very pessimistic, expressing the belief that China could easily plunge into turmoil.

Murray, Geoffrey, *China the Next Superpower: Dilemmas in Change and Continuity* (Curzon, Richmond, Surrey, 1998). Against a tight definition of 'superpower', this book argues that China is emerging as one for the twenty-first century. Murray covers both domestic and international issues, such as contradictions in economic reform, population control, whether China can continue to be fed adequately, the status of women, and 'the China that can say no', including the 'China threat theory'. Although the author is critical of China, his basic standpoint is that of an admirer and one who likes the Chinese greatly (p. viii).

Schell, Orville, and David Shambaugh (eds), *The China Reader: The Reform Era* (Vintage Books, New York, 1999). One of a series of China readers, this is an expertly selected range of extracts on such topics as politics, education, the media, culture, the economy, society and foreign relations covering the period from the late 1970s on. Most of the texts are by Western specialists on China, or Chinese living in the West, but a few are by Chinese leaders and others.

Sexton, John, and Alan Hunter, *Contemporary China* (St Martin's Press, New York, 1999). With a focus on the period of reform, this book takes up such topics as the economy, political life, Chinese culture, international relations, and the future into the twenty-first century. It raises such questions as whether the leaders are taking the country to capitalism and whether China is set to become a world power.

Shambaugh, David (ed.), *Is China Unstable?* (M.E. Sharpe, Armonk NY and London, 2000). Various authors take up issues of order and stability in contemporary China. After an introductory 'typology', the chapters cover the potential for instability in the leadership and at lower levels of administration, in the economy, in the cities and countryside and in the minority areas.

Starr, John Bryan, *Understanding China: A Guide to China's Economy, History, and Political Structure* (Hill and Wang, New York, 1997). Very broad-ranging in its coverage, though with a focus on the present, this book covers such topics as geographical inequalities, the economy, the government, the population problem, the environment, the education system, and foreign relations. The conclusion makes some predictions about the situation in the twenty-first century.

Teather, David, and Herbert Yee (eds), *China in Transition: Issues and Policies* (Macmillan, Basingstoke, 1999). This book has four parts, covering issues in politics and law, foreign policy, economics, and society. The focus is on the very recent past and contemporary times. All authors have worked in tertiary institutions in Hong Kong.

Teiwes, Frederick C., with Warren Sun, *China's Road to Disaster: Mao, Central Politicians, and Provincial Leaders in the Unfolding of the Great Leap Forward 1955–1959* (M.E. Sharpe, Armonk NY and London, 1999). Arranged chronologically, this intensively researched and extremely detailed book analyzes the origins, process and 'cooling down' of the Great Leap Forward and Mao's role in it. The authors argue that Mao Zedong was able to exercise unchallenged political authority in the CCP; they see Mao as changing late in 1957 from a strong-willed and temperamental but essentially rational leader to a dangerous, unpredictable and irrational one who saw everything in terms of political line and enjoyed humiliating those around him.

Wang Gungwu and John Wong (eds), *China's Political Economy* (Singapore University Press/World Scientific, Singapore, 1998). This book is a collection of public lectures and seminar papers, with the focus generally on the 1990s. Despite its title, this book is quite general, with chapters on topics as diverse as history, economic reform, regionalism, the role of Singaporean Chinese in a village in southern China, and Sino-American relations.

Yan Jiaqi and Gao Gao, transl. and ed. D.W.Y. Kwok, *Turbulent Decade: A History of the Cultural Revolution* (University of Hawai'i Press, Honolulu, 1996). Originally in Chinese, this extremely large and detailed book aims 'to investigate the causes of the Cultural Revolution' as well to describe its course and prevent its recurrence (p. xxiv). Apart from several prefaces and an Introduction, the book has 30 chapters, mainly arranged chronologically, beginning with one on the criticism of the drama *Hai Rui Dismissed from Office* (*Hai Rui baguan*) late in 1965 and early 1966 and ending with the fall of the 'gang of four' in October 1976.

Yang, Dali L., *Calamity and Reform in China: State, Rural Society, and Institutional Change Since the Great Leap Famine* (Cambridge University Press, Cambridge, 1996). This is a broad-ranging examination of the political causes and consequences of the major famine that resulted from the Great Leap Forward, with provinces like Anhui, Sichuan, Henan and Guizhou in the forefront. It argues that those areas most devastated by the famine were those that opposed collectivization most seriously when Deng Xiaoping decided to decollectivize.

D POLITICS AND LAW

Baum, Richard, *Burying Mao: Chinese Politics in the Age of Deng Xiaoping* (Princeton University Press, Princeton, 1994). An extremely detailed history of Chinese politics from 1976 to 1993, the book is arranged chronologically. The Introduction explains the framework of emphasis on debates concerning reform among factions and 'cycles of reform', which have 'an oscillating pattern of policy initiative and response, as phases of reform and relaxation alternated with phases of relative restriction and retrenchment' (p. 5).

Brook, Timothy, and B. Michael Frolic (eds), *Civil Society in China* (M.E. Sharpe, Armonk NY and London, 1997). Multidisciplinary in approach, this book examines the concept of civil society and its application to China. Other than an Introduction by the two editors on 'the ambiguous challenge of civil society', there are three general chapters and four case studies relating to higher education, youth, trade unions, and popular religion. The authors recognize the power of the state, but believe that civil society may not threaten the state; the second editor argues that state-led civil society is possible.

Brown, Ronald C., *Understanding Chinese Courts and Legal Process: Law with Chinese Characteristics* (Kluwer Law International, The Hague, London, Boston, 1997). Written by a member of the University of Hawai'i's Law School, this book is organized into four parts: legal process in China; the court and its work; new laws 'professionalizing' enforcers of laws; and Chinese courts now and into the year 2000. With a preface dated May 25, 1997 by Zou Yu, the former Minister of Justice, the book takes a sympathetic view of Chinese law and considers that China deserves much credit for rebuilding its legal and judicial systems given the conditions it faced in 1979 (p. xix).

Chen, Albert Hung-yee, *An Introduction to the Legal System of the People's Republic of China* (Butterworths Asia, Singapore, 1992) covers the basic concepts and principles of procedural and substantive law, as well as history, constitutional structure, sources of law and major legal institutions. Chen sees great strength both in the forces of tradition and in those of Westernization in contemporary China, seeing the country as a good example deserving of study that illustrates the 'transplant of law and legal institutions from one part of the world to another and their interaction with local culture and traditions' (pp. 1–2).

Davis, Michael C. (ed.), *Human Rights and Chinese Values: Legal, Philosophical, and Political Perspectives* (Oxford University Press, Hong Kong, 1995). The emphasis here is on the diversity of Chinese views of human rights. The editor argues that Chinese attitudes to human rights are not monolithic but that opinions different from, or supplementary to, the official view are among those shaping the debate on this topic, one of the most important internationally in the post-Cold War world.

Ding, X.L., *The Decline of Communism in China: Legitimacy Crisis, 1977–1989* (Cambridge University Press, Cambridge, 1994). Originally a doctoral thesis, this book focuses on the role of intellectuals as anti-elite forces in politics. The author sees the clash between the intellectuals and the Party elite as the primary force eroding the CCP's legitimacy in the 1980s.

Domenach, Jean-Luc (transl. A.M. Berrett), *The Origins of the Great Leap Forward: The Case of One Chinese Province* (Westview, Boulder, 1995). This study, a translation from a French original, analyzes political, economic and social developments in

Henan Province from 1949 to the beginning of the Great Leap Forward. Its central question is why the CCP leadership should launch so irrational a movement, the answer being that it was a response to a deep crisis in popular legitimacy.

Dreyer, June Teufel, *China's Political System. Modernization and Tradition* (Macmillan, Basingstoke, 1993, 3rd edn 1999). Designed as a textbook, this work has several chapters of historical background and eight topic-based chapters, such as crime and punishment, the military, quality-of-life issues like health, demography and the environment, ethnic minorities and national integration, and foreign policy.

Dutton, Michael R., *Policing and Punishment in China: From Patriarchy to 'the People'* (Cambridge University Press, Cambridge, 1992). There is a great deal of historical material here, but the focus is on the PRC, including household registration, family, labour reform and policing in the period of reform. A major trend the author perceives since 1978 has been that 'the neighbourhood committees, the local security committees and the neighbourhood work units have combined to both police and educate the population' (p. 340).

Goldman, Merle, *Sowing the Seeds of Democracy in China: Political Reform in the Deng Xiaoping Era* (Harvard University Press, Cambridge, Mass., 1994) deals with the intellectual development of over twenty of the democratic elite from the late 1970s till 1989, showing the maturation of their understanding of democracy over the period.

He Baogang, *The Democratic Implications of Civil Society in China* (Macmillan, Basingstoke, St Martin's Press, New York, 1997). By measuring a set of social groups, such as intellectuals, business groups, student organizations and various associations against a set of benchmarks, the author concludes that what China became in the Deng Xiaoping era was a 'semi-civil society'. One chapter analyzes the role of political organizations outside China. The

author believes the better development of democracy is unlikely without a coalition of reformers both inside and outside the government.

Jia Hao and Lin Zhimin (eds), *Changing Central–Local Relations in China: Reform and State Capacity* (Westview Press, Boulder, 1994) aims to provide a comprehensive picture of central–local relations and the ways they have changed in the reform era. It takes up topics such as institutional change and fiscal politics and presents two case studies, Guangdong and Shanghai. The editors argue that decentralization has brought about local support for reform, but that it has gone much further than its instigators originally intended.

Kent, Ann, *Between Freedom and Subsistence: China and Human Rights* (Oxford University Press, Hong Kong, 1993) offers definitions of human rights and covers civil and political rights as well as economic, social and cultural rights. Chapters deal separately with the period from 1949 to 1979 and 1979 to 1989, with special treatment of the crisis of 1989 and its aftermath.

Kwong, Julia, *The Political Economy of Corruption in China* (M.E. Sharpe, Armonk NY and London, 1997). Chapters include 'the meanings of corruption', 'the social context', 'the dynamics of corruption', and 'a look to the future'. Coverage focuses on the periods of Mao Zedong and of Deng Xiaoping, up to 1989. The author sees culture rather than political economy as a major cause of corruption.

Lieberthal, Kenneth, *Governing China: From Revolution Through Reform* (Norton, New York, 1995. This very large study gives a complete account of Chinese politics, which ranges from 'the legacies of imperial China', the history of the CCP, and analysis of China's political system to dictatorship and corruption, economic development, state-society relationships and the prospects for the future. The author emphasizes China's weak political institutions and lack of mechanisms for political participation, which he sees as sources of instability.

Lo, Carlos Wing-Hung, *China's Legal Awakening: Legal Theory and Criminal Justice in Deng's Era* (Hong Kong University Press, Hong Kong, 1995). This book includes a detailed study of the influence of ideological changes on the legal system as well as case studies based on the legal periodical *Minzhu yu fazhi* (*Democracy and the Legal System*). While acknowledging that what has replaced 'rule by man' under Mao is not the 'rule of law' but the use of law by rulers as a means to rule, the author argues that a genuine legal awakening took place in China under Deng Xiaoping through the establishment of a formal criminal justice system and the development of an embryonic socialist theory of law.

Lubman, Stanley B. (ed.), *China's Legal Reforms* (Oxford University Press, Oxford, 1996; republished from the *China Quarterly* 141 [March 1995]). The authors discuss various aspects of legal reform, including family law, foreign investment law and criminal law and human rights, as well as the barriers to further reform. The editor sees many accomplishments but believes that the decay of those institutions which have held the Chinese party-state together 'will act to limit the possibility of major change in the leadership's goals for legal development' (p. 21).

MacFarquhar, Roderick (ed.), *The Politics of China*; 2nd edn retitled *The Eras of Mao and Deng* (Cambridge University Press, Cambridge, 1997). First published in 1993, this book aims, in six chapters plus a very brief Introduction, 'to provide a comprehensive account of the politics of the People's Republic of China from 1949 to the mid–1990s' (p. vii). The first four chapters are drawn from the *Cambridge History of China*, but two were added specifically to bring the story up to the mid–1990s.

Nathan, Andrew, *China's Transition* (Columbia University Press, New York, 1998). The theme is democracy in China, and the transition is to democracy. There are sixteen chapters altogether on topics such as 'Mao and his court', 'left and right in Deng's China' and 'human rights and American China policy'. The focus is the pre–1997 PRC, but there are chapters on Taiwan and Hong Kong as well. Nathan, a foremost specialist on democracy in China, sees no reason why democracy should not be achieved there.

Nathan, Andrew J., with Hong Zhaohui and Steven R. Smith (eds), *Dilemmas of Reform in Jiang Zemin's China* (Lynne Rienner, Boulder, 1999) explores the dilemmas of the new and more challenging phase of complex economic reform and change as the leadership faces pressures for political liberalization. It covers such aspects as legitimacy crisis in politics in the late 1990s, the political economy of reform, unemployment, and China's economic prospects.

O'Brien, Kevin J., *Reform Without Liberalization, China's National People's Congress and the Politics of Institutional Change* (Cambridge University Press, Cambridge, 1990). There are three parts: Introduction, the National People's Congress under Mao Zedong, and the same body under Deng Xiaoping. O'Brien considers that the 1980s saw progress towards rationalization and inclusion, but also a continuing rejection of liberalization. 'Despite notable efforts to reduce capriciousness and to broaden the base of the regime, the reforms of the 1980s did little to increase political competition or to institutionalize responsiveness' (p. 6).

Potter, Pitman B. (ed.), *Domestic Law Reforms in Post-Mao China* (M.E. Sharpe, Armonk NY, 1994). There are three parts: Conceptual and Institutional Foundations; Economic and Civil Law; and Public Law Relations. An Introduction draws out some themes in law reform taken up by the various chapters, including the importance of 'rights consciousness' shared not only by 'Chinese bureaucrats and legal professionals' but also 'the populace at large' (p. 11).

Seymour, James D., and Richard Anderson, *New Ghosts, Old Ghosts: Prisons and Labor Reform Camps in China* (M.E. Sharpe, Armonk and London, 1998). Covers the history of the reform through labour system in China, but focuses on three regions: Gansu, Qinghai and Xinjiang. The authors conclude that the reason for a likely increase in prison numbers is because of local requirements in the three areas and rising crime rates in China, rather than intensifying totalitarian control.

Tanner, Harold M., *Strike Hard! Anti-Crime Campaigns and Chinese Criminal Justice, 1979–1985* (Cornell University East Asia Program, Ithaca, 1999). The focus here is on crime prevention and campaigns against common crime in the first few years of reform, although there is also some background material covering the 1950s to 1970s. The author sees a major function of criminal law in social control.

Tanner, Murray Scot, *The Politics of Lawmaking in Post-Mao China, Institutions, Processes and Democratic Prospects* (Clarendon Press, Oxford, 1999). In four parts, this book covers theoretical considerations, lawmaking institutions, case studies in lawmaking, and conclusions. The last chapter finds that the NPC, by building a 'solid permanent bureaucracy and subcommittee structure', has made progress towards involvement in lawmaking (p. 250).

Teiwes, Frederick C., *Politics at Mao's Court: Gao Gang and Party Factionalism in the Early 1950s* (M.E. Sharpe, Armonk NY, 1990). This is a highly focused account of elite politics in China in the early 1950s. There are six chapters and eight substantial appendices. Chapter 6 opens with: 'The one indisputable conclusion to emerge from this study is the central role of Mao Zedong' (p. 142).

Teiwes, Frederick C., *Politics and Purges in China: Rectification and the Decline of Party Norms, 1950–1965*, 2nd edn (M.E. Sharpe, Armonk NY, 1993). This is a revised edition of Teiwes's superb 1979 work of the same name, which concerned elite politics before the Cultural Revolution. This edition adds a lengthy Introduction but does not change interpretations.

Tien Hung-mao and Chu Yun-han, *China under Jiang Zemin* (Lynne Rienner, Boulder, 1999). This book covers the politics of the Jiang Zemin period so far, including the political landscape as his period of control opened, economic policy and social conditions. It also comments on the various other main personalities in China's politics and the strategies Jiang has successfully employed to consolidate his position.

Unger, Jonathan (ed.), *The Pro-Democracy Protests in China, Reports from the Provinces* (M. E. Sharpe, Armonk NY, 1991; most of the thirteen chapters were originally published in *The Australian Journal of Chinese Affairs*). After an Introduction by the editor, this book contains five parts, which are about the student protests of 1989 in Beijing, Manchuria (Changchun and Shenyang), the Interior (Xi'an, Chongqing, Changsha and an individual from Hunan), the southeast coast (Fujian) and the Yangzi Delta (Hangzhou and Shanghai). The authors record on-the-spot experience. The editor identifies the main demand of the students as one for an autonomous political space, a demand the authorities resolutely opposed (pp. 5–7).

Wang, James C.F., *Contemporary Chinese Politics: An Introduction*, 6th edn (Prentice Hall, Englewood Cliffs, 1999). This textbook, rich in detail on government, covers the history of the CCP, ideology, political institutions, elites and the cadre system, the provinces and the military, as well as the politics of modernization. The first edition appeared in 1980.

Womack, Brantly (ed.), *Contemporary Chinese Politics in Historical Perspective* (Cambridge University Press, Cambridge, 1991). Eight scholars take up themes from the PRC, mainly in the reform period after 1976, and offer perspectives based on history. Topics include political and economic theories, bureaucracy and bureaucrats, foreign policy, and the democracy movement of 1989 and its suppression.

Wu, Hongda Harry (transl. Ted Slingerland), *Laogai: The Chinese Gulag* (Westview, Boulder, 1992). This account focuses on reform through the labour system, covering such topics as political prisoners and forced labour. In an Afterword, the author stresses that, despite changes in labour reform camp policies and measures, in the early 1990s the prison camps remained a 'central part of the Communist Party's control structure, and over forty years their political function has not changed' (p. 143).

E BIOGRAPHY, AUTOBIOGRAPHY

Breslin, Shaun, *Mao* (Addison Wesley Longman, London, 1998). The first few chapters take a basically chronological approach, including a considerable emphasis on the Cultural Revolution. Chapters 6 and 7 deal with 'Mao and the World' and 'The Politics of De-Maoisation'.

Bryan, John and Pack, Robert, *The Claws of the Dragon: Kang Sheng, The Evil Genius behind Mao and his Legacy of Terror in People's China* (Simon & Schuster, New York, 1991). Based on declassified American archives and restricted PRC material, this book is the first scholarly biography of Kang published in the West. It paints a damning picture of a man who was one of Mao Zedong's main supporters during the Cultural Revolution.

Evans, Richard, *Deng Xiaoping and the Making of Modern China* (Hamish Hamilton, London, 1993; 3rd rev. edn, Penguin, Harmondsworth, 1997). The author was British Ambassador to China from 1984 to 1988 and had access to good materials and conducted his own interviews. This biography takes a chronological approach, but emphasizes the PRC, attributing Deng's success to his unique combination of political conservatism and economic radicalism and noting among his personal qualities 'resilience, tenacity and perhaps above all an ability to win loyal friends' (p. 319).

Goldstein, Melvyn, William Siebenschuh and Tashi Tsering, *The Struggle for Modern Tibet: The Autobiography of Tashi Tsering* (M.E. Sharpe, Armonk NY and London, 1997). The central figure of this autobiography is a Tibetan who left Tibet in the late 1950s, despite hating the old system and becoming a homosexual sex-toy for a well-connected monk. He lived in India and the United States but then returned in 1964. He supported the Cultural Revolution but became its victim, being imprisoned for several years. After his release he became a professor of English at Tibet University in Lhasa and contributed greatly to Tibetan education. In contrast to most accounts by Tibetans published outside Tibet itself, he appears to prefer progress within the current system to independence.

Goodman, David S.G., *Deng Xiaoping and the Chinese Revolution: A Political Biography* (Routledge, London and New York, 1994). This extensive biography of Deng Xiaoping takes a chronological approach, with chapters on his early life, 1904–37, and military service, 1937–52, through to his role in the beginnings of reform, 1979–84, and later stage of reform and retirement, from 1984 on. There are also an Introduction and 'a preliminary assessment', as well as a very extensive list of Deng's speeches and writings. The 'preliminary assessment' is basically positive, emphasizing Deng's role as a reformer, although 'a conservative reformer, a traditionalist who wanted to restore what he considered had been the CCP's traditions, set aside during the Cultural Revolution' (p. 124).

He Liyi, with Claire Anne Chik, *Mr China's Son: A Villager's Life* (Westview Press, Boulder, 1994). An autobiography of the first-named author, this book traces his life throughout the course of the PRC. It offers a microcosm of PRC history, society and economy, especially from the point of view of a Bai (see Chapter 9) and a villager in Yunnan.

Li Zhisui, ed. Anne F. Thurston (transl. Tai Hung-chao), *The Private Life of Chairman Mao: The Inside Story of the Man who Made Modern China* (Chatto & Windus, London, 1994). This account is based on Li Zhisui's experience as Mao Zedong's personal physician from 1955 to 1976, when Mao died. The picture is sharply negative, Mao emerging as a power- and sex-crazed tyrant whom nobody dared defy or criticize. The study gives an excellent account of the atmosphere in Mao's court, but is replete with questionable claims and interpretations.

Ruan Ming, Nancy Liu, and Peter Rand (transl. and ed. Lawrence R. Sullivan), *Deng Xiaoping: Chronicle of an Empire*, Westview Press, Boulder, Oxford, 1994. First published in Taipei in Chinese in 1992 and in French translation the same year, this book focuses on the period from 1976 to 1989. The book is harshly critical of Deng, the 'empire' being Deng's China, which the author sees as having been destroyed by the Beijing massacre.

Salisbury, Harrison E., *The New Emperors, China in the Era of Mao and Deng* (Avon, New York, 1993). The 'new emperors' being Mao Zedong and Deng Xiaoping, this book emphasizes the importance of the past for China's present. The author, a very well known journalist and winner of the Pulitzer Prize, has a eye for the detail of human interaction. He clearly prefers the economic revolutionary Deng to the violent political and social revolutionary Mao, but admits that Deng was no humanist.

Shambaugh, David (ed.), *Deng Xiaoping: Portrait of a Chinese Statesman* (Clarendon Press, Oxford, 1995; reprinted from *China Quarterly*, no. 135 (September 1993), entitled *Special Issue, Deng Xiaoping: An Assessment*) This book has one chapter on Deng before 1949 and several on his 'key dimensions' (p. 3), including politician, economist, social reformer, soldier and statesman. Although judgments about Deng vary, he is recognized as 'one of the world's pre-eminent leaders of the late 20th century' whose impact 'will be felt well into the next century' (p. 1).

Shao, Kuo-kang, *Zhou Enlai and the Foundations of Chinese Foreign Policy* (St Martin's Press, New York, 1996). Designed as a 'focused analysis of Zhou's negotiating skills and his conduct of Chinese foreign policy in the years 1949 to 1976' (p. ix), this book emphasizes Zhou's pragmatism: 'Zhou believed that the new China's foreign policy must be grounded in reality rather than political ideology' (p. 259). A little over half the book treats the PRC period, with a chapter each on Zhou's role in China's relations with the Soviet Union and the United States, and one on nuclear weapons and the United Nations in his foreign policy strategies.

Teiwes, Frederick C. and Warren Sun, *The Tragedy of Lin Biao: Riding the Tiger during the Cultural Revolution, 1966–1971* (Hurst, London, 1996). This excellent study of Lin Biao and his role in the Cultural Revolution criticizes all aspects of the official view of Lin, which damns him for trying to assassinate Mao. Among many other interesting conclusions, the authors argue that Lin was not particularly ambitious and was essentially loyal to Mao. He 'was content with an inactive albeit honoured position and was thrust into a leading role by Mao and subsequently cast aside for reasons that had little to do with any wishes he may have had for greater power' (p. 7).

Wu, Harry, and Carolyn Wakeman, *Bitter Winds: A Memoir of My Years in China's Gulag* (John Wiley & Sons, New York, 1994) is an autobiographical account focused on the first author's experience in China's labour camps from 1960 to 1979. Wu, 'who was reimprisoned for two months in 1995, paints an extremely cruel picture of prison life in China, and has probably done more than any other single person to promote a negative view of China's human rights record.

Yan Jiaqi and David S.K. Hong (transl. Denis C. Mair), with a foreword by Andrew Nathan, *Toward a Democratic China: The*

Intellectual Autobiography of Yan Jiaqi (University of Hawaii Press, Honolulu, 1992). Yan Jiaqi was a victim of the Cultural Revolution and took part in many of China's most dramatic events. In the period of reform he became an 'establishment' intellectual and political thinker but took an active part in the democracy movement of 1989 and, when it was suppressed, fled to the West. His autobiography is thus also highly relevant to democratic thinking and political development in China.

Yang, Benjamin, *Deng: A Political Biography* (M.E. Sharpe, Armonk NY, 1998). Taking a basically chronological approach, this study traces Deng Xiaoping's career from his birth in 1904 to 1996. It is based on over ten years' research, some connections with Deng's family, and other materials. The book provides enormous detail on elite-level CCP politics, Ross Terrill's Foreword claiming that the biography's 'single greatest contribution' is 'to lay bare the political mind of Deng' (p. xi).

F FOREIGN RELATIONS

Chan, Gerald, *Chinese Perspectives on International Relations: A Framework for Analysis* (Macmillan, Houndmills and London, St. Martin's Press, New York, 1999). Focusing on the 1990s Chinese views of international relations and international politics, this book aims to bridge the gap 'between Western studies of Chinese international relations and China's own perception of its international relations' (p. x). The author laments the lack of a research on international relations theory in China, but acknowledges efforts in that direction.

Chen Jian, *China's Road to the Korean War: The Making of the Sino-American Confrontation* (Columbia University Press, New York, 1994). Based on published Chinese sources and interviews with Chinese, this book looks very closely at the period leading up to China's entry into the Korean War in October 1950. The author believes that Mao, believing conflict with the United States inevitable, brought China into the Korean War fundamentally because he saw Western imperialism as the main enemy of the Chinese people and revolution.

Christensen, Thomas J., *Useful Adversaries: Grand Strategy, Domestic Mobilization, and Sino-American Conflict, 1947–1958* (Princeton University Press, Princeton, 1996). This book focuses on two periods: 1949–50 and the Taiwan Straits crisis of 1958. It argues that American domestic politics had already confirmed the hostility between the two countries well before the Korean War and was the determining factor in the hostile relations of the 1950s.

Economy, Elizabeth, and Michel Oksenberg (eds.), *China Joins the World: Progress and Prospects* (Council on Foreign Relations Press, New York, 1999). Includes chapters on China's participation in the United Nations, the international economy and telecommunications, as well as on human rights, environmental protection, and international finance. The main conclusion is that China has been very keen to join the world, but takes care to avoid intrusions in its national sovereignty.

Faust, John R., and Judith F. Kornberg, *China in World Politics* (Lynne Rienner, Boulder, 1995). This book looks at China's options in the 1990s, with the basic question whether it will become a major world actor or remain reactive. Also covered are China's relations with the United States, the Soviet Union/Russia, Asian neighbours, including Japan, and others aspects of China's international relations. The conclusion moots several scenarios for the future.

Foot, Rosemary, *The Practice of Power: U.S. Relations with China Since 1949* (Oxford University Press, Oxford, 1995). After a theoretical chapter, in which such factors as culture, ideology and institutions are given space as foreign policy determinants, this study takes up various facets of American policy towards China, such as China's role in the United Nations, trade, the effect of public opinion, the perception of threat, and the role of nuclear weapons. The author demonstrates how such factors as American domestic politics have affected attempts to isolate, confront or engage with China.

Garson, Robert, *The United States and China Since 1949: A Troubled Affair* (Pinter, London, 1994). This book aims to be an introduction, not to supersede other research. It has eight chapters, arranged chronologically, including one dealing with the eight years preceding 1949 and the last dealing with the period from 1989 to Clinton's early years as president. The author sees the Sino-American relationship as a 'troubled affair'. He believes the United States no longer wishes to be an international policeman but that it 'remains convinced as ever that in China, as elsewhere, a free market in goods will inevitably be followed by the market of ideas' (p. 219).

Garver, John W., *Foreign Relations of the People's Republic of China* (Prentice Hall, Englewood Cliffs, 1993). Designed as a textbook, this comprehensive survey of China's foreign relations from 1949 to 1992 takes a primarily thematic approach. Six sections and fifteen chapters cover such topics as historical influences, relations with the superpowers, China as a revolutionary power, international economics, external threat and internal security, and the future of Chinese power.

Goodman, David S.G., and Gerald Segal (eds), *China Rising: Nationalism and Interdependence* (Routledge, London and New York, 1997) analyzes 'the nature and implications of . . . rising China' (p. 1). Based on a 1996 conference, its focus is on the 1980s and 1990s and it takes up issues such as whether China has an arms control policy, China's role in the WTO and APEC, and the extent to which the PLA makes foreign policy. In the final chapter '"Enlitening" China?', Segal develops the concept that China must be made to adapt to interdependence with the world and, though 'given more space in the international system', must be 'constrained when it undertakes unwanted action' (p. 189).

Harding, Harry, *A Fragile Relationship: The United States and China Since 1972* (Brookings Institution, Washington, 1992). Taking a basically chronological approach this book examines Sino-American relations in great detail from the Nixon visit to the early 1990s. Looking into the future, the author believes the relationship 'is likely to be a less central one for the United States as the result of a more diverse and multipolar world' in the 1990s (p. 359).

Harris, Stuart, and Gary Klintworth (eds), *China as a Great Power: Myths, Realities and Challenges in the Asia-Pacific Region* (Longman, Melbourne and St Martin's Press, New York, 1995). A collection of essays dealing primarily with Beijing's relations with particular global regions or states across a range of topics. One of the conclusions the two editors draw in their final chapter, 'China and the Region After Deng', is that both the region and the West suffer from the lack of a coherent policy in dealing with a more influential and self-confident China (p. 366).

Johnston, Alistair Iain, and Robert S. Ross, *Engaging China: The Management of an Emerging Power* (Routledge, London, 1999). The authors provide a theoretical background to the issues involved in the strategies and options that various countries can adopt in the 'management' of China as a rising power. There are also individual chapters devoted to particular countries, including the United States, Japan, Singapore, Korea, Malaysia, and Indonesia, and a chapter on Taiwan's view.

Kent, Ann, *China, The United Nations, and Human Rights: The Limits of Compliance* (University of Pennsylvania Press, Philadelphia, 1999). This study considers the PRC's interaction with United Nations human rights bodies, such as the International Labour Organization, against the background of its own evolving human rights policies. It also takes up themes such as China and torture. It documents the extent of China's compliance with the norms and rules of international treaties, and of the effectiveness of the international human rights regime, concluding that 'the UN human rights regime has clearly made a difference, to both China and the international community' (p. 250).

Lewis, John Wilson, and Xue Litai, *China's Strategic Seapower: The Politics of Force Modernization in the Nuclear Age* (Stanford University Press, Stanford, 1994). The emphasis is on the post-Mao period, but there is a good deal of historical treatment as well. The book deals with the history and present condition of China's seapower, its nuclear submarines and its fleet ballistic missile weapons systems.

Nathan, Andrew J., and Robert S. Ross, *The Great Wall and the Empty Fortress: China's Search for Security* (W.W. Norton, New York, 1997). This book takes up China's relations with various countries as well as themes such as human rights. The authors argue against the 'China threat' theory. They believe that China is essentially vulnerable, with many rivals and potential enemies, and that its foreign policy has been essentially cautious and aimed at preserving stability.

Robinson, Thomas W., and David Shambaugh (eds), *Chinese Foreign Policy: Theory and Practice* (Clarendon Press, Oxford, 1994). Based on a conference held in 1990, this comprehensive account covers both domestic and international sources of Chinese foreign relations, as well as giving treatments of China's bilateral relations with such major countries as the United States and Soviet Union. The appendix is a valuable bibliographical essay by David Shambaugh.

Ross, Robert S. (ed.), *After the Cold War: Domestic Factors and U.S.–China Relations* (M.E. Sharpe, Armonk NY, 1998). Covering political and economic relationships, including the USA–China–Taiwan triangle, this book argues that domestic American politics exercise too great an influence in determining relations between China and the United States. The authors believe there is a tendency to sacrifice Sino-American relations to narrow interest groups, and are very keen to prevent issues like the place of Taiwan from poisoning relations altogether.

Ross, Robert S., *Negotiating Cooperation: The United States and China, 1969–1989* (Stanford University Press, Stanford, 1995). Based on a realist understanding of international relations, this study takes up case studies showing how China and the United States negotiated their bilateral relations over two decades. The author sees perceptions of the Soviet threat as the major determinant affecting cooperation, but for China Taiwan and national security were paramount.

Roy, Denny, *China's Foreign Relations* (Rowman & Littlefield, Lanham and Oxford, 1998). This takes an approach which is basically neo-realist and adopts the political science of international relations with the focus on China. The book covers the PRC, with a background 'historical overview of Chinese foreign relations', covering mainly the nineteenth and twentieth centuries. It also takes up themes such as China and the world economy, defending the PRC, China and global politics, and the future of China's foreign relations.

Segal, Gerald (ed.), *Chinese Politics and Foreign Policy Reform* (Kegan Paul International, London and New York for The Royal Institute of International Affairs, London, 1990). This collection of fourteen essays is essentially about the relationship between domestic and international affairs in China. Part One deals with domestic reforms, Part Two with the impact of the international system. While the issue is complex, the trend of argument is that domestic reform has affected foreign policy reform more than the other way around.

Segal, Gerald, and Richard H. Yang (eds), *Chinese Economic Reform: The Impact on Security* (Routledge, London and New

York, 1996). Based on a conference held in July 1994, the contributors analyze various aspects of how China's economic reforms have influenced its security, defence and foreign relations. None of the authors consider China an immediate threat, but Segal predicts that China could have the world's largest GDP and defence spending by 2020.

Stokes, Mark A., *China's Strategic Modernization: Implications for the United States*, (Strategic Studies Institute, US Army War College, Carlisle, 1999). This book explores the state of China's modern technologies and weapons systems and finds that it is placing a very high priority in these areas, largely with the aim of countering any potential American intervention in a conflict with Taiwan. The author argues for a more cautious American approach to China.

Sutter, Robert, *U.S. Policy Toward China: An Introduction to the Role of Interest Groups* (Rowman & Littlefield, Lanham, and Goulder, New York and Oxford, 1998) examines all the interest groups that tried to influence American China policy, with the focus on 1991–97.

Swaine, Michael D., *China: Domestic Change and Foreign Policy* (National Defense Research Institute, Rand Corporation, Santa Monica, 1995) analyzes the potential impact of China's domestic political, economic and social trends on foreign relations down to about 2010. The author predicts no dramatic change.

Tan, Qingshan, *The Making of US China Policy: From Normalization to the Post-Cold War Era* (Lynne Rienner, Boulder, 1992). The focus here is the processes leading to the formulation of American China policy, including Taiwan, arms sales, trade and MFN status. The author argues that American public opinion and political institutions play a major role in this formulation, which means that the relationship should not be reduced to the assertion of balance of power.

Westad, Odd Arne (ed.), *Brothers in Arms: The Rise and Fall of the Sino-Soviet Alliance,*

1945–1963 (Stanford University Press, Stanford, 1998). Based on newly available material, such as Soviet archives, this volume takes up major themes in Sino-Soviet relations, including economic relations, Soviet aid to China in the 1950s, military cooperation, and the impact of the Korean War. Relations between Stalin and Mao Zedong occupy an important place in the account. There is a long appendix of documents to which the authors refer.

Zhang, Yongjin, *China in International Society Since 1949: Alienation and Beyond* (Macmillan, Basingstoke, and St Martin's Press, New York, 1998). The author argues that China did not isolate itself in the 1950s and 1960s but was systematically excluded from multilateral diplomacy. Although this process was reversed in the following decades, China maintains an 'entrenched ambivalence' towards full integration into international society (p. 246).

Zheng, Yongnian, *Discovering Chinese Nationalism in China: Modernization, Identity, and International Relations* (Cambridge University Press, Cambridge, 1999) covers the rise of nationalism in China in the 1990s. The author sees two forms of nationalism, popular and official, and believes the two are in contradiction with each other, the authorities being able to constrain the more virulent popular nationalism. He regards nationalism as 'due to external stimulation' not to China's rapid development (p. 159), with the result that it unlikely to lead to chauvinism and need not concern foreign countries.

G THE ECONOMY, POLITICAL ECONOMY

Becker, Jasper, *Hungry Ghosts: China's Secret Famine* (John Murray, London, 1996). This book focuses on the famine of 1958 to 1962 resulting from the Great Leap Forward. The author argues that the famine was mainly man-made, not natural, and affected all parts of China.

Bian, Yanjie, *Work and Inequality in Urban China* (State University of New York Press,

Albany, 1994). Based on a sample survey of 1000 Tianjin resident in 1988 as well as on interviews and Chinese-language and other sources, this book examines urban work units in the period of reform. It has many conclusions, some of them different from conventional wisdom, for example that while relationships (*guanxi*) assist in gaining first employment, they do not necessarily help in later promotions.

Breslin, Shaun, *China in the 1980s: Centre–Province Relations in a Reforming Socialist State* (Macmillan, Basingstoke, 1996) covers mainly economic and political relations between the centre and provinces. The author argues that reform has produced a 'national economic structure that is characterized by provincial autarky' (p. 11).

Chai, Joseph C.H., *China: Transition to a Market Economy* (Clarendon Press, Oxford, 1997). Arranged by topic, this study gives a highly detailed overview of China's economic development in the period of reform. Topics include agriculture, industry, the price system, finance, foreign trade and investment, and the non-state sector. The final chapter makes comparisons with other transition economies.

Draguhn, Werner, and Robert Ash (eds), *China's Economic Security* (Curzon, Richmond, Surrey, 1999). The seven chapters cover such issues as energy future, unemployment, regional disparities, the grain problem and the environment. The book's assumption is that China's economic security is a major issue in regional stability, making it a topic of great importance.

Fewsmith, Joseph, *Dilemmas of Reform in China: Political Conflict and Economic Debate* (M.E. Sharpe, Armonk NY, 1994). Based on written sources, including official documents and economic journals, as well as interview material, this book traces the history of rural and urban reform since the late 1970s, with a strong emphasis on the relevant debates within the leadership. The author argues for more attention to be given to elite politics as a way of understanding the evolution of reform.

Findlay, Christopher, Andrew Watson and Harry X. Wu (eds), *Rural Enterprises in China* (Macmillan, Basingstoke, and St Martin's Press, New York, 1994). Based on surveys carried out on 90 rural enterprises in three provinces, this volume examines the enormous impact such enterprises have created on China's economic transformation in the 1980s and 1990s. The conclusion sees capital accumulation as more important than productivity for the generation of growth in the rural enterprises.

Gu Shulin, *China's Industrial Technology, Market Reform and Organisational Change* (Routledge in association with the UN University Press, London and New York, 1999) covers the evolution of science and technology reform policy and examines major approaches to institutional restructuring, especially the reform of the research and development system in China's machinery industry. In the final section, Gu tries to explain the changes she has discussed; she argues that market reform and organizational change depend on each other, which means that organizational design must be reformed to accord with market reform.

Hay, Donald, Derek Morris, Guy Liu and Yao Shujie, *Economic Reform and State-Owned Enterprises in China, 1979–1987* (Clarendon Press, Oxford, 1994). A highly technical work based on data from 400 of the larger state-owned enterprises, this book covers industrial policy and such matters as employment and wages, productive efficiency and costs, investment, and profits, the final chapter taking up ownership reform and relevant future options.

Hinton, William, *The Great Reversal: The Privatization of China, 1978–1989* (Monthly Review Press, New York, 1990) is primarily about economic change in the countryside from 1978 to 1989. The last chapter is a highly condemnatory critique of the 'Tiananmen Massacre', which the author considers 'the ultimate result of having betrayed the revolution ten years ago' (p. 189).

Howell, Jude, *China Opens Its Doors: The Politics of Economic Transition* (Lynne Rienner, Boulder, 1993). The focus here is on economic policy, foreign trade and foreign direct investment as ways of understanding China's economic relations with the capitalist world economy in the 1980s. There is some emphasis on the special economic zones and a special study of the Xiamen Special Economic Zone.

Huang, Yasheng, *Inflation and Investment Controls in China: The Political Economy of Central–Local Relations During the Reform Era* (Cambridge University Press, Cambridge, 1996). In this book a central question is why China has been able to avoid hyperinflation. The author believes the main reason is strong political centralization combined with economic decentralization. China remains authoritarian, with central power very strong through personnel decisions and provincial power, mainly economic. He argues strongly against the thesis that China will disintegrate.

Institute of Geography, Chinese Academy of Sciences, State Planning Committee, the State Economic Information Centre and the Institute of Statistics, State Statistical Bureau (comp.), *The National Economic Atlas of China* (Oxford University Press, Hong Kong, 1994) contains over 250 maps in ten sections, eight of them economic, with one on population, one on the provinces. There are also essays and booklets with extensive commentary.

Lardy, Nicholas R., *China in the World Economy* (Institute for International Economics, Washington, DC, 1994). The focus is on themes such as trade balances and trends, foreign investment, and Sino-American trade relations, all of which bear on the role that China's economy plays internationally. Also included are the prospects for the future and some policy recommendations.

Lardy, Nicholas R., *Foreign Trade and Economic Reform in China, 1978–1990* (Cambridge University Press, Cambridge, 1992). This wide-ranging analysis of changes in China's foreign trade system gives focus to the relationship between China's foreign trade reforms and domestic economic reform. It thus not only analyzes but also explains the transformation that has taken place.

Liew, Leong, *The Chinese Economy in Transition From Plan to Market* (Edward Elgar, Cheltenham, UK, and Brookfield, USA, 1997). This work concerns 'the transformation of China from a planned to a market economy' (p. 3). The focus is on three main areas, agriculture, industry and macroeconomic management, with attention given to political as well as economic problems.

Lin, Justin Yifu, Cai Fang, and Li Zhou, *The China Miracle: Development Strategy and Economic Reform* (Chinese University Press, Hong Kong, 1996). Putting forward an extremely positive view of the Chinese economy, this book asks such questions as why China has developed so rapidly since 1979 and whether it can continue doing so. Its approach is historical and comparative, and grounded in mainstream economics.

Naughton, Barry, *Growing out of the Plan: Chinese Economic Reform 1978–1993* (Cambridge University Press, Cambridge, 1995). Organized chronologically, this study traces the main trends in China's economic reform process, with emphasis on industry and macroeconomic policy. The author suggests that, though there was originally no careful plan for reform, a coherent package did eventually emerge; he argues that the Chinese experience shows that gradual change away from the command economy is feasible.

Oi, Jean C., *Rural China Takes Off: Institutional Foundations of Economic Reform* (University of California Press, Berkeley, 1999) discusses rural industries and development and entrepreneurship since 1976. The author argues that China's move from a rural planned economy to a market economy is largely the result of giving local officials fiscal incentives to build collectively owned factories and to reform the socialist economy gradually from the bottom up. This 'local state corporatism' is the main explanation for China's astounding rural economic success.

Park, Jung-Dong, *The Special Economic Zones of China and their Impact on Its Economic Development* (Praeger, Westport, Conn. and London, 1997). Originally published in Chinese, Japanese and Korean, this book focuses on the 1980s and is based mainly on interviews and fieldwork. There is general, interpretive coverage of the significance of the special economic zones, with chapters on the reasons for their formation and on their characteristics, as well as a study of nineteen Japanese and Korean enterprises.

Pearson, Margaret M., *China's New Business Elite: The Political Consequences of Economic Reform* (University of California Press, Berkeley, Los Angeles and London, 1997). In 1991 and 1995 the author carried out over 50 intensive interviews with Chinese in managerial positions in the foreign and private sectors, a new class created by economic reform and relatively autonomous from the state. The main aim was to find out if economic reform leads to political change by examining the attitudes of the 'new business elite'. The conclusion is that it does not necessarily do so and that democratization will not follow economic reform in China. Rather, the new elite are a hybrid of socialist clientelism and corporatism.

Putterman, Louis G., *Continuity and Change in China's Rural Development: Collective and Reform Eras in Perspective* (Oxford University Press, New York, 1993). This study, which focuses on the late years of Mao's rule and the period of reform, uses a township in Hebei Province as a case study but also places its findings in a national setting. Topics covered include changing efficiency, growth, and incentive structures.

Selden, Mark, *The Political Economy of Chinese Development* (M.E. Sharpe, Armonk NY, 1992). A collection of previously published articles, with an Introduction. Although there is a good deal about the Maoist period, the author's main concern is the period of Deng Xiaoping. The topics covered include socialism and the relationship between agriculture and the state. The focus is on questions of economic growth and investment, as well as rising inequality caused by the reform policies, on which the author's overall judgment is very mixed.

Shirk, Susan L., *The Political Logic of Economic Reform in China* (University of California Press, Berkeley, 1993). This book seeks to explain why China was able in the 1980s to adopt economic without political reform, while the Soviet Union was not. The explanation lies in Chinese institutions, which are examined in great detail. Much of the book is dedicated to a detailed account of policy-making in the field of state-owned industrial management and finance in the first decade of reform.

Solinger, Dorothy J., *China's Transition from Socialism: Statist Legacies and Market Reforms* (M.E. Sharpe, Armonk NY, 1993). A collection of previously published articles, with an Introduction. The main concerns are the urban economic reforms and the emergence of a new merchant class. The author see the whole economic reform program as a mechanism for bringing about 'a few fundamental and overarching statist ends' (p. 3).

Steinfeld, Edward S., *Forging Reform in China: The Fate of State-Owned Industry* (Cambridge University Press, Cambridge, 1998). This book examines the reform of the SOEs mainly through case studies of three very large examples: the Anshan, Ma'anshan, and Capital Iron and Steel Works. The author argues that private ownership cannot work in China's current system.

Tang Wenfang and William Parish, *Chinese Urban Life under Reform: The Changing*

Social Contract (Cambridge University Press, Cambridge, 2000). Based on recent national surveys, the authors show how rapid change from a planned to a market economy has affected urban life, including that of workers, civil servants, intellectuals, and women. Among other social factors the book analyzes emerging patterns of economic inequality, including gender inequality.

Tisdell, Clement A., and Joseph C.H. Chai (eds), *China's Economic Growth and Transition: Macroeconomic, Environmental and Social/Regional Dimensions* (Nova Science Publishers, Commack, NY, 1997). Eighteen chapters include an Introduction by the editors, eight on 'reforms and economic growth', three on 'environmental issues' and six on 'social and regional dimensions and more on efficiency: growing disparities'. The editors consider China's economic growth since 1978 impressive, but raise questions about the environmental impact and 'consequences for inequality of income in China especially regionally, by locality and according to ethnic groups' (pp. 1–2).

Vermeer, Eduard B., Frank N. Pieke and Woei Lien Chong (eds), *Cooperative and Collective in China's Rural Development: Between State and Private interests* (M.E. Sharpe, Armonk NY, 1998). This collection of conference papers examines various aspects of how the change from Mao Zedong's policies to those of the reform period have affected development in the countryside, with the emphasis on the role of the state and of local actors. Vermeer's Introduction is on 'China's new rural organization'. Besides some theoretical material, several chapters take up a particular place and topic, such as pastoral rangeland management in Ningxia, a comparison of two villages in Hebei, and the revival of a temple in a village in Western Sichuan.

Walder, Andrew (ed.), *China's Transitional Economy* (Oxford University Press, Oxford, 1996). Based on issue no. 144 of *China Quarterly* (December 1995), a special issue with the same title, this book collects studies that examine the interaction and interrelationship of politics and economics. It takes up topics such as historical background, institutions and incentives, and, in observing the sharp contrasts with Eastern European economies, explores the theoretical relevance of the Chinese case for transitional economies.

Wang Liming and John Davis, *China's Grain Economy: The Challenge of Feeding More than a Billion* (Ashgate, Aldershot, Hampshire, 2000) includes extensive empirical and theoretical material. The book covers government policy and agricultural development, grain supply and demand, projections for the future, and the trade implications of grain supply.

Waters, Harry J., *China's Economic Development, Strategies for the 21st Century* (Quorum Books, Westport, Conn. and London, 1997). The focus is on predicting China's economic future from an analysis of the present and recent past. The book covers such topics as industrial growth, investment, rural issues, and infrastructure. Its overall thrust is very optimistic.

White, Gordon, *Riding the Tiger: The Politics of Economic Reform in Post-Mao China* (Macmillan, Basingstoke and London, 1993). With the focus on the period of reform, this book covers such areas as the failure of the Maoist development state and the politics of agrarian and industrial reform, as well as the social impact of economic reform. It explores the basic dilemma that by achieving their aim, economic reforms 'set in train basic social and political changes which undermine the legitimacy and effectiveness' of the socialist state (p. 12).

Xing You-tien, *Making Capitalism in China: The Taiwan Connection* (Oxford University Press, Oxford and New York, 1998). Based on intensive research and interviews among Taiwanese investors in Guangdong, Fujian, Taiwan and elsewhere, this book discusses their role in South China's economy. It shows that Taiwanese investors deal directly with local officials, not the central bureaucracy, and effectively transmit a capitalist ideology to local factory workers. The success of the links between local officials and entrepreneurs is seen as based on a common culture, ethnicity and language.

Xu Gang, *Tourism and Local Economic Development in China: Case Studies of Guilin, Suzhou and Beidaihe* (Curzon, Richmond, Surrey, 1999) has five parts: theoretical and empirical background; the growth and structure of tourist demand; tourism infrastructure development; economic effects; and summary, prospects and policy issues. The conclusion takes a hard-headed look at the benefits of tourism, arguing that 'it seems clear that a short-cut to local prosperity via the vehicle of tourism, as has been hoped, does not exist' (p. 216), and makes some suggestions about the direction tourism should take, especially in Guilin and Suzhou.

Xu Xiaoping, *China's Financial System under Transition* (Macmillan, Basingstoke, and St Martin's Press, New York, 1998) reviews China's financial system from 1979 to 1992. The main argument is that the rapid growth in the number of financial institutions and markets has had a very beneficial effect on the economy; financial reform has greatly strengthened the ability of the financial system to mobilize savings, but has not been so efficient in allocating these savings.

You Ji, *China's Enterprise Reform: Changing State/Society Relations after Mao* (Routledge, London and New York, 1998). This book has four parts: on reshaping state and society relations; depoliticization; and two on 'de-statisation'. It examines the process of reform of China's units (*danwei*) and finds that economic liberalization in the period of reform has weakened CCP control at the factory level and tended to turn the units into corporations: 'de-danweiisation'. The author argues that this process will tend to democratize China.

Young, Susan, *Private Business and Economic Reform in China* (M.E. Sharpe, Armonk NY, 1995). Covering the revival of private enterprise in the period of reform, this book is based mainly on Chinese-language sources and interviews with private businesspeople, officials and scholars undertaken in the late 1980s and early 1990s. It posits changing power relations between local and central officials and private business, which the author sees as important for 'the kind of society and economy to develop from the reforms' (p. 9).

Zhou, Kate Xiao, *How the Farmers Changed China: Power of the People* (Westview Press, Boulder, 1996). With the focus on the countryside in the period of reform, this study covers such topics as markets, rural industries, migration to the cities, population, and women. The author argues forcefully that the farmers, not the CCP, have been the major force driving economic and social reform in China.

H POPULATION

Day, Lincoln H., and Ma Xia (eds), *Migration and Urbanization in China* (M.E. Sharpe, Armonk NY, 1994) is based on a survey carried out in 1986 in 74 towns and cities spread throughout sixteen provinces. It includes overviews, and topics such as urban–rural migration, differences between permanent and temporary migrants, inter-regional migration, and the demographic and family traits of migrants. There are many findings, such as that temporary migrants have come to outnumber permanent ones.

Peng Xizhe, *Demographic Transition in China: Fertility Trends since the 1950s* (Clarendon Press, Oxford, 1991). The chapters are on provincial family-planning programs, the determinants of fertility transition, national trends in fertility and nuptuality, and fertility transition in both urban and rural China, the arguments being supported by many tables and figures. Peng concedes the urgency and stringency of population control, but recommends that 'voluntary co-operation rather than coercion' will be more appropriate for the future program, and that population policy 'should be stabilized, without any rash changes, for a fixed period' (p. 294).

Poston, Dudley L., and David Yaukey (ed.), *The Population of Modern China* (Plenum Press, New York and London, 1992). This comprehensive study covers the PRC period, with brief historical background and some focus on the 1980s, as well as an Epilogue on the 1990 census. Topics include international migration, mortality, fertility, age and sex structure, marriage and family, ethnic composition and internal migration, and urbanization.

Qu Geping and Li Jinchang (transl. Jiang Baozhong and Gu Ran), ed. Robert B. Boardman, *Population and the Environment in China* (Lynne Rienner, Boulder, 1994). A translation of the Chinese-language *Zhongguo renkou yu huanjing* (1990), this book has a good deal of historical material but focuses on the PRC and its population policy. The authors argue that China's excessive population is the main reason for its environmental degradation.

Wang, Gabe T., *China's Population: Problems, Thoughts and Policies* (Ashgate, Aldershot, 1999). There are eight chapters, including on China's population thought since 1949, population distribution, minority population and future perspectives on China's population. The Conclusion points to the significance of China's population for the world.

Wang Jiye and Terence H. Hull (eds), *Population and Development Planning in China* (Allen & Unwin, Sydney, 1991). There are thirteen chapters by a range of authors covering various aspects of population, including its relation to resource management, the environment, urbanization, fertility and employment. Although the authors are not always in agreement with each other, the editors claim they 'share a strong admiration for the accomplishments of China's population policies' over the fifteen years to January 1988.

I GEOGRAPHY, BOOKS ABOUT SPECIFIC REGIONS

Barnett, A Doak, *China's Far West: Four Decades of Change* (Westview Press, Boulder, San Francisco and Oxford, 1993). This extraordinarily detailed book is based on the author's travels in western China in the late 1980s. Since he had extensive experience in the late 1940s, as well as from the early 1970s on, he was well placed to observe change. The particular places covered include Baotou in Inner Mongolia, Ningxia, Gansu, Qinghai, Xinjiang, Ganzi in Sichuan and Yunnan, most of them minority areas. The author foresees continued modernization and affirmative action for minorities, but no hesitation to use force on the part of leaders 'whenever and wherever there are direct challenges to Beijing's ultimate authority or Chinese sovereignty' (p. 660).

Blecher, Marc, and Vivienne Shue, *Tethered Deer: Government and Economy in a Chinese County* (Stanford University Press, Stanford, 1996). Based mainly on fieldwork, this book focuses on Shulu County in Hebei Province from 1970 to 1990. Through chapters on topics like county government, industry and industrialization, and commercial, urban and rural development, the authors argue that what changed over the period was not the development direction of local government but the mechanisms available to implement policy.

Chan, Anita, Richard Madsen and Jonathan Unger, *Chen Village under Mao and Deng* 2nd edn (University of California Press, Berkeley, 1992). This is a close examination of a village near Hong Kong. The second edition expands and updates the earlier one of 1984 through consideration of the period of reform, based on the authors' travels to Chen Village and other sources.

Dai Qing (comp.), John G. Thibodeau and Philip B. Williams (eds) (transl. Yi Ming), *The River Dragon has Come! The Three Gorges Dam and the Fate of China's Yangtze*

River and its People (M.E. Sharpe, Armonk NY, 1998). A collective book originally written in Chinese, this focuses most attention on the issue of the resettlement of people to make way for the Three Gorges Dam project. Dai Qing has long taken a strong stand against the project, as shown in such earlier works as Dai Qing (ed.), *Yangtze! Yangtze! Debate Over the Three Gorges Project* (Probe International, London, 1994). This book continues that opposition, her own introductory chapter being entitled 'The Three Gorges Project: A Symbol of Uncontrolled Development in the Late Twentieth Century'.

Forster, Keith, *Zhejiang in Reform* (Wild Peony, Sydney, 1998). Taking up Zhejiang's politics and economy in the reform period, this book seeks to explain why Zhejiang has done so well by comparison with other provinces. The author points to Zhejiang's traditional commercial culture as a major factor.

Gao, Mobo C.F., *Gao Village: A Portrait of Rural Life in Modern China* (Hurst, London, 1999). About the author's home village in Jiangxi Province, the book discusses several aspects of life since 1949, including population, living standards, health, education and change and continuity, as well as the impact of specific periods, such as the Great Leap Forward, the Cultural Revolution and the period of reform. His picture is considerably less damning of the Cultural Revolution and less enthusiastic about reform than most studies of China.

Hendrischke, Hans J., and Feng Chongyi (eds), *The Political Economy of China's Provinces: Comparative and Competitive Advantage* (Routledge, London, 1999) takes up seven case studies, showing their different economic and political development. The book argues that rather than being a single entity or market, China's provinces are in competition with each other and have different economic and political roles.

Ho, Samuel P.S., *Rural China in Transition: Non-Agricultural Development in Rural Jiangsu, 1978–1990* (Clarendon Press, Oxford, 1994) deals with industrial development and other non-agricultural enterprises in a single province, with information on a wide variety of topics, including economic conditions, ownership, structural change and standard of living. The author argues that control by local governments over the rural non-agricultural sector remains considerable enough to cast doubt on claims of the free market.

Hook, Brian (ed.), *Beijing and Tianjin: Towards a Millennial Megalopolis* (Oxford University Press, Hong Kong, 1998). Taking the Beijing–Tianjin Region as a single region, this book contains chapters on the history and culture, government and politics, geography and natural resources, human resources and economic development of the two cities. Because of its strategic location for international trade and other reasons, the editor envisages that the region's economic importance will grow greatly in the first decade of the new millennium.

Ikels, Charlotte, *The Return of the God of Wealth: The Transition to a Market Economy in Urban China* (Stanford University Press, Stanford, 1996) examines the Guangdong capital, Guangzhou, in the period of reform. It covers some of the city's history as well as many aspects of its contemporary life.

Linge, Godfrey J. R. (ed.), *China's New Spatial Economy: Heading Towards 2020* (Oxford University Press, Hong Kong, 1997). An update on G. J. R. Linge and D. K. Forbes (eds), *China's Spatial Economy* (Oxford University Press, Hong Kong, 1990). Apart from chapters on problems and linkages among China's regional economies, the book examines economic development in four coastal regions: the southeastern provinces, Shanghai, the Bohai Sea Rim and the northeast. The editor's Conclusion places great emphasis on the regional character of China and suggests that, despite better communications, the regions are in some ways growing apart and retain extremely different characteristics.

Lyons, Thomas P., *Poverty and Growth in a South China County: Anxi, Fujian, 1949–1992* (Cornell University, Ithaca, NY, 1994). Based on a county which the author claims as neither special nor advantageous, the book traces its experience of great poverty under Mao Zedong's policies to comparative prosperity in the period of reform. Although there is still poverty, standards of living have risen greatly.

Ruf, Gregory A., *Cadres and Kin: Making a Socialist Village in West China, 1921–1991* (Stanford University Press, Stanford, 1998) discusses how particular families and individuals have affected political, economic and social change in the village of Qiaolou in Meishan County, Sichuan. The author carried out his research mainly in 1990, revisiting Qiaolou briefly four years later. He shows how the relevant families and cadres were able to use major changes of the 1980s and 1990s, such as the introduction of village elections, to their own advantage in maintaining and even expanding control.

Walder, Andrew (ed.), *Zouping in Transition: The Process of Reform in Rural North China* (Harvard University Press, Cambridge, Mass., 1998) is a case study of rural industrialization in Zouping County, Shandong Province, based on field research by many researchers over the years 1988 to 1993. Spectacular improvement is shown in the standard of living and the economy generally, brought about by giving play to local officials' initiative in rural economic development.

White, Lynn T. III, *Unstately Power*: vol. 1, *Local Causes of China's Economic Reforms*; vol. 2, *Local Causes of China's Intellectual, Legal, and Governmental Reforms* (M.E. Sharpe, Armonk NY and London, 1998). These two volumes are a large-scale study of the Shanghai delta region. Volume 1 covers political economy and Volume 2 such topics as ideology, religion, arts, law, welfare and administration. White sees traditional networks of local power-holders as persisting in importance, but also the growth of institutions that could well lead to democratic governance in the future.

Yeung, Y.M., and K.Y. Chu, *Guangdong: Survey of a Province Undergoing Rapid Change* (Chinese University Press, Hong Kong, 1994). Focusing on the reform period since 1979, this large volume seeks to analyze change in many aspects of Guangdong's development. These include political, economic, social and environmental change, with the economic area covering agriculture and forestry, energy, industry and trade, money and banking and transport and communications. There is also a chapter on changing central–Guangdong relations. An updated edition was published in 1998.

Yeung, Y.M., and Sung Yun-wing (eds), *Shanghai, Transformation and Modernization under China's Open Policy* (Chinese University Press, Hong Kong, 1996). This very large and scholarly book focuses on Shanghai in the period of reform. It takes up political and economic issues, as well as those connected with urban and social infrastructure, such as housing and education, and 'topical perspectives' such as population, environment and 'Shanghai as a regional hub'. The Introduction argues (p. 19) that circumstances in the mid–1990s were the most propitious in more than half a century for Shanghai's future role in China.

J THE MINORITY NATIONALITIES

Barnett, Robert (ed.), *Resistance and Reform in Tibet* (Hurst, London, 1994). The editor's preface sees the book as a response to a 'dearth of studies on contemporary Tibet' (p. ix). Other than two introductory historical chapters, the focus here is on Tibet from 1950 to 1990. There is coverage of Tibetan identity, language and art, as well as on movements of resistance to Chinese rule, with strong emphasis on the years 1987–90.

Benson, Linda, and Ingvar Svanberg, *China's Last Nomads: The History and Culture of China's Kazaks* (M.E. Sharpe, Armonk NY and London, 1998). Of the seven chapters, four deal with a history of this Turkic minority of northwestern Xinjiang since 1949. There is also a chapter on their early history and one from 1912 to 1949. The final chapter deals with relations with Kazakhstan, a state undergoing revival of Kazakh cultural identity. The issue of pollution caused by nuclear testing is seen as very pressing, but the authors believe that China can easily quieten 'increasingly restive minorities like the Kazaks' (p 205).

Donnet, Pierre-Antoine (transl. Tica Broch), *Tibet: Survival in Question* (Zed Books, London, 1994). Written by a French journalist who visited Tibet in 1985, this book, an updated translation of the original French version, traces the history of Tibet under the PRC, with a background pre–1950 chapter. The author believes that Tibetan identity will not last long.

Du Ruofu, and Vincent F. Yip, *Ethnic Groups in China* (Science Press, Beijing, New York, 1993). Separate chapters are devoted to each of China's 56 nationalities. There are numerous and excellent coloured photographs.

Gladney, Dru, *Muslim Chinese, Ethnic Nationalism in the People's Republic* (Council on East Asian Studies, Harvard University, distributed by Harvard University Press, Cambridge, Mass. and London, 1991). Against a historical background and theoretical framework, this large-scale study takes up four Hui Muslim communities as case studies, emphasizing diversity. The author argues that the Hui people, 'once members primarily of religious communities . . . now very much see themselves as a bona fide ethnic group' (p. 323).

Goldstein, Melvyn C., and Matthew T. Kapstein (eds), *Buddhism in Contemporary Tibet: Religious Revival and Cultural Identity* (University of California Press, Berkeley, 1998). Although there is historical material, including a survey of the period since 1949, the core of this book is the revival of Buddhism in the Tibetan areas of China since 1978. The book examines the monastic life, pilgrimages, and 'ritual, ethnicity and generational identity'. The main theme of the book revolves around the link between Tibetan religion and identity.

Grunfeld, A. Tom, *The Making of Modern Tibet* (M.E. Sharpe, Armonk NY, 1996). This is an extremely detailed and thoroughly researched account of Tibetan history, nearly two-thirds of it dealing with the period since 1950. It is the second revised edition of a work originally published in 1987, and adds a chapter called 'The Last Decade, 1985–1995'. Two valuable appendices discuss Tibet's population and present the various attitudes towards Tibetan independence. The author's aspiration is towards 'disinterested and dispassionate history' (p. 5). This book is less critical of the Chinese and their role in Tibet than most English-language accounts of Tibet, but in his Conclusion he states that 'the future looks to me, at the moment, bleaker than a decade ago' (p. 247).

Hansen, Mette Halskov, *Lessons in Being Chinese, Minority Education and Ethnic Identity in Southwest China* (University of Washington Press, Seattle, 1999). Based on field research and historical sources, this book is a comparative study of education among the Naxi of Lijiang in northern Yunnan and the Dai of Sipsong Panna in the province's south, with the focus on the period of reform. The author argues that state policy, although intended to be applied uniformly across all minority regions, has proven much more successful in some places than others.

Kaup, Katherine Palmer, *Creating the Zhuang: Ethnic Politics in China* (Lynne Rienner, Boulder, 2000). This study considers the culture of China's most populous minority, the Zhuang, showing the CCP's skilful balancing of ethnic and regional loyalties since it came to power. It shows the greater demands for special treatment that the Zhuang have begun to make on the central government.

Lemoine, Jacques, and Chiao Chien (eds), *The Yao of South China: Recent International Studies* (Pangu, Editions de l'A.F.E.Y., Paris, 1991). This book is a collection of the papers given at a colloquium on Yao studies held in Hong Kong in May 1986. All are in English, despite the place of publication. There is a great deal of historical material, but most deals with the PRC. The topics covered include language, family and kinship, economy and religion, and arts and literature.

Mackerras, Colin, *China's Minorities: Integration and Modernization in the Twentieth Century* (Oxford University Press, Hong Kong, 1994). This book has three sections: the background; tradition and foreign impact 1900–49; and socialism within tradition: the People's Republic, 1949–93, the last part being by far the longest. The author considers policies towards the minorities, their economies, population problems and the implications of the minorities for China's foreign relations. He believes that the twentieth century has generally seen a correlation between integration and modernization and that the break-up of China due to secessionist problems, while possible, is far from inevitable.

Mackerras, Colin, *China's Minority Cultures: Identities and Integration Since 1912* (Longman, Melbourne, and St Martin's Press, New York, 1995). Other than the Introduction, the book has two chapters each (one covering the Republican period, the other the People's Republic) on religion, education, marriage, divorce and gender issues, and literature and the performing arts. The author does not expect a general cultural assimilation but believes that the minorities 'will maintain their own recognisable cultures—some of them powerfully' (p. 221).

Oakes, Tim, *Tourism and Modernity in China* (Routledge, London, New York, 1998). Emphasizing the relationship between tourism and modernity, this book examines the social, political and economic aspects of tourism. It analyzes the advantages and disadvantages of opening areas to tourism, with emphasis on the falsity of the modern tourist experience. Despite its title, its focus is on Guizhou Province and the minorities there.

Olivier, Bernard Vincent, *The Implementation of China's Nationality Policy in the Northeastern Provinces* (Mellen Research University Press, San Francisco, 1993). Despite its title, this book is actually about China's Korean minority. Basically chronological, Part One deals with the pre–1949 period, Part Two with the era of Mao Zedong, and Part Three from 1978 to 1989. The author, who bases himself on fieldwork and a wide range of Chinese-language, English-language, Russian, Korean and other sources, writes that the book attempts 'to illustrate the limits, but also the actual achievements of the party's nationality policy in the Northeastern provinces' (p. 7).

Rudelson, Justin Jon, *Oasis Identities: Uyghur Nationalism Along China's Silk Road* (Columbia University Press, New York, 1997). Based on fieldwork in Xinjiang in 1989 and 1990, especially in Turpan and Ürümqi, this book examines the ideas of various groups of Uygurs, the main minority of the Autonomous Region. It concludes that Uygur identity is rising, but doubts that this will lead to independence from China.

Safran, William (ed.), *Nationalism and Ethnoregional Identities in China* (Frank Cass, London, Portland, Or., 1998). Other than an Introduction by the editor, this book contains eight essays on various aspects of China's minorities, including language, the politics of identity, preferential policies, and religion and its impact on social relations. Regions covered include Xinjiang, Hainan, Inner Mongolia and Lijiang, Yunnan.

Schein, Louisa, *Minority Rules: The Miao and the Feminine in China's Cultural Politics*

(Duke University Press, Durham, 2000). Based on extensive fieldwork, this book is an ethnography of the Miao people. It focuses on the construction of Miao ethnicity in the period of post-socialist reform, and its reworking by the state, non-state elites and the Miao themselves.

Shakya, Tsering, *The Dragon in the Land of Snows: A History of Modern Tibet since 1947* (Pimlico, London, 1999). Based on Western, Chinese and Tibetan sources, this extremely detailed and copiously documented study takes a chronological approach to the history of modern Tibet. The author, a Western-trained Tibetan, states that the study was inspired by 'the generalised treatment' of the Tibetan issue internationally and 'the simplistic manner in which it was discussed' (p. xxi).

K EDUCATION

Cherrington, Ruth, *China's Students: The Struggle for Democracy* (Routledge, London and New York, 1991) takes up the history of student movements and political activism in the PRC, with the main focus on the student movement of 1989. The author was an eyewitness of much of the story she relates; she was 'caught up in the pro-democracy "fever"' (p. 170) of May 1989, but had to leave Beijing just after the movement was suppressed during the night of June 3–4.

Cherrington, Ruth, *Deng's Revolution: Young Intellectuals in 1980s China* (Macmillan, London, and St Martin's Press, New York, 1997). This study of China's educated youth in the 1980s is based on interviews, other primary data collected in China, and primary sources. It discusses China's youth and especially educated youth in the 1980s. It characterizes them as disaffected and cynical, with a brief period of political activism towards the end of the decade being shattered by the suppression of the student movement in June 1989.

Cleverley, John, *The Schooling of China* 2nd rev. edn (Allen & Unwin, Sydney, 1991). Takes a basically chronological approach,

with Chapters 5 to 15 about the PRC. The second edition updates the first, which came out in 1985, for example adding a section on the 'pro-democracy movement' of the late 1980s, the author commenting that 'the student demonstrations of the 1980s should be seen as part of their historical role in modern China' (p. 320).

Du Ruiqing, *Chinese Higher Education: A Decade of Reform and Development (1978–1988)* (Macmillan, Houndmills and London, 1992). Apart from a background historical chapter, this book covers such topics as management and structure, curriculum, faculty, students and exchanges with other countries. The material is based on policy documents, journal reports and interviews or correspondence with Chinese students, scholars and educational leaders. It concludes with a series of recommendations.

Epstein, Irving (ed.), *Chinese Education: Problems, Policies, and Prospects* (Garland, New York and London, 1991). In sixteen chapters, and an Introduction by the editor, this book covers such topics as education at various levels from early childhood to universities and adult education, teaching, gender, the administration of education and political education. The focus is educational change in the period of reform, and a major aim is 'to place Chinese educational policies within the broader social context of Chinese development' (p. xiii).

Hayhoe, Ruth (ed.), *Education and Modernization: The Chinese Experience* (Pergamon Press, Oxford, 1992). Of the thirteen chapters, the first three deal with dynastic and pre–1949 education, the fourth from the late 1950s to the late 1970s. Later chapters deal with the period of reform and take up particular issues relevant to modernization and education, such as the eradication of illiteracy, workers' education, distance education, teachers, moral-political education, curriculum, women's education and the education of minorities.

Pepper, Suzanne, *China's Education Reform in the 1980s: Policies, Issues, and Historical*

Perspectives (Institute of East Asian Studies, University of California, Berkeley, 1990). This fairly comprehensive study looks at how historical views on ideology and education have affected the 1980s, especially primary, secondary and higher education. There is also some commentary on the educational aspects of the 1989 crisis.

Pepper, Suzanne, *Radicalism and Education Reform in 20th-Century China* (Cambridge University Press, Cambridge, 1996). Other than a general explanatory Introduction, this book has three parts. The first deals with the Republican period, and the second with 'Learning from the Soviet Union', which two parts the author designates as 'a search for the origins of radical reform' (p. 4). The third part deals with the Cultural Revolution; there is brief coverage of its aftermath, but, since the book is about radicalism, there is no focus on the period of reform.

Peterson, Glen, *The Power of Words: Literacy and Revolution in South China, 1949–95* (University of British Columbia Press, Vancouver, 1997). In eleven chapters focusing mainly on Guangdong Province, this book covers not only 'literacy and society in modern China' and 'literacy and economic development in the post-Mao era', but also many matters relating to education under the PRC, such as 'the contested priorities of early postrevolutionary mass education' and 'the problem of the teachers'. The author argues a strong impact by power-brokers on the social definition of literacy; and the failure of policies on literacy to redress social inequalities, even in a rich province such as Guangdong.

Events that have featured in China's foreign relations since 1949 are given in detail in a special category in Chapter 1, while Chapter 4 devotes a section to the substantial literature on the same topic. This is an enormous topic, and manageability requires it to be severely restricted. Apart from listing China's diplomatic relations with the countries of the world, this chapter takes up a small selection of those relationships and issues of greatest importance to China and the world, with a very strong emphasis on the years since 1990. This involves omitting some relationships of great importance, such as China's with Japan and Vietnam, as well as with the countries of Western Europe (other than Britain over the single issue of Hong Kong).

China's overwhelming foreign relations aims since 1949 have been the defence of its own security and interests, and the desire for international respect. Consequently, its dominant concerns have been first with the United States and the Soviet Union and its main successor state Russia; second with the nations, interests and conflicts of its own region; and third with general international bodies, in particular the United Nations. Although China has tried to befriend most of the nations of the Third World, these countries have rarely loomed as large in its thinking as any of the categories of nations and issues mentioned above; nor have they been as important as China's public pronouncements might suggest.

RELATIONS WITH THE SOVIET UNION

The Soviet Union recognized the new PRC on October 2, 1949, formal diplomatic relations being established the next day. Mao Zedong and Zhou Enlai visited Moscow shortly afterwards and the Sino-Soviet Treaty of Friendship, Alliance and Mutual Assistance was signed in Moscow on February 14, 1950. The excellent relations China enjoyed with the Soviet Union thereafter began to deteriorate after Khrushchev's de-Stalinization speech at the Twentieth Congress of the Communist Party of the Soviet Union (see Chapter 1, A. February 25, 1956). In April 1960 China charged, through an article in its main ideological journal *Red Flag*, that the Soviet Union was changing and negating Lenin's concept of imperialism, and thus began serious polemics with its former ally.

National issues quickly assumed much more importance than ideological ones. The Soviet Union believed the Great Leap Forward and the establishment of the people's communes in 1958 to be not only un-Marxist but also exercises in madness, and in the summer of 1960 withdrew all its experts from China, causing serious problems for a Chinese economy that was already in dire straits. According to a later Chinese claim, the Soviet Union refused to fulfil a nuclear-sharing agreement it reached with the Chinese leadership in 1957.

The Soviet Union also denounced the Cultural Revolution in strong terms. In 1969 Sino-Soviet relations reached a nadir, with armed clashes along the border. By then China had reached the conclusion that Soviet social imperialism was an even more serious threat to its security and to the peace of the world than United States imperialism.

The death of Mao Zedong in 1976 at first opened the possibility of a thaw in relations, but the Chinese soon let it be known that they still regarded opposition to Soviet interests as the linchpin of their foreign policy. A long article published in *People's Daily* on November 1, 1977 fulsomely praised Mao Zedong's theory of the 'three worlds', and in foreign policy terms gave top prominence to its anti-Soviet implications. In the late 1970s China's relations with the Soviet Union again worsened, due to the Soviet invasion of Afghanistan, which began at the end of 1979, and other factors.

In 1982 the Soviet Union began very tentatively to seek a normalization of relations with

China, which responded by setting down 'three obstacles': troops along the Sino-Soviet and Sino-Mongolian borders; Soviet support for Vietnam's occupation of Kampuchea; and the Soviet occupation of Afghanistan. At first progress towards normalization was extremely slow, but it gathered momentum following Mikhail Gorbachev's accession to power in 1985. In a major speech made in Vladivostok (see Chapter 1, **A**. July 28, 1986), he made several concrete proposals to improve relations, including cooperation in space exploration. In mid-May 1989, Gorbachev made a major visit to Beijing and Shanghai, during which relations were declared 'normalized' in a joint communiqué.

Jiang Zemin led a high-ranking delegation to the Soviet Union in May 1991, marking the best situation in Sino-Soviet relations since the relationship had begun to deteriorate in 1956. This was only the highest in level of a number of bilateral visits since Gorbachev's to China in May 1989. It signalled the ironical fact that Sino-Soviet relations had reached a peak when the Soviet Union fell at the end of 1991. China's reaction to the declaration that the Soviet Union had been replaced by the Commonwealth of Independent States (December 25, 1991) was to declare its respect for the wishes of the individual republics and its wish to continue amicable relations with all of them. On December 27, it sent cables of recognition to all but one of the newly independent republics. The exception was Latvia, which had declared its intention to establish consular relations with Taiwan.

CHINA AND THE COMMONWEALTH OF INDEPENDENT STATES

In general, China has enjoyed better relations with the non-Communist Russia than it had with the Soviet Union. Jiang Zemin made several visits to Russia and other countries that had formerly been part of the Soviet Union. While he was there in May 1991, the two countries had signed an agreement ending their dispute over the eastern section of their common border, the agreement being ratified by both parliaments in February 1992. During Jiang Zemin's visit to Russia in September 1994, the leaders agreed on a 'constructive partnership' of equality, mutual benefit and friendship. They also agreed not to target their strategic missiles at each other. Perhaps most important, they presided over the signature by their foreign ministers of an agreement on demarcation of the shared borders in the west, thus settling almost all the two countries' mutual borders and ending bitter disputes that had even erupted into military clashes in the past.

Russian President Boris Yeltsin visited China in December 1992. He described the visit as heralding the dawn of a new epoch, and the two countries agreed to regard each other as friends. Even more striking, the Japanese news agency Kyodo reported that a secret document was signed during Yeltsin's visit calling for closer military cooperation between the two countries as a means of breaking the Western embargo on the transfer of military technology.[1] He visited China several more times during the 1990s. The joint statement of April 25, 1996, signed during one of Yeltsin's visits to China, expresses great confidence in the strength of bilateral relations and offers mutual support concerning major questions of sovereignty; for instance China supports Russia's attempts to maintain national unity, including its position on Chechnya (with which Russia was fighting a war to prevent its secession from the Federation), while Russia recognized both Taiwan and Tibet as inalienable parts of China. On April 23, 1997, during another visit by Jiang Zemin to Moscow, Russia and China signed a joint statement which pledged that 'the two sides shall, in the spirit of partnership, strive to promote the multipolarization of the world and the establishment of a new international order'.

There was also much attention to China from the other states of the former Soviet Union. The presidents of several of them visited China towards the end of 1992, including those of Ukraine, Moldova and Turkmenistan, while Qian Qichen visited

Uzbekistan, Kyrgyzstan, Kazakhstan and Russia. For its part, China was particularly keen to maintain good relations with these countries, especially those with common borders. In April 1996 the presidents of China and the four countries of the former Soviet Union with which it shared borders, namely Russia, Kazakhstan, Kyrgyzstan and Tajikistan, began an annual series of meetings to discuss mutually important matters, such as trade, overall international affairs, building confidence along the borders, and ensuring mutual recognition of each others' ethnic and other interests. (See Chapter 1, **A**. April 25, 1996, April 24, 1997, July 3, 1998, August 25, 1999).

When the Kosovo crisis erupted in 1999 (discussed in greater detail below), China and Russia found themselves on the same side against NATO. Russia was very quick to offer sympathy when NATO aircraft bombed the Chinese Embassy in Belgrade on May 7. Boris Yeltsin immediately sent former premier Viktor Chernomyrdin, who had been trying to broker a peace deal in Yugoslavia, to Beijing for talks with Chinese leaders. The talks showed a shared interest and view between the two countries, and it was clear that the crisis had driven them even closer together.

Later the same year, the Russian government blamed bombing incidents, in which apartment buildings in Moscow were blown up, on Islamic 'terrorists' from Chechnya and decided once again to destroy the secessionist leadership there. The war was carried out fiercely but involved significant civilian casualties and drew hostile comments from the West. However, Russia found support from China. In mid-October 1999, Foreign Ministry Spokesperson Zhang Qiyue told a news conference that the Russian government had an obligation to 'safeguard its national unification, territorial integrity and social stability' and declared the Chechnya crisis an internal matter for Russia. When Yeltsin made his final visit to China as president (see Chapter 1, **A**. December 9–10, 1999) he was assured by Jiang Zemin of China's support for his war

in Chechnya. One section of the final communiqué read: 'The Chinese side supports the government of the Russian Republic's action in fighting terrorism and splitism forces', while Russia expressed its support for China's sovereignty over all its provinces.

RELATIONS WITH THE UNITED STATES AND THE WEST

Relations under Mao Zedong

The PRC's relations with the main capitalist countries of the world began on a bad footing. In August 1949, even before the establishment of the PRC, the US government issued a white paper denouncing Mao Zedong's statement of the previous month, that China under the CCP would 'lean to one side', namely that of the Soviet Union. Great Britain, however, recognized the PRC in January 1950.

It was the Korean War of June 1950 to July 1953 that solidified hostility between the PRC and the capitalist countries, by far the most important of which was the United States. A UN resolution of June 27, 1950 called on UN members to assist the Republic of Korea, and several Western countries, including the United States, Britain and Australia, sent troops. China immediately denounced the resolution as illegal, and in October its troops began fighting on behalf of the Democratic People's Republic of Korea. This meant that Chinese troops and those of several Western countries were taking part on opposing sides. Each side declared the other to be the aggressor in Korea, but China also feared for its own security, and even accused the United States of air intrusions and the use of germ warfare in its northeast.

Several issues kept Sino-American relations at a low ebb in the late 1950s and early 1960s. These included a crisis in the Taiwan Straits between August and October 1958 and Tibet. The United States was among many countries condemning the Chinese for violating human rights in Tibet and suppressing the uprising there in March 1959, while China accused the United States of directly assisting the old ruling classes to mount the rebellion in the first place (see Chapter 1, **B**. March 1959 and Chapter 9).

United States intervention in Vietnam (with combat troops from 1965 on) made relations with China even more bitter than in the preceding few years, since China supported the left-wing forces that were fighting against the United States. However, in contrast to the Korean War, Chinese troops never intervened in Vietnam, nor did United States ground troops actually invade North Vietnam; as a result, Chinese and American troops never fought against each other in Vietnam. For China, the poison tended to go out of relations with the United States as those with the Soviet Union worsened in the late 1960s.

It was during the 1970s that most of the capitalist countries and others friendly with them established diplomatic relations with the PRC. The US president, Richard Nixon, visited China in February 1972, resulting in a vast improvement in China's image in the West.

RELATIONS UNDER DENG XIAOPING TO 1989

Early in 1979, to enormous fanfare, Deng Xiaoping visited the United States just after the formal establishment of relations between the two countries at ambassadorial level. This represented one of the most intense points of China's friendship with the West and hostility towards the Soviet Union.

During most of the 1980s, China proclaimed its foreign policy to be 'independent'. The Western countries and Japan were happy to contribute to China's modernization programs; consequently its overall relations with them remained generally positive. Economic and sociocultural ties between China on the one hand, and the Western countries and Japan on the other, expanded to represent a substantial investment by each side in the other.

In the case of the United States, the major problem in the early 1980s remained the issue of Taiwan. China expressed extreme displeasure over the continuation of United States arms sales to Taiwan. In August 1982, a joint communiqué was signed in Beijing by Chinese and American representatives, in which the United States declared it would eventually cease the arms sales, but gave no timetable for doing so. Although the communiqué did not really resolve the issue, neither side chose to allow it to disrupt bilateral relations unduly.

In 1987, Tibet re-emerged as an issue in Sino-American relations. In September, during a visit to the United States, the Dalai Lama called for Tibet to be designated a 'zone of peace' and denounced China's policies and actions there. Immediately afterwards, pro-independence disturbances broke out in Lhasa and were suppressed by the Chinese authorities. The United States condemned China for human rights breaches, while China demanded that the United States stop interfering in its domestic affairs (see also Chapter 1, **B**. September 27, October 1 and 6, 1987). A series of similar disturbances among the Tibetans followed over the following months, the worst occurrence being in March 1989. These events produced similar condemnations in the United States and counter-reactions from the Chinese government.

For Great Britain, Hong Kong was the main issue in relations with China in the 1980s and much of the 1990s. In September 1982, in response to a statement by British Prime Minister Margaret Thatcher that the treaties of the nineteenth century should continue to be regarded as valid, the Chinese Foreign Ministry reaffirmed its commitment to the reassertion of China's sovereignty over Hong Kong. In December 1984, Thatcher and Chinese Premier Zhao Ziyang signed the Sino-British Joint Declaration on Hong Kong, under which China would resume sovereignty over Hong Kong from July 1, 1997. Despite many issues of disagreement, attempts to work together for a reasonable transfer of power yielded some results.

RELATIONS WITH THE WEST IN THE AFTERMATH OF THE BEIJING MASSACRE

All Western and other advanced capitalist industrialized nations reacted with strong horror and condemnation to the Beijing massacre of early June 1989. Although none of them actually broke off diplomatic or economic relations, China was downgraded in their priorities and they took concrete measures of various kinds to show their disapproval, provoking pained and hostile reactions from China (see Chapter 1, A. 1989). Western and Japanese tourism to China declined sharply, and China's image in the West suffered severely. Human rights violations against pro-democracy dissidents were added to those against the Tibetans as a major issue in China's relations with the Western countries, and the United States in particular, occupying a far higher priority in Western diplomacy than had been the case before.

In an article on 'New China's Diplomacy: 40 Years On', marking the fortieth anniversary of the PRC's establishment in October 1989, the Minister of Foreign Affairs, Qian Qichen, claimed that China was still following a stand independent of the United States and the Soviet Union. He also attacked 'some Western countries' for regarding 'their values as absolute truth', and criticized them for interfering, exerting political pressure and applying economic sanctions.

The Chinese began an active human rights diplomacy by issuing a document in November 1991 entitled 'Human Rights in China'. Among many other points this argued that:

- in the right to subsistence, the foremost of all human rights, China's performance had been very good;
- it was necessary to take culture and history into account before making judgments on such matters as human rights; and
- China was in favour of international dialogue on human rights, but would never permit countries to interfere in its internal affairs using human rights as a pretext.

One of the results of the crackdown on the student movement of 1989 was debate over MFN status, which China had enjoyed with the United States since 1979. It meant that the tariffs which the United States government

imposed on trade with China were akin to those with non-communist countries instead of the higher and less favourable rate required of other communist countries. On July 10, 1991 the US House of Representatives rejected President Bush's decision to renew MFN unconditionally and adopted a resolution that the renewal of MFN should depend on China's fulfilling certain human rights conditions. Although the vote was not sufficient to reverse Bush's decision, China reacted furiously and attacked the House action as a dangerous signal for the future. In 1992 further legislation was passed by the Congress to the same effect, to the fury of the Chinese, but again Bush vetoed it (September 28).

All international relations throughout the world were affected by the collapse of the Soviet Union at the end of 1991. This event signalled the end of the bipolar world and Cold War which had dominated the globe for so long and left the United States as the single, and undisputed, superpower.

HONG KONG AND RELATIONS WITH BRITAIN, 1989–97

In Hong Kong, the crisis of mid–1989 had caused enormous worries about the future. Large-scale demonstrations occurred attacking the Chinese government from the time martial law had been declared in May 1989, and they were even larger after the crackdown. Nevertheless, China adopted its Basic Law on Hong Kong in 1990 (see Chapter 1, B. April 4, 1990), which followed the Joint Declaration of 1984.

There was acrimonious argument over the building of a new airport in Hong Kong, with the Chinese demanding to be consulted over a matter that would cost an enormous amount of money and would affect post–1997 Hong Kong, but Britain determined to press ahead regardless of what the Chinese might think. An agreement was reached on this matter in 1991 (see Chapter 1, A. September 3, 1991). However, it was not until much later that the two signed an agreement on the financing of the airport (see Chapter 1, A. November 4, 1994).

Relations worsened when Chris Patten took over as the last British governor of Hong Kong in July 1992. Much less well disposed towards the Chinese than his predecessor Lord David Wilson had been, he quickly made it clear that he would be less amenable to Chinese requests. In October 1992, he presented plans to expand the voting rights of Hong Kong citizens before 1997. The Chinese reacted angrily, seeing this move as contrary to the Joint Declaration of 1984 and the Basic Law of 1990. When Patten visited China in October 1992 it became clear that the Chinese leaders were in deep disagreement with his policies and the next month the Standing Committee of the NPC declared that China would not abide by Patten's reforms after it took control in 1997.

Even worse followed in mid–1993 when Patten got a bill on the initial procedures for elections passed by Hong Kong's Legislative Council (LegCo). China was convinced that Patten had turned his back on the 1984 Joint Declaration and, although Patten denied this, its spokespersons attacked him vigorously. When he visited the United States in May 1993 to push for the renewal of MFN, thinking he was doing the Chinese a favour by promoting their cause, China reacted very negatively and one Chinese source in nearby Shenzhen attacked him as a 'whore' who 'wanted a monument erected to his chastity'.[2] (Such attacks did not divert Patten from subsequently visiting the United States to support MFN for China.) In mid-December, when Patten took part of his electoral reform package to LegCo, Director Lu Ping of the State Council's Hong Kong and Macau Affairs Office declared that any person elected by Patten's elections would have to step down on June 30, 1997. However, despite Beijing's protests, Patten brought in the first stage of democratic reforms in February 1994, with the first democratic elections actually being held in September the same year; the NPC Standing Committee had just legislated (September 1) that all political structures which Britain established thereafter in Hong Kong would be abolished from July 1, 1997. In mid-September 1995 the first elections for all 60 seats in the LegCo resulted in victory for only sixteen of the Beijing-backed candidates, a Foreign Ministry spokesmen arguing that the elections were unfair and unreasonable and contrary to the December 1984 Joint Declaration.

Other arguments arose, such as over the recognition of British nationality of Hong Kong residents and whether they would be able to enter Britain freely after July 1, 1997. However, relations were somewhat better in the two years leading up to the handover than had been the case in the two years following Chris Patten's appointment as governor. The handover itself was attended by a range of British and Chinese dignitaries, notably Prince Charles and Jiang Zemin (see Chapter 1, **A**. June 30–July 1, 1997). Contrary to the expectations of many Western journalists, this magnificent ceremony occurred without any major mishaps.

SINO-AMERICAN RELATIONS UNDER CLINTON

Under US President Bill Clinton, relations between China and the United States were uneven and difficult, despite his policy of engagement, as opposed to containment. Individual events are recorded in Chapter 1.

A few months after coming to office in January 1993, Clinton announced extension of MFN status to China (see Chapter 1, **A**. May 29, 1993), but also his intention of attaching human rights and other conditions to renewal the following year. China condemned the statement as politicization of trade and interference in its internal affairs. The following year Clinton made a statement that effectively delinked trade and human rights (see Chapter 1, **A**. May 26, 1994), even though it also incorporated some expectations on China's part, including an improvement in human rights. China took the announcement as a major victory for its diplomacy. Human rights activists in the United States generally agreed with this verdict, although they thought the decision a disaster which simply promoted business interests above the morality inherent in an emphasis on human rights.

In 1997 Chinese President Jiang Zemin visited the United States and his American counterpart made a return visit the following year, both visits improving the overall relationship. Indeed, the joint statement that Jiang Zemin and Bill Clinton issued on October 29, 1997, during Jiang's visit, stated that 'the two Presidents are determined to build toward a constructive strategic partnership between China and the United States through increasing cooperation to meet international challenges and promote peace and development in the world'.

In April 1999, in conjunction with a visit Premier Zhu Rongji made to Washington, Clinton made a major speech on China which, despite some sharp criticisms, was strongly positive about the overall direction in which China was moving. In a detailed analysis of the situation in China he stated that 'in the last twenty years, China has made incredible progress in building a new economy, lifting more than 200 million people out of absolute poverty'. He praised China for having assisted the United States in several major foreign policy objectives, for example persuading North Korea to freeze its production of plutonium and averting a nuclear confrontation in South Asia. He denounced those who would 'contain' China and reminded his listeners that the American debate over China was mirrored by a similar debate in China over the United States. Nobody, he declared, could possibly gain from a Sino-American cold war 'except for the most rigid, backward-looking elements in China itself'.[3]

However, there were a number of issues that continued throughout most or all of Clinton's presidency to cause difficulties for the relationship. These included:

- problems over the status of Taiwan and Taiwan's increased attempts to operate as a state in the world community
- disagreements over human rights, their nature and the obligations they involve, and differing perceptions of each other's human rights performance
- the Chinese perception from about 1993 that influential circles in the United States

were again beginning to castigate China as a threat
- disagreements over trade and intellectual property rights
- the status of Tibet, with a large and vocal lobby not only charging China with human rights abuses there but actively pushing for Tibet's independence (see also Chapter 9)
- the difficulty of agreeing on terms by which the USA would support membership of the WTO (set up in January 1995).

Some of these are discussed below, as is a further issue emerging towards the end of the Clinton presidency: the Kosovo crisis of 1999.

Taiwan

Among these problems, the most serious was the question of Taiwan, because for China it bore on the issue of sovereignty. This and other issues made 1995 and 1996 particularly bad years for Sino-American relations, despite the Jiang–Clinton summit towards the end of 1995. (See several entries in Chapter 1, A. 1995.) The years 1999 and 2000 also showed this issue affecting the relationship.

When Taiwan President Lee Teng-hui visited the United States in June 1995, China reacted with real anger. Despite American protestations that Lee's was a private and unofficial visit, China feared that the United States was giving tacit support to an attempt it saw by Lee to separate Taiwan from China or to create 'two Chinas'. When Lee was in the United States, a PRC spokesman, Shen Guofang, commented that to allow Lee the visit had 'seriously damaged the foundation of Sino-US relations' and described it as 'this willful action on the part of the US government'.[4] The Chinese press issued a barrage of criticism against Lee Teng-hui for splitism, especially as supposedly expressed in his speech given at his alma mater Cornell University, and against the United States for encouraging him and giving him a forum.

In March 1996 the dispute over Taiwan escalated further when China carried out military exercises very near Taiwan, just before and even during the Taiwanese presidential election of March 23. The main motive was to express disapproval of Lee Teng-hui and any trend towards the independence of Taiwan. The United States responded by sending into the area the largest group of American military vessels assembled in Asia since the Vietnam War, including those with nuclear power, appearing to signal that, in the event of a Chinese attack, they would likely intervene. Each side regarded the other's action as provocative. At a news conference on March 11, 1996, Chinese Foreign Minister Qian Qichen responded to a question on the sending of the US *Independence* aircraft carrier into the Taiwan Straits area by remarking: 'It is preposterous for some people in the US to call openly for interference on the Taiwan issue by the Seventh Fleet, or even for protecting Taiwan. Maybe they have forgotten that Taiwan is part of China's territory, not a protectorate of the United States.'[5]

The issue of arms sales to Taiwan did not die completely. In mid–1999, the US Defense Department announced the sale of Hellfire missiles and electronic warfare equipment worth nearly US$90 million to Taiwan. China objected furiously, pointing out that this was in direct conflict with the agreement the two sides had signed on August 17, 1982 (see Chapter 1, **A**. August 17, 1982) and charging the United States with interference in China's internal affairs.

On the other hand, the United States did not support Taiwan's abandonment of the 'one China' principle, which it announced on July 12, 1999 (see Chapter 1, **B**. July 13, 1999). About a week after the announcement, President Clinton reaffirmed his commitment to the 'one China' policy during a telephone conversation with Jiang Zemin. Lee Teng-hui's view, put forward in an interview with German radio journalists on July 9, was that Taiwan's relations with the mainland were a matter of state-to-state relations. PRC spokespersons castigated this view sharply and consistently as the 'theory of two states'

(*liangguo lun*), since the PRC viewed these relations as those between two parts of one China. Although Taiwan's position gained advocates among many influential people in the United States, including some in Congress, the US Administration under Clinton offered it no support.

The issue became even more tense in 2000. On February 21, the PRC's Taiwan Affairs Office and the Information Office of the State Council issued a paper entitled 'The One-China Principle and the Taiwan Issue', in which it adopted an uncompromising stand on the Taiwan question. It denounced the position, taken by many in Taiwan and in the West, that the issue of democratization and democracy was central to this issue, despite the presidential election about to be held in Taiwan (March 18, 2000). One passage in particular caused anxiety and controversy generally, especially among concerned people in the West and Taiwan.

To safeguard the interests of the entire Chinese people including compatriots in Taiwan and maintain the peace and development of the Asia-Pacific region, the Chinese government remains firm in . . . doing its utmost to achieve the objective of peaceful reunification. However, if a grave turn of events occurs leading to the separation of Taiwan from China in any name, or if Taiwan is invaded and occupied by foreign countries, or if the Taiwan authorities refuse, sine die, the peaceful settlement of cross-Straits reunification through negotiations, then the Chinese government will only [*sic*] be forced to adopt all drastic measures possible, including the use of force, to safeguard China's sovereignty and territorial integrity and fulfill the great cause of reunification.[6]

The Taiwan election of March 18, 2000 brought the Democratic Progressive Party candidate Chen Shui-bian to power. The PRC reacted calmly but with dismay, reiterating its one-China stand but declaring it would wait and see how things developed under his leadership. Meanwhile Clinton's reaction to the election was to declare it a victory for democracy with the potential to bring about peaceful reunification between the mainland of China and Taiwan.

For China, an issue of considerable moment at the end of the twentieth century was Theater Missile Defense, an American proposal to use an anti-missile system to defend Japan, South Korea and even Taiwan. TMD was derived from a more general proposal for a national missile defence system. While in China in mid–1998, Clinton turned down a Chinese suggestion to exchange American refusal to involve Taiwan in the TMD for a Chinese pledge not to sell missiles to Iran. In August 1999, Taiwan's President Lee Teng-hui declared it desirable and in its own interests to belong to the TMD system, to the great anger of the PRC (see Chapter 1, **A.** August 20, 1999). In an interview in mid-August 2000, Chen Shui-bian appeared less certain, but signalled Taiwan's participation in TMD as likely. Despite American disclaimers that NMD and TMD were aimed against 'rogue states' such as Iran, Iraq and North Korea, China argued that so substantial a defence system was hardly needed against such countries and was convinced that NMD (and hence also TMD) were aimed against itself, specifically in the event of war over Taiwan. Russia and China were at one in their stand on NMD and TMD and, during July 2000, expressed their strong public agreement during meetings in Dushanbe, the capital of Tajikistan, and in Beijing.

In mid-July Israel cancelled an agreement made with Jiang Zemin during his recent visit there (see Chapter 1, **A.** April 12, 2000) to sell advanced weaponry to China. The United States had placed pressure on Israel, fearing that China would use the weaponry in any war over Taiwan.

Human rights

Although the human rights issue had become prominent in 1989, it continued as one of the main issues in Sino-American relations throughout the presidency of Bill Clinton.

Lobby groups in the United States and other Western countries demanded that their governments press the Chinese on human rights, and these were very willing to acquiesce in such a demand.

Throughout the 1990s, American Administration and government personnel, among others, made known their concern and demands concerning such matters as freedom of religion, especially in Tibet, the treatment of dissidents, and other matters relating to human rights. On several occasions, a Chinese show of conformity to American human rights demands was taken as a sign for a favour to be granted by the American Administration to China. A good example of this was the case of Harry Wu, an American Chinese whom the Chinese authorities had accused of espionage and arrested (see Chapter 1, **A.** July 8 and August 24, 1995). Wu's release after conviction was the cue for the Americans to agree both that President Clinton's wife Hillary should attend the forthcoming World Conference on Women (see below) and that a presidential summit should take place the following year in the United States. Sometimes the United States appeared simply to ignore China's sensitivities but then to make a conciliatory gesture. Thus, in April 1993, Clinton, who had just come to power, 'twitted' the Chinese leadership 'by receiving its old nemesis the Dalai Lama, Tibet's God King, at the White House',[7] knowing full well that the Chinese regarded the Dalai Lama as a splitter and strongly opposed such a meeting. But at the end of May he duly extended MFN, albeit with conditions.

American concern over human rights showed no sign of waning as the twentieth century drew to its conclusion. Americans reacted with great hostility to the news that, at the end of 1998, the Chinese authorities had cracked down on the new China Democratic Party, which had appeared to be gaining in support as a force for the kind of democracy favoured by the United States. When Secretary of State Madeleine Albright attended a reception to celebrate the twentieth anniversary of the establishment of diplomatic relations between the United States and China (January 1, 1979), she felt called on to criticize the crackdown, while some members of Congress refused to meet with a Chinese human rights delegation which was in the United States at the time. This was despite the fact that the delegation had come for the revival of the human rights dialogue that resulted from Clinton's visit to China in the middle of 1998. Yet human rights discussions did indeed take place over two days in Washington early in 1999, with agreements being reached on several major matters. Both sides agreed that human rights are universal, and that they should be treated in a comprehensive manner, meaning that economic, social and cultural rights as well as political and civil rights should be given equal importance.

In 1999 and 2000, the suppression of the Falungong added a further issue in the realm of human rights and freedom of religion. Many in the United States regarded this as a straight-forward case of religious persecution. The fact that the Falungong leader Li Hongzhi lived in the United States and was given protection there, against the opposition of the Chinese authorities, brought a foreign affairs dimension into China's policy towards the Falungong. On the other hand, because of the problems cults have created in the the United States, China's assertion that the Falungong was not a religion but a harmful cult did carry some weight with the American Administration and reduced the damage to bilateral relations involved in China's suppression of the Falungong.

In 2000, the United States tried again to have China censured by the UN Commission for Human Rights in Geneva. In response China broke off its human rights dialogue with the United States. In March Madeleine Albright actually addressed the Commission, arguing strongly that China's human rights had deteriorated in 1999 and demanding censure. On April 18, however, the annual meeting of the Commission voted 22–18 to refuse permission for full-scale discussion of the United States resolution, the ninth time

since 1990 that the anti-China motion had failed.

The 'China threat'

Hostility to China in the United States and other Western countries was due largely to criticism of its human rights record. But this hostility also bred a renewal of the notion that China was a threat to American and world security. This was fuelled strongly by the crisis over Taiwan in 1996 (see above), because the Chinese lobbing of missiles appeared to many in the United States as aggressive and threatening behaviour. But correspondingly the Chinese government reacted to such notions as ridiculous and merely a sign that many influential Americans wanted to prevent China's economic development and modernization, because of a fear that it would eventually challenge the American supreme place in the world.

In March 1999, Taiwan-born scientist Lee Wen-ho was dismissed from his position at a Los Alamos weapons research centre on suspicion of having given nuclear weapons secrets to China in 1988. Congressional Republicans took the cue to charge China with espionage and demand a review of China policy. Clinton denied the charges of Chinese espionage and restated his policy of engagement, categorically rejecting Republican demands for a review of China policy. Beijing responded to the affair quite caustically, with a mid-March commentary in the *People's Daily* declaring that the nuclear spying charges were not only groundless nonsense but had arisen from 'the rotten wood of the theory of a China threat', proponents wishing 'fundamentally to contain China's development and uphold America's world hegemony'.[8]

Late in May 1999, an American congressional investigative panel headed by Republican Christopher Cox, which had been working on the issue for eleven months, released a 700-page report that accused China of having stolen the secrets to every key American nuclear warhead made since the 1970s and even, apart from using the data itself, passing some of it to the enemies of the United States (see Chapter 1, **A.** May 25, 1999). China immediately charged that the report's results were not only absurd and without basis but also laden with ulterior motives. On July 15, 1999, the Information Office of the State Council issued a lengthy attack on the Cox report, charging it with deliberate deception and distortion on a grand scale. The Cox report was described as 'a farce with the aim of instigating anti-China sentiments and undermining Sino-US relations'.

The Kosovo crisis of 1999

In the meantime another divisive issue had arisen of great importance to both sides: the crisis in Kosovo, Yugoslavia. Late in March, NATO began bombing Yugoslavia on the grounds that it had refused to sign an agreement granting Kosovo more autonomy from Serbia and allowing NATO troops to supervise this greater autonomy. Hundreds of thousands of Albanian refugees immediately fled from Kosovo to Albania and Macedonia, an exodus that NATO blamed on Serbian 'ethnic cleansing'. China followed the Serbian line that it was the result of the NATO bombing. However, China regarded the bombing as immoral and was deeply concerned by the fact that NATO felt it had the right to bomb another country without UN authorization. For China the implication was that the United States would feel free to intervene in Taiwan or Tibet against China's wishes and even bomb China. The bombing was still going on during Zhu's visit to the United States.

The Kosovo issue assumed new seriousness as a divisive issue when NATO missiles hit the Chinese embassy in Belgrade, killing three Chinese (see Chapter 1, **A.** May 7, 1999 and **F.** May 8, 1999). China insisted on an emergency meeting of the UN Security Council, using it to denounce NATO and (unsuccessfully) to demand sanctions against NATO (see Chapter 1, **A.** May 7 and 8, 1999). Anti-American and anti-NATO demonstrations immediately broke out in Beijing and other major cities, with the Chinese

authorities endorsing the actions, but warning that they must stay within the law (see Chapter 1, **B.** May 8 and 9, 1999). The demonstrations in Beijing went on daily for four days, with similar protests in two dozen other cities, notably Shanghai, Guangzhou, Shenyang, Xi'an and Chengdu. Although they stopped on government order, the feelings of nationalism and anti-Americanism proved durable.

The United States acknowledged both that it had been American missiles that had struck the Chinese embassy and that the building had been targeted, but claimed to have believed that it was a Yugoslav government building with military significance; they were using out-of-date maps. President Clinton on several occasions described the bombing as a tragic mistake, denying absolutely that it was deliberate. This apology was inadequate to China, where official opinion, and most of the population, simply did not believe that such an attack could be accidental. On May 10, 1999, Foreign Ministry spokesman Zhu Bangzao declared that, as a protest against the bombing, China had decided to postpone high-level military contacts with the United States, its consultations in the fields of proliferation prevention, arms control and international security, and its human rights dialogue. Senior Chinese statesmen, such as Jiang Zemin and Zhu Rongji, who had been known for their pro-American feelings, began to withdraw from their stance. What was quickly clear was that the effect of the bombing, whether accidental or not, would produce a long-term and hostile effect on China's view of the United States and on Sino-American relations.

Negotiations followed over apology and compensation. On December 16, 1999, a deal was announced by which the US Administration would ask Congress to appropriate US$28 million as compensation for the bombing of the Embassy and the deaths of the three Chinese, while China would pay US$2.87 million to compensate for damage done by protestors to American consular facilities in China. In April 2000, the Central

Intelligence Agency announced punishments, mainly reprimands, to officials it blamed for the inaccurate information leading to the disaster. However, China continued to refuse to believe that the bombing of its Belgrade embassy was other than deliberate.

The World Trade Organization

The WTO was set up in 1995 in succession to the GATT with the primary aim of liberalizing international trade. China had withdrawn from the GATT in 1950 but began negotiating to rejoin in the mid–1980s. It was refused permission to join the WTO as a founding member, and negotiations thereafter, though sometimes intense, came to nothing. According to one authority, 'Obstacles to membership included US efforts to link WTO membership to political issues and China's concern at the adjustment costs that the removal of protections and subsidies might bring to domestic manufacturing and agriculture'.[9] During Zhu Rongji's April 1999 visit to the United States, he offered a range of concessions to reach an agreement with the United States through which China could join the WTO but, although 'progress' was made on the issue, no conclusion was reached, the United States refusing at the last minute to commit itself to China's entry.

Late in 1999 (see Chapter 1, **A.** November 15, 1999), the United States and China finally signed an agreement by which the Americans allowed China into the WTO. Considering they had been arguing over the issue for thirteen years, this was a significant breakthrough with the potential to improve Sino-American relations greatly, as well as to bring China into the international economy much more thoroughly. Under the agreement, China won:

- crucial American support to join the WTO on the basis of being a developing economy rather than, as the United States had consistently insisted, a developed one
- a promise that Clinton would persuade Congress to grant China permanent normal trading relations
- substantial concessions in the area of textiles.

The United States won:

- reduced import duties (from an average of 22.1 per cent to an average of 17 per cent after WTO entry)
- far greater access to China's telecommunications, cinema and financial services markets
- greatly reduced tariffs on automobiles and automobile parts, and selected agricultural products, such as cotton and rice.

In mid-February 2000, Clinton requested Congress to support permanent NTR, arguing that this would assist trade in the interests both of the United States and China, and that it would assist the rise of democratic values and politics and improve human rights in China. However, a coalition including the following main groups attempted to defeat passage of permanent NTR:

- the labour movement, which argued that China's low-waged and non-unionized labour would make America non-competitive and thus increase unemployment in the United States
- the environmental movement, which argued that it would merely contribute to the destruction of China's environment
- human rights activists, who believed it would permanently break the link between NTR and human rights
- those who believed that permanent NTR merely helped China to strengthen militarily, posing a threat to its neighbours and, ultimately, to the United States.

Ironically, opposition to permanent NTR for China was far stronger in Clinton's own Democratic Party than among the Republicans. On May 24, 2000 the House of Representatives voted in favour of permanent NTR for China, subject to the establishment of a Congressional human rights commission to monitor China's record, with 237 votes in favour and 197 against. The Senate voted in favour of permanent NTR in September 2000.

CHINA AND THE UNITED NATIONS

A major factor in China's acceptance by many of the world's nations, especially those of the

West, was its entry into the United Nations. In 1961 the UN General Assembly had adopted a resolution sponsored by the United States and four other countries designating the PRC's admission to occupy the China seat as an 'important question' requiring a two-thirds majority. This resolution, together with other factors, including the Cultural Revolution in China itself, had the effect of keeping the PRC out of the UN until October 25, 1971. On that day there were two votes on the China seat. One, concerning whether Taiwan's expulsion was an important question, was lost by 59 votes to 55, with fifteen abstentions. The other, the resolution calling for the restoration of the PRC's lawful rights in the UN and its related organizations, and for the immediate expulsion of Chiang Kaishek's representatives, was passed by 76 votes to 35 with seventeen abstentions.

China has taken an active role in the United Nations, including involvement in the UN's various councils and specialized agencies. It has participated in numerous UN-connected or UN-sponsored international conferences and meetings, and has used the UN and associated international gatherings as a forum for its own policies on a wide range of international issues. In its first year of UN membership, formal decisions had been reached for China to join ten UN specialized agencies, and other main bodies (the first being UNESCO on October 29, 1971); and by 1996 it was a member of some 45 UN organs, specialized agencies and commissions.

In the 1990s, China increased its role in the UN, partly as a result of the expanded role of the UN as an organization itself. For instance, in November 1992 it opposed sanctions imposed by the UN Security Council on Yugoslavia, arguing that such action would only exacerbate the already serious war going on in Bosnia-Herzegovina. Also, in 1992, it took part in a peacekeeping force for the first time, by sending 47 military observers and an engineering battalion of 400 men to Cambodia. In 1999 China decided to send civilian policemen to join the UN Special Mission to East Timor. In addressing the UN General Assembly on September 27, 1995 on the occasion of the UN's fiftieth anniversary, Chinese Minister of Foreign Affairs Qian Qichen declared that the UN was 'the most universal and authoritative intergovernmental organization of sovereign states' and was 'irreplaceable by any other international organizations'. On the whole, however, it was still true in the 1990s, as it had been earlier, that China did not attempt to assume a leadership role in the UN commensurate with its size or population.

Possibly the most important occasion showing Chinese participation in the UN was holding the Fourth UN World Conference on Women in September 1995. A number of very senior women from around the world addressed the Conference, including Benazir Bhutto, Prime Minister of Pakistan, Susanna Agnelli, Foreign Minister of Italy, and Hillary Clinton, wife of US President Bill Clinton. Mrs Clinton attacked China for its human rights record but emphasized that female rights were a major part of human rights. In her speech Peng Peiyun, Chinese Minister in Charge of the State Family Planning Commission, spoke of the work the Chinese government was undertaking on behalf of women. This included:

- an emphasis on full female participation in economic construction
- the promotion of female educational development
- improvement of women's health
- the protection of the rights and interests of women and girls
- an increase in women's participation in political life.

A Platform for Action was drafted by 189 countries and adopted at the end of the Conference. It specifies twelve areas of concern for women and urges action to accelerate the advancement of women and the achievement of full gender equality. At about the same time as the UN Conference was the Non-Governmental Organizations Forum on Women held in Huairou outside Beijing, in which some 30 000 delegates took part in about 5000 workshops.

CHINA AND NUCLEAR WEAPONS

China's reaction to the Partial Nuclear Test Ban Treaty of 1963 was negative. It advocated instead the total destruction of nuclear weapons. But it carried out its own first nuclear test in October 1964, at the same time declaring that 'at no time and in no circumstances will China be the first to use nuclear weapons'. The Chinese government defended its nuclear program by arguing that it was necessary for China to secure itself against nuclear attack while the superpowers were still developing large nuclear arsenals.

At the Special UN General Assembly Session on Disarmament held in 1978, China's Foreign Minister Huang Hua repeated China's frequently stated position demanding the total destruction of nuclear weapons. He condemned both superpowers for their nuclear (and other military) expansion and for hypocrisy in claiming to be maintaining peace, but his attacks on the Soviet Union were much more intense and hard-hitting than those on the United States.

In the 1980s China stressed its demand that, since the two superpowers together possess 95 per cent of all the world's nuclear weapons, they should take the initiative to stop the arms race. China's reaction to the various steps taken by the Soviet Union and United States in this direction has been positive, but very low-key. Most importantly, it welcomed the signing of the Intermediate-range Nuclear Forces Agreement of December 1987 as a positive step towards reducing international tensions, but cautioned against over-optimism.

In the first major statement which China made to the UN on the subject of nuclear arms after the fall of the Soviet Union, China's Ambassador to the UN Hou Zhitong made the following main points (see also Chapter 1, A. October 21, 1992):

- The world has become more turbulent and the gap between rich and poor countries widened in recent years.
- China welcomes the initiatives taken by the United States and Russia in the direction of disarmament.
- Because the United States and Russia still have much the largest and most advanced nuclear arsenals, they have special responsibility for disarmament.
- The Chinese government has consistently stood for complete prohibition and thorough destruction of nuclear weapons.
- China supports the Treaty on the Non-Proliferation of Nuclear Weapons (see Chapter 1, A. March 11, 1992).
- China proposes the following transitional measures towards the aim of total destruction of nuclear weapons:
  - all nuclear-weapon states should follow China in committing themselves not to be the first to use nuclear weapons or ever to use them against non-nuclear states
  - all nuclear states should follow China in supporting proposals for nuclear-free zones
  - all countries with space capabilities should observe the principle of the peaceful use of outer space and cease all development of space weapons.

Following this declaration, China undertook several underground nuclear tests (included in Chapter 1), for which it came under increasing international criticism, notably from Japan and Australia. At the same time China continued to take part in the deliberations concerning a Comprehensive Test Ban Treaty. On July 29, 1996, it conducted a further nuclear test, announcing that this would be its last and that a total moratorium would come into effect the next day.

In a statement issued on August 15, 1996, China declared that it had several reservations about the Treaty, especially with regard to on-site inspection. In particular, it criticized the failure of the proposed Treaty to make any distinctions between the international monitoring system and national means like satellite data and news reports. Since only a few developed countries possessed advanced national means, China regarded the use of such means as subjective and discriminatory, and likely to lead to abuse of the right of on-site inspection by a few countries. Talks on the Comprehensive Test Ban Treaty collapsed on August 20, 1996, not because of China's reservations but because of a veto by India.

Nevertheless, on September 24, 1996, China signed the Comprehensive Test Ban Treaty, along with the United States, Russia, Britain and France, at the same time issuing a statement opposing the abuse of verification procedures, notably those infringing on the sovereignty of other countries.

ALPHABETICAL LIST OF COUNTRIES WITH DIPLOMATIC RELATIONS WITH THE PRC

This list includes all those countries which, as of August 2000, had diplomatic relations with the PRC. In a few cases of countries which had once established relations but had since broken them, the date of rupture is also given. In some instances, a further formal title is added for a country in order to distinguish among two or more rival claimants to government. This does not imply that the formal name of any country with which China holds diplomatic relations in 2000 is the same as it was when the relations were established. For example, China established diplomatic relations in 1950 with the Democratic Republic of Vietnam (North Vietnam), but the name of the united Vietnam with which diplomatic relations were held in 2000 was the Socialist Republic of Vietnam.

The principal issue for China in the establishment of diplomatic relations has been the status of Taiwan, which the CCP continues to claim as a province of China. This issue has assumed particular priority in the case of international bodies such as the UN, and those countries—like the Western nations or Japan—which had strong and good relations with Taiwan until they recognized the PRC in the 1970s and which have continued to maintain flourishing unofficial and commercial relations since then. For this reason, comments are often made in the following list concerning a country's attitude to the Taiwan question.

Afghanistan—January 20, 1955.

Albania—November 23, 1949.

Algeria—December 20, 1958.

Andorra—June 29, 1994.

Angola—January 12, 1983. In the communiqué, Angola recognizes the PRC government as 'the sole legal government representing all the Chinese people, and that Taiwan is an inalienable part of the territory of the PRC'.

Antigua and Barbuda—January 1, 1983. In the communiqué, Antigua and Barbuda recognizes the PRC government as 'the sole legal government representing all the Chinese people, and that Taiwan is an inalienable part of the territory of the PRC'.

Argentina—February 19, 1972. In the communiqué, Argentina 'takes note' of China's position on Taiwan.

Armenia—April 6, 1992.

Australia—December 21, 1972. In the communiqué, Australia 'acknowledges (*chengren*) the position of the Chinese government that Taiwan is a province of China' and recognizes it as 'the sole legal government of China'.

Azerbaijan—April 2, 1992.

Austria—May 28, 1971. In the communiqué, China 'respects the status of neutrality' and Austria recognizes the PRC government as 'the sole legal government of China', but there is no mention of Taiwan.

Bahamas, The—May 23, 1997.

Bangladesh—October 4, 1975.

Barbados—May 30, 1977.

Belgium—October 25, 1971. In the communiqué, Belgium 'takes note' of China's position that Taiwan is 'an inalienable part of the territory' of the PRC and recognizes that the PRC government is 'the sole legal government of China'.

Belize—March 6, 1987. On October 11, 1989, Belize established diplomatic relations with Taiwan; the PRC reacted by suspending diplomatic relations on October 23.

Benin—November 12, 1964.

Byelorussia—January 20, 1992.

Bolivia—July 9, 1985. In the communiqué, Bolivia recognizes the PRC government as 'the sole legal government of China' and Taiwan as 'an inalienable part of the territory' of the PRC.

Bosnia-Herzegovina—April 3, 1995.

Botswana—January 6, 1975. In the communiqué, Botswana recognizes the PRC government as the 'sole legal government representing the entire Chinese people, and Taiwan province as an inalienable part of the territory' of the PRC.

Brazil—August 15, 1974. In the communiqué, Brazil recognizes the PRC government as 'the sole legal government' of the Chinese people and 'takes note' of China's reaffirmation that Taiwan is an inalienable part of its territory.

Brunei—September 30, 1991.

Bulgaria—October 4, 1949.

Burkina—September 15, 1973. On February 4, 1994, the Chinese government broke off diplomatic relations with Burkina, when the latter restored diplomatic relations with Taiwan on February 2.

Burma—*see* Myanmar.

Burundi—December 21, 1963. Relations were suspended by Burundi on January 29, 1965, but restored on October 13, 1971.

Cambodia—July 19, 1958. China continued diplomatic relations with the government of Norodom Sihanouk following his overthrow on March 18, 1970, including the Democratic Kampuchea with which he was associated, nominally or otherwise, after the seizure of Phnom Penh by the Khmer Rouge on April 17, 1975. China never recognized the Khmer Republic of Lon Nol, which came to power in Phnom Penh after Sihanouk's overthrow but was itself defeated in April 1975. Nor did China recognize the People's Republic of Kampuchea, renamed the State of Cambodia in 1989, a state established and based in Phnom Penh after a Vietnamese invasion of Kampuchea which took that city on January 7, 1979. However, China recognized and supported the Supreme National Council set up in September 1990, hosted a meeting of the four factions which composed it in July 1991 and recognized the series of governments that followed the peace agreement signed in Paris on October 23, 1991.

Cameroon—March 26, 1971. In the communiqué, China supports the policy of non-alignment of the Cameroon government, and Cameroon recognizes the PRC government as 'the sole legal government which represents the entire Chinese people' but does not specify Taiwan as an inalienable part of Chinese territory.

Canada—October 13, 1970. In the communiqué, Canada recognizes the PRC government as 'the sole legal government' of China and 'takes note' of China's position that Taiwan is 'an inalienable part of the territory' of the PRC.

Cape Verde—April 25, 1976.

Central African Republic—September 29, 1964. Relations were ruptured by the Central African Republic on January 6, 1966, but restored on August 20, 1976. Relations were again ruptured on July 18, 1991, after the Central African Republic transferred its diplomatic relations to Taiwan, but on January 29, 1998, the country again transferred its diplomatic relations back to the PRC.

Chad—November 28, 1972. Following Chad's announcement on August 12, 1997, that it would resume diplomatic relations with Taiwan, China stated on August 15 that it was severing relations with Chad, effective immediately.

Chile—December 15, 1970. In the communiqué, Chile recognizes the PRC government as 'the sole legal government' of China and 'takes note' of China's statement that Taiwan is an inalienable part of PRC territory.

Colombia—February 7, 1980.

Comoros—November 13, 1975.

Congo (People's Republic)—February 22, 1964.

Congo (Democratic Republic of the)—
February 20, 1961. Relations were
ruptured on September 18, 1961 but re-
established on November 24, 1972.

Cook Islands—July 25, 1997.

Croatia—May 13, 1992.

Cuba—September 28, 1960.

Cyprus—December 14, 1971. Date of the
signature of the communiqué, issued on
January 12, 1972, in which Cyprus
recognizes the Chinese government as the
sole legal government of the entire Chinese
people but makes no reference to Taiwan.

Czechoslovakia—October 6, 1949.

Dahomey—November 12, 1964. Relations
were ruptured on January 2, 1966, but
resumed on December 29, 1972.

Denmark—May 11, 1950.

Djibouti—January 8, 1979.

Ecuador—January 2, 1980.

Egypt—May 30, 1956.

Equatorial Guinea—October 15, 1970. In the
communiqué, Equatorial Guinea
recognizes the PRC government as 'the
sole legal government of the entire Chinese
people' but makes no reference to Taiwan.

Eritrea—May 24, 1993.

Estonia—September 11, 1991.

Ethiopia—November 24, 1970. In the
communiqué, Ethiopia describes the PRC
government as 'the sole legal government
representing the entire Chinese people'
but makes no reference to Taiwan.

Fiji—November 5, 1975.

Finland—October 28, 1950.

France—January 27, 1964.

Gabon—April 20, 1974. In the communiqué,
Gabon describes the PRC government as
'the sole legal government representing
the entire Chinese people' but makes no
reference to Taiwan.

Gambia—December 14, 1974. Diplomatic
relations were suspended on July 25,
1995, after Gambia established relations
with Taiwan the same month.

Georgia—June 9, 1992.

Germany (Democratic Republic)—October
27, 1949. This joined the Federal Republic
in October 1990.

Germany (Federal Republic)—October 11,
1972. The communiqué includes nothing
about China's position on the two
Germanies and nothing about Federal
Germany's position on the status of
Taiwan; there is not even any reference to
the PRC government as the sole legal
government of China.

Ghana—July 5, 1960. Relations were
suspended by Ghana on October 20,
1966, with China closing its embassy on
November 5, 1966, but were resumed on
February 29, 1972.

Greece—June 5, 1972. In the communiqué,
Greece 'takes note' of China's position that
Taiwan is 'an inalienable part of the
territory' of the PRC and recognizes that
the PRC government is 'the sole legal
government of China'.

Grenada—October 1, 1985. On August 7,
1989, the Ministry of Foreign Affairs
issued a statement suspending diplomatic
relations with Grenada, after the
government of Grenada had announced
on July 19, 1989 that it had established
diplomatic relations with Taiwan.

Guinea—October 4, 1959.

Guinea-Bissau—March 15, 1974. In the
communiqué, Guinea-Bissau recognizes
that the PRC government is 'the sole legal
government of the entire Chinese people
and that Taiwan province is an inalienable
part of the territory of the People's
Republic of China'. On May 31, 1990,
China announced that it would sever
diplomatic relations, following Guinea-
Bissau's decision to establish diplomatic
relations with Taiwan, and did so June 11.
However, on April 23, 1998, Guinea-
Bissau again transferred its diplomatic
relations back to the PRC.

Guyana—June 27, 1972.

Hungary—October 6, 1949.

Iceland—December 8, 1971. In the
communiqué, Iceland 'takes note' of
China's position that Taiwan is 'an
inalienable part of the territory' of the PRC
and recognizes that the PRC government
is 'the sole legal government of China'.

India—April 1, 1950.

Indonesia—June 9, 1950. On October 9, 1967, the Indonesian government decided to declare an official suspension of diplomatic relations with the PRC; on October 31, 1967 a Chinese aircraft dropped all Indonesian Embassy staff in Jakarta and picked up its own Embassy staff, thus completing the rupture of Sino-Indonesian diplomatic relations. On August 8, 1990 China and Indonesia formally re-established diplomatic relations. In the communiqué, signed in Beijing on July 3, 1990, Indonesia 'maintains only economic and trade relations of non-governmental nature with Taiwan'.

Iran—August 16, 1971. Iran recognizes the PRC as the 'sole legal government of China'.

Iraq—August 20, 1958.

Ireland—June 22, 1979.

Israel—January 24, 1992. In the communiqué, Israel recognizes the PRC as the sole legal government of all China and states that Taiwan is an inalienable part of PRC territory.

Italy—November 6, 1970. In the communiqué, Italy recognizes the PRC government as 'the sole legal government' of China and 'takes note' of China's statement that Taiwan is 'an inalienable part of the territory' of the PRC.

Ivory Coast—March 2, 1983. The Ivory Coast recognizes the PRC government as 'the sole legal government representing the entire Chinese people' and declares that it 'has taken note' of the Chinese government's statement that Taiwan is an inalienable part of PRC territory.

Jamaica—November 21, 1972.

Japan—September 29, 1972. In the communiqué, signed the same day, Japan recognizes the PRC government as 'the sole legal government of China' and 'fully understands and respects' China's stand that Taiwan is an inalienable part of PRC territory.

Jordan—April 7, 1977. Date of the signature of the communiqué, announced on April 14, 1977; Jordan 'recognizes the government of the People's Republic of China as the sole legal government representing the entire Chinese people, and Taiwan province as an inalienable part of the territory of the People's Republic of China'.

Kampuchea—see Cambodia.

Kazakhstan—January 4, 1992.

Kenya—December 14, 1963.

Kiribati—June 25, 1980.

Korea (Democratic People's Republic of)—October 6, 1949.

Korea (Republic of)—August 24, 1992. Chinese and South Korean Foreign Ministers Qian Qichen and Lee Sang-ock sign a communiqué in which the Republic of Korea recognizes the Government of the PRC as the sole legitimate government of China, and the fact that Taiwan is an inalienable part of Chinese territory.

Kuwait—March 22, 1971.

Laos—April 25, 1961.

Latvia—September 12, 1991.

Lebanon—November 9, 1971. In the communiqué, Lebanon 'takes note of China's stand that Taiwan is an inalienable part of PRC territory and recognizes the PRC government as 'the sole legal government of China'.

Lesotho—April 30, 1983. In the communiqué, Lesotho 'recognizes that the government of the PRC is the sole legal government of China and that Taiwan is an inalienable part of the PRC'. On April 2, 1990, Lesotho re-established diplomatic relations with Taiwan, after which the PRC decided on April 7 to break diplomatic relations with it. On January 12, 1994, China and Lesotho reestablished diplomatic relations at ambassadorial level.

Liberia—February 17, 1977. On October 2, 1989, Liberia announced its re-establishment of diplomatic relations with Taiwan, signing a communiqué to that effect on October 9. The PRC responded by announcing its suspension of diplomatic relations on October 10.

Relations were again restored on August 10, 1993, but again ruptured for the same reason on September 9, 1997.

Libya—August 9, 1978.

Lithuania—September 14, 1991.

Luxembourg—November 16, 1972.

Macedonia—October 12, 1993. On January 27, 1999, the foreign ministers of Taiwan and Macedonia signed, in Taipei, a communiqué to establish diplomatic relations, but on January 29, 1999, the Macedonian President Kiro Gligorov stated his refusal to recognize these relations. Later, Macedonia's decision in favour of Taiwan was confirmed, as a result of which China severed relations with Macedonia on February 9, 1999.

Madagascar—November 6, 1972.

Malaysia—May 31, 1974. In the communiqué, Malaysia recognizes the PRC government as the sole legal government of China and 'acknowledges' the PRC position that Taiwan is an inalienable part of PRC territory.

Maldives—October 14, 1972.

Mali—October 25, 1960.

Malta—January 31, 1972.

Marshall Islands—November 16, 1990. Relations were terminated December 11, 1998 shortly after the Marshall Islands established diplomatic relations with Taiwan.

Mauritania—July 19, 1965.

Mexico—February 14, 1972.

Micronesia—September 11, 1989.

Moldova—January 30, 1992.

Mongolia—October 16, 1949.

Morocco—November 1, 1958.

Mozambique—June 25, 1975.

Myanmar—June 8, 1950.

Namibia—March 22, 1990.

Nepal—August 1, 1955.

Netherlands—October 19, 1954, at chargé d'affaires level, raised to ambassadorial level on May 18, 1972. In the communiqué, the Netherlands 'respects' the stand of the Chinese government that Taiwan is a province of the PRC and recognizes it as 'the sole legal government

of China'. On May 5, 1981, China downgraded the relationship to chargé d'affaires level; the Netherlands reciprocated on May 11, 1981. Relations were raised again to ambassadorial level February 1, 1984.

New Zealand—December 22, 1972. In the communiqué, New Zealand 'acknowledges' the position of the Chinese government that Taiwan is an inalienable part of PRC territory and recognizes it as 'the sole legal government of China'.

Nicaragua—December 7, 1985. Nicaragua recognizes the PRC government as 'the sole legal government of China' and Taiwan as an inalienable part of the territory of China. However, following Nicaragua's restoration of ties with Taiwan, the PRC announced its suspension of diplomatic relations on November 7, 1990.

Niger—July 20, 1974. In the communiqué, Niger recognizes the PRC government as 'the sole legal government representing the entire Chinese people, and Taiwan province as an inalienable part of the territory of the PRC'. China broke off diplomatic relations on July 30, 1992, after Niger confirmed it had established diplomatic relations with Taiwan on July 22, 1992, but resumed them on August 19, 1996 at ambassadorial level.

Nigeria—February 10, 1971.

Norway—October 5, 1954.

Oman—May 25, 1978.

Pakistan—May 21, 1951.

Papua New Guinea—October 12, 1976. The communiqué makes no mention of Taiwan, nor is there reference to the PRC government's being the sole legal government of China. On July 5, 1999, Papua New Guinea and Taiwan signed a communiqué establishing diplomatic relations during a visit by Prime Minister Bill Skate to Taiwan. However, on July 7, Skate resigned and on July 14 was replaced by Sir Mekere Marauta. On July 21, the new government negated its predecessor's decision, arguing that proper procedures had not been followed, as a result of which diplomatic relations remained with the PRC.

Peru—November 2, 1971. In the communiqué, Peru 'takes note' of China's position that Taiwan is 'an inalienable part of the territory' of the PRC and recognizes that the PRC government is 'the sole legal government of China'.

Philippines—June 9, 1975. In the communiqué, the Philippines recognizes the PRC government as 'the sole legal government of China' and 'fully understands and respects' China's position that Taiwan is an integral part of China's territory.

Poland—October 7, 1949.

Portugal—February 8, 1979.

Qatar—July 5, 1988.

Romania—October 5, 1949.

Ruanda—November 12, 1971. In the communiqué, Ruanda recognizes the PRC government as 'the sole legal government of China', but makes no reference to Taiwan.

Russia—*see* Union of Soviet Socialist Republics.

Saint Lucia—September 1, 1997.

San Marino—May 6, 1971.

São Tomé and Principe—July 12, 1975. Relations were suspended, as of July 11, 1997, following São Tomé and Principe's decision to establish relations with Taiwan.

Saudi Arabia—July 21, 1990.

Senegal—December 7, 1971. In the communiqué, Senegal recognizes the PRC government as 'the sole legal government of China', but makes no reference to Taiwan. On January 9, 1996, China broke off diplomatic relations following Senegal's establishment of relations with Taiwan on January 3.

Seychelles—June 30, 1976.

Sierra Leone—July 29, 1971. In the communiqué, Sierra Leone recognizes the PRC government as 'the sole legal government representing the entire Chinese people'.

Singapore—October 3, 1990

Slovenia—May 13, 1992.

Somalia—December 14, 1960.

South Africa—January 1, 1998.

Spain—March 9, 1973. In the communiqué, Spain 'acknowledges the position of the Chinese government that Taiwan is a province of China'.

Sri Lanka—February 7, 1957.

Sudan—February 4, 1959.

Surinam—May 28, 1976. In the communiqué, Surinam recognizes the PRC government as 'the sole legal government' of China.

Sweden—May 9, 1950.

Switzerland—September 14, 1950.

Syria—August 1, 1956.

Tajikistan—January 4, 1992.

Tanzania—April 26, 1964. China had previously established diplomatic relations with Tanganyika since its independence from Britain on December 9, 1961, and with Zanzibar since December 11, 1963, the day after its independence, before the unification of the two states into a United Republic on April 26, 1964.

Thailand—July 1, 1975. In the communiqué, Thailand recognizes the PRC government 'as the sole legal government of China' and 'acknowledges the position of the Chinese government that there is but one China and that Taiwan is an integral part of Chinese territory'.

Togo—September 19, 1972. In the communiqué, Togo recognizes the PRC government as 'the sole legal government of China'.

Tonga—November 2, 1998.

Trinidad and Tobago—June 20, 1974.

Tunisia—January 10, 1964. Relations were formally ruptured on September 26, 1967, but resumed on October 8, 1971.

Turkey—August 4, 1971. In the communiqué, Turkey recognizes the PRC government as 'the sole legal government of China'; both sides undertake to 'facilitate the performance' of their diplomatic missions' functions. Turkey had earlier voted in the UN against the resolutions to place the PRC in the China seat there.

Uganda—October 18, 1962.

Ukraine—January 4, 1992.

Union of Soviet Socialist Republics—October 3, 1949. With the collapse of the Union at the end of 1991, the Russian Federation automatically succeeded.

United Kingdom of Great Britain and Northern Ireland—January 6, 1950 was the day Britain notified Beijing of its intention to establish diplomatic relations. On June 17, 1954 both countries' governments agreed to send a chargé d'affaires to each other's capital. On March 13, 1972, both agreed to raise the status of their diplomatic relations to ambassadorial level. In the communiqué, Britain 'acknowledges the position of the Chinese government that Taiwan is a province of China' and recognizes it as 'the sole legal government of China'.

United States of America—January 1, 1979. In the communiqué, issued on December 16, 1978 in Beijing (December 15 according to Washington time), the United States recognizes the PRC government as 'the sole legal government of China', but 'will maintain cultural, commercial, and other unofficial relations with the people of Taiwan'. In addition, the United States 'acknowledges the Chinese position that there is but one China and Taiwan is part of China'.

Uzbekistan—January 4, 1992.

Vanuatu—March 26, 1982. In the communiqué, Vanuatu recognizes the PRC government as 'the sole legal government' of China, but makes no reference to Taiwan.

Venezuela—June 28, 1974.

Vietnam—January 18, 1950.

Western Samoa—November 6, 1975. In the communiqué, Western Samoa 'acknowledges' China's position on the status of Taiwan.

Yemen (Arab Republic)—September 24, 1956.

Yemen (Democratic People's Republic)— January 31, 1968.

Yugoslavia—January 2, 1955.

Zambia—October 29, 1964.

Zanzibar—December 15, 1963. (See also under Tanzania.)

Zimbabwe—April 18, 1980. Chinese Foreign Minister Huang Hua attended the ceremony of April 17–18 declaring Zimbabwe independent of Great Britain.

6 CHINA'S ECONOMY

With over a fifth of global population, China is a poor third-world country. Since 1978, it has introduced transition reforms in order to move away from Soviet-style central planning and become a market economy. The process is not yet at an end and the two systems coexist, although the state-owned sector has gradually reduced in size as the market has expanded.[1]

After the death of Chairman Mao Zedong in 1976, the need for economic reform was recognized at high levels of the Party, although there was disagreement about the process. After two years of political struggles, it was determined that a move towards the market was acceptable. This began slowly in agriculture, where market reform of production is now essentially complete, although this takes place on land leased from the state as private ownership is not yet allowed. The reform process gradually picked up momentum and was tentatively extended to industry and the financial sectors, where there is still much to be done.

With some exceptions, the state sector is characterized by large, often unwieldy, bureaucratic companies with overstaffing and low efficiency. The market sector typically has smaller, more dynamic firms, as well as those companies that have some degree of foreign investment, including the totally foreign-owned; large companies are common in the totally foreign-owned portion. 'Town and village enterprises' make up an unusual hybrid of firms with both private and local state capital investment, and they may have similarly mixed management personnel. These vary greatly; some on the political Left claim them as a significant Chinese contribution to socialist industrial structure, although mainstream observers discount this.

The process of reform has been gradual rather than 'big bang' and although stop-go cycles exist it has been a strikingly successful example of the transition economy, particularly when compared with some East European models. A summary of the Chinese economy is provided in Table 6.1.

Table 6.1 The main economic indicators, 1998

Population (mills, at year end)	1 248.1
GDP (yuan bills, current prices)	7 955.3
GNI per head (previously GNP) (US $)	860 [b]
GNI per head ppp [a] (US $)	3 070 [b]
Real growth in GDP (%)	7.8
Real increase in average consumption per head (%)	3.2 [b]
Change in General Index of Retail Prices (%)	−2.6
Unemployment (%)	3.1
Grain output (mill metric tons)	490.0
Grain output, change in year (%)	−0.8
Exports (US $ mills, f.o.b.) [c]	183 527
Imports (US $ mills, f.o.b.) [c]	136 914
External debt (US $ mills, at year end)	146 697 [b]
Debt service ratio (%) [d]	8.6 [b]
First place in the world for the production of:	cement, cereal grains, cloth, coal, cotton, fertiliser, fruit, groundnuts, meat, rape seed, steel, tobacco
Second place in the world for the production of:	electricity, greasy wool, tea

Notes:
[a] Purchasing power parity
[b] 1997 figure
[c] IMF figure
[d] Debt service payments as a percentage of exports of goods and services in that year.

RESOURCES AND INFRASTRUCTURE

Natural resources

China is the third largest country in the world and stretches from the permafrost border areas of Russia to a small area of tropics in the south. Much of the land is inhospitable and unsuitable for agriculture, which is concentrated along the coast and in the main river basins. The north is dry and in many years suffers a drought, while the south is wet and in many years suffers floods. (See more detail in Chapter 8.)

China has the world's greatest reserves of antimony, molybdenum, rare earth, titanium, tungsten and vanadium, and large reserves of asbestos, coal, copper, iron, lead-zinc, mercury, nickel, phosphorus, silver and tin. Despite this, the country is the world's third largest importer of minerals, and both iron ore and copper can be in short supply. Many minerals are located in the north or inland areas of China and getting them to the main coastal markets is often not easy.

Transport and Communications

Despite much effort since 1949, transport in China has been inadequate for the needs of development. Since 1950, measured by increased mileage available, the greatest increase has been in civil aviation (92 times), followed by road transport (11 times), then rail (2.4 times). This is, however, misleading in terms of transport importance, for the keystone of the transport system is the railway network, which carries over a third of all goods and people. Congestion is common and passenger tickets can be hard to get.

For many years the road system was poor but, given the domination of the transport system by the railways, acceptable. With the rapid development of the past two decades and the advent of the private motor car, the road system is less capable of meeting demand than previously. In 1984, private vehicles numbered only 173 500 but by 1998 there were 4 236 500, a 24-fold increase. Over the same period, the length of highways increased only 1.4 times, from 926 700 km to 1 278 500 km. As much private mileage is confined to urban areas, the congestion there grew particularly rapidly.

The ports are constantly congested, although improving slowly. The main port is Shanghai, and Hong Kong was added in 1997.

Telecommunications have enjoyed a major boom since the 1990s. For many years the telephone service was frankly appalling, but recently it has shown substantial improvement, both in quality and in availability. Heavy investment has occurred: 820 000 km of optical cable trunk lines were installed by 1998, and various satellite communication systems are now in operation. The number of telephone sets has increased from 12.3 million in 1990 to 131.2 million in 1998.

Energy

China is the second largest consumer of energy in the world, after the United States. Coal dominates the energy sector. Throughout the 1950s it provided 95 per cent of all energy output, but this fell to around 70 per cent in the late 1970s mainly because of the development of the oil industry. Petroleum production grew rapidly after the mid-1960s, and its share of all energy hit a peak of 24.7 per cent in 1976, after which the share gradually diminished to hover below 20 per cent. Offshore oil, once the subject of great hopes and hype, has been something of a disappointment. In 1993 China became a net importer of petroleum, as domestic supply could not keep pace with demand. Despite the slowdown, in 1995 China was still the sixth largest oil producer in the world.

For many years energy shortages were a feature; consumers could find themselves without power supply in normal waking hours and offices in tall buildings could find themselves without working lifts. By 1999, steady expansion of power output, together with increased efficiency in use, closed much of the gap between supply and demand, although admittedly the economic slowdown helped to take the pressure off the system. Localized shortages still regularly arise, particularly when the economy is booming.

Coal still supplies three-quarters of all energy consumed but is mostly found in the north and west, remote from where it is needed, which accounts for the congestion on the railways. The coal is generally of low quality, badly processed, often not washed, and when burned is a major source of air pollution. The coal industry uses much out-of-date technology and suffers from thousands of accidental deaths each year.

China has immense hydroelectric power potential, the greatest in the world, which is located mostly in the south. As so often is the case, the necessary conditions of mountain valleys and rivers do not occur close to the major industrial and residential areas. The controversial Three Gorges project on the Yangzi River is intended to supply electricity downstream to Shanghai and the adjacent areas.

Pollution and the Environment

China's environment has long been polluted: for centuries few would willingly drink unboiled water, and the burning of wood and low-quality coal for fuel ensured a low quality of urban air. The heavy industrialization program of the 1950s added serious industrial air and water pollution to all major cities. The emphasis on growth since 1978 has increased the problem, particularly from the small new enterprises which cannot afford, and have little interest in, clean production. Many of these seem to be township and village enterprises (TVEs). Air pollution from the rapidly increasing numbers of private motor vehicles is an additional worry.

There is some confusion in official attitudes. On the one hand, protection of the environment is seen as a basic national policy; on the other, there is a widespread view that growth and development must come first and that environmental degradation is the short-term price that must be paid; when China becomes rich it will be time to deal with the pollution problem. The latter view tends to prevail.

Land and forests are being lost to development. According to the World Bank, the forested area of China is 1 333 000 sq. km (14.3 per cent) and each year it reduces by about 866 sq. km. Much is in out-of-the-way areas, and few forests are visible around the populated areas.

Since 1978 many new houses, factories and roads have sprung up and reduced the amount of land available to agriculture. The statistics are still to be verified but they show a net loss of cultivated land of 4.5 per cent, from 99 389.5 thousand hectares in 1978 to 94 970.9 thousand hectares in 1999. Equally worrying is the fact that much of the lost land was fertile and planted to crops like vegetables for the local market. Rapid urbanization adds to the problem: in 1980 a fifth of the population resided in urban areas, but by 1998 this had increased to a third. With only 7 per cent of global cultivated land and 22 per cent of the world's population to feed, the loss of crop land is a serious matter.

The world's largest dam at the Three Gorges on the Yangzi River, scheduled for completion in 2009, is seen as essential to provide energy for development. It is regarded with suspicion by many outside China, and some within, because of the severe environmental effects, the millions of people who will be displaced, and the destruction of a natural tourist spot which earns valuable foreign exchange. It is claimed that the electricity produced will save on coal use and thereby help reduce air pollution.

THE DOMESTIC SECTORS

Agriculture

The main crops produced are grain (including rice, wheat and maize), cotton, sugar cane, sugar beet, oil-bearing crops (including rapeseed and peanuts), and soybeans.

Immediately after the CCP came to power in 1949, the average increase in agricultural output was high, but this could not be sustained. Grain crops proved particularly difficult, mainly because of the low purchase price set by the state. After 1978 the increased freedom to choose what to plant allowed a swing from grain to cash crops as quotas and price controls were relaxed. During the 1990s it proved difficult to reach the high growth rates achieved in the past, although crops with a high income elasticity of demand, such as fruit, pork, beef and mutton, sugar cane and oil-bearing crops, did well. The output of more mundane crops, such as wheat, rice and tea, grow more slowly.

The changes in agriculture in the early 1980s led to substantial increases in output. However, once the new incentives had achieved their effect, the reallocation of land from less to more suitable crop use had been achieved, and the slack had been taken up from investment made earlier but previously under-used, it became difficult to continue the improvement. Small family farming has been successfully reestablished, but future growth in output will increasingly require more modern farming methods, such as the increased use of farm equipment as well as pesticides and fertilisers (and proper instruction in their use).

Other problems exist. Environmental degradation has caused soil erosion and increased the dangers of floods. Additionally, in the past the state has reneged on payment for crop deliveries or paid by IOUs. Local officials have a habit of imposing illegal taxes or fines on peasants, or withholding supplies of pesticides or insecticides, or charging overly high prices for them. All such behaviour acts as disincentives to the producers.

An ongoing problem is that peasants do not own the land, they only have the use of it, and this uncertainty reduces the incentive for them to invest. Soil degradation is a danger if the land is mined rather than properly farmed. In the longer term, the family farms will be too small and amalgamations will be required.

Industry

Since 1949, industrial development has been rapid, with the fastest growth achieved in the 1950s. Following the demise of the Great

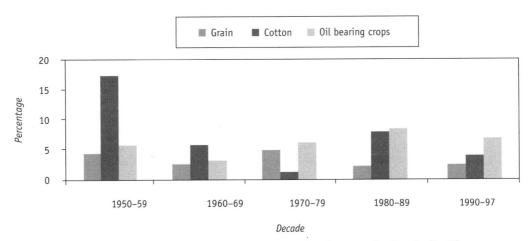

Figure 6.1 The average change in output p.a. of major crops by decade (in %)

Table 6.2 The output of main crops, 1990 and 1998 (in million tons)

	1990	1998	Percentage change
All grain crops, of which:	446.240	512.295	14.80
wheat	98.23	109.73	11.70
rice	189.33	198.713	4.96
Tea (thousand tons)	540	665	23.15
Cotton	4.508	4.501	−0.16
Sugar cane	57.620	83.438	44.81
Oil-bearing crops	16.132	23.139	43.44
Pork, beef & mutton	2 513.5	4 598.2	82.94

Leap Forward, industrial development continued but at a slower rate over the 1960s. Since then, the average rate of industrial growth has increased with each decade.

During the 1990s, growth has not been steady: a boom occurred from 1992 to 1994, and the economy achieved a soft landing by 1996. After that, gross industrial output continued to increase but at a slower rate. This was in large part influenced by the Asian financial crisis that began in 1997. Chinese exports to Asia suffered, foreign direct investment (FDI) was reduced, and China entered into a period of what, for China, was tantamount to a recession. Prices began to fall in October 1997 and surplus capacity emerged in several industries in 1998.

Industrial ownership has changed substantially over the past two decades; measured by gross industrial output value, between 1978 and 1998, the share of state-owned industry fell substantially as collective ownership increased, individually owned firms emerged, and enterprises with foreign investment grew from nothing to 15 per cent.

Much of the recent industrial growth has come from private industry and TVEs. Both sectors are relatively new. Private industry disappeared by the mid–1950s in the whirlwind of nationalization and was prohibited until the 1980s. Once reestablished, private firms grew rapidly: measured by output value, between 1990 and 1998 they grew at an average of 36.1 per cent a year, compared with 20.3 per cent for collectively owned, and only 5.6 per cent for state-owned industry.

The output of modern consumer durables, such as cameras, colour TVs and household refrigerators, has increased to meet the rapidly growing demand, while the production of bicycles, now something of an 'inferior good' in China, has decreased.

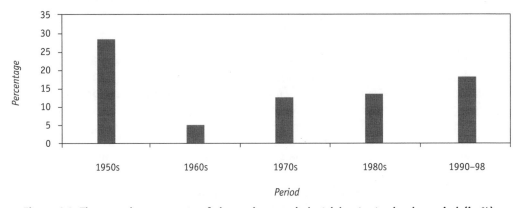

Figure 6.2 The annual average rate of change in gross industrial output value by period (in %)

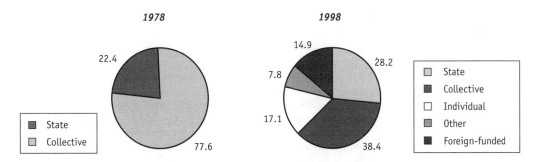

Figure 6.3 The ownership of industry 1978 and 1998 by gross industrial output value

Note: In 1998, enterprises with foreign funding are partially included in the other categories; relatively few firms are totally foreign owned.

The rapid economic development has resulted in a substantial change in the composition of output. China still has a large rural economy but its importance is falling as tertiary industry (services) has increased substantially. In 1978 primary industry made up 28.1 per cent of the economy, secondary 48.2 per cent and tertiary industry 23.7 per cent. By 1998 these figures were 18.7, 49.2 and 32.1 per cent respectively.

THE EXTERNAL SECTORS

Foreign trade

Prior to 1970, foreign trade had been little developed. During the 1950s, trade made up an average of 10.2 per cent of GDP, but this fell to 6.9 per cent in the 1960s, following the collapse of the Great Leap Forward. The first serious increase in foreign trade for many years occurred in 1972, as China began its movement back into world affairs. This trend accelerated after 1979 when the new policies required greater imports of machinery, technology and materials to support development. Exports had to increase to pay for these needed imports. After China began to open its economy to the world, the proportion of GDP taken by foreign trade more than doubled, from an average of 8.3 per cent in the 1970s to 19.8 per cent in the 1980s. This increase continued during the 1990s when foreign trade increased to average 35.7 per cent of GDP in 1990–98.

The balance of payments

Despite the high rates of growth, which normally suck in imports and produce a deficit on visible trade in the balance of payments, China has largely managed to avoid this. Between 1990 and 1998, the only year to record a deficit was 1993. Less praiseworthy are some of the methods used, which have often relied on increases in quotas, or other short-term measures to restrain imports.

In part to encourage foreign trade, but more importantly to try to meet the necessary conditions for entering the WTO and to satisfy the demands of the United States for greater market access, during the 1990s China made substantial reductions in its level of protection. In 1996 decreases were made in over 4000 tariffs, which reduced the average from 36 per cent to 23 per cent, and China further announced that it would replace 179 non-tariff barriers by tariffs. Additional tariff cuts in October 1997 reduced the average to 17 per cent. Tariff levels and quotas are still severe enough to promote a healthy smuggling industry, despite valiant efforts on the part of the authorities to curb this.

China's trade composition and trading partners

Since the 1950s, on the export side China has steadily moved towards its comparative advantage, reducing its reliance on the ex-

Table 6.3 The output of major industrial products, 1990 and 1998

		1990	1998	Percentage change
Light industry				
Bicycles	millions	31.416	23.1249	−26.39
Cameras	millions	2.1322	55.2187	2489.75
Cloth	billion metres	18.88	24.1000	27.65
Colour TVs	million sets	10.3304	34.9700	238.52
Refrigerators	millions	4.6306	10.6000	128.91
Washing machines	millions	6.6268	12.0731	82.19
Beer	million tons	6.9200	19.8767	187.24
Heavy industry				
Cement	million tons	209.71	536.0000	155.59
Chemical fertilizers	million tons	18.80	30.1000	60.13
Coal	100 million tons	10.80	12.5000	15.74
Crude oil	million tons	138.31	161.0000	16.41
Crude steel	million tons	66.35	115.5900	74.21
Motor vehicles	millions	0.51	1.6300	217.12
Pig iron	million tons	62.38	118.6367	90.18

ports of agricultural produce (in a land-short country), first increasing its reliance on exports of labour-intensive light industrial goods, then later adding machinery.

International tourism is an increasingly important earner of foreign exchange for China. In 1990 1.75 million foreign tourists visited China, and total earnings of foreign exchange (including from Overseas Chinese and Hong Kong or Macau visitors) were US$2218 million or 3.6 per cent of total exports. By 1998, 7.11 million foreign tourists visited China and total foreign

exchange earnings reached $12 602 million or 6.9 per cent of total exports.

China sells largely to the developed areas of Asia, such as Hong Kong, Japan, and South Korea, and the developed Western world of the United States and Western Europe. The richer countries buy the products of Chinese manufacturing industry that they find too expensive to produce for themselves.

Exports have become more concentrated over two decades. In 1998 the main six destinations between them took 68 per cent of all Chinese exports (63 per cent in 1980) and

Table 6.4 China's balance of payments, 1996–98 (in US$ millions)

	1996	1997	1998
Exports of goods f.o.b.	151 077	182 670	183 527
Imports of goods f.o.b.	-131 542	-136 448	-136 914
Trade balance	19 535	46 222	46 613
Exports of services	20 601	24 581	24 057
Imports of services	-22 585	-30 306	-28 980
Balance on goods and services	17 551	40 497	41 690
Other income received	7 318	3 174	5 583
Other income paid	-19 755	-19 097	-22 227
Balance on goods and services	5 114	24 574	25 046
Current transfers received	2 368	5 477	4 661
Current transfers paid	-239	-333	-382
Current balance	7 243	29 718	29 325
Capital account (net)	–	-21	-47
Direct investment abroad	-2 114	-2 563	-2 634
Direct investment in China	40 180	44 236	43 751
Portfolio investment assets	-628	-899	-3 830
Portfolio investment liabilities	2 372	7 703	97
Other investment assets	-1 126	-33 929	-35 040
Other investment liabilities	1 282	8 430	-8 620
Net errors and omissions	-15 504	-16 818	-16 754
Overall balance	31 705	35 857	6 248

Table 6.5 China's main exports, 1997 (in US$ millions and % by SITC category)

All commodities	182 791.7	100.0
0 Food and live animals	11 050.8	6.0
05 Vegetables and fruit	3 138.0	1.7
2 Crude materials (inedible) except fuels	4 151.6	2.3
3 Mineral fuels, lubricants etc.	6 992.5	3.8
33 Petroleum, petroleum products etc.	4 252.9	2.3
5 Chemicals and related products	10 102.4	5.5
6 Basic manufactures	35 158.4	19.2
65 Textile yarn, fabrics etc.	14 028.9	7.7
652 Woven cotton fabrics (excluding narrow or special fabrics)	3 091.9	1.7
7 Machinery and transport equipment	43 614.4	23.9
76 Telecommunications and sound equipment	10 303.8	5.6
77 Other electrical machinery, apparatus etc.	13 016.5	7.1
8 Miscellaneous manufactured articles	69 636.4	38.1
84 Clothing and accessories (excluding footwear)	31 875.5	17.4

the top three alone, Hong Kong, the United States and Japan, took 58 per cent (53 per cent in 1980).

On the import side, the government has a tendency to operate an active industrial policy, influencing and controlling what it can. Generally the government encourages the import of what is seen as essential, such as machinery and transport equipment, and discourages imports of 'non-essentials' such as most consumer goods.

In contrast to exports, the sources of Chinese imports have become marginally less concentrated. In 1998 the top six nations supplied 65 per cent of total imports (64 per cent in 1980), but the share of the top three suppliers, Japan, the United States and Taiwan, were responsible for only 44 per cent (the top three in 1980, Japan, United States and West Germany, 52 per cent). China's imports

are largely aimed at assisting the process of development, and include raw materials and much machinery and equipment.

China and the WTO

China first applied to join GATT, the precursor of the WTO, in 1986. It was not possible for China to be allowed in immediately, because it clearly did not meet the rules of admission. From China's point of view, the main disadvantage of not being a member of the WTO was that it could not routinely claim NTR treatment, which meant that restrictions could more easily be placed on Chinese exports, and, in practical terms, the important American market was not automatically available. Each year China had to renegotiate access. (See also Chapter 5.)

The essential principles involved in membership are:

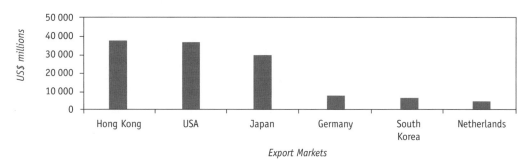

Figure 6.4 China's main export markets 1998 (in US$ millions)

Table 6.6 China's main imports, 1997 (in US$ millions and % by SITC category)

	All commodities	142 370.4	100.0
0	Food and live animals	4 288.2	3.0
2	Crude materials, excluding fuels	11 727.6	8.2
26	Textile fibres and waste	3 691.7	2.6
3	Mineral fuels etc.	10 364.3	7.3
33	Petroleum and its products	9 389.1	6.6
4	Animal and vegetable oil and fats	1 680.1	1.2
5	Chemicals and related products not elsewhere specified	19 046.8	13.4
562	Fertilizer manufacture	2 989.3	2.1
8	Plastic materials	9 210.4	6.5
6	Basic manufactures	32 909.0	23.1
65	Textile yarn and fabrics	12 527.5	8.8
67	Iron and steel	6 737.8	4.7
7	Machinery and transport equipment	52 722.9	37.0
71	Power-generating equipment	3 717.9	2.6
72	Machinery for special industries	9 704.9	6.8
8	Miscellaneous manufactured goods	8 352.3	5.9
84	Clothing and accessories	1 117.6	0.8

- Normal Trade Relations (NTR) treatment: this prevents discrimination against any other member nation, or favour to any, by insisting that the best terms given to any one country be extended to all.
- National treatment: imported goods must be treated exactly the same as domestically produced ones, thus preventing discrimination against foreigners.
- Non-tariff barriers: protection for domestic industry must be through clearly visible tariffs, and not made via concealed barriers, such as placing restrictions or charges on foreign products.
- Tariff concessions: when applying for membership, a country must submit a list of tariff concessions that it has agreed with other members. After the WTO admits the country, these rates cannot be increased, although they may be reduced.

The process of admission is twofold: first a WTO Working Party examines the applicant's economic and trade policies in depth, then bilateral negotiations take place between the applicant and concerned members of the WTO about the terms of accession. The results are combined into a protocol of accession that must be approved by a two-thirds majority of the members.

China faces special problems because of its socialist market economy. These include the presence of planned and market sectors, each with different rules; various subsidies and quotas; administratively set prices; differential treatment of foreign and local firms (as well as between different types of local firms); some secret rules; and high tariffs. China argues that its many changes over two decades should be seen as meeting the rules for admission but not all members yet agree.

Foreign exchange

As a result of a healthy balance of payments, China's gold and foreign exchange reserves are more than adequate. At December 31, 1998, the reserves stood at US$145 billion and were enough to cover eleven months' imports; this was a far cry from the situation in 1978 when the reserves would have purchased only one month's imports.

During the central planning period, China ran a fixed exchange rate system, with the currency inconvertible on international markets and usually heavily overvalued. A small black market existed in Hong Kong, and after the opening to tourists and business in the 1970s, an illegal kerbside market developed in China. In the 1980s China ran a dual exchange rate system, with a different rate set for foreigners doing business in China, including tourists. Foreigners used Foreign Exchange Certificates, which at least in the major cities began to spill over into society generally.

Swap markets developed where foreign and some trading businesses could buy or sell yuan at a rate closer to the market than the official high rates. This system altered on January 1, 1994 when Foreign Exchange Certificates started to be dropped, and the dual rate system ended with the combination

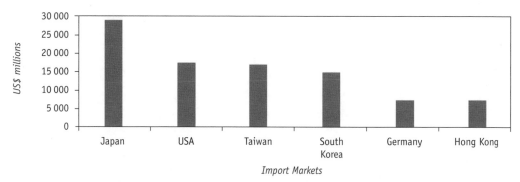

Figure 6.5 Main sources of imports 1998 (in US$ millions)

The External Sectors

of the swap and official rates. The currency was effectively made current account convertible on December 1, 1996. This means that all receipts and payments arising from international trade can be converted, for example profits on investment by foreign companies can be remitted, but the FDI itself, foreign loans and the trading of securities are still firmly controlled.

China's exchange rate in the 1990s

Since a large devaluation in 1994, the exchange rate has fluctuated around 8 to 8.5 yuan to the US dollar.

The Asian crisis of 1997 forced many Asian countries to devalue, but China resisted. It was able to do this because it had relatively little foreign hot money that could easily be removed. Once China stated that it would not devalue, national pride became involved and it was impossible to backtrack. Chinese exports languished and a devaluation would almost certainly have helped China, although globally it would have made it harder to end the Asian crisis and might have sparked off a further round of competitive devaluations.

Foreign capital

Since 1949, there have been only two periods when China has been prepared to accept foreign capital. The first was immediately after the new government took over, when the economy was in chaos and had to be restored and then developed. Loans were accepted from the Soviet Union and used to establish an industrial base, with the focus on heavy industry. From 1958 on, China entered an extended period of economic self-isolationism, which was to last until the early 1970s when foreign trade began to expand. Foreign investment did not become acceptable again until late in the 1970s, when a limited use was allowed.

In recent years, China has actively sought both international loans and FDI, and the amount secured depends on the willingness of foreigners to put money into the country. This varies year by year, but as a market, China always seems attractive to many. Even after the political crisis and Beijing massacre of 1989, FDI continued to grow, but briefly at a slower rate.

In order to attract FDI, since 1980 China has gradually reduced barriers to foreign investment and altered tax and profit rules in an effort to keep China competitive with other Third World nations. In this it has been successful. The restrictive rules on establishing joint ventures were eased in 1990 and assurances against nationalization given. A year later, preferential tax treatment was improved for wholly owned foreign enterprises, as well as for foreigners investing in preferred sectors such as energy. Foreign investors were allowed to purchase 'B' shares on the Shenzhen and Shanghai stock exchanges.

Foreign capital actually used (the agreed figure for investment is always higher than the utilized amount) averaged US$2888 million a year from 1979 to 1983, and during the

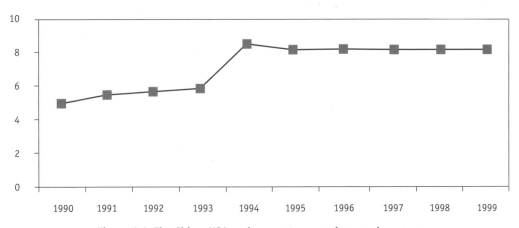

Figure 6.6 The China–USA exchange rate, yuan:$, annual average

China's Economy

1980s rose slowly to around US$10 000 million a year. It was 1993 before foreign capital utilized suddenly surged, and by 1997 it reached $64 408 million, before falling away in 1998 during the Asian crisis.

Foreign investment is valuable but not crucial for China: according to the World Bank, in 1997 FDI totalled US$60 828 million, but this made up only 4.9 per cent of GDP.

The sources of foreign capital, including both loans and FDI, have varied over time, but Hong Kong, Japan and the United States are regularly near the top and Taiwan has increased in importance. In 1988 the supply of foreign capital was heavily concentrated: Japan headed the list, followed by Hong Kong and Macau combined, and they supplied almost two-thirds of the total, while contributions from international organizations such as the World Bank made up another 11 per cent.

By 1997 the sources of foreign capital were more diverse: a third came from Hong Kong (now a part of China), but Japan in second place supplied under 10 per cent (see Table 6.8). The UK had slipped to seventh place from third in 1988. Over the past decade and excluding Hong Kong, Taiwan has become the largest investor in the country.

One problem with the Hong Kong figures is that some of the capital is already owned in China and has been moved to Hong Kong, then sent back to China in order to gain tax or other advantages. This so-called 'round tripping' confuses the figures, both for origin and total.

Foreign loans from international organizations can be sizeable. In 1993 the combined loans from the World Bank, the International Fund for Agricultural Development and the Asian Development Bank amounted to US$2 268.71 million, equivalent to 20.3 per cent of all foreign loans. The contribution of international organizations varies over the years: back in 1988 these three international bodies accounted for 10.8 per cent of total foreign capital supplied, including loans and investment. Almost all came from the World Bank.

Foreign debt

Despite accepting large quantities of foreign capital, China's foreign debt is easily manageable. The debt service ratio, measured by total debt service payments as a proportion of the export of goods and services (which raise the foreign exchange to service the debt), was below 12 per cent between 1990 and 1997, a low figure. Furthermore, the debt service ratio fell gradually over the decade.

MACROECONOMIC POLICIES

China's impressive economic achievements over the past two decades have been the result of government policies, events outside

Table 6.7 The flow of foreign capital (actually utilized) (in US$ millions)

1979–82	1983	1984	1985	1986	1987	1988	1989	1990
12 457	1 981	2 705	4 647	7 258	8 452	10 226	10 059	10 289

1991	1992	1993	1994	1995	1996	1997	1998
11 554	19 202	38 960	43 213	48 133	54 804	64 408	58 557

Table 6.8 The main sources of foreign capital in 1997 (in US$ millions)

Rank	Source	US$ millions	% of total
1	Hong Kong	21 651.11	33.6
2	Japan	6 325.97	9.8
3	USA	4 161.17	6.5
4	Taiwan	3 342.34	5.2
5	Singapore	2 806.96	4.4
6	Republic of Korea	2 242.63	3.5
7	UK	2 019.96	3.1
8	Virgin Islands	1 717.30	2.7
Total of 8		44 267.44	68.8

China, and a generous helping of luck. Together they have resulted in the country beginning the process of globalization, rapid economic growth, a reasonable average rate of inflation, a rise in the standard of living, a widening in income distribution, an increase in overt unemployment, and an enlargement of budget deficits.

Before Mao Zedong's death in 1976, China was in the grip of extremist ideology-driven ideals. After 1976, there were two years of political struggle and economic dithering before Deng Xiaoping emerged a clear winner to set in train a reform program at the Third Plenum of the Eleventh CCPCC in December 1978 (see Chapter 2). China now has two sectors, a planned one that has diminished in size but still covers those sectors regarded by the state as crucial (largely in heavy industry) and a market one, which includes private firms that have grown lustily from nothing and the preexisting collectively owned firms. The new TVEs are part of the collective sector. They are a mixed group of firms, partly or entirely owned by local authorities, or local officials, and often with some private input.

The reform program after 1978 required a new economic system. The earlier method of administrative decisions for all important economic matters was no longer adequate. Prices were to be allowed to fluctuate, labour and capital markets had to be set up, and fiscal and monetary instruments developed. A host of new laws in areas as diverse as labour, tax, banking, export, import, patents, copyright, company law, accounting, foreign investment and insurance was required.

The domestic reform program began in agriculture with contracts being signed with farmers to supply produce to the state, allowing them limited freedom to make production decisions and sell surpluses in the reopened local markets. Collective agriculture was abandoned before the mid-1980s, and family farming on state-owned land was established. Since then prices have gradually been freed and by 1998, when cotton could be sold on the market, grain was the only major crop still subject to state control.

Reforms were introduced more slowly in state-run industry, partly because the problem was more difficult. Instead, private firms were first allowed and later encouraged to set up alongside the planned sector so that a dual industrial structure emerged. In 1983, banks, which previously merely gave SOEs whatever funds the state plan dictated, began to lend to them instead, and the firms were allowed to retain part of their profit as an incentive measure. In 1986 the jobs-for-life system, which encouraged laziness and resulted in low productivity, began to be tackled by issuing labour contracts, although these were not rapidly and widely adopted. It was 1995 before a real Labour Law brought in minimum wages, arbitration committees, and labour contracts for those who still did not have them.

Before 1978, prices were set by the state. They were gradually freed up, starting with minor agricultural produce. A dual price system, one for planned goods, the other for market goods, was established in 1985 and planned prices were gradually increased towards market ones. By the early 1990s, the government claimed that free prices operated for 95 per cent of consumer goods and 85 per cent of industrial inputs.

Table 6.9 China's debt service ratio, selected years (in US$ millions)

	1980	1990	1991	1992	1993
Total debt stock	4 504	55 301	60 259	72 428	85 928
Debt service paid	930	7 057	8 305	8 618	10 168
Debt:service ratio		11.7	11.9	10.2	11.1
	1994	1995	1996	1997	
Total debt stock	100 457	118 090	128 817	146 697	
Debt service paid	11 135	15 066	15 756	18 445	
Debt:service ratio	8.9	9.9	8.7	8.6	

Table 6.10 The major reforms

1971	Early reform policy: to increase the use of foreign trade to promote development.
1977	Early reform policy: to encourage the inflow of foreign capital.
1979	The start of the transition process. State agricultural purchase prices were increased to promote production.
	A joint venture law was passed to encourage foreign firms to set up in China.
1980	The responsibility system was introduced in agriculture, as were contracts to supply the state with produce. The sale of surplus output in newly reopened markets was permitted, the aim being to promote production.
	Four Special Economic Zones were established in South China to stimulate foreign capital inflow and economic development.
1981	Private individual enterprises, previously forbidden, were encouraged in commerce and industry.
1983	To promote industrial output, enterprises were allowed to retain part of their profits. To encourage managerial efforts in SOEs, banks were instructed to lend to them rather than merely handing over state allocations as in the past.
1984	The reforms accelerated in agriculture and communes were largely abandoned in favour of family farming on state-owned land. The government started to free prices and continued to remove state controls over agriculture.
	Fourteen Open Cities were established outside the Special Economic Zones to further encourage foreign investment and promote local initiatives.
	The People's Bank of China began to move towards being a central bank, and four new banks were established.
1985	A dual price system was introduced, with prices for the planned sector and higher ones for private firms and the market.
1986	Labour contracts were introduced to end the jobs-for-life policy in industry in an attempt to stimulate worker enthusiasm and move towards a market for labour.
1987	Further price relaxation saw all prices placed in three groups: market-determined, government-guided, and government-set.
1988	To try to stimulate industrial reform, a contract responsibility system and a bankruptcy law were introduced to industry.
1989/90	Purchase prices were raised to encourage agricultural production. The central government found it increasingly difficult to raise revenues.
1992	SOEs were given more power to make decisions as plan targets and price controls over them were weakened.
	Deng Xiaoping's tour of south China accelerated the reform movement, which was showing signs of lagging.
1994	Agricultural purchase prices were again raised to encourage production.
	Major fiscal and monetary reform began; the People's Bank of China was turned into a central bank.
1995	The Labour Law of January 1 strongly promoted labour contracts and accelerated the movement towards a labour market.
1996	The transformation and mergers of struggling industrial firms was encouraged to promote efficiency.
	In a movement towards globalization, tariff cuts were reduced from an average of 36 per cent to 23 per cent.
	Agricultural purchase prices were raised again to encourage production.
1997	New tariff cuts in October reduced the average to 17 per cent.
1998	The reform of agriculture was almost completed when the state freed the price of cotton, leaving grain the last remaining crop under direct control.
	The problem of SOE inefficiency began to be tackled seriously after a decade of increasing pressure on them. The SOEs began to dismiss workers, which increased the level of unemployment.
1999	The dismissed redundant SOE workers and those pensioned off faced serious standard of living difficulties, so the state increased their basic living allowance or pension.

The banking sector began to shuffle slowly towards a Western-style system but as it is forced to lend to SOEs with no hope of repayment, it is riddled with non-performing loans and is technically bankrupt. Nineteen eighty-four saw the creation of four banks: the Agricultural Bank of China, the Industrial and Commercial Bank of China, the People's Construction Bank of China (subsequently renamed China Construction Bank) and the Bank of China. A proliferation of small banks, credit cooperatives and other financial institutions mushroomed after that. The People's Bank of China now functions as a normal central bank.

In the external sector, foreign investment began to arrive in a limited way in the late 1970s then rose steadily, until by the early 1990s China was the largest recipient in the developing world. By 1997, China took 37 per cent of all direct foreign investment flowing to developing countries. Foreign investment provided new technology, foreign management skills, access to foreign markets and much-needed competition for China's domestic industry.

As the reform process proceeded, the central government began to find it harder to raise revenues, as SOE profits declined and local authorities gained at central expense. Expenditures, particularly subsidies, became a drain. In a major fiscal and monetary reform in 1984, efforts were made to improve the centre's position relative to the provincial one. Central and local taxes were separated and a value added tax was brought in.

The existing SOEs were frequently inefficient, overstaffed and of low productivity, and in dire need of reform, but forcing rapid improvement here would have led to unemployment for large numbers of workers. The state chose to go cautiously until 1998, when mergers and closures resulted in many unwanted staff and workers being dismissed. Naturally the level of unemployment rose and social hardship worsened. To ameliorate the effects, in 1999 the government increased the basic living allowance for redundant workers from SOEs and improved pensions in the

SOE sector as well as paying off the arrears of delayed pension payments.

The problems of the unemployed are compounded by massive urban drift. The introduction of market efficiency into agriculture and slackening of controls has meant that many peasants move to the cities, where they eke out a living as best they can. Although lowly paid and usually despised by locals, who blame them for most of the growing criminal activity, any job still pays substantially more than their earnings in the fields.

The collapse of the Soviet Union in 1991 led to a struggle over the economy within the leadership. The choice was to freeze change or push forward towards a thorough market economy. This was settled in 1992 when Deng Xiaoping won the dispute after a much-publicized tour of southern China, which strongly signalled his preferences for a full-blown market economy. If 1978 was a watershed in economic policy, 1992 was the year that established the permanency of the reform policy.

The 1997 Asian financial crisis hurt China as it resulted in a diminution of FDI flows in 1998, while total exports barely increased and aggregate demand fell, as did economic growth. Since then, the economy has been growing at around 7–8 per cent.

Macroeconomic control of the economy, although improved, is still deficient. Since 1997, faced with low demand and (for China) relative stagnation, the government has tried to induce a domestic expansion by a series of interest rate reductions. But demand did not pick up, indicating that monetary policy is either subject to huge lags or is as yet ineffective. As a result, the government was forced into more Keynesian methods of expansion by increasing spending on infrastructure. Internal demand currently remains weak but exports are picking up as Asia pulls out of the earlier crisis.

Much of the vast improvement in growth and standard of living that has occurred over two decades can be attributed to the reform program, which has been implemented gradually without causing chaos or excessive political upheaval. This has resulted in:

- the better allocation of land, labour and capital, by dealing with the mismatches inherited from the period of planning and then by using them to produce goods and services demanded domestically or abroad
- improved incentives for individuals and enterprises in agriculture, industry and commerce
- the growth of a dynamic private sector alongside the state one, together with the new TVEs
- improved financial and administrative systems, which includes a start on moving towards instituting the rule of law
- the use of foreign capital and expertise via loans, aid and direct investment
- more use of foreign trade, involving selling the goods and services at which China is proficient, in exchange for the goods and services required for development
- increased competition from enterprises with foreign capital in them, and from imports, for the previously heavily protected domestic enterprises
- the shedding of unnecessary workers from productive and administrative government enterprises.

THE MACROECONOMIC PERFORMANCE

Growth rates

Since the establishment of the CCP government in 1949, China's economic growth has fluctuated markedly. The highest average growth rates of GDP were recorded in the 1950s, which averaged 11.0 per cent, the best recorded rate being 21.3 per cent in 1958 (although data in that year were heavily exaggerated). The nadir was the 1960s with a worst year in 1961 of −27.3 per cent. Since the reform policies began in 1978, the average annual growth rate has been just under 10 per cent per annum over two decades (best year 1984, 15.2 per cent). There has been a tendency for growth to be faster in periods of more market-oriented policies; during or shortly after periods of political extremism, the economy suffered and growth could become negative, for instance 1960–62, and 1967–68.

Recent growth has been more than satisfactory. After a slow start in 1990 (3.8 per cent), the 1990s showed noteworthy economic success. Double-digit growth of real GDP occurred between 1992 and 1995 and the average for 1990–98 was a commendable 9.1 per cent per annum. There is some reason to believe that the statistics may be exaggerated, so these figures must be treated with caution.

Inflation rates

Over the past two decades the inflation rate has fluctuated but averaged just over 7 per cent per annum, after low official rates were recorded during the earlier planned period when inflation was concealed.

The average price increase between 1990 and 1998 was 7.1 per cent per annum, but this disguises both a major inflationary boom, which peaked in 1994 when the increase in prices reached 21.7 per cent, and deflation in

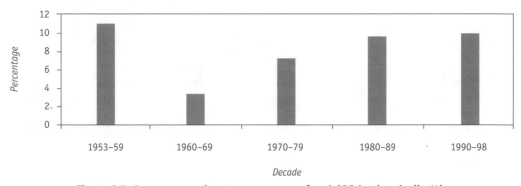

Figure 6.7 Average growth rates per annum of real GDP by decade (in %)

1998–99. The fall in prices helped consumers but caused problems for many companies in China.

Wages

The wages of staff and workers have increased substantially in recent times. Between 1990 and 1998 they rose by an average of 5.4 per cent per annum after adjustment for changes in the cost of living. Progress, however, has not always been smooth. In the high inflation years of 1988–89, real wages fell as the rise in prices outstripped wage increases.

Certain sectors have lagged behind the general improvement, especially those working in the government sector, where wages are fixed by the state. The major gains have gone to those working in modern private industry or in firms with foreign capital involvement. In an effort to rectify this, and to encourage consumption, in 1999 the government increased the wages of civil servants and raised the urban minimum living guarantee standard.

Peasant income is harder to measure, but in 1998 the farmers' annual net income per capita stood at only 2162 yuan, as compared with the 7479 yuan average wage for an urban staff or worker. The cost of living is of course lower in rural areas but facilities are poorer; peasant incomes also fluctuate more than urban ones.

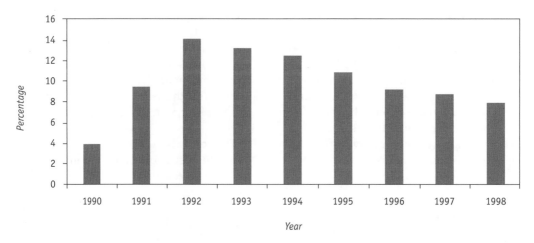

Figure 6.8 Real rate of growth of GDP, 1990–98 (in %)

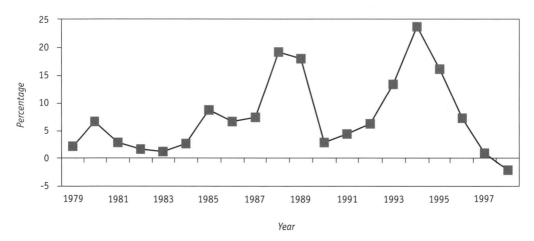

Figure 6.9 The inflation record: General Index of Retail Prices, 1978–98

Although peasants receive a great deal less than their urban counterpart, they improved their position vis-à-vis urban workers between 1978 and 1998. In 1978 the ratio of peasant household income to wages was 1:4.6, but by 1998 it had risen to 1:3.5

The standard of living

The standard of living can be measured in several ways. National income per capita is the easiest, but because prices vary between countries and are significantly lower in China, it is better to adjust the measure on

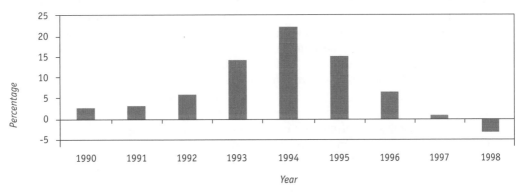

Figure 6.10 Inflation in the 1990s: General Index of Retail Prices

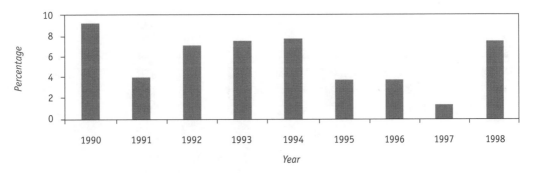

Figure 6.11 The change in real wages of staff and workers, 1984–98 (in %)

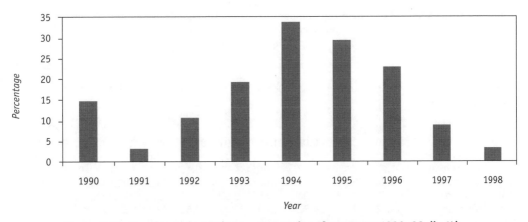

Figure 6.12 The change in net income per capita of peasants, 1990–98 (in %)

The Macroeconomic Performance

the basis of purchasing power parity, in other words, what a dollar will buy locally. On this basis, in 1990 China had a GDP per head of US$1990 and by 1997 it had increased to US$3130.

The standard of living can also be indicated by the private consumption of goods and services accompanied by the provision of public goods and services.

In China, each decade since 1949 shows an increase in the level of private consumption of goods and services, with particularly high growth in the 1980s and 1990s of around 7 per cent per annum.

The improvements can be seen if we examine the actual consumption of goods. In a poor country such as China, an increase in the consumption of items such as washing machines, electric fans, refrigerators, television sets and cameras indicates a rising standard of living. In recent years, both urban and rural dwellers have done well, as Table 6.11 shows.

Although the absolute level of ownership by peasants is lower, the index shows that during the 1990s they managed to increase their possession of desirable consumer goods faster than urban dwellers. The exception is bicycle ownership: most urban families already have one or more and some are switching to motor vehicles.

On the rise in education see Chapter 10. Health standards have improved substantially, so much so that the sizeable reduction in death rates ahead of birth rates was an important contributor to the population

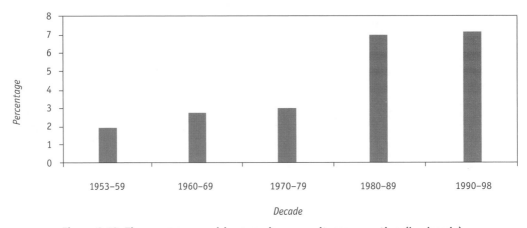

Figure 6.13 The average annual increase in per capita consumption (by decade)

Table 6.11 The standard of living: the number of consumption goods owned per 100 urban and rural households year end, 1990–98

	1990	1991	1992	1993	1994	1995	1996	1997	1998	Index 1990=100
Washing machines urban	78.41	80.58	83.41	86.36	87.29	88.97	90.06	89.12	90.57	115.5
Washing machines rural	9.12	10.99	12.23	13.82	15.30	16.90	20.54	21.87	22.81	250.1
Electric fans urban	135.50	143.48	146.03	151.64	153.79	167.35	168.07	165.74	168.37	124.3
Electric fans rural	41.36	53.3	60.08	71.79	80.91	88.96	100.46	105.93	111.59	269.8
Refrigerators urban	42.33	48.7	52.6	56.68	62.10	66.22	69.67	72.98	76.08	179.7
Refrigerators rural	1.22		2.17	3.05	4.00	5.15	7.27	8.49	9.25	758.2
Colour TVs urban	59.04	68.41	74.81	79.46	86.21	89.79	93.50	100.48	105.43	178.6
Colour TVs rural	4.72		8.08	10.86	13.52	16.92	22.91	27.32	32.59	690.5
Cameras urban	19.22	21.32	24.32	26.48	29.83	30.56	32.13	33.64	36.26	188.7
Cameras rural	0.70	0.87	1.0	0.99	1.16	1.42	1.94	2.06	2.22	317.1

problem (see Chapter 7). Between 1949 and 1998, the provision of doctors per thousand people has increased 2.4 times and that of hospital beds 15.5 times.

In one respect, the provision of health has worsened for China's rural population. By the mid–1970s around 90 per cent of rural dwellers in communes were covered for basic medical care, however limited this was, but since the passing of the communes only around 10 per cent of farmers have health coverage and the rest must rely on private treatment.

A different way of measuring prosperity was invented by the World Bank at the start of the 1990s. This is the 'Human Development Index', which examines a country and rates it on the basis of life expectancy, educational attainment, and income. China, as a medium-level country for human development, has improved steadily since the mid–1980s (see Figure 6.15), and in 1997 ranked 98th of the 174 countries in the world for which there is data. Canada, Norway and the United States came top, with Sierra Leone, Niger and Ethiopia at the bottom.

On the United Nations' poverty measure of living on a dollar a day or less, some 29.4 per cent of China's population is below the poverty line, but using China's own measure of poverty, which is less stringent, it is only 11 per cent.

Employment

The official figures for unemployment are not particularly meaningful. First, the way they are defined excludes many people normally regarded as unemployed, such as any of the

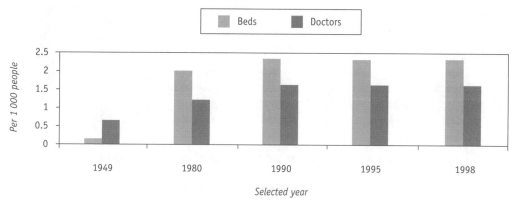

Figure 6.14 The standard of living: hospital beds and doctors per thousand people (selected years)

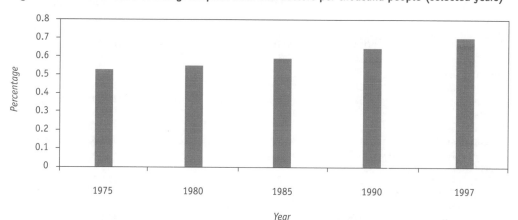

Figure 6.15 China's Human Development Index (selected years)

Note: The theoretical maximum is 1.0; medium-level countries are defined as those scoring between 0.500 and 0.799.

The Macroeconomic Performance

500 million people who work in agriculture, those who migrate to the cities (possibly numbering 100 million or more), and those in urban areas aged above 50 years for males or 45 for females. Second, many people with little reason to be kept on are retained in unproductive work rather than being made redundant. Third, the figures may be fudged and kept low for reasons of national pride. With these caveats in mind, the figures are presented in Figure 6.16.

No one can be certain, but if all those currently excluded, and all those underemployed in government organizations and SOEs were to be included, figures perhaps eight to eleven times those reported might not surprise.

The government budget

It is difficult for the central government to control income and expenditure and so achieve its budget. In 1998 the government budgeted for a deficit of RMB¥44.8 million, in an effort to expand the flagging economy, but the outcome was a deficit of 96.0 million. This result was the consequence of central expenditures increasing faster than budgeted (11.7 per cent over budget) and also increasing faster than revenues (3.1 per cent over bud-

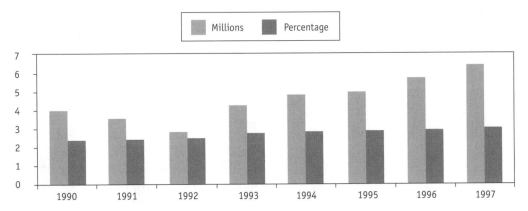

Figure 6.16 The number and percentage of urban unemployed

Table 6.12 Government finances, 1998–99 (in million yuan)

	1998 Budget	1998 Outcome	Difference		1999 Budget	1999 Budget change over previous year's outcome
	Billions yuan	Billions yuan	Billions yuan	% of budget	Billions yuan	%
Central government budget						
Total state revenue	532.0	548.3	16.3	3.1	588.6	7.3
Total state expenditure	576.8	644.3	67.5	11.7	738.9	14.7
Balance	−44.8	−96.0	−51.2	114.3	−150.3	–
Revenue						
Centrally collected	471.1	488.5	17.4	3.7	528.8	8.2
Local authority remitted	59.8	59.8	0	0.0	59.8	0.0
Expenditure						
Central expenditure	275.3	312.0	36.7	13.3	411.1	31.8
Remitted to local authorities	301.7	332.3	30.6	10.1	327.8	−1.4
Local budgets						
Revenues	798.9	829.1	30.2	3.8	879.9	6.1
Expenditures	798.9	824.9	26	3.3	879.9	6.7
Local surplus	0.0	4.2	4.2		0.0	n.a.

get). Local authorities, which were targeted to spend 58.1 per cent of the total of central and local expenditures, exceeded the figures on both revenue and expenditure, but as the excess revenues exceeded excess expenditure, on balance they had a net contractionary effect.

The real government deficit is greater than the figures indicate, because the country's practice is to count borrowings as income, which is not standard practice. In addition, part of the expenditure on the military is hidden, and although some may appear in the budget in disguised form, not all of it seems to be included. Finally, forcing the banks to make loans to loss-making SOEs with no hope of repayment should probably be counted in the budget as a direct subsidy.

Economic cycles

The Chinese economy is prone to suffer from economic cycles. When economic growth increases rapidly it leads to a rise in prices; the normal response of the government is to introduce an austerity program in order to contain the inflation and slow the rate of growth.

The economic boom of 1987–88 was fuelled by consumption. The peasants had enjoyed substantial increases in incomes, especially in 1987, and wished to spend; urban workers outside the state-run sector had received substantial income increases in 1985–88; and people generally had the chance to make up for the austerity years of the Cultural Revolution.

The next boom, which began in 1992 and peaked in 1994, was investment-led, especially in the construction industry in coastal locations. It was assisted by an uncontrolled expansion of the money supply and a rise in extra-budgetary funds. The boom was contained and tailed off into single-digit steady growth so that by 1996 China achieved a soft landing.

Investment booms led by local authorities are common. The decentralization of authority as part of the reform program has increased the power of local governments and some have returned to the traditional pattern of behaving as local fiefdoms, which has decreased the ability of the central government to exercise control. With the recent rapid economic development and periodic surges in the rate of growth, the construction industry is particularly volatile.

ECONOMIC PROBLEMS

Since the decisions of the Third Plenum of the Eleventh CCPCC in December 1978, the overall goal has been to revitalize the country by increasing the use of a market economy. China is both an 'economy in transition' as it moves from central planning to the market, and a developing country. At the same time the overriding goal has been to keep the CCP in power. China has been highly successful in its efforts, yet economic problems still exist. Some of these were inherited, but most are connected with the effort to introduce market structures and policies, while a few are the result of external forces.

The main economic problems inherited at 1976–78

- Poverty and low living standards
- Growth less than needed to solve such problems as poverty and cope with population increases
- Reduced work ethic, the result of the powerful experience of being punished for trying to do better; also a lack of incentives to work hard
- Extremely poor resource allocation of land, labour and capital, the legacy of planners' mistakes and political interference in the economy
- Low productivity levels, backward technology
- Regional income disparities
- Lack of agreement among top Party and government leaders on what direction to take and what economic policies to pursue
- No experience of economic policies other than primitive central planning together with the dominant role of political movements

The main current economic problems
Macroeconomic problems
- Reduced domestic demand and slow growth in total exports in late 1997 led to slower economic growth.
- Deflation emerged in October 1997 and continued at least to the end of 1999.
- Surplus capacity emerged in 1998–99 in many industries, as new capacity came on line at a time when demand was lowered.
- Official cartels were promoted by government in an unsuccessful attempt to arrest price falls; these cartel arrangements may limit competition in the future.
- It was difficult to encourage consumer demand in order to boost the economy. The earlier spending splurges were finished and increasing uncertainty about employment prospects, as well as housing, medical care and pension provision, encouraged consumer caution. Government efforts to expand the economy in 1999 were not conspicuously successful, although domestic sales picked up in the latter half of the year and export earning began to grow again.

Efficiency, productivity and labour problems
- The number of laid-off workers increased; difficult to supply enough work to stop unemployment rising further. A real attempt to reduce unemployment is needed at some stage.
- It is difficult to improve productivity levels and efficiency levels without forcing even higher rates of unemployment. A formidable balancing act is needed.
- How should the SOEs be reformed? These are particularly poor, with low productivity, low profits and overstaffing, which results in large subsidies and financial predicaments for banks and the state. The problem is the result of mismanagement, waste and fraud.
- How should the banking system be reformed to make it efficient, deal with the bad debts and worthless assets, and get it

out of technical bankruptcy. An end is needed to the policy of soft-lending, which means easy loans to SOEs, irrespective of underlying assets or likely ability to repay.
- Pension funds were instituted for SOEs in 1997, but low profits or a lack of financial provision, and the ageing population, mean a shortfall in pension funds.
- Domestic innovation is weak and most technology must be imported. Education standards need to be raised to increase creativity and reduce learning by rote.
- Growth in investment is slower than in the past.

Resource allocation and cycles problems
- Boom and bust pattern in urban housing and construction is common.
- How can agricultural output, especially food output, be kept growing?
- What can be done about underemployed labour in rural areas? An expansion of market towns is planned.

Socio-politico-economic problems that affect the economy
- Corruption is endemic in society.
- The rule of law is in its infancy.
- What can be done about beggars and peasants who have moved to urban areas?
- Bureaucracy and red tape continues, although it is being attacked.
- There is widening income distribution and an increase in envy of the nouveaux riches with their conspicuous consumption.
- There is disillusionment with the CCP and a feeling that there is little to support or believe in.

International problems
- Maintaining the growth in exports to eat into the industrial surplus capacity and compensate for low domestic demand.
- Appeasing the USA on the balance of trade deficit that it has with China.
- Encouraging FDI and persuading foreign investors that China is still a desirable place in which to invest.

7   POPULATION

TOTAL POPULATION

More people have lived under a single central government in China for much of that country's history than anywhere else on Earth. Since coming to power in 1949, the PRC government has reacted to this situation with a variety of policies, ranging from pride in the size of China's population during some periods to strong attempts at others to curb population growth rates, especially during the 1980s and 1990s.

    The population of China remains predominantly rural. However, the urban:rural ratio has risen steadily since 1949, and gathered momentum in the 1980s. A readjustment of the criteria for building towns in 1984 resulted in large numbers of newly built towns, which partly explains the sudden rise in the proportion of the urban population in that year shown in Table 7.1.[1] The figures in the table cover all the provinces, autonomous regions and province-level cities of the Chinese mainland. In the last column, 'urban:rural ratio', the urban population includes all those people living within areas under the jurisdiction of cities, while the rural population includes the population of counties, but not of towns.

Table 7.1 Total population figures

Year	Population (in millions)	Growth rate over previous year (per '000)	Male:Female ratio (%)	Urban:Rural ratio (%)
1949	541.67	16	51.96/48.04	10.6/89.4
1950	551.96	18.99	51.94/48.06	11.2/88.8
1951	563.00	19.60	51.92/48.08	11.8/88.2
1952	574.82	20.99	51.90/48.10	12.5/87.5
1953	587.96	22.85	51.82/48.18	13.3/86.7
1954	602.66	25.00	51.84/48.16	13.7/86.3
1955	614.65	19.89	51.75/48.25	13.5/86.5
1956	628.28	22.18	51.79/48.21	14.6/85.4
1957	646.53	29.05	51.77/48.23	15.4/84.6
1958	659.94	20.74	51.82/48.18	16.2/83.8
1959	672.07	18.38	51.91/48.09	18.4/81.6
1960	662.07	−14.88	51.78/48.22	19.7/80.3
1961	658.59	−5.26	51.44/48.56	19.3/80.7
1962	672.95	21.80	51.29/48.71	17.3/82.7
1963	691.72	27.89	51.37/48.63	16.8/83.2
1964	704.99	19.18	51.27/48.73	18.4/81.6
1965	725.38	28.88	51.18/48.82	18.0/82.0
1966	745.42	27.63	51.23/48.77	17.9/82.1
1967	763.68	24.50	51.22/48.78	17.7/82.3
1968	785.34	28.36	51.22/48.78	17.6/82.4
1969	806.71	27.21	51.18/48.82	17.5/82.5
1970	829.92	28.77	51.43/48.57	17.4/82.6
1971	852.29	26.95	51.41/48.59	17.3/82.7
1972	871.77	22.86	51.40/48.60	17.1/82.9
1973	892.11	23.33	51.42/48.58	17.2/82.8
1974	908.59	18.47	51.43/48.57	17.2/82.8
1975	924.20	17.18	51.47/48.53	17.3/82.7
1976	937.17	14.03	51.49/48.51	17.4/82.6
1977	949.74	13.41	51.50/48.50	17.6/82.4
1978	962.59	13.53	51.49/48.51	17.9/82.1

Table 7.1 (cont.)

Year	Population (in millions)	Growth rate over previous year (per '000)	Male:Female ratio (%)	Urban:Rural ratio (%)
1979	975.42	13.33	51.46/48.54	19.0/81.0
1980	987.05	11.92	51.45/48.55	19.4/80.6
1981	975.42	13.33	51.46/48.54	19.0/81.0
1982	1 015.41	14.68	51.52/48.48	20.8/79.2
1983	1 030.08	14.45	51.58/48.42	23.5/76.5
1984	1 043.57	13.10	51.59/48.41	23.0/77.0
1985	1 058.51	14.32	51.70/48.30	23.7/76.3
1986	1 075.07	15.64	51.70/48.30	24.5/75.5
1987	1 093.00	16.68	51.50/48.50	25.3/74.7
1988	1 110.26	15.79	51.52/48.48	25.8/74.2
1989	1 127.04	15.11	51.55/48.45	26.2/73.8
1990	1 143.33	14.45	51.52/48.48	26.4/73.6
1991	1 158.23	13.03	51.34/48.66	26.4/73.6
1992	1 171.71	11.64	51.05/48.95	27.6/72.4
1993	1 185.17	11.49	51.02/48.98	28.1/71.9
1994	1 198.50	11.25	51.10/48.90	28.6/71.4
1995 (Feb)	1 200.00	n.a.	n.a.	n.a.
1995	1 211.21	10.60	51.03/48.97	29.0/71.0
1996	1 223.89	10.47	50.82/49.18	29.4/70.6
1997	1 236.26	10.11	51.07/48.93	29.9/70.1
1998	1 248.10	9.53	50.98/49.02	30.4/69.6
1999	1 259	8.77	n.a	30.9/69.1

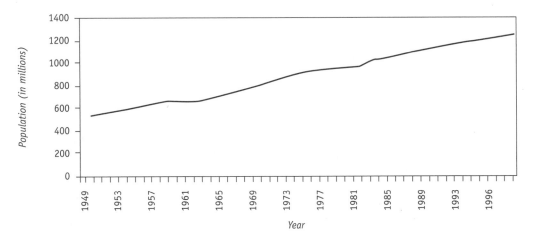

Figure 7.1 Total population figures (in millions)

There have been five censuses held in the People's Republic of China, in 1953, 1964, 1982, 1990 and 2000, applying in the first four cases to July 1 and in the last to November 1. In addition, there have been two sample censuses, applying to July 1, 1987 and October 1, 1995. Table 7.2 shows the main results of each of the censuses and sample censuses. They include only those areas under the control of the PRC's government, in other words not Taiwan, Hong Kong or Macau.

The figures in Table 7.1 are based on the State Statistical Bureau's published figures, and on the State Statistical Bureau's annual communiqués of China's

Table 7.2 Main results of the PRC's censuses and sample censuses

1953 census

Total population: 582 603 417 (601 938 035 if 11 743 320 Overseas Chinese and Chinese students studying overseas, and 7 591 298 people in Taiwan are included)
Males: 297 553 518
Females: 276 652 422
Male:female proportion: 51.82:48.18
Sex ratio (females taken as 100): 107.56
Average size of households (persons): 4.34
Percentage living in cities and towns: 13.26

1964 census

Total population: 694 581 759
Males: 356 517 011
Females: 338 064 748
Male:female proportion: 51.33:48.67
Sex ratio (females taken as 100):105.46
Average size of households (persons): 4.41
Percentage living in cities and towns: 14.1

1982 census

Total population: 1 008 175 288
Growth rate over preceding year (per thousand): 14.55
Birth rate over preceding year (per thousand): 20.91
Death rate over preceding year (per thousand): 6.36
Males: 519 433 369
Females: 488 741 919
Male:female proportion: 51.5:48.5
Sex ratio (females taken as 100): 106.3
Average size of households (persons): 4.41
Percentage living in cities and towns: 20.60

1987 sample census

Total population: 1 072 330 000
Growth rate over preceding year (per thousand): 14.8
Birth rate over preceding year (per thousand): 21.2
Death rate over preceding year (per thousand): 6.4
Males: 547 960 630
Females: 524 369 370
Male:female proportion: 51.1:48.9
Sex ratio (females taken as 100): 104.5

1990 census

Total population: 1 133 682 501
Growth rate over preceding year (per thousand): 14.70
Birth rate over preceding year (per thousand): 20.98
Death rate over preceding year (per thousand): 6.28
Males: 584 949 922
Females: 548 732 579
Male:/female proportion: 51.6:48.4
Sex ratio (females taken as 100): 106.6
Average size of households (persons): 3.96
Percentage living in cities and towns: 26.23

1995 sample census (from 1.04 per cent of the total population)

Total population: 1 189 130 000
Growth rate over preceding year (per thousand): 10.55
Birth rate over preceding year (per thousand): 17.12
Death rate over preceding year (per thousand): 6.57
Males: 605 279 000
Females: 583 851 000

Table 7.2 (cont.)

Male:female proportion: 50.9:49.1
Sex ratio (females taken as 100): 103.67
Average size of households (persons): 3.7

2000 census
    Total population: 1 265 830 000 (1 295 330 000 including Taiwan, Hong Kong and Macau)
    Average annual growth rate since 1990 (per thousand): 10.7
    Percentage of population aged under 14: 22.9
    Percentage of population aged 65 and over: 6.96
    Number of people aged 65 and over: 88.1 million
    Male/female proportion: 51.63/48.37
    Sex ratio (females taken as 100): 106.74
    Average size of households (person): 3.44
    Percentage living in cities and towns: 36.09

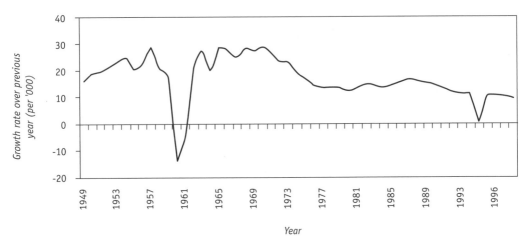

Figure 7.2 Total population figures (Growth rate over previous year per '000)

socioeconomic development. For the year 1995, a figure is added for February 15, since that was the day on which the Chinese government estimated the country to have reached the crucial figure of 1.2 billion.[2] In the case of four of the census years, 1953, 1964, 1982 and 1990, or the sample census years 1987 and 1995, they differ slightly from the figures given by the census, or sample census, for two main reasons:

- They are less precise.
- They refer to the end of the year, whereas the census or sample census figures in each case refer to the middle of the year, or, in the case of the 1995 sample census, to October 1.

The Chinese government was extremely reticent about releasing population (and other) statistics from the late 1950s until the end of the 1970s. Even the existence, let alone the results, of the 1964 census was not revealed until years after the event. The census figures have become much more detailed and reliable with the passage of time. Table 7.3 shows population figures in millions for some years; the direct sources of these figures are other than Chinese.[3]

The figures shown in this table are consistently lower than the official statistics. Whereas the official version is that the population reached 1.2 billion early in 1995, this table does not show it moving so high until two years later.

In 1980, at the Third Session of the Fifth NPC, Premier Hua Guofeng formally announced the policy of restricting each couple (except among the minority nationalities) to one child only, and to limiting the total population to 1.2 billion by the end of the twentieth century. The 1990 census showed some successes in restricting population growth, but also some failures. At the news conference following the release of the 1990 census results, Zhang Sai, president of the State Statistical Bureau, stated his view that there would have been 200 million more babies born in the previous decade but for the one-child-per-couple policy. And at the Twenty-third General Population Conference of the International Union for Scientific Study of Population, held in Beijing in October 1997, Premier Li Peng stated that there had been 300 million births less from the mid–1970s to the present, because of the population policy.[4] But at the same time, the figures showed that the population growth rate had actually risen. The result was a renewed, indeed strengthened, commitment to the policy of population restriction in the 1990s, the figures in Table 7.1, the sample census of 1995 and the 2000 census suggesting some success. Yet the goal of limiting the Chinese population to 1.2 billion by the turn of the century was shown to be over-optimistic by the fact that, according to official sources, the population reached that figure in February 1995. In September that year the Fifth Plenum of the Fourteenth Central Committee formally revised the goal to limiting the population to within 1.3 billion by 2000 and 1.4 billion by 2010 (see also Chapter 1, C. September 28, 1995). Even in the 1980s, there were exemptions for minority nationalities (see Chapter 9) and for some peasants whose first child was a girl. At the end of January 2000, it was announced that couples who were themselves born into single-child families would themselves be allowed up to two children, with the critical period being around 2005 when a large number of only children, born in the 1980s, would reach reproductive age. By that time, the fertility rate had sunk below replacement level. Authorities were afraid the one-child policy could eventually create a society in which there were not enough adult children for the care of old parents. This did not indicate any relaxation of the population control policy. In March 2000 the CCP Central Committee and State Council declared that China would attempt to create a better population control system that would limit population growth to 1.5 per cent per year (see Chapter 1, E. March 2, 2000). On May 7, 2000, NCNA stated that 'the country will continue to encourage marriage and childbearing at later ages and call for one child per couple while some couples will be allowed to have a second child in accordance with the law'.

A survey conducted by the State Statistical Bureau between January 1987 and October 1988 indicated that 16.75 per cent of babies born in that period were not registered. In the cities the incidence of non-registration was 2.35 per cent, but in the countryside it was 31.85 per cent. This serious problem of under-registration indicates that the population figures for the late 1980s may be substantial undercounts.[5]

Most of the under-registration is of girls and due to the continuing wish for the single child to be male, which remains especially strong in the countryside. The 1990 census found the sex ratio of the zero age group to be

Table 7.3 Population figures in millions for selected years

Year	Population	Year	Population	Year	Population	Year	Population
1973	811	1983	1015.4	1989	1103.9	1995	1178
1975	820	1984	1034.5	1990	1119.9	1996	1191
1978	958	1985	1042.0	1991	1151.3	1997	1200
1979	971	1986	1050.0	1992	1158.2	1998	1215
1981	985	1987	1062.0	1993	1149.5	1999	1227.2
1982	1008.0*	1988	1087.0	1994	1162		

Note: * Including residents of Hong Kong and Taiwan.

Total Population

111.75, at age 1 to be 111.59, and at age 2 to be 110.11. The 1995 sample census showed the sex ratio at the zero age group to be 116.57 and at age 1 to be 121.08, in other words even higher than in the 1990 census.[6] In most countries about 103 to 106 baby boys are born for every 100 baby girls. In countries such as South Korea, China and India, sex ratios at birth have been higher than this, and a sex ratio of just under or even over 120 demands explanation. The main one is under-registration of girls, but selective abortion has been rising and common in the 1990s, when the technology enabling the discovery of the sex of the baby well before birth has been widespread.[7] Female infanticide also exists, but its extent is unknown.

One factor making the task of supervising, let alone controlling, birth quotas very difficult is the existence of the 'floating' population. The first decade of reform after 1978 saw the movement around the country of about 50 million people. They included many women of child-bearing age who (or whose families) took advantage of the lack of permanent address to evade birth control authorities.[8] In the 1990s the 'floating population' continued to expand. A national conference on the subject in 1995 estimated it at 80 million, though with some 44 million registered with public security organizations as 'temporary residents'.[9] There are many categories of these migrants. However, it appears that the socially motivated mobile population, of the kind that may wish or be able to avoid scrutiny in order to be able to have more than their quota of children, is lower than in the early years of the reform period.[10]

POPULATION DENSITY

China may be the most populous country in the world, but it is not the most densely populated. The area of those territories currently ruled as part of the People's Republic of China totals 9.6 million square kilometres. Omitting Hong Kong and Macau, the 1964, 1982 and 1990 censuses show, respectively, a rise in the population density in the People's

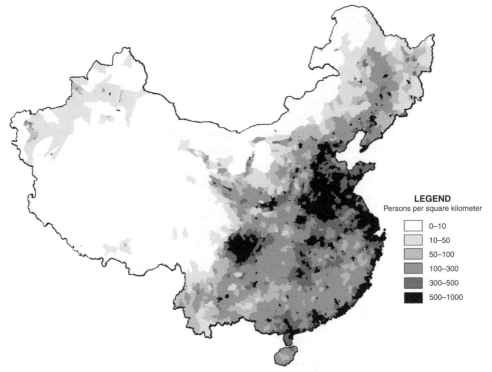

LEGEND
Persons per square kilometer

	0–10
	10–50
	50–100
	100–300
	300–500
	500–1000

Map 7.1 Population density by county and city, 1995
Map supplied by ACASIAN, Griffith University

Republic from 72.35 persons to 105.02 persons, and 118.09 persons per square kilometre. Population density is also extremely uneven, being heavily concentrated in the areas near the coast. In the sparsely populated autonomous regions and provinces of Tibet, Xinjiang, Qinghai, Gansu and Ningxia, which take up about 45 per cent of China's total area, the population density in 1964 was 6.15 persons per square kilometre, but this had risen to 10.25 by 1982, and 11.82 by 1990.

POPULATION BY PROVINCE

There were 33 provinces or territories at province level in the PRC as of mid–2000. This number had increased over the years.

Table 7.4 Census population by province

Province	1953	1964	1982	1990	2000
Beijing	2 768 149	7 568 495	9 230 663	10 819 407	13 820 000
Tianjin	2 693 831	part of Hebei	7 764 137	8 785 402	10 010 000
Hebei	35 984 644	45 687 781	53 005 507	61 082 439	67 440 000
Shanxi	14 314 485	18 015 067	25 291 450	28 759 014	32 970 000
Inner Mongolia	6 100 104	12 348 638	19 274 281	21 456 789	23 760 000
Liaoning	18 545 147	26 946 200	35 721 694	39 459 697	42 380 000
Jilin	11 290 073	15 668 663	22 560 024	24 658 721	27 280 000
Heilongjiang	11 897 309	20 118 271	32 665 512	35 214 873	36 890 000
Jehol[a]	5 160 822	–	–	–	–
Shanghai	6 204 417	10 816 458	11 859 700	13 341 896	16 740 000
Jiangsu	41 252 192	44 504 608	60 521 113	67 056 519	74 380 000
Zhejiang	22 865 747	28 318 573	38 884 593	41 445 930	46 770 000
Anhui	30 343 637	31 241 657	49 665 947	56 180 813	59 860 000
Fujian[b]	13 142 721	16 757 223	25 872 917	30 048 224	34 710 000
Jiangxi	16 772 865	21 068 019	33 185 471	37 710 281	41 400 000
Shandong	48 876 548	55 519 038	74 419 152	84 392 827	90 790 000
Henan	44 214 594	50 325 511	74 422 573	85 509 535	92 560 000
Hubei	27 789 693	33 709 344	47 804 118	53 969 210	60 280 000
Hunan	33 226 954	37 182 286	54 010 155	60 659 754	64 400 000
Guangdong	34 770 059	42 800 849	59 299 620	62 829 236	86 420 000
Guangxi	19 560 822	20 845 017	36 421 421	42 245 765	44 890 000
Hainan[c]	–	–	–	6 557 482	7 870 000
Sichuan	62 303 999	67 956 490	99 713 246	107 218 173	83 290 000
Xikang[d]	3 381 064	–	–	–	–
Chongqing[e]	–	–	–	–	30 900 000
Guizhou	15 037 310	17 140 521	28 552 942	32 391 066	35 250 000
Yunnan	17 472 737	20 509 525	32 553 699	36 972 610	42 880 000
Tibet	1 273 969	1 251 225	1 892 224	2 196 010	2 616 300
Shaanxi	15 881 281	20 766 915	28 904 369	32 882 403	36 050 000
Gansu	12 928 102	12 630 569	19 569 191	22 371 141	25 620 000
Qinghai	1 676 534	2 145 604	3 895 695	4 456 946	5 180 000
Ningxia	incl. with Gansu	2 107 490	3 895 576	4 655 451	5 620 000
Xinjiang	4 873 608	7 270 067	13 081 538	15 155 778	19 250 000
Others	11 743 320	3 361 655	–	–	–
People's Liberation Army	never announced	never announced	4 238 210	3 199 100	2 500 000
Total	582 603 417	694 581 759	1 008 180 738	1 130 483 401	1 264 776 300[f]

Notes:

[a] Jehol was abolished and parts of it merged with Hebei, Liaoning and Inner Mongolia in July 1955.

[b] This figure does not include the population of Quemoy and Matsu, under Guomindang control.

[c] Hainan was made a province in 1988, having formerly been part of Guangdong.

[d] Xikang was merged into Sichuan in July 1955.

[e] Chongqing became a province-level municipality in 1997.

[f] Discrepancy with figure on p. 212 due to rounding.

Hainan was declared to be a province in April 1988, while in March 1997 the NPC decided to split Chongqing Municipality off from Sichuan. In the middle of 1997 Hong Kong reverted to China as a special administrative region with province level, with Macau following in December 1999. Territories at province level include autonomous regions and municipalities. There are enormous variations in the population levels of China's provinces. In the 1990 census Sichuan had the largest population and Tibet the smallest. But figures derived from a 1997 sample survey on population change showed the most populous province as Henan (with 93.916 million), followed by Shandong (89.178 million), with Sichuan only third (85.642 million). The reason for the change was the

splitting off of Chongqing Municipality (with its 30.904 million people) from Sichuan.

Some provincial boundaries have changed between these censuses, which explains some of the apparently unusually rapid or slow rates of growth.

THE LARGEST CITIES

In China, population figures for cities include those people within a fixed administrative area, which covers only the 'urban areas' of the relevant city in parentheses. Although the four most populous cities are province-level administrative areas in their own right, the administrative area counted for the Chongqing, Shanghai, Beijing and Tianjin figures in Table 7.6 represents only the 'urban areas' of these cities. This is much smaller than the

Table 7.5 Households and sex ratios by province, 1990 census

Province	Number of households	Total males	Total females	Sex ratio female=100
Beijing	3 132 379	5 593 669	5 225 738	107.04
Tianjin	2 552 087	4 470 923	4 314 479	103.63
Hebei	15 369 258	31 210 985	29 871 454	104.48
Shanxi	7 187 159	14 958 605	13 800 409	108.39
Inner Mongolia	5 294 429	11 156 291	10 300 507	108.31
Liaoning	10 837 730	20 152 625	19 307 072	104.38
Jilin	6 289 838	12 624 226	12 034 495	104.90
Heilongjiang	8 915 127	18 048 627	17 166 246	105.14
Shanghai	4 100 320	6 806 773	6 535 123	104.16
Jiangsu	17 900 152	34 123 509	32 933 010	103.61
Zhejiang	11 767 679	21 364 779	20 081 151	106.39
Anhui	13 377 949	29 026 355	27 154 458	106.89
Fujian	6 643 832	15 434 927	14 613 297	105.62
Jiangxi	8 398 607	19 493 985	18 216 296	107.01
Shandong	21 976 486	42 915 180	41 477 647	103.47
Henan	19 829 242	43 813 581	41 695 954	105.08
Hubei	13 123 043	27 828 775	26 140 435	106.46
Hunan	15 748 571	31 501 434	29 158 320	108.04
Guangdong	13 648 447	32 152 701	30 676 535	104.81
Guangxi	8 913 562	22 157 660	20 088 105	110.30
Hainan	1 404 158	3 418 689	3 138 793	108 92
Sichuan	28 625 768	55 549 979	51 668 194	107.51
Guizhou	7 246 292	16 769 818	15 621 248	107.35
Yunnan	8 045 831	18 995 951	17 976 659	105.67
Tibet	406 973	1 098 694	1 097 316	100.13
Shaanxi	7 826 202	17 071 411	15 810 992	107.97
Gansu	4 802 170	11 592 811	10 778 330	107.56
Qinghai	923 894	2 310 499	2 146 447	107.64
Ningxia	999 655	2 389 525	2 265 926	105.45
Xinjiang	3 376 052	7 821 328	7 334 450	106.64
Total	278 662 892	581 854 315	548 629 086	106.06

Table 7.6 China's most populous cities, 1990 census

City	Province	Total population	Male	Female
Shanghai	Shanghai	8 214 436	4 262 216	3 952 220
Beijing	Beijing	7 362 425	3 841 942	3 520 483
Tianjin	Tianjin	5 855 068	2 987 240	2 867 828
Shenyang	Liaoning	5 827 089	2 967 168	2 859 921
Nanjing	Jiangsu	5 168 121	2 697 112	2 471 009
Wuhan	Hubei	4 039 881	2 106 384	1 933 497
Guangzhou	Guangdong	3 935 195	2 056 856	1 878 339
Chongqing	Sichuan	3 127 161	1 630 991	1 496 170
Harbin	Heilongjiang	2 990 915	1 513 476	1 477 439
Chengdu	Sichuan	2 954 909	1 542 935	1 411 974
Shijiazhuang	Hebei	2 921 431	1 503 045	1 418 386
Xi'an	Shaanxi	2 872 558	1 502 691	1 369 867
Zibo	Shandong	2 484 206	1 271 192	1 213 014
Dalian	Liaoning	2 483 783	1 272 119	1 211 664
Ji'nan	Shandong	2 403 946	1 241 934	1 162 012
Changchun	Jilin	2 192 320	1 119 999	1 072 321
Qingdao	Shandong	2 101 809	1 069 228	1 032 581
Taiyuan	Shanxi	2 051 558	1 084 011	967 547
Liupanshui	Guizhou	1 844 463	963 772	880 691
Zhengzhou	Henan	1 796 766	944 504	852 262
Zaozhuang	Shandong	1 793 103	926 506	866 597
Guiyang	Guizhou	1 664 708	880 268	784 440
Lanzhou	Gansu	1 617 770	856 068	761 702
Kunming	Yunnan	1 611 969	851 323	760 646
Tangshan	Hebei	1 517 750	779 930	737 820
Hangzhou	Zhejiang	1 476 223	775 976	700 247
Anshan	Liaoning	1 442 220	703 012	707 155
Qiqihar	Heilongjiang	1 424 861	735 065	702 060
Taian	Shandong	1 412 806	722 801	692 331
Fuzhou	Fujian	1 402 581	720 475	672 947
Pingxiang	Jiangxi	1 388 432	729 634	672 998
Fushun	Liaoning	1 388 011	721 957	684 999
Changsha	Hunan	1 377 805	715 434	655 848
Nanchang	Jiangxi	1 369 125	709 069	660 056
Yancheng	Jiangsu	1 366 779	702 116	664 663
Jilin	Jilin	1 320 170	667 985	625 182
Neijiang	Sichuan	1 289 184	662 339	626 845
Datong	Shanxi	1 277 310	680 915	596 395
Suining	Sichuan	1 259 603	644 413	615 190
Baotou	Inner Mongolia	1 248 416	644 683	603 733
Huainan	Anhui	1 239 957	648 500	591 457
Changde	Hunan	1 231 548	633 312	598 236
Ürümqi	Xinjiang	1 217 162	631 204	585 958
Luoyang	Henan	1 202 204	622 898	579 306
Nanning	Guangxi	1 163 949	612 868	551 081
Weifang	Shandong	1 151 764	592 588	559 176
Handan	Hebei	1 151 670	635 246	516 424
Ningbo	Zhejiang	1 142 432	586 191	556 241
Hefei	Anhui	1 110 781	597 441	513 340
Zhanjiang	Guangdong	1 099 585	576 596	522 989
Leshan	Sichuan	1 070 150	547 001	523 149
Jingmen	Hubei	1 042 930	531 289	511 641
Tianshui	Gansu	1 039 757	539 716	500 041
Chaozhou	Zhejiang	1 027 564	531 070	496 494
Daqing	Heilongjiang	1 025 930	526 452	499 478
Wuxi	Jiangsu	1 013 606	519 573	494 033

area for the province-level municipalities of the same name, which explains why the populations given above are so much smaller than in the census provincial figures of 1990 shown in Table 7.5. Chongqing is not counted as a province-level unit in the 1990 census, since it did not become such until 1997. Table 7.6 includes all cities whose urban-area population was over 1 million according to the 1990 census, ranking them in order of population and including both male and female populations. According to the 1990 census, there were 56 cities in China with urban-area populations of over 1 million.

The following table shows the populations of all China's provincial capitals at the end of 1997 and of 1998. The figures are those described as 'non-agricultural'. The figures are in millions and given in descending order of 'non-agricultural' population in 1998. The name given in parentheses is the province-level administrative unit to which the city is attached.

THE AGE OF THE CHINESE POPULATION

China's is a fairly young population.[11] The proportions of the total population aged

Table 7.7 The populations of China's provincial capitals (millions)

City	Non-agricultural population		City	Non-agricultural population	
	1997	1998		1997	1998
Shanghai (Shanghai)	9.43	9.54	Taiyuan (Shanxi)	1.92	1.94
Beijing (Beijing)	7.23	7.34	Changsha (Hunan)	1.71	1.74
Chongqing (Chongqing)	5.95	6.14	Kunming (Yunnan)	1.64	1.69
Tianjin (Tianjin)	5.15	5.21	Nanchang (Jiangxi)	1.62	1.65
Wuhan (Hubei)	4.23	4.28	Fuzhou (Fujian)	1.50	1.55
Harbin (Heilongjiang)	4.23	4.27	Lanzhou (Gansu)	1.51	1.54
Shenyang (Liaoning)	4.23	4.24	Guiyang (Guizhou)	1.38	1.42
Guangzhou (Guangdong)	4.11	4.17	Hefei (Anhui)	1.30	1.33
Chengdu (Sichuan)	3.18	3.27	Ürümqi (Xinjiang)	1.24	1.28
Changchun (Jilin)	2.72	2.77	Nanning (Guangxi)	1.10	1.14
Nanjing (Jiangsu)	2.70	2.76	Hohhot (Inner Mongolia)	0.86	0.89
Xi'an (Shaanxi)	2.68	2.72	Xining (Qinghai)	0.68	0.69
Ji'nan (Shandong)	2.29	2.26	Yinchuan (Ningxia)	0.51	0.53
Hangzhou (Zhejiang)	2.04	2.11	Haikou (Hainan)	0.42	0.44
Zhengzhou (Henan)	1.98	2.04	Lhasa (end 1996) (Tibet)	0.12	n.a.
Shijiazhuang (Hebei)	1.92	1.98			

Table 7.8 Proportion of persons aged under 15 to the total

1953 census	35.41	1987 sample census	28.76
1964 census	40.41	1990 census	27.69
1982 census	33.59	1995 sample census	26.73

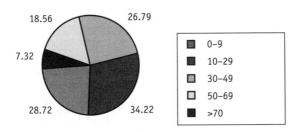

Figure 7.3 China's age structure, 1953 census (in %)

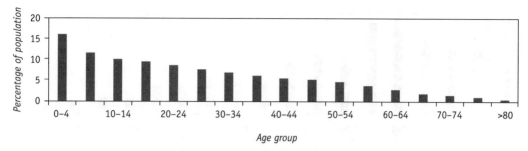

Figure 7.4 China's age structure, 1953 census (in %)

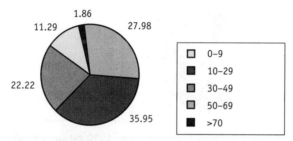

Figure 7.5 China's age structure, 1964 census (in %)

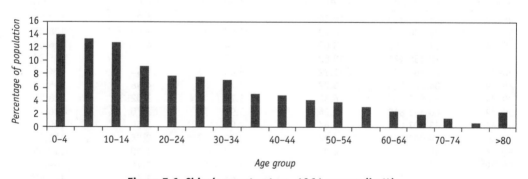

Figure 7.6 China's age structure, 1964 census (in %)

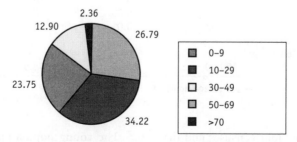

Figure 7.7 China's age structure, 1982 census (in %)

The Age of the Chinese Population

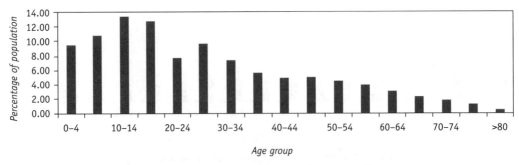

Figure 7.8 China's age structure, 1982 census (in %)

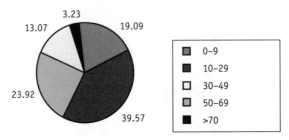

Figure 7.9 China's age structure, 1990 census (in %)

Table 7.9 China's age structure and sex ratios, 1990 census

Age	Total persons	Percentage	Male	Female	Sex ratio
0–4	116 438 419	10.30	5.40	4.90	110.22
5–9	99 336 743	8.79	4.57	4.22	108.22
10–14	97 226 692	8.60	4.44	4.16	106.68
15–19	120 158 421	10.63	5.45	5.18	105.37
20–24	125 761 174	11.12	5.68	5.44	104.40
25–29	104 267 525	9.22	4.74	4.48	105.43
30–34	83 875 707	6.30	3.28	3.02	108.80
35–39	86 351 812	7.64	3.94	3.70	106.67
40–44	63 707 664	5.64	2.95	2.69	109.76
45–49	49 087 941	4.34	2.29	2.06	111.29
50–54	45 619 559	4.04	2.13	1.90	112.09
55–59	41 709 335	3.69	1.93	1.76	109.92
60–64	33 976 254	3.01	1.55	1.46	105.99
65–69	26 332 520	2.33	1.14	1.19	96.29
70–74	18 050 580	1.60	0.74	0.86	85.96
75–79	10 933 924	0.96	0.41	0.55	75.09
80–84	5 352 690	0.47	0.18	0.30	59.37
85–89	1 907 544	0.17	0.05	0.12	46.21
90–94	351 602	0.03	0.01	0.02	36.77
95–99	57 851	–	–	–	33.60
100 and over	6 681	–	–	–	30.34
Total	1 130 510 638	100.00	51.47	48.53	106.04

Note: There are slight errors in the percentage figures due to rounding.

under 15 years in the four censuses and the two sample censuses were as in Table 7.8.

The young population rose very steeply indeed over the period 1953 to 1964 but has

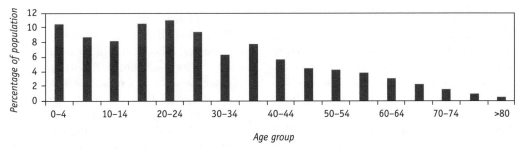

Figure 7.10 China's age structure, 1990 census (in %)

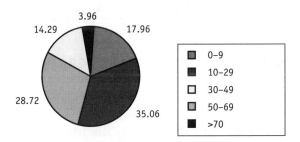

Figure 7.11 China's age structure, 1995 sample census (in %)

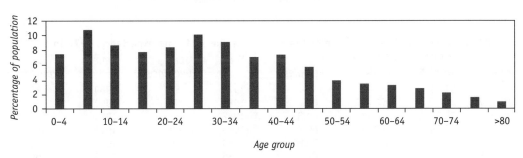

Figure 7.12 China's age structure, 1995 sample census (in %)

Table 7.10 China's age structure and sex ratios, 1995 sample census

Age bracket	Percentage	Sex ratio	Age bracket	Percentage	Sex ratio
0–4	7.28	118.38	55–59	3.85	107.62
5–9	10.68	110.19	60–64	3.47	104.22
10–14	8.77	107.93	65–69	2.73	99.38
15–19	7.38	106.08	70–74	1.96	89.91
20–24	8.74	98.17	75–79	1.15	77.25
25–29	10.17	99.14	80–84	0.59	64.26
30–34	8.82	100.47	85–89	0.21	47.88
35–39	6.95	104.51	90–94	0.05	35.22
40–44	7.41	102.90	95–99	–	23.98
45–49	5.54	104.51	100 and over	–	44.16
50–54	4.24	105.78			

tended to fall since then. This appears to reflect policy, but other factors no doubt play a part, such as the modernization process taking place, especially since the late 1970s.

Between 1991 and 1995 the number of people aged 65 and over grew at an average 4.9 per cent, 2.25 times higher than five years earlier. The proportion of elderly to the total population rose 1.12 percentage points. Over the fifty years of the PRC, China moved from high birth rates and high mortality rates to low birth and low mortality rates. In 2000, China's 65 and over constituted 6.96 per cent of the total, while those of under fifteen were about 25 per cent, which means that China has moved quite rapidly towards an ageing society.

LIFE EXPECTANCY IN CHINA

The average life expectancy has risen dramatically in recent decades. When the PRC was established the average life expectancy was around 35 years. Judith Banister states that 'Life expectancy at birth in China rose from only about 24 years in 1929–31 to approxi-

mately 63 years by the mid–1970s and, by 1981, to around 66 years. According to official sources, it has risen still further in recent years'.[12] The State Statistical Bureau put the average lifespan in China in 1996 at 70.8 years, although United Nations figures put life expectancy in the same year at only 69 (as against 77 in the United Kingdom, 64 in Indonesia and 62 in India).[13] The 1988 official claim for the infant mortality rate in 1981 was 35 per thousand,[14] while the 1995 sample census showed the infant mortality rate was 32.3.[15]

LAND, GRAIN AND POPULATION

Population pressure on China's available land resources has intensified since the relatively prosperous period of the mid-eighteenth century. The figures in Table 7.13 show that even by 1995 the average per capita share of grain per *mu* was well below what it had been

Table 7.11 Reported male and female life expectancy, 1957–99[16]

Year	Total	Males	Females
1957	57.00	–	–
1970–75	–	67	69
1975	68.25	67.17	69.32
1978	68.28	66.95	69.55
1979	–	68.00	70.00
1980–85	–	66	69
1981	67.88	66.43	69.35
1990	–	67.58	70.91
1996	70.8	68.71	73.04
1997	70.83	68.7	73.2
1998	–	68	71

Table 7.12 Life expectancy, 1976 to 1997[17]

Year	Life expectancy	Year	Life expectancy
1976	62	1989	66
1981	68	1990	68
1982	65	1991	69
1983	69	1992	69
1984	65	1993	69
1985	65	1994	69
1986	64	1995	69
1987	66	1996	69
1988	66	1997	70

Table 7.13 China's population, cultivated land and grain[18]

Year	Population (millions)	Cultivated land (million mu)	Per capita share (mu)	Grain yield (kg per mu)	Per capita output (kg)
1368–1644	over 60	700	12.7	90	over 1000
1741	143.41	588	4.1	140	574
1840	412.81	842	2.1	150	over 300
late 1940s	455.59	1275	2.7	110	c.300
1952	574.82	1860	3.2	90	c.280
1962	672.95	1820	2.7	nearly 90	240
1979	975.42	1810	1.8	180	340
1985	1050.44	1450	1.4	260	365
1990	1133.68	1435	1.3	311	394
1995	1189.83	1425	1.2	327	392

around the middle of the eighteenth century, let alone what it had been under the Ming dynasty (1368–1644). (There are approximately 15 *mu* in each hectare or 1500 in each square kilometre.) The two great population explosions from the mid-eighteenth to mid-nineteenth centuries and for the first three decades of the PRC have produced lasting effects. Although cultivated land expanded in the first decades of the PRC, one of the effects of the industrialization process has been that land formerly used for agriculture has been taken over by industry. Although grain yields grew in the late twentieth century, the shrinkage in cultivated land areas and the continuing population growth has an effect on output per person.

This chapter provides an overview of China's main geographical divisions and, within these, its provinces and their cities, especially capital cities. Information is given on history, economic geography, and the principal features of interest of each province or province-level unit, including natural topographical features and climate, and man-made objects of interest. Some information is also provided on the climate, significant features and history of provincial capitals, and other places of special historical interest are also noted.[1]

ECONOMIC GEOGRAPHY

A general overview of the economic base of each province/municipality/autonomous region is presented, followed, as relevant, by a listing of the region's main products grouped roughly, according to generic order, under industrial manufacturing materials and manufactured products, naturally derived products, and agricultural produce.

POPULATION

The population of each province or province-level administrative unit and of its capital city is given in Chapter 7 (Tables 7.4 and 7.7 respectively), while China's most populous cities are listed, together with province-level administrative unit, in Table 7.6.

CLIMATE

Data presented show the capital's climatic situation at the beginning and middle of the year (specifically 1997). The information includes temperatures in degrees celsius for the coldest and hottest months, which are indicated in parentheses; rainfall in millimetres for the driest and wettest months respectively (shown in parentheses); and hours of sunshine for the sunniest and dullest months respectively (shown in parentheses).

PRINCIPAL TOPOGRAPHICAL FEATURES

Mountain ranges
Himalayas (8848 m)
Karakorum (8611 m)
Kunlun (7724 m)
Pamir (7579 m)
Hengduan (7556 m)
Tianshan (7435 m)
Nyainqentanglha (7111 m)
Gangdise (7095 m)
Tanggula (6137 m)
Qilian (5826 m)
Altai (4374 m)

Rivers
The figures given in parentheses are length in kilometres and annual flow in 100 million cubic metres (includes only rivers lying entirely within China):
Yangzi River (Changjiang) (6300 km; 9513 m cu. m)
Yellow River (Huanghe) (5464 km; 661 m cu. m)
Sungari River (Songhuajiang) (2308 km; 762 m cu. m)
Pearl River (Zhujiang) (2214 km; 3338 m cu. m)
Liaohe (1390 km; 148 m cu. m)
Haihe (1090 km; 228 m cu. m)
Huaihe (1000 km; 622 m cu. m)

Lakes
Poyang (Jiangxi: 3583 km^2)
Dongting (Hunan: 2824 km^2)
Taihu (Jiangsu: 2425 km^2)
Qinghai (Qinghai: 4584 km^2, saltwater)
Nam Co (Tibet: 1925 km^2, saltwater)

NORTH CHINA

Beijing Municipality (previous names Cambaluc or Khanbaliq, City of the Khan; Beiping; Peking)

Climate: temp.: –3.8°C (Jan.) and 28.2°C (July); rain: 0.0 mm (Feb.) and 139.8 mm (July); sun: 120.9 hrs (Nov.) and 279.0 hrs (Oct.).

Economic geography: Beijing is China's capital, and is also the nation's political and cultural centre, although in economic terms it does not rank among the highest of China's province-level units. Beijing has good transport facilities, and is an important communications and aviation centre for China. In the western hills around the city there are some mineral and coal reserves. Beijing is noted for traditional handicrafts including cloisonné enamels, ivory and jade carvings, carpets and silk flowers. Since 1978, attempts have been made to move heavy industry away from the city centre to avoid excessive pollution, but despite various measures and laws, including a total ban on smoking in public places, Beijing remains a heavily polluted city. Beijing is also China's most important centre for foreign tourists. In 1990 the number of foreign tourists was 657 500, the figure growing to 1.78 million in 1998. It has become a leading centre for overseas investments. As of 1997, 143 of the world's 500 leading multinational corporations were investing in projects in Beijing, and the same year the municipality attracted US$2.5 billion overseas investments, which was 10.6 per cent above the preceding year.

Products: Heavy industry rose as a proportion of industrial value-output from about 50 per cent in 1990 to 68 per cent in 1995. Heavy industrial products include cars, machine tools, steel, and cement, with automobile production taking up a significant proportion of foreign investment. Beijing is also home to light industries, including food processing, electronics and printing.

Features and history: Tiananmen Square, the Palace Museum, Temple of Heaven, Summer Palace, Ming Tombs, Great Wall of China. Beijing is among the world's ancient cities. In the wave of invasions which destroyed the Northern Song Dynasty, the city became the secondary capital of the Khitans' Liao Dynasty 907–1115 and in 1151 became the capital of the Jurchens' Jin Dynasty, the imperial palaces being completed the following year. Destroyed in the thirteenth century, Khubilai Khan restored it as the capital of the Mongol Yuan Dynasty in 1264. The first Ming emperor's capital was in Nanjing, but in 1421 the third Ming emperor, Yongle, moved it back to Beijing, and it was during his reign that the Imperial Palaces or 'Forbidden City' were constructed. The city was taken over by the Manchu Qing Dynasty in 1644. The Old Summer Palace, Yuanmingyuan, was initially completed in 1709, but Qianlong later added to it greatly, the whole complex including buildings in French and Italian style. The Yuanmingyuan was destroyed by Western invaders in 1860. Later, the Empress Dowager built another Summer Palace (Yiheyuan), which remains one of Beijing's main attractions. The Great Wall, now partially restored at Badaling and elsewhere, was originally built in small sections in the fifth century BC, and first linked by the first emperor of the Qin dynasty (Qinshihuang) in the third century BC. Like the present-day imperial palaces, the remaining wall is the result of Ming restoration. One of Beijing's most important cultural assets is the Beijing Opera (*Jingju*), which developed from the late eighteenth century and is certainly China's most important form of regional theatre. Tiananmen Square has been the site of many significant historical events, including the demonstrations of the May Fourth Movement of 1919, the establishment of the PRC in October 1949 and the student demonstrations of April to June 1989, climaxing in their violent suppression on the night of June 3–4.

Tianjin Municipality

Climate: temp.: −4.9°C (Jan.) and 28.8°C (July); rain: 8.0 mm (Jan.) and 102.9 mm (Sept.); sun: 107.7 hrs (Nov.) and 276.2 hrs (Oct.).

Economic geography: Tianjin, also known by the romanization Tientsin, is a large commercial and industrial centre. The city is still one of northern China's most important trading ports, and is a transport centre where imports and exports are handled. Links with other parts of China are good. Since 1949, Tianjin has become an industrial centre, with a wide range of industry and products, including a large textile industry and a machine-building industry. The municipality's mining sites include coal and iron ore. Tianjin was one of the first fourteen cities opened in 1984 and in 1994 was approved as a national comprehensive reform experimental city.

Products: Major products in the late 1990s include motor vehicles, ethylene, seamless steel pipes, chemical fibres, mobile telecommunication equipment and motorcycles.

Features and history: Established as a prefecture in 1731, and became a treaty port in 1861, playing a significant role in China's modernization. Although ravaged in July 1976 by the Tangshan earthquake, Tianjin's architecture still retains many distinctive features with its blend of Western and Chinese styles. Examples include the Friendship Club and former English Country Club. Restaurants offer fresh seafood, and the Viennese coffee shop Qishilin (Kiesling's) is a well-known landmark.

Hebei Province

Topographical features: North China Plain, 1 500 000 km² of highly fertile loess or yellow earth plateau up to 100 m deep.

Economic geography: Hebei Province is best known for its vast mineral resources and high level of agricultural production, particularly grain farming. In the mid–1990s it accounted for about 7 per cent of China's total arable land. More than 80 minerals have been discovered in the province, and there are extensive reserves of coal. Since the founding of the PRC, industry has developed considerably, and the province is now an important producer of coal, petroleum, iron, steel and textiles. Structural reform has led to preeminence of five main industries: pharmaceuticals, building materials, metallurgy, motor vehicles and food processing.

Products: Major products include cooking coal, petroleum and iron ore. Recently emphasized major products include refined chemicals, chemical fibres, antibiotics, high-grade building materials, wine and beverages. Tangshan remains a major producer of iron and steel and ceramics. Handan and Shijiazhuang are major industrial cities. Major producer of cotton and grain, as well as fruit, being especially famous for pears; coastal areas produce fish and salt.

Capital: Shijiazhuang.

Climate: temp.: −2.2°C (Jan.) and 29.6°C (July); rain: 0.4 mm (Jan.) and 65.5 mm (July); sun: 85.0 hrs (Dec.) and 270.4 hrs (May).

Features and history: Shijiazhuang was a small village of little significance until industrialization brought the Beijing–Hankou (Wuhan) railway at the beginning of the twentieth century. It was the communist capital for the period 1947–49, between the fall of Yan'an to Guomindang forces and the capture of Beijing by the communists. There are few sites of historical interest, apart from a military cemetery with a pair of twelfth-century Jin Dynasty bronze lions. In nearby Zhengding is Longxing Temple, featuring a tenth-century statue of Guanyin, the Goddess of Mercy.

Other places of interest:

Chengde, previously Jehol or Warm River—resort of Manchu emperors. The Kangxi Emperor constructed the palace to blend in with the natural scenery, and around it the Qianlong Emperor added eight temples, seven of which still remain.

Beidaihe—On Bohai Gulf, this Western-style seaside resort was built at the turn of the century.

Shanhaiguan—An ancient walled town at the eastern end of Great Wall with a gate, built in 1639, inscribed 'First Pass under Heaven'.

Tangshan—Developed in the late Qing, becoming a major railway and coalmining centre. Was the main site of the great Tangshan earthquake of July 28, 1976, which was among the most devastating in all human history in terms of casualties. The Chinese Seismological Society reporting in November 1979 that estimated casualties were 242 000 dead and 164 000 seriously wounded.

Shandong Province

Topographical features: Mainly low-lying, with a long coastline (about a sixth of China's total), Shandong contains much of the Great North China Plain as well as the lower reaches and mouth of the great Yellow River. The highest peak is the famous Mt Tai (1524 m). The Shandong Peninsula separates the Bohai and Yellow Seas. Traditionally Shandong has been subject both to flooding and drought, the former because much of the lower reaches of the Yellow River lie above the surrounding plain in its peak season, necessitating the building of dykes.

Economic geography: Shandong Province is rich in mineral resources, and is an important energy-producing area of China. Ore deposits include coal, iron, petroleum, gold, diamonds and aluminium; the province also exports oil and coal. Other industries include iron and steel, chemicals, textiles, and pottery and china manufacture. Shandong's deep-water ports include Qingdao, Yantai, Weihai and Longkou. Shandong's economic growth over the period 1979–94 was considerably above the national average, its agricultural growth being about three times the national average. Shandong's contribution to China's national income rose from 6.5 per cent in 1978 to 9.2 per cent in 1993. Shandong has attracted large amounts of foreign investment and its open cities include Qingdao and Yantai.

Products: Shandong produces wheat, cotton, oil-bearing crops, vegetables and fruit, apples from Yantai and pears from Laiyang being especially well known. Major industrial products include rolled steel, cement, plate glass, refrigerators, washing machines, colour television sets, air-conditioners, motorcycles and clothes. Shandong also produces petroleum and copper, and its gold and diamond deposits are among the best in China.

Capital: Ji'nan.

Climate: temp.: −0.2°C (Jan.) and 30.4°C (July); rain: 0.4 mm (Jan.) and 148.1 mm (Aug.); sun: 106.9 (Nov.) hrs and 257.1 hrs (May).

Features and history: Lying just south of the Yellow River, Ji'nan offers evidence of neolithic settlement and has been a major cultural city throughout most of China's history. The present-day architecture is strongly influenced by early twentieth-century German occupation. Ji'nan is notable for its many pavilions and teahouses overlooking a variety of springs, pools and lakes. In nearby mountain caves, including those of One Thousand Buddhas Mountain, are found Buddhist carvings dating back to the Northern Wei Dynasty of the sixth century.

Other places of interest:

Taishan (*Mt Tai*)—One of China's five sacred mountains and a site of imperial sacrifices to heaven. It rises impressively from the surrounding plain, with many shrines and temples. Some 7000 carved steps lead to the main temple at the summit. At the mountain's foot is the enormous Confucian temple Tai Miao.

Qufu—Birthplace of Confucius and capital of the ancient state of Lu, containing a major Temple to Confucius as well as the graveyard of the Kong family, including that of Confucius himself, and a mansion traditionally belonging to the Kong family.

Qingdao—An early twentieth-century German coaling station on the southern Shandong Peninsula, and also a popular seaside resort, Qingdao is now Shandong's main industrial city. The Germans also founded the Qingdao (Tsingtao) Brewery here. It is currently one of China's open coastal cities, at the end of 1997 having 5183 overseas-funded businesses.

Henan Province

Topographical features: The Yellow River, with its fertile loess, flows through the province into Shandong, the name Henan actually meaning 'south of the Yellow River'. Its plains and mountainous regions each take up about half its territory, the plains being in the east, the mountains in the west.

Economic geography: Henan is another province that has undergone major industrial development since the founding of the PRC. Its industries include metallurgy, coal, machine-building, power, chemicals, textiles and paper-making. Luoyang, a machine-building centre, is home to China's largest tractor plant, bearings plant and mining machinery factory. Henan has abundant mineral resources, with very large prospective coal reserves. The Xiaoqinling goldmines are among China's largest, and the province's bauxite deposits rank second in the country. Thanks to the Beijing–Guangzhou railway and other railway lines, Henan is one of China's major communications centres. Henan is also a major agricultural province.

Products: A very significant producer of grain, including both wheat and rice, also corn, cotton, oil-bearing crops, tobacco, tea, vegetables, fruits, and aquatic products. Among China's main producers of raw coal and crude oil, as well as agricultural machinery, especially tractors, bearings, industrial arts and ceramics, and cigarettes.

Capital: Zhengzhou.

Climate: temp.: 0.0°C (Jan.) and 27.9°C (July and August); rain: 2.3 mm (Oct.) and 77.9 mm (Sept.); sun: 89.4 hrs (Nov.) and 255.6 hrs (August).

Features and history: Zhengzhou has been a site of continuous settlement for over 3500 years, and was the second capital of the Shang Dynasty (*c.* 1500–1066 BC). Remains of the Shang city walls and dwellings are still visible in the eastern suburbs, and the Henan Provincial Museum preserves evidence of early settlement. In 1910 foreign industrial expansion brought railways to Zhengzhou, which was the site of a bloody strike by Beijing–Hankou railway workers in 1923. In 1937 severe flooding was caused and thousands of lives lost when the Guomindang breached the Huanghe dyke 32 km northeast of the city to repel the Japanese invasion; order was not restored to the river until 1947. The city again sustained heavy damage over the following two years, during the civil war, and has since been rebuilt as a modern industrial centre.

Other places of interest:

Luoyang—Now the home of China's best tractors, this ancient city was the Chinese capital for nine dynasties, 1027 BC–AD 937: it was the principal capital of the Zhou Dynasty (770–256 BC) and the Eastern Han (AD 25–220). Luoyang contains China's earliest Buddhist temple, White Horse Temple (*Baima si*), whose original buildings dated from the first century, and Longmen Buddhist caves, including 1352 caves carved out during the Northern Wei Dynasty, 493–543, and Fengxian Temple Cave, dating from 672–75, containing fine sculpture from the Tang Dynasty, 618–907.

Anyang—Although now a modern industrial city, the nearby village of Xiaotun is the site of ancient Yin, the Shang Dynasty capital *c.* 1400–1050 BC. The royal palace and tombs, workshops and houses have been excavated, and oracle bones and tortoise shells furnishing evidence of early Chinese script have been uncovered.

Kaifeng—Formerly the capital of several dynasties, most notably the Northern Song, AD 960–1126, Kaifeng is now Henan's agricultural centre. Many Shang Dynasty bronzes have been uncovered here. After sacking by Jurchens caused the flight of the Song court to the south in 1126, the city lost its prominent position. Sites of interest include the Old Music Terrace, or Yuwangtai; Xiangguo Monastery, founded in the sixth century and restored during the Qing Dynasty, which contains a fine statue of Guanyin; and the Dragon Pavilion, site of a Ming Dynasty palace.

Shaolin Monastery—Reputedly founded in the fifth century by an Indian monk, Shaolin has long been a training ground for the local version of martial arts. It has been almost destroyed several times, but a few original buildings still remain intact.

Shaanxi Province

Topographical features: The great Northwest China loess plateau forms much of northern Shaanxi's topography. The Yellow River, with its tributary Wei River, forms the borders of Shaanxi, Shanxi and Henan. Huashan, one of China's sacred mountains, rises 2160 m, and is located just southwest of the confluence of the Yellow, Wei and Luo Rivers. North and mainly south of the Wei River is the Guanzhong Plain, the most thickly populated part of the province and site of the capital Xi'an. Southern Shaanxi is much more mountainous and high-lying, being dominated by the Qinlin Mountain Range.

Economic geography: Shaanxi is one of China's important machine-building centres, producing high-voltage transmission and transformation equipment, turbine blowers and turbine compressors, petroleum and coalmining equipment and motors, among other things. The Guanzhong area, which was for centuries until the eighth century China's 'key economic area', remains one of the country's main wheat-growing and textile bases, producing both cotton and woollen textiles. The province has seen rapid development in the electronics industry, and there is also an important coal industry, with extensive coal and other mineral deposits. In view of spectacular historical remains, especially from the ancient period, Shaanxi is a major tourist destination, attracting 154 000 foreigners in 1990, rising to 412 000 in 1998. Shaanxi has opened greatly to foreign investment in recent years, and as of 1997 had the only agricultural hi-tech industrial pilot zone in China.

Products: Prominent products in Shaanxi's economic expansion are electronics, pharmaceuticals, colour television sets, and chemical fertilizers. It is a major producer of lacquer, walnuts, silkworm cocoons and grapes.

Capital: Xi'an, previously called Chang'an.

   Climate: temp.: –0.5°C (Jan.) and 28.3°C (July and Aug.); rain: 0.7 mm (Dec.) and 91.9 mm (July); sun: 32.3 hrs (Dec.) and 236.9 hrs (June).

   Features and history: Shaanxi was the site of China's capitals for the first 2000 years of its recorded history. Xi'an was the capital of the Western Han, 206 BC–AD 25, and Tang Dynasties. Evidence of stone age settlement has been found at nearby Banpo. The tomb of the first emperor to unite China, Qinshihuang (reigned 246–210 BC), with its thousands of terracotta warriors, was discovered by accident in Xi'an in 1974, with archaeological excavation beginning the following year. With the founding of the Han dynasty and establishment of trade with imperial Rome, the city evolved into a major trading centre at the Chinese end of the Silk Road. After the fall of the Tang, Xi'an declined in importance. The Shaanxi Provincial Museum contains a unique collection of neolithic stone carvings and bronze Han bas-relief steles. Big Goose Pagoda, dating from 652, and the Ming Dynasty Bell Tower and Drum Tower are also notable. To the north-west of the city, the tomb of the second Tang emperor, Zhao Ling, is approached through an avenue of gigantic guardian figures and spirits.

Other places of interest:

   Yan'an—Situated on the Yan River, northern Shaanxi, this was the site of the Communist Chinese headquarters 1936–47, when caves were cut out of the cliffs as dwellings.

Shanxi Province

Topographical features: Shanxi Province is bounded along most of its west and much of its south by the Yellow River, which makes a great bend towards the east at the point where Shanxi, Shaanxi and Henan meet. Along its east the great Taihang Mountain Range runs from north to south, and it is from these mountains that Shanxi takes its name, meaning literally 'west of the mountains'. Other than the Yellow River, the province's main river is the Fen, which rises north of the capital Taiyuan and flows into the Yellow River. Shanxi is well endowed with ancient buildings, and contains a great many of China's buildings surviving from the twelfth century or before.

Economic geography: Shanxi is a centre of heavy industry, with one of the biggest iron and steel complexes in the country, mainly engaged in producing special steels of various types and steel plates. There is also a major machine-building industry, producing hoisting equipment and machinery for mining, spinning and weaving, and steel-rolling. The province has vast mineral resources, and its reserves of coal and aluminium rank first in the country, with proven coal deposits of 200 billion tonnes, about a third of the national total, and proven aluminium deposits of over 300 million tonnes— more than a quarter of the country's total. Nearly 90 different types of mineral resources have been discovered, of which the deposits of 24 rank first in China. One of the most bauxite-rich areas in Asia, with verified bauxite reserves of well over 500 million tonnes.

Products: By far China's main producer of coal, the Datong Mining Administration being the country's largest coalmine; highly significant producer of coke and electricity.

Capital: Taiyuan.

   Climate: temp.: –4.6°C (Jan.) and 25.2°C (July); rain: 0 mm (Dec.) and 114.7 mm (July); sun: 118.6 hrs (Dec.) and 271.2 hrs (Oct.).

   Features and history: Located at the northern end of Taiyuan Basin on Shanxi Plateau, Taiyuan was previously a strategic city with a turbulent history as the guardian of the western approach to the North China Plain. Historical sites include Chongshan Temple and Shanxi Provincial Museum. The Jin Ancestral Temple, dating back to the fifth century, is located 26 km from Taiyuan.

Other places of interest:

Datong—Originally a trading centre near the Great Wall, Datong is now in the middle of the coalmining areas on the railway line between Beijing and Inner Mongolia, and was the centre of China's steam locomotive industry. Of historical interest are the Ming Dynasty Nine Dragon Screen, Guanyin Temple with its Three Dragon Screen, and the Upper and Lower Huayan Temples.

Yungang—Just near Datong, this is the site of 53 Northern Wei Buddhist caves cut mainly AD 460–93, with a 17 m statue of Sakyamuni, representing the earliest collection of Chinese Buddhist stone figures.

NORTHEAST CHINA (PREVIOUSLY MANCHURIA)

Heilongjiang Province

Topographical features: The most northeasterly of China's provinces, Heilongjiang borders Russia. Its territory is approximately half mountainous and half plain and plateau, the latter very favourable for agriculture. Most of its border with Russia is marked by the Amur River, called in Chinese the Heilongjiang (Black Dragon River), from which the province takes its name. The province's other greatest river is the Songari (Songhuajiang), on which the capital Harbin lies.

Economic geography: Heilongjiang is situated in a black-earth belt, and its farmland is both very extensive and very fertile. The Sanjiang Plain and Songnen Plain, once known as the Great Northern Wasteland, now form one of China's major cereal-producing regions. Heilongjiang also contains China's largest forestry centre, and is one of the key areas for animal husbandry, particularly horses, oxen, sheep and deer. Heilongjiang has a good network of land, water and air communications, and the longest railway mileage in China, including a section of the continental railway linking Asia with Europe. Like other northern provinces, Heilongjiang has an abundance of mineral resources. There are major deposits of oil, coal and natural gas, together with good deposits of gold, copper, lead, zinc and other minerals. Since the founding of the PRC, Heilongjiang has established itself as an important industrial centre, with a range of industries including coal, oil, timber and machinery, all using advanced technology.

Products: Heilongjiang is a major producer of rice, maize, wheat, soybeans, sorghum and other crops; also the lower reaches of the Nen River are among China's most prominent dairy areas. It is the main producer of crude oil and natural gas, a significant producer of coal, and a major producer of tractors, and rolling stock. Heilongjiang is China's main timber-producing province, accounting for about a quarter of total production.

Capital: Harbin.

Climate: temp.: –17.6°C (Jan.) and 25.1°C (July); rain: 0.4 mm (Feb.) and 195.8 mm (Aug.); sun: 140.2 hrs (Jan.) and 285 hrs (June).

Features and history: Harbin offers neo-classical Russian architecture, including an Orthodox Russian cathedral. Ice-sculptures and ice-sports on the river are popular in winter. Originally a fishing village, Harbin developed into a city when the Siberia–Vladivostok railway was built in the nineteenth century.

Other places of interest:

Daqing—China's largest city for petrochemicals and the site of one of China's largest oilfields. Daqing achieved great fame in 1964 when Mao Zedong called on the whole country to learn from Daqing in industry. Its most famous exemplar was 'iron man' Wang Jinxi who withstood the extremes of cold and isolation to build the country. Wang enjoyed a good political career, even joining the Central Committee in 1969, but died in November 1970 of gastric cancer.

Jilin Province

Topographical features: The southeast part of the province is mostly mountainous, and dominated by the Changbai Mountains. There are borders both with Russia and the Democratic People's Republic of Korea. The central western part of the province is low-lying, dominated by the Songliao Plains. In the northwestern part of the province, grasslands and pastoral areas predominate.

Economic geography: Since 1949, Jilin's industry has developed greatly, some major industries being motor cars, machine-building, basic chemicals and optical instruments, paper-making and food-processing. Recently the government has strongly encouraged international investment in the province and in 1997 itself investment of ¥35.1 billion (RMB) in 90 key construction projects. Jilin's favourable agricultural conditions have made it a granary for northeast China, with major cereal crops being rice, maize, sorghum and millet. Jilin is also a major corn producer, its corn kernels being known for their fine quality, and an important forestry zone. The province is

known for its production of 'the three treasures of north-east China'—ginseng, sable fur, and pilose antlers.

Products: Major products include motor vehicles, passenger railway carriages, tractors, chemicals, ferro-alloy, timber, corn, grape wines and soybeans.

Capital: Changchun.

Climate: temp.: −15.5°C (Jan.) and 25°C (July); rain: 1 mm (Dec.) and 230.1 mm (Aug.); sun: 173.1 hrs (Dec.) and 298.6 hrs (July).

Features and history: Changchun became the capital of the Japanese puppet state of Manzhouguo (Manchuria), 1932–45, and retains some evidence of its previous grandeur in former administrative and other buildings.

Other places of interest:

Changbai Nature Reserve—This is one of China's largest reserves, in which Tianchi (the Heavenly Lake), a small volcanic crater lake, is situated, forming a small part of the border between China and Korea.

Liaoning Province

Topographical features: The southeast is dominated by the great Liaodong Peninsula, which protrudes to the southwest. The east is the western part of the Changbai Mountains, with a border with the Democratic People's Republic of Korea along the Yalu River. In the central part of the province the Liaohe Plain forms the southern part of the great Northeast Plains. The western region is mostly mountainous.

Economic geography: Liaoning is part of China's industrial area, and is the centre of its iron and steel industry, with four major iron and steel complexes at Anshan, Benxi, Fushun and Dalian. Industries involve non-ferrous metals, fuel, electricity, machine-building and oil-processing. The province is also China's major manufacturer of heavy industrial products. At Fushun there is a large open-cut coalmine. Light industry is also well developed. There are abundant mineral resources, including iron ore and boron, and precious metals such as diamonds. The long coast provides abundant sea-salt resources, and the seas are a major fishing ground. Much of Liaoning is fertile agricultural land, and the Liaodong Peninsula is a major fruit-growing area. Liaoning has seen enormous expansion of overseas investment in recent years, enabling reform in many of the state-owned businesses, including the large ones. Liaoning has a very good network of railways, and the expressway linking Shenyang with Dalian, opened in September 1990, was the longest in the Chinese mainland as of the mid–1990s. Liaoning has also increased its exports to foreign countries, including Japan, the United States and the Republic of Korea.

Products: Main producer of steel, major producer of rolled steel, pig iron, coke, soda ash, natural gas and crude oil; of mining equipment, metal-cutting machine tools, locomotives, washing machines, bicycles, textiles, wrist-watches, televisions, radios, sewing machines and chemical fibres. Major producer of beer, silkworm cocoons and fruit, especially apples and pears, maize, paddy rice, sorghum, cotton and peanuts; also significant marine producer, such as of shellfish and seaweed. Main producer of tussah silk.

Capital: Shenyang (previously Mukden).

Climate: temp.: −13.2°C (Jan.) and 26.7°C (July); rain: 3.7 mm (Feb.) and 270 mm (Aug.); sun: 151.8 hrs (Dec.) and 288.1 hrs (July).

Features and history: Shenyang is the communications centre of the extreme north-east (formerly Manchuria), situated in the largest heavy industrial province. Liaoning Exhibition Hall displays its accomplishments. The city was the original Manchu capital of Mukden, with the Imperial Palace built 1625–36, before the move to Beijing with the establishment of Qing Dynasty, 1644, and still retains the imperial palaces and other buildings from that era. It was also the site of the 'Mukden Incident' in September 1931, which led on to the Japanese occupation of all China's northeast and the establishment of their puppet state of Manchuria.

Other places of interest:

Lüda—Formed from agglomeration of the naval base of Lüshun, formerly also called Port Arthur, and Dalian, this is an important industrial port and still exhibits evidence of earlier Japanese and Russian occupation. It is the site of the enormous Dalian Shipyard. It is spaciously laid out with beaches and parks, and contains a large Museum of Natural History.

NORTH-NORTHWEST CHINA

Gansu Province

Topographical features: Principally desert and mountain, with a great deal of high-lying plateau territory, especially in the northwest. The Yellow River flows through the province, in particular through the capital Lanzhou. There is some good agricultural land in the southeast. In ancient times, the Silk Road ran through Gansu province, and nowadays the same is true of the transcontinental Eurasian Railroad, which, since 1990, has linked Lianyungang on the east cost of China to Rotterdam.

Economic geography: Heavy industry is central to the economy of Gansu Province, with metallurgical, petroleum, chemical, power, machine-building and coalmining industries dominating. The most important area of the metallurgical industry in Gansu is the non-ferrous metals sector. Oil prospecting, drilling and refining equipment is produced by the province's machine-building industry. Gansu has water-power resources and rich mineral deposits, with nickel, copper, lead and zinc reserves among the largest in

China. Light industry consists of food-processing, textiles, leather-making, medicine and paper-making. Extensive grassland areas are the basis for animal husbandry of cattle, sheep, horses, donkeys, mules, camels and pigs. The best-known Gansu livestock are the Hequ horses and Gansu plateau fine-wool sheep. Foreign investment has increased greatly in recent years.

Products: Major producer of woollen carpets; significant producer of pears, walnuts and wheat.

Capital: Lanzhou.

Climate: temp.: −3.7°C (Jan.) and 23.0°C (July); rain: 0 mm (Jan., Feb., Oct., Dec.) and 88.3 mm (July); sun: 138.7 hrs (Dec.) and 296.5 hrs (June).

Features and history: Lanzhou is a major new industrial city of the northwest, located at the centre of the railway system.

Other places of interest:

Dunhuang—In the extreme west of Gansu, Dunhuang is the site of the Mogao Caves, also called Qianfo (Thousand Buddhas) Caves, the most spectacular and famous ancient caves in China. The caves date from 366 to the fourteenth century and provide incomparable examples of Chinese art and culture, especially Buddhist sculpture.

Jiayuguan—This is the westernmost outpost of the Great Wall, with a Ming Dynasty gatepost, located on the Silk Road.

Inner Mongolian Autonomous Region

Topographical features: The Mongolian steppes extend from the Altai Mountains in the west to the Manchurian Plateau in the east. There is agricultural land in the south, where the Yellow River makes its great bends first to the east and then to the south, and in the land to the south of the Yellow River, called the Ordos. The north is vast grasslands, which are pastoral areas. The far west is desert, while the far northeast, dominated by the Xing'an Mountains, is rich in forests. Inner Mongolia was the first of China's autonomous regions to be established, on May 1, 1947.

Economic geography: With 30 per cent of China's pasture (about 88 million hectares), the Inner Mongolian Autonomous Region is a major livestock-breeding area. The main animals are sheep, cattle, horses and camels, with

several breeds very highly regarded. Other branches of agriculture include grain and cash crop production. The region is rich in minerals, and is ranked first in the world in rare-earth metals and niobium deposits, first in China in natural soda deposits, and among the first few in the country in coal deposits. Industry has developed since the autonomous region was set up, and now includes iron and steel, coal, electricity, timber, machine-building, chemicals, electronics, building materials and other sectors. A trade fair held in 1997 to mark the fiftieth anniversary of the establishment of the Inner Mongolian Autonomous Region resulted in many millions of dollars of exports and foreign investment.

Products: Significant producer of animal products, such as wool, meat, especially mutton and beef, dairy products and cashmere; as well as of timber, corn, wheat, sugar beat, and soybeans.

Capital: Hohhot.

Climate: temp.: −10.2°C (Jan.) and 23.8°C (July); rain: 0 mm (Jan., Dec.) and 132.6 mm (July); sun: 133.7 hrs (Dec.) and 299.8 hrs (June).

Features and history: Hohhot is a relatively new settlement to the south of the Daqing Mountains. It is the site of the tomb of Han Dynasty princess Wang Zhaojun, sent to marry a Xiongnu chieftain in 33 BC.

Other places of interest:

Baotou—The most populous city in Inner Mongolia, Baotou was greatly expanded after the founding of the PRC. It is now an industrial centre with iron and steel works. Nearby is the eighteenth-century Tibetan Buddhist monastery of Wudangzhao.

Xinjiang Uygur Autonomous Region

Topographical features: The largest in area of all China's province-level administrative units, 1.6 million km², the autonomous region borders Russia, Mongolia, Kazakhstan, Kyrgyzstan, Tajikistan, Afghanistan, Pakistan and India. Its Tianshan Mountains are among the highest in China and run through the centre of the region, while in the far north the Altay range and in the far south the Kunlun Mountains dominate the landscape. The region is generally very dry, with oases the main habitable areas. In the south the vast Takalamakan Desert is not only the largest in China, but among the largest in the world. In the far southwest is the Pamir Plateau. The Turpan (Turfan) Basin is well below sea level and among the lowest land places on earth. The Tarim River, which flows through much of the region north of the Taklamakan Desert, is the longest continental river in China. A significant proportion of the population are Islamic minorities, especially the Uygurs and Kazakhs.

Economic geography: Xinjiang is one of China's chief pastoral areas, with a tradition of animal husbandry, particularly in sheep and horse production. The region is rich in minerals, with deposits including oil, coal, gold, mica, jade and asbestos. The Tarim and Junggar basins have large areas of oil-containing structures with high pressure and good yields. Crops include cereal crops and long-staple cotton, but these depend largely on irrigation. Xinjiang has built up an industrial system including a range of industries such as petroleum, coalmining, iron and steel, and machine-building. In January 2000 the region formally launched a ¥70 billion investment plan involving 30 key construction projects in ten fields such as water conservation, agriculture, electric power, the oil industry, coalmining and transportation.

Products: Major products include grapes, melons, cotton, sugar beet, wheat and millet, silkworms and animal products, especially meat, and milk. Turpan's grapes and Hami's melons are nationally famous.

Capital: Ürümqi.

Climate: temp.:−10.8°C (Dec.) and 24.4°C (July); rain: 0.2 mm (Apr. and Oct.)

and 45.1 mm (May); sun: 54.8 hrs (Dec.) and 321.8 hrs (July).

Features and history: Ürümqi was formerly called Dihua and has Islamic and early twentieth-century Russian architecture. It has become a significant industrial centre, especially since the late 1970s, and has developed into a modern city.

Other places of interest:

Turpan—Historically a centre of Buddhism, Turpan contains the One Thousand Buddha Caves, which once rivalled Dunhuang, but Islam has now more or less entirely replaced Buddhism. The Turpan Basin, nicknamed 'the Oven', experiences temperatures of 48°, and Lake Aydingkol in its centre, at 154 m below sea level, is the second lowest land place on earth. Irrigation enables extensive fruit production, such as grapes and melons. Nearby Gaochang and Jiaohe were flourishing centres on the Silk Road, the former with a population of 50 000 during the Tang Dynasty, but abandoned in the fourteenth century; and the latter with a population of 6000, flourishing between the second and fourteenth centuries.

Kaxgar—In southern Xinjiang, the first place in Xinjiang to adopt Islam and still the site of China's largest mosque, the Idkah, which is still in active use.

Ningxia Hui Autonomous Region

Topographical features: In general the north of the autonomous region is lower-lying than the south. The Yellow River flows right through the north, towards the northeast, with surrounding plateau territory which is dry and requires irrigation to make it fertile. Rainfall in Yinchuan is lower than in any other Chinese provincial capital, even Ürümqi.

Economic geography: Ningxia has a long tradition of agriculture. The Yinchuan Plain has also become an important base for commercial cereals production in northwest China. Crops include wheat, rice, sorghum, maize, millet and broom corn millet. The area also has abundant aquatic products. Sheep and cattle are bred in the pasture lands of the south. Mineral deposits include coal, phosphorus, petroleum, salt, iron and tantalum, an essential element for making surgical instruments and electronic components. The power industry has also seen rapid development since 1949. Other industries include machine-building, metallurgy, chemicals, petroleum and electronic industries.

Products: Include wheat, rice, beet, melons, red pepper, and freshwater fish.

Capital: Yinchuan.

Climate: temp.: −5.5°C (Dec.) and 23.9°C (July); rain: 0.2 mm (Oct.) and 68.2 mm (Aug.); sun: 187.3 hrs (Dec.) and 310.8 hrs (June).

Features and history: Yinchuan was the capital of the Western Xia kingdom, founded in the eleventh century but destroyed in 1227 by the Mongols. Some imperial and other tombs can still be seen outside the city. The Beita, or Northern Pagoda, dates from the fifth century. Ningxia is a Hui area and Islam is strong in Yinchuan. There is a large Islamic theological college, in Middle Eastern style, which was built with financial support from the Islamic Development Bank.

Other places of interest:

Tongxin—A strongly Muslim town in the centre of Ningxia. Its old mosque, which dates from the Ming dynasty and is in Chinese style, was the site where the Chinese Communist Party set up its first county-level political power among the minority nationalities, in October 1936.

CENTRAL CHINA

Jiangsu Province

Topographical features: Located along the lower reaches of the Yangzi River, Jiangsu is almost entirely low-lying plains and is, overall, the lowest-lying and flattest of China's provinces or autonomous regions. In the south is the great Lake Tai (Taihu), while in the north is Lake Hongze. The Grand Canal runs through the province from north to south.

Economic geography: Both industry and agriculture play an important part in Jiangsu's economy, which is among the most developed in China. The province's industry encompasses a range of fields, with textiles, light industry, electronics, chemicals and machine-building being important; Jiangsu's chemicals, silk reeling and silk textiles are especially significant. The cultivation rate of land is about 60 per cent, with a wide variety of crops; the province is a very important grain producer and cotton-producing area. In recent years Jiangsu has attracted very significant overseas investment. The number of foreign tourists visiting it was 219 200 in 1990, which had risen to 695 500 in 1998.

Products: Agricultural products include grain, especially rice, wheat and barley, cotton, hemp and silkworm cocoons, oil-bearing crops such as rapeseed and peanuts, fruit such as pears and grapes, as well as fish, crabs and meat, especially pork. Industrial products include mining equipment and metal-cutting machine tools, as well as goods of daily use such as refrigerators, bicycles, radios and television sets, electric fans, wrist-watches, cameras and recorders. Jiangsu is known for its processed woollen goods, cloth and yarn.

Capital: Nanjing, previously called Jiankang and Jinling.

Climate: temp.: 2.1°C (Jan.) and 27.7°C (Aug.); rain: 15.4 mm (Sept.) and 204.9 mm (Aug.); sun: 84.1 hrs (Dec.) and 225.2 hrs (May).

Features and history: Over its very long history Nanjing has been the capital of eight dynasties, including (for about half a century) the Ming Dynasty. From 1853 to 1864 it was also the capital of the Taiping Heavenly Kingdom, the largest in scale of the many rebellions against the Qing Dynasty. It was also the capital of the Guomindang government from 1927 to 1937, and again from 1946 until it fell in 1949. Outside the city is the vast Sun Yatsen Mausoleum as well as the tomb of the Hongwu Emperor (reigned 1368–98), who founded the Ming Dynasty. The city is also the largest inland river port in China and a strategic railway hub, as well as a major educational centre.

Other places of interest:

Yangzhou—Founded 400 BC and situated on the Grand Canal, this city was famed for its scholarship because its scenic attractions tempted many scholars to retire there. It was also the hub of China's Qing Dynasty salt merchants. Its elegantly carved, narrow canal-side dwellings have escaped modernization, even since the advent of the railway and subsequent decline of the canal in importance.

Suzhou—Founded around 600 BC by the King of Wu not far from the shores of Lake Taihu, Suzhou, like Yangzhou, was an important trading centre on the Grand Canal, especially for silk, for which it remains famous. The city is the site of 107 beautiful gardens created by retired scholars; of those remaining open to the public, the most famed is that of the Master of Fishing Nets. Other attractions are Tiger Hill, the birthplace of Suzhou's founder; the Tang Dynasty Bridge with 53 arches, a museum, and the Silk Embroidery Institute.

Lianyungang—Situated in the far northeast of Jiangsu, this city has been made into a development zone. Its main feature is that it is the eastern extremity of the great Eurasian Railway, which was formally opened in September 1990 and enables transport all the way across the Eurasian continent to western China, through Kazakhstan and eventually to Rotterdam, a total distance of 10 900 km. This makes Lianyungang a port of very great economic and trading importance. In 1997 China and Russia signed a contract for the joint development of a nuclear power station at Lianyungang.

Anhui Province

Topographical features: The province is divided into three sections by the Huaihe River running southwest to northeast across the northwestern end, and the Yangzi River running roughly parallel across the southeastern end. In the centre of the province lies its largest lake, Chaohu. The far south of the province is mountainous, with Huangshan, or the 'Yellow Mountains', standing 1840 m high with numerous peaks.

Economic geography: Anhui has some important mineral reserves, with proven coal deposits amounting to 22.3 billion tonnes, iron reserves amounting to 2.4 billion tonnes and significant copper reserves. The province has an industrial system comprising coalmining, metallurgy, electricity generation, machine-building and electrical appliances, chemicals, building materials, textiles, food-processing and other industries. In 1990 the Anhui authorities developed a strategic plan, based on the above-listed industries in the four cities of

Anqing, Tongling, Wuhu and Maanshan, to develop the Anhui section of the Yangzi River, with the aim of coordinating with the development of the Pudong area in Shanghai, and of rendering mutual economic assistance. Anhui is also an important agricultural area, with some significant rice-producing areas, and commodity cereal production. Tea is produced in certain areas of the province, and Anhui has the largest freshwater fish-farming area in China.

Products: Significant producer of soybeans, rice, wheat and tubers; oil-bearing crops, such as rapeseed and sesame; major producer of hemp, tea, silkworm cocoons, fruit, especially pears and grapes, meat, tobacco and cotton yarn. Major industrial products include coal, steel, pig iron, cement, washing machines and refrigerators.

Capital: Hefei.

> *Climate:* temp.: 2.8°C (Jan.) and 28.5°C (Aug.); rain: 33.4 mm (Jan.) and 117.2 (Mar.); sun: 91.8 hrs (Dec.) and 220.4 hrs (May).
>
> *Features and history:* A small market town prior to 1949, Hefei is now a modern industrial centre and home of the National Science and Technology University. Anhui Provincial Museum contains a 2000-year-old jade burial costume.

Other places of interest:

> Huangshan—One of China's five sacred mountains, Huangshan's scenic grandeur has been renowned throughout history. The most famous of its peaks are Lotus Flower Peak, Bright Summit and Heavenly Capital.

Hubei Province

Topographical features: Hubei is situated along the middle reaches of the Yangzi River, which flows right through the province from west to east. The west of the province is largely mountainous, but the east consists mainly of low-lying plains. In the southeast are many lakes, notably the Honghu. The Dongting Lake is just south of the province, and gives the province its name, *hubei* meaning literally 'north of the lake'.

Economic geography: Hubei's economy has both an industrial and an agricultural base, and the province is rich in minerals such as gypsum, iron and copper. Hubei's industries include iron and steel, machine-building, electronics, shipbuilding, instrument-making and textiles, with several heavy industrial enterprises being of national significance. The province's agriculture has characteristics of both the north and south. The Jianghan Plain is one of China's most important rice and wheat areas. Hubei is also a major freshwater produce centre and an important area for forest reserves. Hubei and Chongqing Municipality are the site of the highly controversial Three Gorges Project, which claims to be the largest project in the history of world hydroelectric power construction. The first phase of the project concluded with the successful damming of the Yangzi River in western Hubei in November 1997 (see Chapter 1, C. 1997), and the whole project is scheduled for completion in 2009. Overseas investment in Hubei has become significant in recent years, focusing on basic industries, infrastructure and hi-tech projects.

Products: Agricultural products include rice, wheat, maize, sugar, jute, tobacco, tea, citrus fruit and pears, cotton, sesame, hemp, freshwater products such as fish and shellfish, meat such as pork, and herbal medicine. Industrial products include steel, rolled steel, pig-iron, motor vehicles and tractors.

Capital: Wuhan.

Climate: temp.: 4.6°C (Jan.) and 29.6°C (Aug.); rain: 21.7 mm (Sept.) and 294.2 mm (July); sun: 73.7 hrs (Dec.) and 260.9 hrs (Aug.). In 1998, a year of exceptional flooding along the Yangzi, Wuhan had 758.4 mm of rainfall in its highest month (July).

Features and history: Wuhan is actually composed of three cities on the confluence of the Yangzi and Han Rivers: Hankou, Hanyang and Wuchang. Hankou, on the north bank of the Han River, is a modern commercial city displaying some colonial-style buildings and boulevards. Hanyang, on the south bank of Han River, is built in more traditional style. Wuchang, on the east bank of the Yangzi River, is an old city with many features of historical interest, most notably that this was where the 1911 Revolution broke out which overthrew the Chinese monarchy. East Lake is the site of many temples and pagodas; Hubei Historical Museum also being situated here.

CENTRAL-SOUTH CHINA

Hunan Province

Topographical features: In the north of the province is the Dongting Lake, the second largest freshwater lake in China. This lake gives the province its name, *hunan* meaning literally 'south of the lake'. The Dongting Lake and the plains to the south take up some 20 per cent of the province's area, and include Changsha, the capital. The Xiang River, on which Changsha is situated, is the province's main river and flows from the south into the Dongting Lake. The western part of the province and the far northeast are mountainous.

Economic geography: Hunan is a major centre of China's non-ferrous metallurgical industry. Of 111 kinds of non-ferrous ores discovered in Hunan, reserves of 83 have been verified. In terms of their reserves, antimony and tungsten are in the world's forefront, while several rank first or second among all provinces of China, including bismuth, realgar, fluorite, lead, zinc, mercury, kaolin clay and graphite. Hunan embroidery, the origin of which dates back some 2000 years, is known for its lifelike designs and bright colours, while silk products and chinaware are also of a high order. Hunan is one of China's major grain suppliers. Its chief cereal crop is rice, and it also has one of the largest outputs of ramie in China. Tea is another major product and Hunan is also well known for its hogs and pig products. In 1988 Hunan set up a number of experimental zones to promote opening to the outside world, including the scientific and technological experimental zone in Changsha, and investment from overseas has burgeoned, one factor behind a great improvement in the technological level of the economy in Hunan.

Products: Agricultural products include rice, tea, tungseed oil, aquatic products such as marine shellfish and freshwater fish, meat, especially pork, sugar cane, tobacco and fruit. Industrial products include electric locomotives and rolling stock, motor cycles, electronics, air-conditioners and textiles.

Capital: Changsha.

Climate: temp.: 5.7°C (Jan.) and 28.6°C (Aug.); rain: 52.1 mm (Aug. and Apr.) 401.6 mm (June); sun: 30.1 hrs (Feb.) and 199.4 hrs (May).

Features and history: Changsha is divided by the Xiang River, which has formed a long sandbank (changsha means literally 'long sand') at that point. On the southern extremity of the sandbank, which is called Juzizhou, is the Juzizhoutou Memorial Pavilion in memory of Mao Zedong, who received his education here. Yuelu Hill offers panoramic views of the city, now dominated by modern architecture, although it dates back to the Warring States Period, as part of the Kingdom of Chu. The provincial museum contains treasures from the Western Han tomb of Mawangdui. Puppet shows are a feature of modern Changsha.

Zhejiang Province

Topographical features: The north is very well watered and a fertile part of the Yangzi Basin, while the south and west are mountainous. Zhejiang is a coastal province and includes some 2000 offshore islands, the largest number for any of China's provinces, notably Zhoushan Island and the Zhoushan Archipelago.

Economic geography: Industry in Zhejiang is mainly light and small-scale, with its paper-making, wine-making and silk textiles industries important to China's economy. Other industrial focuses are on machinery, electronics, petrochemicals and pharmaceuticals. Zhejiang is known as 'the home of silk', having produced silk for about 4000 years. Most of the yellow rice wine of China is produced here. The province has quite rich non-metallic mineral reserves, with deposits of fluorine ranking first in the country. Zhejiang has a high level of agricultural production. The diverse economy includes farming, forestry, animal husbandry and fishery. Rice is the primary crop, and silk and tea are also important.

Products: Major industrial products include generators and metal-cutting machine tools, washing machines, refrigerators, electric irons, aluminium household utensils, and tinned food. Agricultural products include silk, woollen goods, tea, silkworm cocoons, over 60 kinds of fruit, rice, hemp, sugar cane, walnuts and milk. Famous local products include Hangzhou brocade and fans. Zhejiang is also one of China's main producers of aquatic products, including both marine and freshwater fish and shellfish.

Capital: Hangzhou.

Climate: temp.: 4.5°C (Jan.) and 27.7°C (July); rain: 25.9 mm (Sept.) and

432.6 mm (July); sun: 50.5 hrs (Dec.) and 209.7 hrs (May).

Features and history: Situated at the southern extremity of the Grand Canal between West Lake and Qiantang River, it is said of this city with its lovely scenery, 'above is Heaven; below are Hangzhou and Suzhou'. Hangzhou has been one of China's principal silk producers for many centuries, and the Hangzhou Silk Printing and Dyeing Complex is the largest in China. Hangzhou is the home of the two great poets Bai Juyi (772–846) and Su Shi (1036–1101). During the sixth century, when there were settlements on surrounding hills, West Lake was a shallow bay in Qiantang River, which gradually became silted up. After 610, when the Grand Canal reached Hangzhou, the city's development began, and Hangzhou finally became the capital of the Southern Song Dynasty, 1127–1279. In the thirteenth century Marco Polo described the city as the most prosperous and magnificent in the world. However, it declined in importance from the Ming Dynasty onwards. The Pagoda of Six Harmonies (*Liuhe ta*) and Lingyin Temple date from 970 and 326 respectively. The place where the famous Dragon Well tea is grown is very near the West Lake.

Other places of interest:

Shaoxing—This was the birthplace of China's most famous modern writer, Lu Xun (1881–1936), whose life and works are enshrined in the Lu Xun Museum. Attractions include old wood and stone buildings, including canal-side dwellings similar to those in Suzhou. Shaoxing was also the home of China's early female revolutionary, Qiu Jin, beheaded in 1907 at the age of 28, whose house is now a museum.

Jiangxi Province

Topographical features: Fertile alluvial lowlands, lakes and rivers in the north,

bounded by the Yangzi River to the north. The Poyang Lake in the central north is the largest freshwater lake in China. The south, east and west are mostly mountainous, taking up nearly two-thirds of the province's total area.

Economic geography: Jiangxi has a diverse range of products, including minerals, fine porcelain and agricultural products. The province has the second largest tungsten reserve in China, and its copper reserves rank first in China. Jiangxi porcelain, made at Jingdezhen, is world-famous and the city is known as 'the capital of porcelain'. Agriculture is important to Jiangxi's economy, and the province is one of China's commodity grain-producing centres, most importantly rice. Jiangxi is one of China's main tea-growing areas and is also an important timber-producing area, with well over half its total area covered by forests.

Products: Industrial products include generators; five minerals are sometimes referred to as 'five golden flowers': tungsten, copper, rare earth, uranium and tantalum. Main producer of ceramics, significant producer of rice, sugar cane, tea, citrus fruit, pine resin and Chinese medicine, as well as freshwater produce, including fish and shellfish; also source of forestry products.

Capital: Nanchang.

Climate: temp.: 6.0°C (Jan.) and 27.9°C (Aug.); rain: 23.6 mm (Oct.) and 268.8 mm (June); sun: 38.8 hrs (Dec.) and 175 hrs (May).

Features and history: Nanchang was the birthplace of the Red Army following the uprising led by Zhou Enlai and Zhu De on August 1, 1927, August 1 still being celebrated as Army Day.

Other places of interest:

Lushan—One of China's five sacred mountains, Lushan's cluster of peaks rises to 1426 m above Lake Poyang and the Yangzi River, with the resort town of Guling at 1098 m. Here can be seen the Daoist Cave of Immortality (*Xianren dong*), a subalpine Botanical Garden and the former residence of Chiang Kaishek, as well as the site of the famous Lushan Plenum of August 1959 (see Chapter 1, **D**. August 16, 1959).

Shanghai Municipality

Climate: temp.: 3.9°C (Jan.) and 27.6°C (Aug.); rain: 11.1 mm (Feb.) and 435.3 mm (Aug.); sun: 84.4 hrs (Dec.) and 199.8 hrs (May).

Topographical features: Lying at the mouth of the Yangzi River, Shanghai is all low-lying and consists mainly of a peninsula, a large island and a number of smaller islands. The main part of the city, the peninsula, lies on the Huangpu and Wusong Rivers, while on the far west is the Dianshan Lake.

Economic geography: Shanghai is China's most powerful industrial centre, its largest port, and one of the largest ports in the world. It is primarily a centre of industrial processing, with a good balance of large and small enterprises and of light and heavy industries. Since 1990, the Pudong New Area has developed at an extraordinary speed, and consists of the Waigaoqiao Bonded District, the Lujianzui Banking and Trading District, the Jinqiao Exports Processing District and the Zhangjiang Hi-Tech Garden District. By 1997, 79 of the world's 500 leading multinational corporations had invested in the Pudong New Area, including General Motors, Motorola, Kodak, Mitsubishi and Philips. Shanghai contributes far more to the Chinese economy and far more finances to the central government than any other single province-level unit. Enterprises in Shanghai generally have a high degree of scientific and technological expertise. Major industries are steel, metallurgy, chemicals, machine-building, shipbuilding, electronics, instruments and meters, textiles and handicrafts, while the automobile, aviation and spacecraft industries are also developing. Shanghai is also China's most important commercial and financial centre, and is the site of many of China's best universities and other institutions of learning and higher learning.

Products: Steel and rolled steel, pig-iron, coke and ferro-alloy, motor cars and metal-cutting machine tools. The electronics industry produces complete sets of electronic instruments, meters and computers. Products of the city's chemical industry include sulphuric acid, caustic soda, chemical fertilizers, medicines, pesticides, chemical fibres, synthetic rubber and plastics. Light and textile industries are well developed, with products such as televisions, radios, bicycles, washing machines, sewing machines, electric irons, cameras, watches, clothing and shoes. Agriculture remains important on the city's outskirts, with rice, wheat, cotton, rape and vegetables being the main crops. Shanghai also produces aquatic products, such as fish and shellfish.

Features and history: Five thousand years old, Shanghai began as a small trading centre on the Huangpu, or Whampoa, Creek. Although it has been a flourishing port for centuries, it grew in importance with the nineteenth-century establishment of Western treaty ports, and was among the cities opened to foreign trade by the Sino-British Treaty of Nanjing in 1842. It was the main site of the *coup* through which Chiang Kaishek seized power and suppressed the Chinese Communist Party in 1927. The architecture of Nanjing Road and the waterfront area, or Bund, still display marks of the International Concession. In the old Chinese quarter is found the Yu Garden, dating from the Ming Dynasty, and the Huxingting Teahouse, while the Longhua Pagoda dates back to the Song Dynasty. The enormous Shanghai Museum is probably the best in China for the arts and history of the imperial period and for the minority nationalities. The Lu Xun Museum, Residence and Tomb commemorate China's greatest modern writer.

SOUTH CHINA

Guangdong Province

Topographical features: Guandong is a
coastal province with rich alluvial valleys
and plains and the tropical Leizhou
Peninsula, located opposite Hainan Island.
Hilly country dominates the north. The
West River (*Xijiang*) flows east and then
southeast through the province, while the
capital Guangzhou lies on the Pearl River
(*Zhujiang*), which fans out into a large and
fertile delta area.

Economic geography: Guangdong contains
cities which early became special
economic zones. These have helped make
the province's economy develop very
rapidly since the early 1980s, and attract
foreign investments and overseas high-
grade technology on a large scale.
Guangdong is a developed light industrial
centre, textile and food-processing
industries being of major importance.
Heavy industries include iron and steel,
electricity, rubber, machinery, petroleum,
coal, chemicals, non-ferrous metals and
shipbuilding. Guangdong is also known
for its rich underground mineral deposits
of rare and non-ferrous metals. There are
good iron ore reserves, oil shale deposits
and offshore oilfields. Guangdong's
handicrafts, such as ivory and jade
carvings, are famous internationally. The
Pearl River delta is one of China's major
silk-cocoon producing centres, and
Guangdong is among the country's main
cultivators of tropical and subtropical
plants and fruit, including bananas,
pineapples and lichees. Fisheries also
contribute significantly to Guangdong's
economy. Tourism is a major industry in
Guangdong, and in 1998 its total number
of tourists, at 7.98 million, was the highest
of any province-level administrative unit
on the Chinese mainland, while the
number of foreign tourists, 1.32 million,
was second only to Beijing. China's first
large nuclear power station is located at
Daya Bay in southern Guangdong.
Zhongshan University in Guangzhou is
among the best comprehensive
universities in China and is the best of
many universities and other educational
institutions in Guangdong.

Products: Industrial products include colour
televisions, refrigerators, air-conditioners,
washing machines, sewing machines,
bicycles, motorcycles, electric fans,
watches, radios, textiles, knitwear, tinned
food, umbrellas, arts and crafts, and paper.
Other products are salt, sulphuric acid
and cement, silk, silkworm cocoons, sugar
and sugar cane, herbal medicine, fruit,
rice, tubers, tea, oil-bearing crops such as
peanuts, rubber, pine resin, freshwater
and marine products such as fish and
shellfish and freshwater crustaceans, and
meat, including pork.

Capital: Guangzhou, or Canton.

Climate: temp.: 13.9°C (Feb.) and 28.0°C
(Aug.); rain: 9.7 mm (Nov.) and
468.6 mm (June); sun: 49.5 hrs (Apr.)
and 156 hrs (Nov.).

Features and history: Situated on the Pearl
River estuary, Guangzhou was already a
thriving port, with Arab traders among
its populace, by the Tang Dynasty:
Huaisheng Mosque, built in 627, is said
to be China's oldest mosque. From the
sixteenth century until the signing of
the Treaty of Nanjing in 1842
Guangzhou was the only Chinese port
open to European traders. In 1840, the
first Sino-British War (the Opium War)
started here, and after the Treaty was
signed Guangzhou lost its unique

status. However, Guangzhou's modern World Trade Fair illustrates the continuing importance of international trade to the city. The Cantonese supported their local leader, Sun Yatsen, in the 1911 Revolution, and the Sun Yatsen Memorial Hall is located here. Mao Zedong and Zhou Enlai's efforts to educate Guangdong peasants later in the 1920s are commemorated by the National Peasant Movement Institute. Other interesting features are the History Museum, Hualin Temple, and Guangxiao Monastery. Nearby are Shamian Island, still retaining evidence of its foreign occupation in its architecture.

Other places of interest:
   Shenzhen, adjoining Hong Kong, *Zhuhai*, adjoining Macau, and *Shantou* have all experienced very rapid economic growth rates and technology transfer since becoming special economic zones in 1980. *Zhongshan*, the place where Sun Yatsen (Sun Zhongshan) was born, was formerly called Xiangshan but was renamed in honour of its most famous son. The house where Sun was born is still a museum, with a more recently built exhibition hall displaying pictures and objects concerning his life.

Hainan Province

Topographical features: China's most southern province, lying entirely within the tropics and studded with palm trees, consists of Hainan Island and several much smaller islands and island chains. About two-thirds of the area of Hainan Island is flat and low-lying, but the interior of the southern half includes the Wuzhi Mountains.

Economic geography: Hainan has reserves of over 50 minerals, including limestone, marble, quartz and iron ore. It is also well endowed with tropical rainforests. Fisheries are important. Industries that have established a base are rubber, processed food, sugar, timber and industrial arts. Tourism has recently become a major trade, with 87 100 foreigners visiting the island in 1998.

Products: The province produced 48 per cent of China's total rubber output in 1997. Other products include coffee, coconuts, sugar, tea, pineapples, bananas and pearls.

Capital: Haikou.
   Climate: temp.: 17.7°C (Feb.) and 29.3°C (Aug.); rain: 0 mm (Nov.) and 462.3 mm (Sept.); sun: 35.4 hrs (Feb.) and 226.4 hrs (July).

Features and history: Sometimes called 'the pearl of the southern seas', Hainan was also a place of exile in traditional times. It was made into a prefecture in the Ming period (1368–1644). It was part of Guangdong Province but split off to become a province by itself in 1988. Haikou's places of interest include the tomb of Hai Rui, the famous just sixteenth-century official; a play about him was used to spark the Cultural Revolution in 1965–66. The Wugong ci is a temple dedicated to five prominent men of the Tang and Song periods who, as exiles, made contributions to Hainan's agriculture and development. It includes an exhibition of the achievements of Su Shi (1036–1101), a major figure of the Song dynasty who was exiled to Hainan in the last years of his life, dying the same year as he was recalled and rehabilitated.

Other places of interest:
   Sanya, at the southern tip of Hainan Island, is the most southern major population centre in China. In the 1990s the vast Nanshan si (Monastery of the Southern Mountain) was built nearby. Though there are monks in residence, the monastery is mainly a tourist attraction and a shrine to the environment.

Guangxi Zhuang Autonomous Region

Topographical features: Guangxi borders Vietnam to the southwest, with a fairly short coastline on the south. There is low-lying plain territory along the coast and in the southeast part of the province, but it is mostly mountainous elsewhere. Limestone karst formations, with caves and multiple peaks, are a feature of Guangxi.

Economic geography: Heavy industry includes machine-building, metallurgy, power generation, chemicals, iron and steel, and cement; light industry includes sugar refining, paper-making, canneries and tannery plants. Agriculture is central to the region's economy, with rice being the main cereal crop, together with maize, sugar cane and tea leaves. The southern part of Guangxi is a major tropical and subtropical plant development area. The region is known for its fruits and also has a forestry industry and fishery. It has significant mineral deposits, its reserves of tin being the largest in China.

Products: Rolling stock, tinned food, sugar and sugar cane, fruit such as citrus fruit and bananas, rubber, Chinese cinnamon, aquatic products, especially marine, such as fish and crustaceans. Mineral products include aluminium, tin, antimony, zinc, lead and limestone.

Capital: Nanning.

Climate: temp.: 14.4°C (Feb.) and 28.5°C (Aug.); rain: 6.3 mm (Nov.) and 256.1 mm (Aug.); sun: 21.2 hrs (Dec.) and 149.2 hrs (Aug.).

Features and history: Though an ancient city, Nanning was of comparatively little significance before the twentieth century, but it has become an important light industrial centre. It is located on the Yong River, which is the name of the West River in its upper reaches.

Other places of interest:

Beihai—Guangxi's main port. An ancient city, it was once part of Guangdong, and became a municipality in 1950 and an open port in 1984. It is now an industrial city, with machine and shipbuilding industries. Along with Fangcheng, to its west, it serves as a port also for the landlocked provinces of Yunnan, Guizhou and Sichuan.

Guilin—On the Li River, founded in the third century BC, Guilin has long been known for its limestone karst scenery. At the base of Fubo Hill, on the Li River, are found caves with Tang and Song Buddhist carvings.

Yangshuo—Eighty kilometres upstream from Guilin, Yangshuo, perched high on rocky cliffs above the river, is a frequent destination of tourist boats travelling up the Li River. Stone steps lead up cliffs to the old town with its still-thriving marketplace and an ancient stone washpool in its centre.

Fujian Province

Topographical features: Extremely mountainous (over four-fifths of the area) with narrow but fertile river valleys. There is a narrow low-lying strip along the coast, the long coastline being opposite Taiwan and characterized by many harbours and offshore islands.

Economic geography: Fujian's industries have developed in low-technology areas such as sugar, paper, tinned food, plastics, pottery and porcelain. Other industries include coalmining, cement, electric appliances, timber-processing, clothes and handicrafts. The province has a wide range of mineral deposits, including iron, tungsten, tantalum, barite, quartz and pyrophyllite. Fujian produces mainly grain crops, with rice as the staple. The province is among China's main forestry areas, one of its sugar-producing areas, and a major centre for growing tea and fruit. The province is the homeland of a great many overseas Chinese and has profited enormously from their interest in the province and their investment in its enterprises.

Products: Sugar, sugar cane and bananas, lichees and pineapples, tea, rubber, aquatic products, including marine fish and crustaceans, seaweed, and freshwater shellfish, and flowers such as the narcissus.

Capital: Fuzhou.

Climate: temp.: 11.1°C (Jan.) and 28.1°C (July); rain: 48.7 mm (Jan.) and

282.7 mm (June); sun: 63.9 hrs (Feb.) and 158.8 hrs (July).

Features and history: On the banks of the Min River, surrounded by hills, Fuzhou was a thriving trading centre by the thirteenth century, with Muslim, Jewish and Christian traders among its populace. It is now an open city with a great deal of overseas investment, and a Taiwan Investment Zone has been established to promote investment from Taiwan. Its major manufactured goods are leather footwear, garments, machinery, and household electrical appliances.

Other places of interest:

Xiamen Special Economic Zone, previously known as Amoy—On the coast at the mouth of the Jiulong River. Being the homeland of large number of people from Taiwan and other overseas Chinese has helped this area economically. There have been enormous advances in overseas investment in recent years and by the end of 1997 Xiamen had 3448 overseas-funded businesses in such areas as machine-building, electronics, chemicals, steel-making, aviation, real estate, entertainment, schools and roads.

SOUTH-WEST CHINA

Chongqing Municipality

Topographical features: Mostly mountainous and high-lying, the topography of this most recently established of China's province-level municipalities (see Chapter 1, **B.** March 14, 1997) is dominated by the upper reaches of the Yangzi River, which flows right through it towards the northeast. The city of Chongqing itself is situated at the confluence of the Yangzi and Jialing Rivers.

Economic geography: Chongqing Municipality is a major area involved in the Three Gorges Project, and its capital Chongqing is the largest industrial city on the upper reaches of the Yangzi. There are over 40 kinds of minerals with deposits in the municipality, those with verified reserves including coal, natural gas, strontium, manganese, limestone, marble, spar, fluorite, quartz, mercury and rock salt; the strontium reserves are the largest in China, and the municipality has China's largest natural gas field. There are many kinds of trees, farm crops, medicinal herbs and aquatic products. The three pillars of the municipality's industry are machine-building and the metallurgical and chemical industries. By the end of 1999 the municipality had established more than 1700 foreign-funded industrial enterprises, using US$1 billion in foreign investment.

Products: Main primary products include grain, pork, tobacco, silkworm cocoons, citrus fruit, livestock, timber and fish, industrial products such as acoustical, optical, electronic and computer science instruments and machinery, meters, textiles, chemicals and medicine.

Capital: Chongqing.

Climate: temp.: 8.6°C (Dec.) and 30.9°C (Aug.); rain: 13.1 mm (Dec.) and 170.8 mm (May); sun: 1.0 hr (Dec.) and 246.5 hrs (Aug.).

Features and history: An ancient city, Chongqing was the capital of Chiang Kaishek's government from 1938 to 1946. The main section is situated on a large peninsula with the Yangzi to the south and the Jialing to the north, and there are now bridges over both rivers.

Other places of interest:
   Three Gorges Scenic Area is beside the
      Yangzi just across the border from
      Hubei. Much of this scenery will be
      inundated with the completion of the
      dam project.
   Dazu, near the border with Sichuan, is the
      site of magnificent stone carvings
      dating from the late ninth to the
      thirteenth centuries. Although the
      grottoes are Buddhist, many of the
      carvings depict ordinary secular life,
      while many of the Buddhist figures are
      shown as normal human beings in
      scenes of everyday life.

Sichuan Province

Topographical features: Fertile plains in the
   eastern Sichuan Basin, especially the
   Chengdu Plains. The western part is very
   mountainous. The upper reaches of the
   Yangzi River run through the southern
   part of the province, forming a border
   with Yunnan for much of its length.
Economic geography: Sichuan is a major
   centre for the metallurgical, engineering,
   electronic and chemical industries. One of
   China's two space centres is located in
   Xichang in the far southwest of the
   province. It has enormous forests and also
   grasslands, making it an important timber,
   pasture and animal husbandry region.
   However, due to the degrading effect of
   development on forests, the province
   launched a pilot project in 1999 to return
   200 000 hectares of farmland to forest in
   120 counties over two years. Well known
   for its mineral resources, Sichuan has
   large deposits of natural gas, phosphorous
   and salt. Sichuan is among the leaders in
   Chinese agriculture. It was at the forefront
   of reform, instituting reform policies
   under Zhao Ziyang even before they were
   being officially promoted from the centre.
Products: Products include natural gas and
   chemical fertilizer, salt, coal, electricity and
   hydropower, pig-iron, steel, cement,
   timber, sulphuric acid, chemical fertilizer,
   cigarettes and colour television sets. A

major area for the production of rice,
   wheat, maize, rapeseed, silkworm cocoons,
   sugar cane, tea leaves, tobacco, and fruit.
   Sichuan also produces livestock in large
   numbers, especially pigs, cattle and goats.
Capital: Chengdu, formerly Jinjiangcheng.
   Climate: temp.: 7.0°C (Jan.) and 26.8°C
      (Aug.); rain: 3 mm (Dec.) and 195 mm
      (Aug.); sun: 8.1 hrs (Feb.) and
      175.2 hrs (Aug.).
   Features and history: Dating back 2500
      years, Chengdu was a minor town
      during the Warring States Period, rising
      to prominence as the capital of the state
      of Shu during the Three Kingdoms
      Period. During the Eastern Han
      Dynasty it was named Jinjiangcheng, or
      Brocade City, since the silk industry
      flourished here. The city was devastated
      during the thirteenth century by
      Mongols after Sichuanese resistance to
      their invasion. In the seventeenth
      century Chengdu was briefly the
      headquarters of an independent
      Sichuanese state. It was also one of the
      last Guomindang strongholds in the
      late 1940s. Interesting sights in or near
      Chengdu include Wuhou Temple,
      commemorating Zhuge Liang, Shu's
      great military leader, and the home of
      the great poet Du Fu (712–70).
Other places of interest:
   Leshan—This is the home of great modern
      writer and scientist Guo Moruo
      (1892–1978), where the world's largest
      stone Buddha is found, carved in cliffs
      above the Min River.
   Mt Emei—One of China's five sacred
      mountains, with many Buddhist
      monasteries and famous for its
      beautiful scenery.

Yunnan Province

Topographical features: Borders Laos,
   Vietnam and Myanmar. A central
   limestone plateau with Lake Dianchi,
   China's sixth largest freshwater lake, in
   the middle. Major rivers include the
   Yangzi, known as the Jinsha at this point

and also forming part of the northern border, and the Lancang, which flows right through the province into Laos, becoming known as the Mekong at that point. Much of Yunnan is mountainous, especially in the northwest. The region is subject to earthquakes.

Economic geography: Yunnan has rich mineral deposits, with reserves of tin, lead and zinc that rank high in China. Proven coal deposits total more than 14 billion tonnes, and there are rich marble deposits. Industries include mining, metallurgy, power, coal, chemicals, machine-building, building materials, food-processing, textiles, electronics, cement and paper-making. The province has a complex cultivation system and a wide variety of crops, although rice production accounts for about half of its total cereals output. The northern part of the province is a major forestry area, while the southern section is an important production base for tropical and subtropical crops and fruit. Tourism is a major money-spinner, Yunnan having spectacularly beautiful scenery, a generally benign climate, and many places of interest.

Products: Producer of rice, maize, wheat, sugar cane, tea leaves and tobacco, tuber crops, peas, beans, phosphorus, lead, zinc, tin, marble, cigarettes, walnuts, rubber, lacquer, and freshwater crustaceans. Handicrafts and fine arts are a major form of product, including some special to Yunnan's many minority nationalities, such as Dai brocade and carpets.

Capital: Kunming, also known as City of Perpetual Spring, having among the least variations in temperature of China's capitals.

  Climate: temp.: 8.6°C (Jan.) and 20.4°C (June and Aug.); rain: 14.7 mm (Jan.) and 368.4 mm (July); sun: 44.5 hrs (July) and 253.8 hrs (May).

  Features and history: Kunming is an ancient city, with several surviving temples dating from the Yuan. On the shores of nearby Lake Dianchi is the Daguan Park, and in the cliffs above the

lake is the Dragon Gate, surmounted by two Yuan Dynasty temples.

Other places of interest:

  Stone Forest (*Shilin*)—Found in Lu'nan Yi Autonomous County 120 km from Kunming, this 30 m high karst 'forest' is composed of jagged limestone columns interspersed with lakes.

  Xishuangbanna Dai Autonomous Prefecture—This area features tropical forests with 60 species of mammals, including elephants and gibbons, and 400 types of birds, situated on the Burmese–Lao border. Its population includes people from many minority groups, with the Dai dominating.

  Dali—An old city beside the Erhai, the largest lake in Yunnan after the Dianchi. The capital of the Dali Bai Autonomous Prefecture, it features many beautiful Bai villages.

Guizhou Province

Topographical features: High-lying mountainous and plateau province, occupying the northeastern section of the great Yungui (Yunnan and Guizhou) Plateau, with many basins and river valleys. The province is noted for its karst limestone formations, including many limestone caverns.

Economic geography: Guizhou's mineral deposits play an important part in the province's economy and industry. Coal deposits are widespread and the province is rich in phosphorus, bauxite, antimony, tungsten, mercury and rare earth. Guizhou's industry, which did not begin to see significant development until the 1960s, consists mainly of coal, metallurgical, chemical, machine-building and power industries, with coal the key sector. The province is one of China's most important metallurgical bases for non-ferrous metals. Light industries and winemaking are significant. Guizhou is also one of China's important fir-tree producers.

Products: Mercury and cinnabar, coal, tobacco and cigarettes, rapeseed, sugar cane, textiles, paper, fur, leather and silk cloth, walnuts, tussah, machinery, processed foods, and several products special to the province such as Anshun batik, the world-famous spirit *maotai*, and certain types of lacquerware.

Capital: Guiyang.

    Climate: temp.: 6.0°C (Feb.) and 24.8°C (Aug.); rain: 8.6 mm (Nov.) and 183.8 mm (July); sun: 11.8 hrs (Dec.) and 176.1 hrs (Aug.).

    Features and history: Guiyang is an industrial city, the Ming-Dynasty Hongfu Monastery being a point of special interest.

Other places of interest:

    Huangguoshu Falls—Near Anshun, these falls, 50 m wide and with a drop of 70 m among cliffs with many caves, are China's most famous and largest.

TIBET AND QINGHAI

Tibetan Autonomous Region

Topographical features: Borders India, Nepal, Sikkim, Bhutan and Myanmar. Extremely high-lying with many mountains and lakes, Tibet is sometimes called 'the roof of the world'. The Qinghai-Tibet Plateau is the highest and largest tableland in the world, with an average altitude of about 4000 m. The Himalayan Mountains, including the world's highest peak Qomolangma (Mt Everest), are along the southwestern border; Yarlung Zangbo River (India's Brahmaputra) with its watershed in the Himalayas, flows south through the region; Lake Nam Co, 1925 km², is the largest saltwater lake in Tibet.

Economic geography: Before the 1960s there was no real industry apart from handicrafts; however, although at the beginning of the twenty-first century Tibet's industrial base remains weak, there are many hundreds of factories, and industries include coalmining, power, chemicals, machine-building, building materials, textiles and leather-processing. Tibet has good mineral reserves, those of ferrochrome, copper, borax and salt being among the largest in China, and it also has abundant geothermal resources. Agriculture is the mainstay of Tibet's economy, with highland barley the principal grain crop. Animal husbandry is important, the main livestock being sheep, cattle and yaks. The region's dense primeval forests form one of the important natural forest zones in China. In the 1990s about 60 economic construction projects were undertaken, including mainly infrastructure, such as water supply, electricity, roads, power, telecommunications, schools and hospitals. At the beginning of the twenty-first century, there are about 20 000 km of roads, and a fibre-optic cable leads from Lhasa to Lanzhou and Xining, as well as other cities in Tibet, although there are still no railways. Tourism is a money-earner, in view of Tibet's mystique in the Western world and its wonderful monasteries and spectacular scenery; and although permission is not easily granted for individuals, 87 000 foreign tourists visited Tibet in 1998.

Products: Yaks, cattle and sheep, beef, mutton and milk; minerals, such as chromium, iron, copper, lead, zinc, borax, salt, mica and gypsum; timber; crops, such as barley, peas, broad beans, wheat, buckwheat, and rice; medicines, including medicinal musk; and textiles.

Capital: Lhasa.

    Climate: temp.: − 2.8°C (Jan.) and 16.3°C (July); rain: 0 mm (Feb.) and 88.8 mm (Sept.); sun: 202.1 hrs (Sept.) and 287.9 hrs (May).

Features and history: Lhasa is Tibet's main religious and administrative centre, 3540 m above sea level. After the 1959 rebellion, the Fourteenth Dalai Lama, Tibet's traditional temporal and spiritual ruler, fled to India. In 1980, following a decade of repression during the Cultural Revolution, more lenient policies towards Tibet were announced, with many buildings destroyed before and during the Cultural Revolution restored. However, 1987 and 1989 saw further disturbances and riots. The Potala Palace is the former seat of the Dalai Lama. A palace was first constructed on this site by Tibet's first recorded ruler, the seventh-century King Songtsan Gambo. The present Potala Palace, one of the world's great traditional buildings, dates from the seventeenth century. There are also main monasteries in Lhasa itself: Jokhang, from the seventh century, and Sera and Drepung, from the fifteenth century.

Other places of interest:

Xigaze or Shigatse—Tibet's second city and home of the second most revered leader after the Dalai Lama, the Bainqen Lama, whose seat is Tashilhunbo, a monastery built in 1447.

Qinghai Province

Topographical features: In the northwest of the province is the Qaidam Basin, 240 500 km² of desert and saltmarsh. In the northeast is the Qinghai (Kokonor) Basin, which includes Lake Qinghai, which gives the province its name; it is saltwater and, 4585 km² in area, China's largest inland lake. In the south is the northern part of the Qinghai-Tibet Plateau, which provides the source of both the Yangzi and Yellow Rivers.

Economic geography: Minerals are very important to Qinghai's economy, with reserves of lake salt, sylvite, magnesium, salt, lithium, iodine, natural sulphur, bromine, limestone, quartz and asbestos ranking high in the country. Prospecting in the 1990s confirmed large reserves of natural gas. There was no industry before 1949, but industries that have developed over the past five decades include metallurgy, coal mining, machine-building, textiles, chemical, and petroleum. Since the 1990s, provincial authorities have given great emphasis to the generation of hydroelectricity and to the development of the Golmud-Kunlun Economic Development Zone. Animal husbandry is important, since Qinghai has more than 33 million hectares of pasture land, making it one of China's largest pastoral areas. Sheep and cattle are the main livestock and Qinghai is one of China's major horse producers.

Products: Sheep, yak and horses, mutton, beef and milk. Potassium chloride, petroleum, lake salt, limestone, lithium and other minerals. Medicinal materials, including caterpillar fungus, antlers, musk and rhubarb.

Capital: Xining.

Climate: temp.: –7°C (Dec.) and 16.8°C (July); rain: 0.5 mm (Jan.) and 105.2 mm (Aug.); sun: 204.5 hrs (Dec.) and 259.4 hrs (July).

Features and history: Xining is an industrial city with only the Guandong Mosque and the Beishan Temple of historical and architectural interest. However, near Xining is the Taersi or Kumbum Monastery, one of the great monasteries of Tibetan Buddhism, almost a town in its own right, with ancient temple buildings, stupas and shrines and a small market complex.

Officially, China still adopts Stalin's definition of a nationality: a historically constituted community of people having a common territory, a common language, a common economic life and a common psychological make-up that expresses itself in a common culture. The Chinese government recognizes 56 nationalities in China, the majority Han grouping and 55 minority nationalities. Although there are peoples with members who consider that they ought to be recognized as a separate nationality, the Chinese state remains extremely resistant to granting recognition to any further nationalities.

These 56 are extremely diverse. Some of the minorities, including the Hui and Zhuang, are very similar to the Han; others are very different, for instance the Turkic peoples of the west such as the Uygurs or Kazakhs, or the Iranian Tajiks. The minority nationalities occupy more than 60 per cent of China's territory, including, above all, the vast western areas.

Chinese policy officially opposes forced assimilation and allows autonomy to the minority nationalities, so that they can retain their own characteristics. Under this policy, the government has set up numerous autonomous areas throughout China. The policy's real effect, however, can best be described as integration.

Both policy and reality are fiercely opposed to outright secession, which the government has suppressed brutally on several occasions. Most of the minorities have succeeded in integrating reasonably well with the Han, but independence or secessionist movements and wishes have remained strong among a few, particularly the Tibetans and Uygurs, and these are discussed briefly below.

THE POPULATIONS OF THE NATIONALITIES

Excluding members of the army, the total population of the minority nationalities in the first four censuses was: July 1, 1953—34 013 782, or 5.89 per cent of China's total population; July 1, 1964—39 883 909, or 5.77 per cent of the total; July 1, 1982—66 434 341, or 6.62 per cent of the total; and July 1, 1990—90 567 245, or 8.01 per cent. The 2000 census put the minorities' population at 8.41 per cent of China's total. The sample census taken on July 1, 1987 showed that the minority nationalities represented 8.0 per cent of the total population, while that of 1995 showed the proportion of the minorities' population to the total at 8.98, with a total of 108.46 million people.

Table 9.1 gives the minorities' population, according to the first four censuses. The order is by population in the 1990 census.[1]

In the 1964 census, there were 183 nationalities registered, among which the government recognized only 54. Of the remaining 129

nationalities, 74 were considered to be part of the officially recognized 54, 23 were classified as 'other nationalities' and the remaining 32 were classified as 'indeterminate'.

Almost all the minorities are exempt from the single-child-per-couple rule introduced in the 1980s. There are, however, still controls in virtually all areas, though they vary sharply from nationality to nationality and from urban to rural areas.[2] Other than natural increase, the most important reason for the population growth among the minority nationalities between the 1964 and 1982, and 1982 and 1990 censuses was the reregistration of people as members of minority nationalities. For the former census the best illustration of this is the Tujia, who are not very different from the Han. The growth by 5.4 times is largely explained by Han people simply reregistering as Tujia, an action that brought with it personal social benefits. A similar explanation is the principal reason for the large growth of the Manchu population between 1982 and 1990. The large rise in the proportion of the

Table 9.1 Total population figures according to nationality and percentage increases

Nationality	1953 Census	1964 Census	1982 Census	1990 Census
Han	542 824 056	651 296 368	936 674 944	1 039 187 548
Zhuang	6 864 585	8 386 140	13 383 086	15 555 820
Manchus	2 399 228	2 695 675	4 304 981	9 846 776
Hui	3 530 498	4 473 147	7 228 398	8 612 001
Miao	2 490 874	2 782 088	5 021 175	7 383 622
Uygurs	3 610 462	3 996 311	5 963 491	7 207 024
Yi	3 227 750	3 380 960	5 453 564	6 578 524
Tujia	–	524 755	2 836 814	5 725 049
Mongolians	1 451 035	1 965 766	3 411 367	4 802 407
Tibetans	2 753 081	2 501 174	3 847 875	4 593 072
Bouyei	1 237 714	1 348 055	2 119 345	2 548 294
Dong	712 802	836 123	1 426 400	2 508 624
Yao	665 933	857 265	1 411 967	2 137 033
Koreans	1 111 275	1 339 569	1 765 204	1 923 361
Bai	567 119	706 623	1 132 224	1 598 052
Hani	481 220	628 727	1 058 806	1 254 800
Li	360 950	438 813	887 107	1 112 498
Kazakhs	509 375	491 637	907 546	1 110 758
Dai	478 966	535 389	839 496	1 025 402
She	–	234 167	371 965	634 700
Lisu	317 465	270 628	481 884	574 589
Gelo	–	26 852	54 164	438 192
Lahu	139 060	191 241	304 256	411 545
Dongxiang	155 761	147 443	279 523	373 669
Va	286 158	200 272	298 611	351 980
Shui	133 566	156 099	286 908	347 116
Naxi	143 453	156 796	251 592	277 750
Qiang	35 660	49 105	102 815	198 303
Tu	53 277	77 349	159 632	192 568
Sibe	19 022	33 438	83 683	172 932
Mulam	–	52 819	90 357	160 648
Kirghiz	70 944	70 151	113 386	143 537
Daur	–	63 394	94 126	121 463
Jingpo	101 852	57 762	92 976	119 276
Salar	30 658	34 664	69 135	87 546
Blang	–	39 411	58 473	82 398
Maonan	–	22 382	38 159	72 370
Tajiks	14 462	16 236	26 600	33 223
Pumi	–	14 298	24 238	29 721
Achang	–	12 032	20 433	27 718
Nu	–	15 047	22 896	27 190
Ewenki	4 957	9 681	19 398	26 379
Jing	–	4 293	13 108	18 749
Juno	–	–	11 962	18 022
Benglong or Deang	–	7 261	12 297	15 461
Uzbeks	13 626	7 717	12 213	14 763
Russians	22 656	1 326	2 917	13 500
Yugurs	3 861	5 717	10 568	12 293
Bonan	4 957	5 125	9 017	11 683
Moinba	–	3 809	1 140	7 498
Oroqen	2 262	2 709	4 103	7 004
Drung	–	3 090	4 633	5 825
Tatars	6 929	2 294	4 122	5 064
Hezhen	–	718	1 489	4 254
Gaoshan	329	366	1 650	2 877
Lhoba	–	–	1 066	2 322
Others not yet identified	1 017 299	32 411	799 705	752 347

minority nationalities between 1982 and 1995 (6.7 to 8.98 per cent) is also mainly due to the reregistration of significant numbers of Han people as members of minority nationalities, although it also relates to the substantial (though not total) exemption of members of minority nationalities from the family planning policy. The violent fluctuation in the Moinba figures, although with small numbers, is probably due to reregistration with the very similar Tibetans. There are no 1964 figures for the Juno and Lhoba because they were not then recognized as minority nationalities. The figures do not include Taiwan, where there is, for instance, a substantial Gaoshan community.

The figures for the Tibetan populations given by exile communities also differ substantially from the official Chinese figures. The reasons for the decline in the Tibetan population between the 1953 and 1964 censuses are highly controversial. There are two likely explanations. The first is that the population was continuing a decline which had been occurring for centuries as the result of a high proportion of the population being in the monastic estate. Second, the 1959 rebellion and its suppression caused a large number of refugees to leave China, as well as some deaths. The Legal Inquiry Committee of the International Commission of Jurists carried out two investigations,[3] which suggested that breaches of human rights may have occurred on a scale that could have affected Tibetan demography in the period between 1953 and 1960. On the other hand, a Chinese analysis of the lower count of Tibetans in 1964 than in 1953 suggested mainly that the 1953 census overcounted the Tibetans. The figure for Tibet itself was based on estimates given to the central government by the local regime, which was still dominated by the old rulers. These exaggerated the population figures because they followed the principle that 'the larger the population the greater the power'.[4]

AUTONOMOUS AREAS

PRC minority nationality policy encourages the establishment of autonomous areas at sev-

eral levels: autonomous regions, equivalent in level to provinces; prefectures; and counties (termed banners in Inner Mongolia). (See the section *The Government* in Chapter 2 for more detail.) Table 9.2 lists China's autonomous regions, together with the autonomous prefectures and counties or banners. Capitals (in parentheses) are given for autonomous regions and autonomous prefectures, as well as the province (in the case of all places except autonomous regions) and the date of establishment of all autonomous places.[5]

Under the policy of autonomy, the minority nationalities were to hold effective control in their own areas. One implication is that cadres in minority nationality areas should, as far as possible, belong to the relevant minorities. In 1982 the State Nationalities Affairs Commission reported that there were 1.03 million cadres from the minority nationalities. By the end of 1988 there were about 1.84 million minority cadres; it was claimed that this figure was 33 times greater than in 1950 and 1.2 times greater than in 1978.[6] A government report of September 1999 specifically devoted to the minorities claimed that at that time the number of minority cadres was 2.7 million. In the particularly sensitive region of Tibet, the same report claimed that in 1998 Tibetan cadres accounted for 74.9 per cent of the total in the Tibetan Autonomous Region.[7] A work conference on minority cadres concluding on June 27, 2000 stated that at the end of 1999 there were 2.824 million minority cadres, which was 6.9 per cent of the total national figure. The total rise in the number of minority cadres since 1993 had been 452 000, the annual rate of increase being 3 per cent, which over the seven years was 7.7. percentage points higher than the rise in the number of cadres of all nationalities throughout China.[8]

SOME ECONOMIC AND CULTURAL INDICATORS IN NATIONALITY AREAS

The minority nationalities' economic development and standard of living have both improved dramatically under the PRC.

Table 9.2 PRC autonomous areas (with capital city)

	Name of province	Date of establishment
1. Inner Mongolian Autonomous Region (Hohhot)		May 1, 1947
2. Xinjiang Uygur Autonomous Region (Ürümqi)		Oct. 1, 1955
3. Guangxi Zhuang Autonomous Region (Nanning)		Mar. 15, 1958
4. Ningxia Hui Autonomous Region (Yinchuan)		Oct. 25, 1958
5. Tibetan Autonomous Region (Lhasa)		Sept. 9, 1965
6. Yanbian Korean Autonomous Prefecture (Yanji)	Jilin	Sept. 3, 1952
7. Enshi Tujia–Miao Autonomous Prefecture (Enshi)	Hubei	Dec. 1, 1983
8. Western Hunan Tujia–Miao Autonomous Prefecture (Jishou)	Hunan	Sept. 20, 1957
9. Ganzi Tibetan Autonomous Prefecture (Kangding)	Sichuan	Nov. 24, 1950
10. Liangshan Yi Autonomous Prefecture (Xichang)	Sichuan	Oct. 1, 1952
11. Ngawa Tibetan–Qiang Autonomous Prefecture (Maerkang)	Sichuan	Jan. 1, 1953
12. Southeast Guizhou Miao–Dong Autonomous Prefecture (Kaili)	Guizhou	July 23, 1956
13. South Guizhou Bouyei–Miao Autonomous Prefecture (Duyun)	Guizhou	Aug. 8, 1956
14. Southwest Guizhou Bouyei–Miao Autonomous Prefecture (Xingyi)	Guizhou	May 1, 1982
15. Xishuangbanna Dai Autonomous Prefecture (Jinghong)	Yunnan	Jan. 24, 1953
16. Dehong Dai–Jingpo Autonomous Prefecture (Luxi)	Yunnan	July 24, 1953
17. Nujiang Lisu Autonomous Prefecture (Liuku)	Yunnan	Aug. 23, 1954
18. Dali Bai Autonomous Prefecture (Dali)	Yunnan	Nov. 22, 1956
19. Diqing Tibetan Autonomous Prefecture (Zhongdian)	Yunnan	Sept. 13, 1957
20. Honghe Hani–Yi Autonomous Prefecture (Gejiu)	Yunnan	Nov. 18, 1957
21. Wenshan Zhuang–Miao Autonomous Prefecture (Wenshan)	Yunnan	Apr. 1, 1958
22. Chuxiong Yi Autonomous Prefecture (Chuxiong)	Yunnan	Apr. 15, 1958
23. South Gansu Tibetan Autonomous Prefecture (Xiahe)	Gansu	Oct. 1, 1953
24. Linxia Hui Autonomous Prefecture (Linxia)	Gansu	Nov. 19, 1956
25. Yushu Tibetan Autonomous Prefecture (Yushu)	Qinghai	Dec. 25, 1951
26. South Qinghai Tibetan Autonomous Prefecture (Gonghe)	Qinghai	Dec. 6, 1953
27. Huangnan Tibetan Autonomous Prefecture (Tongren)	Qinghai	Dec. 22, 1953
28. North Qinghai Tibetan Autonomous Prefecture (Menyuan Hui Autonomous County)	Qinghai	Dec. 31, 1953
29. Golog Tibetan Autonomous Prefecture (Maqen)	Qinghai	Jan. 1, 1954
30. West Qinghai Mongolian–Tibetan Autonomous Prefecture (Delingha)	Qinghai	Jan. 25, 1954
31. Bayingolin Mongolian Autonomous Prefecture (Korla)	Xinjiang	June 23, 1954
32. Bortala Mongolian Autonomous Prefecture (Bole)	Xinjiang	July 13, 1954
33. Kizilsu Kirghiz Autonomous Prefecture (Artux)	Xinjiang	July 14, 1954
34. Changji Hui Autonomous Prefecture (Changji)	Xinjiang	July 15, 1954
35. Yili Kazakh Autonomous Prefecture (Gulja)	Xinjiang	Nov. 27, 1954
36. Mengcun Hui Autonomous County	Hebei	Nov. 30, 1955
37. Dachang Hui Autonomous County	Hebei	Dec. 7, 1955
38. Qinglong Manchu Autonomous County	Hebei	May 10, 1987
39. Fengning Manchu Autonomous County	Hebei	May 15, 1987
40. Weichang Manchu Mongolian Autonomous County	Hebei	June 12, 1990
41. Kuancheng Manchu Autonomous County	Hebei	June 16, 1990
42. Harqin Left Wing Mongolian Autonomous County	Liaoning	Apr. 1, 1958
43. Fuxin Mongolian Autonomous County	Liaoning	Apr. 7, 1958
44. Fengcheng Manchu Autonomous County	Liaoning	Jan. 17, 1985
45. Xinbin Manchu Autonomous County	Liaoning	Jun. 7, 1985
46. Xiuyan Manchu Autonomous County	Liaoning	Jun. 11, 1985
47. Qingyuan Manchu Autonomous County	Liaoning	June 6, 1990
48. Benxi Manchu Autonomous County	Liaoning	June 8, 1990
49. Huanren Manchu Autonomous County	Liaoning	June 10, 1990
50. Kuandian Manchu Autonomous County	Liaoning	June 12, 1990
51. Beizhen Manchu Autonomous County	Liaoning	June 29, 1989
52. Qian Gorlos Mongolian Autonomous County	Jilin	Sept. 1, 1956

Table 9.2 (cont.)

	Name of province	Date of establishment
53. Changbai Korean Autonomous County	Jilin	Sept. 15, 1958
54. Yitong Manchu Autonomous County	Jilin	Aug. 30, 1989
55. Dorbod Mongolian Autonomous County	Heilongjiang	Dec. 5, 1956
56. Jingning She Autonomous County	Zhejiang	Dec. 24, 1984
57. Changyang Tujia Autonomous County	Hubei	Dec. 8, 1984
58. Wufeng Tujia Autonomous County	Hubei	Dec. 12, 1984
59. Tongdao Dong Autonomous County	Hunan	May 7, 1954
60. Jianghua Yao Autonomous County	Hunan	Nov. 25, 1955
61. Chengbu Miao Autonomous County	Hunan	Nov. 30, 1956
62. Xinhuang Dong Autonomous County	Hunan	Dec. 5, 1956
63. Zhijiang Dong Autonomous County	Hunan	Sept. 27, 1987
64. Jingzhou Miao–Dong Autonomous County	Hunan	Feb. 19, 1987
65. Mayang Miao Autonomous County	Hunan	Apr. 1, 1990
66. Liannan Yao Autonomous County	Guangdong	Jan. 25, 1953
67. Lianshan Zhuang–Yao Autonomous County	Guangdong	Sept. 26, 1962
68. Ruyuan Yao Autonomous County	Guangdong	Oct. 1, 1963
69. Longsheng Multinational Autonomous County	Guangxi	Aug. 19, 1951
70. Jinxiu Yao Autonomous County	Guangxi	May 28, 1952
71. Rongshui Miao Autonomous County	Guangxi	Nov. 26, 1952
72. Sanjiang Dong Autonomous County	Guangxi	Dec. 3, 1952
73. Longlin Multinational Autonomous County	Guangxi	Jan. 1, 1953
74. Du'an Yao Autonomous County	Guangxi	Dec. 15, 1955
75. Bama Yao Autonomous County	Guangxi	Feb. 6, 1956
76. Fuchuan Yao Autonomous County	Guangxi	Jan. 1, 1984
77. Luocheng Mulam Autonomous County	Guangxi	Jan. 10, 1984
78. Huanjiang Maonan Autonomous County	Guangxi	Nov. 24, 1987
79. Dahua Yao Autonomous County	Guangxi	Dec. 23, 1987
80. Gongcheng Yao Autonomous County	Guangxi	Oct. 15, 1990
81. Baisha Li Autonomous County	Hainan	Dec. 30, 1987
82. Baoting Li Autonomous County	Hainan	Dec. 30, 1987
83. Changjiang Li Autonomous County	Hainan	Dec. 30, 1987
84. Ledong Li Autonomous County	Hainan	Dec. 28, 1987
85. Lingshui Li Autonomous County	Hainan	Dec. 30, 1987
86. Qiongzhong Li Autonomous County	Hainan	Dec. 28, 1987
87. Muli Tibetan Autonomous County	Sichuan	Feb. 19, 1953
88. Ebian Yi Autonomous County	Sichuan	Oct. 5, 1984
89. Mabian Yi Autonomous County	Sichuan	Oct. 9, 1984
90. Xiushan Tujia–Miao Autonomous County	Chongqing	Nov. 7, 1983
91. Xiyang Tujia–Miao Autonomous County	Chongqing	Nov. 11, 1983
92. Pengshui Miao–Tujia Autonomous County	Chongqing	Nov. 10, 1984
93. Qianjiang Tujia–Miao Autonomous County	Chongqing	Nov. 13, 1984
94. Shizhu Tujia Autonomous County	Chongqing	Nov. 18, 1984
95. Weining Yi–Hui–Miao Autonomous County	Guizhou	Nov. 11, 1954
96. Songtao Miao Autonomous County	Guizhou	Dec. 31, 1956
97. Sandu Shui Autonomous County	Guizhou	Jan. 2, 1957
98. Zhenning Bouyei–Miao Autonomous County	Guizhou	Sept. 11, 1963
99. Ziyun Miao–Bouyei Autonomous County	Guizhou	Feb. 11, 1966
100. Guanling Bouyei–Miao Autonomous County	Guizhou	Dec. 31, 1981
101. Yuping Dong Autonomous County	Guizhou	Nov. 7, 1984
102. Wuchuan Mulam–Miao Autonomous County	Guizhou	Nov. 26, 1987
103. Daozhen Mulam–Miao Autonomous County	Guizhou	Nov. 29, 1987
104. Yanhe Tujia Autonomous County	Guizhou	Nov. 23, 1987
105. Yinjiang Tujia–Miao Autonomous County	Guizhou	Nov. 20, 1987
106. Eshan Yi Autonomous County	Yunnan	May 12, 1951
107. Lancang Lahu Autonomous County	Yunnan	Apr. 7, 1953

Table 9.2 (cont.)

	Name of province	Date of establishment
108. Jiangcheng Hani–Yi Autonomous County	Yunnan	May 18, 1954
109. Menglian Dai–Lahu–Va Autonomous County	Yunnan	June 16, 1954
110. Gengma Dai–Va Autonomous County	Yunnan	Oct. 16, 1955
111. Ninglang Yi Autonomous County	Yunnan	Sept. 20, 1956
112. Gongshan Drung–Nu Autonomous County	Yunnan	Oct. 1, 1956
113. Weishan Yi–Hui Autonomous County	Yunnan	Nov. 9, 1956
114. Lu'nan Yi Autonomous County	Yunnan	Dec. 31, 1956
115. Lijiang Naxi Autonomous County	Yunnan	Apr. 10, 1961
116. Pingbian Miao Autonomous County	Yunnan	July 1, 1963
117. Hekou Yao Autonomous County	Yunnan	July 11, 1963
118. Cangyuan Va Autonomous County	Yunnan	Feb. 28, 1964
119. Ximeng Va Autonomous County	Yunnan	Mar. 5, 1965
120. Nanjian Yi Autonomous County	Yunnan	Nov. 27, 1965
121. Mojiang Hani Autonomous County	Yunnan	Nov. 28, 1979
122. Xundian Hui–Yi Autonomous County	Yunnan	Dec. 20, 1979
123. Yuanjiang Hani–Yi–Dai Autonomous County	Yunnan	Nov. 22, 1980
124. Xinping Yi–Dai Autonomous County	Yunnan	Nov. 25, 1980
125. Weixi Lisu Autonomous County	Yunnan	Oct. 13, 1985
126. Jingdong Yi Autonomous County	Yunnan	Dec. 20, 1985
127. Jinggu Dai–Yi Autonomous County	Yunnan	Dec. 25, 1985
128. Jinping Miao–Yao–Dai Autonomous County	Yunnan	Dec. 7, 1985
129. Luquan Yi–Miao Autonomous County	Yunnan	Nov. 25, 1985
130. Puer Hani–Yi Autonomous County	Yunnan	Dec. 15, 1985
131. Yangbi Yi Autonomous County	Yunnan	Nov. 1, 1985
132. Shuangjiang Lahu–Va–Blang–Dai Autonomous County	Yunnan	Dec. 30, 1985
133. Lanping Bai–Pumi Autonomous County	Yunnan	May 5, 1988
134. Zhenyuan Yi–Hani–Lahu Autonomous County	Yunnan	May 15, 1990
135. Tianzhu Tibetan Autonomous County	Gansu	May 6, 1950
136. North Gansu Mongolian Autonomous County	Gansu	July 29, 1950
137. Dongxiang Autonomous County	Gansu	Sept. 25, 1950
138. Zhangjiachuan Hui Autonomous County	Gansu	July 6, 1953
139. South Gansu Yugur Autonomous County	Gansu	Feb. 20, 1954
140. Aksay Kazakh Autonomous County	Gansu	Apr. 27, 1954
141. Jishi shan Bonan–Dongxiang–Salar Autonomous County	Gansu	Sept. 30, 1981
142. Menyuan Hui Autonomous County	Qinghai	Dec. 19, 1953
143. Huzhu Tu Autonomous County	Qinghai	Feb. 17, 1954
144. Hualong Hui Autonomous County	Qinghai	Mar. 1, 1954
145. Xunhua Salar Autonomous County	Qinghai	Mar. 1, 1954
146. Henan Mongolian Autonomous County	Qinghai	Oct. 16, 1954
147. Datong Hui–Tu Autonomous County	Qinghai	July 10, 1986
148. Minhe Hui–Tu Autonomous County	Qinghai	June 27, 1986
149. Yanqi Hui Autonomous County	Xinjiang	Mar. 15, 1954
150. Qapqal Sibe Autonomous County	Xinjiang	Mar. 25, 1954
151. Mori Kazakh Autonomous County	Xinjiang	July 17, 1954
152. Hoboksar Mongolian Autonomous County	Xinjiang	Sept. 10, 1954
153. Taxkorgan Tajik Autonomous County	Xinjiang	Sept. 17, 1954
154. Barkol Kazakh Autonomous County	Xinjiang	Sept. 30, 1954
155. Oroqen Autonomous Banner	Inner Mongolia	Oct. 1, 1951
156. Ewenki Autonomous Banner	Inner Mongolia	Aug. 1, 1958
157. Morin Dawa Daur Autonomous Banner	Inner Mongolia	Aug. 15, 1958

Agricultural, and especially industrial, production growth rates have been high.

However, the improvements have been uneven, and the gap between the regions near the coast, inhabited mainly by the majority Han nationality, and the western regions, where many of the minorities live, has widened. According to official figures cited by economist Dong Funai, annual economic growth in the eastern half of China approached 13 per cent, but was less than 9 per cent for the western. Per capita GDP in the eastern regions was 40 per cent above national average, but only 60 per cent of the national average in the western. Of China's poorest people, 90 per cent lived in the west. In an attempt to overcome these problems, the government decided early in 2000 to shift the focus of economic construction from the eastern coastal provinces to the western

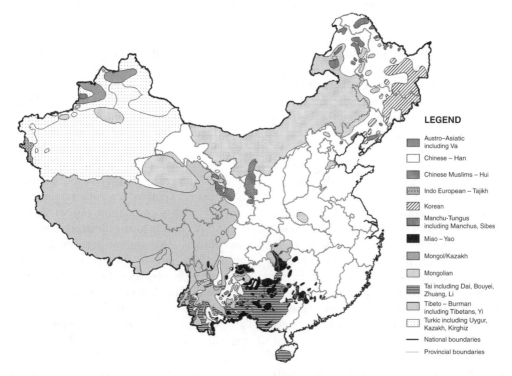

LEGEND

Austro–Asiatic including Va

Chinese – Han

Chinese Muslims – Hui

Indo European – Tajikh

Korean

Manchu-Tungus including Manchus, Sibes

Miao – Yao

Mongol/Kazakh

Mongolian

Tai including Dai, Bouyei, Zhuang, Li

Tibeto – Burman including Tibetans, Yi

Turkic including Uygur, Kazakh, Kirghiz

— National boundaries

— Provincial boundaries

Map 9.1 Minority nationalities in China
Map supplied by ACASIAN, Griffith University

Table 9.3 Economic figures for nationality areas

	1952	*1965*	*1978*	*1986*	*1990*	*1998*
Grain (millions of tonnes)	15.82	22.17	31.24	40.65	53.73	71.50
Cotton (thousands of tonnes)	31.40	88.70	59.70	224.00	470.00	1410.00
Large livestock (millions)	24.39	33.73	38.07	49.51	52.86	55.65
Sheep and goats (millions)	40.30	85.95	95.80	99.88	113.62	128.44
Pigs (millions)	11.37	21.51	32.60	48.69	56.65	70.47
Steel (thousands of tonnes)	–	394	1285	2481	3683	6330
Pig-iron (thousands of tonnes)	9	558	1682	2951	4170	7020
Raw coal (millions of tonnes)	1.78	20.29	60.81	88.76	120.77	175.70
Electricity (millions of kwh)	80	3340	17 400	40 080	173 900	135 700
Railways (thousands of km)	3.787	n/a	9.018	12.60	13.10	17.10
Roads (thousands of km)	25.90	125.50	208.00	250.90	293.70	376.40
Hospital or sanitorium beds (thousands)	5.711	93.23	253.50	301.00	378.90	391.80
Hygiene technical personnel (thousands)	17.90	156.90	279.40	435.90	488.70	498.70

regions. Drawing attention to the rich natural resources and potential markets of the western regions, the government claimed that such a policy could succeed in developing the western regions and the national economy in the long term, and even begin closing the gap with the eastern seaboard; it also conceded serious obstacles and problems, such as the lack of water and technology, and the risks of ecological damage.[9]

As suggested by the figures in Table 9.4, growth in education and culture has also been generally impressive.[10]

In 1996, the State Ethnic Affairs Commission began a program to help the students of 22 nationalities, with populations of less than 100 000 each and a combined population of about half a million, to achieve the goal of nine years' compulsory education to 85 per cent of the students by the end of the century. The government's policy was to provide aid to the smaller groups first and to use the experience to help larger groups. The government has increased overall investment in those areas where poverty is particularly serious and has attempted to provide better training for teachers in primary and secondary schools, where both Modern Standard Chinese and the local ethnic languages are taught.[11]

Literacy rates vary enormously among the minorities, but on the whole are significantly below the national average. Official claims are that literacy has improved enormously under the CCP, especially since the reform period began at the end of the 1970s. Among the more populous minorities, the Tibetans represent the less literate end of the spectrum, with a falling but still very high rate of illiteracy. It is claimed that, whereas 95 per cent of children in old Tibet were illiterate, about 81.3 per cent of school-age children attended school as of 1999, and the illiteracy rate was 48 per cent. At the other end of the spectrum are the Koreans. By the end of the twentieth century, the Yanbian Korean Autonomous Prefecture had more or less fully implemented nine-year compulsory education. In 1998, 99.97 per cent of school-age children in this prefecture were in primary schools, with 99.98 per cent of them entering a higher grade. Among the primary school graduates, 95.2 per cent entered a regular junior middle school, with a graduation rate of 96.8 per cent.[12] According to an official account issued in February 2000, the gap between the school attendance rate in the areas inhabited by minority peoples and the average national level went down from 3.7 percentage points to 0.7 percentage points.[13]

One factor of considerable interest is the extent to which the cultures of the minorities are preserved in the education system. In fact the curriculum is the same everywhere in

Table 9.4 Figures on minority nationality education and culture ('000s)

	1952	1965	1978	1985	1994	1997
Minority students enrolled						
Tertiary level	2.9	21.9	36.03	94.1	177.9	217.0
Secondary level	92.0	390.7	2 526	2 361	3 474	4 597
Primary level	1 474	5 219	7 686	9 548	11 492	12 483
Minority teachers						
Tertiary level	0.623	3.311	5.876	12.775	21.101	50
Secondary level	4.45	16.14	116.95	140.27	237.83	381.00
Primary level	59.8	133.2	310.2	397.8	478.8	633.0
Volumes published in minority languages	6 612	24 800	31 790	36 290	45 520	49 990
Magazines published in minority languages (volumes)	1 686	2 680	3 130	10 350	12 470	9 700
Newspapers published in minority languages (issues)	29 333	39 550	70 720	114 020	125 260	105 270

China, but in cultural classes, such as music, minorities can include their own dances and musical instruments. Moreover, in the 1980s and 1990s the government has followed a policy of encouraging schools in the minority areas to use the local language and employ teachers belonging to the relevant nationality. At primary level this policy had come, by the mid–1990s, to be followed well in most of those nationality areas where there is only one nationality represented in the schools. The higher up the education system one proceeded, the less likely it was that instruction would be in the local language.

One area where the language of instruction has been especially controversial has been Tibet. This is because of the accusation that the Chinese are destroying Tibetan culture, including preventing Tibetan children from being educated in their own language. Tibetan-language textbooks were already in use in primary schools in the mid–1990s. In September 1999, both primary and secondary schools in the Tibetan Autonomous Region began to use a new set of Tibetan-language textbooks. According to official statistics ethnic Tibetans made up over 85 per cent of the faculty in the region's 814 primary schools and 3314 teaching stations, as well as about half the teachers in the 108 secondary schools and secondary polytechnic and vocational schools in Tibet.[14]

Religion is of great importance to many of the minorities, in general more so than to the Han. The two most important, and strongest, religions are Islam, which the Chinese state regards as a marker of being non-Han, and Tibetan Buddhism, which is the traditional religion of the Tibetans, Mongolians and several others. The Chinese Constitution specifies religious freedom, as long as it poses no threat to the state, and allows the establishment of mosques, monasteries, temples, churches and shrines. As noted below, the Chinese state does not hesitate to suppress religious movements which have any link with secessionist actions.

Official figures claim that the number of Muslim believers in 2000 was over 18 million, with 30 000 mosques and 40 000 imams and other clergy. In Xinjiang there were said to be 8.1 million religious believers, the great majority of them Muslims, with 23 000 places of religious worship, including over 20 000 mosques, and 29 000 clergy, the great majority of them Islamic. Tibet was claimed to have over 1700 Tibetan Buddhist monasteries or temples, with 46 000 monks and lamas.[15]

SECESSIONIST AND RELATED PROBLEMS SINCE THE LATE 1980s

At all times the Chinese government has firmly opposed secessionism. By far the main places it has occurred are Tibet and Xinjiang.

After a lull since 1959, when a rebellion broke out in Tibet (see Chapter 1, B. March 1959), there was a resurgence of secessionist activity in Tibet in 1987 (see Chapter 1, B. September 27, October 1 and 6, 1987). This continued at intervals, climaxing in major demonstrations on behalf of independence in March 1989 (see Chapter 1, B. March 5–7, 1989). These were suppressed by the Chinese authorities, who declared martial law, the first time this had happened under the PRC.

In the 1990s, the number of secessionist demonstrations declined, a major one taking place on May 24–25, 1993. However, problems related to Tibetan identity and the role of the Dalai Lama persisted. In 1995 there was a major dispute between the Chinese government and the Fourteenth Dalai Lama over who should decide on the identity of the Bainqen (Panchen) Lama. The Tenth had died in January 1989, and the Dalai Lama's choice for the Eleventh was different from that of the Chinese (see also Chapter 1, D. May 14 and December 8, 1995). Both selected their own candidate, the Dalai Lama's supporters accusing the Chinese of imprisoning his appointee. The one formally enthroned in Tibet was the Chinese choice.

On July 16, 1996 the Dalai Lama made a major speech to the British Parliament in London. In it he criticized the Chinese harshly for cultural genocide and human rights abuses, but also suggested that all he demanded for Tibet was genuine autonomy, not full independence. In June 1988 he had put forward a similar proposal in Strasbourg, but formally withdrew it in 1991 when it came up against strong opposition from some factions among his own supporters. His 1996 proposal proved more durable, despite the fact that it has also aroused opposition from some of his own supporters, and he has repeated it strongly on many occasions. China has remained resolutely hostile to the Dalai Lama and to all his proposals, regularly condemning him as a splittist. China expects the independence movement in Tibet to subside after the Dalai Lama dies, even though support for this cause has grown substantially since the late 1980s in the United States and other Western countries and is one of the issues affecting China's relations with them. (See Chapter 5.)

Whereas the thirtieth anniversary of the 1959 Tibetan uprising was marked by major disturbances in Tibet itself, nothing of the kind happened in March 1999. Tibet itself was fairly calm. In a speech given to exiled Tibetans in Dharamsala, the Dalai Lama called on Beijing to resume dialogue to resolve the Tibetan issues, which had been discontinued since November 1998. He emphasized that he was seeking not independence but 'genuine autonomy' for Tibet. He condemned the repressions by the central government in Tibet, which had seriously violated human rights, and attacked Chinese government policies, arguing that they were aimed at eliminating the core of Tibet's culture and identity. A few days later, in an apparent gesture of conciliation, Chinese President Jiang Zemin pledged to consider using 'international norms' in dealing with separatists in Tibet and Xinjiang, while in a BBC interview the Dalai Lama stated that Tibetans would be loyal to Beijing if granted 'meaningful autonomy'.

On December 28, 1999 the 14-year-old Seventeenth Karmapa Lama left home in Tibet for Dharamsala, the capital of the Dalai Lama's government-in-exile, arriving there on January 4, 2000 (see Chapter 1, E. September

27, 1992). Since he was recognized both by Beijing and the Dalai Lama and had been, other than the Eleventh Panchen Lama, the most important Tibetan religious leader still living in China, his departure was a severe setback to Chinese policy on Tibet. It also raised questions about China's relations with India. Both China and India elected to maintain a low profile over the incident, although in mid-January 2000 India announced that it would allow the boy to remain in India if he wished.

Among China's minorities, the Tibetans have attracted greatest attention over human rights abuses. One reason for this is that the Dalai Lama enjoys enormous support in Western countries, notably the United States. American congressional and other reports and Amnesty International regularly put forward strong criticisms of China's policy and behaviour towards Tibet. China's response is to deny reports of abuses as groundless and to denounce interference in its domestic affairs by foreigners.

Although the 1990s thus saw continuing serious problems over Tibet, secessionist movements were actually stronger in Xinjiang. In April 1990, major disturbances erupted in Akto, not far from Kaxgar in southern Xinjiang (see Chapter 1, B. April 5–6, 1990), and trouble continued throughout the decade, including terrorist and separatist disturbances. The main incident occurred in Gulja, capital of the Yili Kazakh Autonomous Prefecture, early in 1997 (See Chapter 1, B. February 5–6 and following). In August 1998 a group calling itself the East Turkistan People's Liberation Front made an attack on an army base, which resulted in 30 casualties and the destruction of five military planes.

In May 1996 the Xinjiang CCP held a work conference to discuss the autonomous region's problems, especially those relating to its stability. Delegates argued that separatists were organizing riots, terrorist activities and bombings, many stirred up from outside China. In a kind of stick-and-carrot approach to solving the problem, the meeting called for the following measures, among others:

- the reorganization of 'weak and lax' CCP branches, especially those dominated by Muslims
- better training of cadres
- better investigation into cases of people who harassed and took revenge against CCP members and cadres
- far greater attempts to improve the economy.

Among these mechanisms the last was the most important. A passage of the final communiqué read as follows:

> Seizing opportunities to speed up economic development and improve the people's livelihood is the most important, basic work to do to ensure Xinjiang's stability. Only by continuing to speed up Xinjiang's economic and social development and narrowing the differences between coastal areas and interior provinces and regions, as well as by accelerating the region's economic development and improving the people's livelihood every year, can we strengthen the conviction of people of all ethnic groups in supporting the CCP leadership, follow the path of building socialism with Chinese characteristics and take the initiative in resisting and combating national separatism and all sorts of sabotage activities.[16]

One of the themes of this conference and following statements was to blame illegal religious activities for the problems in Xinjiang. An official newspaper report charged separatists for with using religion as a cover in order to 'disseminate reactionary religious ideas and preach jihad'. It went on that 'all the disturbance, chaos and violent terrorism cases that have occurred . . . are almost without exception connected to illegal religious activities'.[17]

Just as in the case of Tibet, there are significant foreign relations implications for the situation in Xinjiang. China has taken active measures to improve its relations with Russia and its Central Asian neighbours, one aim being to adopt concerted action against secessionist movements. A series of meetings among the presidents of China, Russia, Kazakhstan, Kyrgyzstan and Tajikistan began in April 1996 and has resulted in much-enhanced border security and strengthened relations among these five countries. (See Chapter 1, A. April 26, 1996 and Chapter 5.)

One of the reasons why China has tried for so long to maintain good relations with Pakistan is to dissuade it from supporting any secessionist movements in Xinjiang based on Islam. China is, for instance, nervous about Pakistan's longstanding support for the Taleban, the militant Afghan Islamic group that took control of the capital Kabul in 1996. China has not recognized the new government and fears that it will try to stir up Islamic secessionism in Xinjiang. Another anxiety for China is the hostile political direction that some Pakistani religious schools teach to Chinese Muslim students.

Although not nearly as strong as those for Tibet, there have also been criticisms of China's human rights violations in Xinjiang, especially as regards the Uygurs. In April 1999, Amnesty International released a long report similar to those it publishes on Tibet accusing China of gross violations of human rights in Xinjiang. It charged that China had discriminated against Uygurs for top jobs and systematically eroded their economic, social and cultural rights over the past few months. It claimed that there were 200 political prisoners in detention in Xinjiang and that torture of political prisoners was carried out systematically in the region. China immediately challenged the report. Foreign Ministry spokesman Sun Yuxi stated that 'there is no such problem of oppression and persecution of Xinjiang Uygurs'. He continued: 'At present, Xinjiang enjoys political stability, ethnic unity, social progress and people there are living in harmony and contentment.'[18] Both the United States and Britain expressed serious concern at the eight-year prison sentence imposed on the rich Uygur businesswoman Rebiya Kadeer in mid-March 2000 for threatening national security.

CHARACTERISTICS OF CHINA'S MINORITY NATIONALITIES[19]

Achang
The Achang are mountain farmers. Some groups believe in primitive spirits and practise ancestor worship, while others follow Theravada Buddhism. They speak a Tibeto-Burman language, but most can also speak Chinese.

Bai
A Tibeto-Burman people, the Bai were a major ethnic grouping and cultural elite in the Nanzhao kingdom that dominated the region to China's southwest from the seventh century until 902. They are rice-growers, whose religions include worship of 'local tutelary spirits', shamanism, Buddhism and Daoism. The Bai have close cultural ties with the Han, and are among the most acculturated of China's minority nationalities.

Benglong
The Benglong speak an Austro-Asiatic language close to that of the Va. They are subsistence farmers and are culturally similar to the Burmese. Some Benglong follow a form of Theravada Buddhism.

Bonan
The Bonan are culturally close to the Hui. They speak a Mongolian language and are Islamic.

Blang
The Blang speak a Mon–Khmer language, and their culture is closely related to those of nearby Burma (Myanmar) and Laos. They are farmers, with an economy based on shifting cultivation. The main traditional religions are Theravada Buddhism, polytheism and ancestor worship. Some people speak Thai, Va or Chinese.

Bouyei
The Bouyei have a similar way of life to the Miao and their language is closely related to those of the Zhuang and Dai. They practise polytheism and ancestor worship.

Dai
The Dai, who have a close affinity with the Thais, were one of the main ethnic groups dominating the Nanzhao kingdom (seventh century to 902). They are Theravada Buddhists and their arts include colourful dancing and singing.

Daur
The traditional occupations of the Daur are grain and vegetable farming and animal husbandry; they also rely on logging, hunting and fishing. This nationality has a strong spoken-language and cultural affinity with the Mongolians. There is a rich oral literature, but no written script. The main religion is shamanism.

Dong
The Dong trace their origins back to about the third century BC. They speak a Thai language and are primarily agricultural. Dong architecture features covered bridges and multistorey drum towers.

Dongxiang
The Dongxiang are closely related to the Mongolians and speak a Mongolian language. However, they are Islamic and mainly agricultural, growing potatoes, wheat and maize, as well as industrial crops.

Drung
These farmers speak a Tibeto-Burman language closely related to Jingpo. Their traditional religion is nature worship, with belief in spirits, but there are also some Christians.

Ewenki
The Ewenki are a Tungus people who speak a Tungus language. Their religions include animal and ancestor worship, shamanism and Tibetan Buddhism. Once migrant hunters, the Ewenki have led a more settled life over the past 40 years, but they still hunt, breed deer, tend flocks and farm.

Gaoshan
The aboriginal mountain people of Taiwan, the Gaoshan are millet farmers and hunters. Until the early 1900s the Gaoshan were headhunters. They speak a Malay-Polynesian language and believe in polytheism

and ancestor worship, although some are Christians.

Gelo

The Gelo are mountain subsistence farmers and hunters. A Gelo language exists but few use it, instead communicating in Chinese, Miao, Yi and Bouyei.

Hani

The Hani are subsistence farmers who speak a Tibeto-Burman language. They practise polytheism and ancestor worship.

Hezhen

Among China's smallest minority nationalities, the Hezhen speak a Manchu-Tungus language. They are farmers who concentrate on rice-growing. Their religion is based on nature worship and shamanism. Their main art form is sung folk narrative.

Hui

The Hui are Muslims who can trace their origins to the seventh century, when Arab and Persian merchants settled in China. They are involved in many occupations, with the Hui working as shop and restaurant keepers, artisans and peasants. Other than their belief in Islam, and all that implies, the Hui culture is basically the same as that of the Han. Nationality members speak and write Chinese. Territorially they are very scattered.

Jing

The Jing cultivate rice and are good fishermen. They have their own language, but many now speak Cantonese. The Jing are descendants of Vietnamese migrants who arrived in China from the fifteenth century on, the word *jing* being the Chinese equivalent of the Vietnamese Kinh, the name given to the majority people of Vietnam. Some are Daoists and a few Catholics.

Jingpo

The Jingpo live in the mountainous areas along the Burma border and speak a Tibeto-Burman language closely related to Drung. The main traditional religion is polytheism, but some practise Christianity. The main staple food is rice, but in some places maize.

Juno

Subsistence farmers, renowned for their fine, colourful fabrics, the Juno speak a Tibeto-Burman language. Of all minorities, the state recognized the Juno as a nationality most recently (in 1979). Their traditional religion is nature and ancestor worship.

Kazakh

Renowned for their horsemanship, the Kazakhs keep Bactrian camels and are wandering herders of goats and sheep. The Kazakh language has two scripts, one based on Arabic, the other on Latin. Kazakh people are mainly Muslims, but shamanism still survives.

Kirghiz

The Kirghiz are pastoral wanderers and herders of goats and sheep. They are a Turkic people who speak a Turkic language. Most are Islamic, but a few follow Tibetan Buddhism.

Korean

Korean migration into Manchuria dates from the seventeenth century, but did not occur in sizeable numbers until the nineteenth. The Koreans are mainly rice-growers, but have also joined China's industrialization. This nationality's culture and language are the same as in Korea.

Lahu

The Lahu have their own language, which belongs to the Yi branch of the Tibeto-Burman languages, but most Lahu speak Chinese or Thai due to a close association with the Han and Dai peoples. They lacked a written script until 1957. Some Lahu practise nature and ancestor worship, but Mahayana Buddhism and Christianity are also found.

Lhoba

The Lhoba speak a Tibetan language, but do not have their own script. Their traditional religion is nature worship. Both the 1982 and 1990 censuses found the Lhoba to be the least populous of all China's nationalities.

Li

Natives of Hainan Island, the Li live mainly in the mountainous areas and are agricultural.

Their area is tropical and rich in tropical crops, such as coconuts, cocoa, pineapples, mangoes and bananas. They speak a Sino-Tibetan language, but many now speak Chinese. They believe in polytheism and nature worship.

Lisu
Subsistence farmers, the Lisu have arranged, monogamous marriages, but prefer free love before marriage. Their language belongs to the Yi branch of the Tibeto-Burman family.

Manchu
Once herders and hunters, the Manchus trace their origins back some 3000 years. They conquered China in the seventeenth century and adopted Chinese manners, language and culture to such an extent that little survives of their own distinctive culture. Very few now speak the Manchu language. The Manchus formerly practised shamanism and ancestor worship. Territorially they are, next to the Hui, the least concentrated of all minorities in China.

Maonan
The Maonan share a love of festivals and colourful dress with the Zhuang, and speak a related language. They are farmers who grow millet and buckwheat.

Miao
The Miao are one of the most ancient of China's nationalities, tracing their origins back more than 4000 years. Before the modernization of farming methods they grew millet and buckwheat using the slash-and-burn method. The Miao language has three main dialects, but there was no unified written script until 1956. Religions include nature and ancestor worship and Christianity.

Moinba
The Moinba are mountain herders. They have a way of life, culture and language similar to the Tibetans and follow Tibetan Buddhism.

Mongolian
The Mongolians once ran a gigantic empire, founded in 1206 by Chinggis Khan, which covered most of the Eurasian continent. The Mongolian language belongs to the Altaic family; there are many mutually understandable dialects. The Mongolian script, still in use in the PRC, dates at least from the early thirteenth century. The main religion is Tibetan Buddhism. Mongolians were traditionally nomadic (some still are), living in hide and felt tents called yurts. However, they are increasingly becoming settled and even urban dwellers. Industry is well developed among the Mongolians.

Mulam
The Mulam are an agricultural people with a self-sufficient village economy. Religions include Buddhism and Daoism. The Mulam language is related to that of the Dong and Chinese characters are used.

Naxi
The Naxi speak a language belonging to the Yi branch of the Tibeto-Burman family. Traditional religions include the national worship of Dongba (a form of shamanism which is nearly extinct), Tibetan Buddhism and Daoism. Most Naxi follow a patriarchal family system, but one section, called the Mosuo, is matrilineal.

Nu
Farmers who are closely related to the Tibetans, the Nu speak a Tibeto-Burman language. Some follow Tibetan Buddhism, while others are nature worshippers or Christians.

Oroqen
A Tungus people who speak a Tungus language, the Oroqen were once semi-nomadic, living in birch and hide tents. They are now more settled and work as hunters, herders of deer, and farmers.

Pumi
The Pumi speak a language related to Tibetan and have a similar lifestyle to Tibetans, but only part of the nationality accepts Tibetan Buddhism; the others have a polytheistic religion and sacrifice to their ancestors.

Qiang
Closely related to Tibetans and speaking a similar language, the Qiang are herders and

farmers. They are, however, polytheists, nature worshippers and shamanists, not Tibetan Buddhists.

Russian

Almost all of China's Russian population arrived in the northeast and Xinjiang after the Russian civil war of 1918–22. Culturally and linguistically they are the same as in Russia.

Salar

Islamic Turkic speakers living in a semi-desert area, the Salar are herders of sheep and some cattle. Their diet consists largely of steamed buns and a variety of noodles made of highland barley, wheat and buckwheat.

She

The She language belongs to the Miao branch of the Miao-Yao family. The origins of the She are unclear, but probably date back to the seventh century. Some are Buddhists, while others are polytheists or ancestor worshippers.

Shui

The Shui have a language close to that of the Dong. Their main diet is rice and fish, supplemented with corn, barley, wheat and sweet potatoes. Most are nature worshippers and polytheists, but a few are Catholics.

Sibe

The Sibe speak a Manchu-Tungus language. They traditionally lived in the northeast of Liaoning with the Manchus, but in 1764 many were moved to the west as border guards on the Russian frontier, where a portion of the Sibe population still lives. They are traditionally polytheistic but a few follow Tibetan Buddhism.

Tajik

Of Iranian stock, the Tajiks speak an Iranian language and follow Islam. By means of extensive irrigation, they grow rice, wheat, fruit and cotton; some are herders. Houses are built of wood and stone, with square flat roofs.

Tatar

The Tatars are Islamic Turkic speakers and farmers. Their diet includes round cakes, with the outside crisp and inside soft. They also eat cheese, dried apricots and rice.

Tibetan

Before the implementation of reforms in 1959, following a major rebellion against Chinese rule, Tibet was a theocratic state. The Tibetans have a highly distinctive culture, mainly based on their own form of Buddhism, and a rich written and oral literature. They are farmers of barley, peas and tubers and herders of yaks, sheep and goats. They are also the only one of China's minority nationalities to have created a major tradition of drama independently of the Han people.

Tu

The Tu trace their origins to the thirteenth century. They speak a Mongolian language and are related to the Mongolians. They have two dialects and a rich oral literature. Originally pastoralists, they have practised agriculture for several centuries. Most follow Tibetan Buddhism, but some still adhere to polytheistic beliefs.

Tujia

The Tujia farm rice and corn, collect fruit and fell trees for lumber. They are good at handicrafts, and in most ways are very similar to the Han people.

Uygur

A Turkic people who ran a major empire centred on what is now Mongolia from 744 to 840, the Uygurs converted to Islam over several centuries. They grow fruit, wheat, cotton and rice through irrigation. Uygur customs, culture and art are similar to those of other Turkic people and they excel in music, song and dance. The Uygur language belongs to the Turkic group of the Altaic family of languages.

Uzbek

The origins of the Uzbeks go back to the fourteenth century. They are Islamic Turkic speakers and farmers with dress and food very similar to those of the Uygurs.

Va

The Va speak a Mon-Khmer Austro-Asiatic language, but had no script until recently. They grow rice, maize, cotton and fruits such as bananas, pineapples, mangoes and oranges. Most are nature worshippers, but some are Theravada Buddhists or Christians.

Yao

The Yao farm sweet potatoes, maize and rice. They have recently developed hydroelectric power and increased irrigation. There are several different mutually incomprehensible Yao languages, and Chinese or Zhuang are often used for communication. Traditional religions include nature worship, ancestor worship and Daoism.

Yi

The Yi speak a Tibeto-Burman language and have their own script. They once had a reputation as fierce warriors and those in Liangshan, Sichuan, formerly had a heavily stratified slave system. They are polytheists, and also have a long tradition of Buddhism, with Daoism and Christianity introduced later.

Yugur

Descended from the Uygurs of the ninth century, the Yugurs are Turkic speakers. They are herders and farmers, with some hunting as a sideline. Most practise Tibetan Buddhism.

Zhuang

The Zhuang are the most populous of China's minority nationalities, and one of the best integrated with the Han. Zhuang origins go back well before the time of Christ. They speak a language related to Thai, but many speak Chinese. The Chinese written language was formerly used, but in 1955 a Zhuang written language based on Latin letters was devised. Religions include Buddhism, Daoism, ancestor worship and Christianity.

BACKGROUND TO EDUCATION IN CONTEMPORARY CHINA

Since before the PRC was established, education has been a high priority for the CCP and universal education a central goal of CCP policy. However, periodic conflict within the Party about the functions of education has seen major shifts in policy. Initially, China depended heavily on the Soviet Union for educational policy and techniques. Political movements such as the 1957 Anti-Rightist Campaign and the Great Leap Forward that followed disrupted progress in education—the former attacking students and teachers for their 'expert' stance, the latter placing more emphasis on political attitudes and participation in manual labour than on formal education.

During the Cultural Revolution, the educational structure of the preceding period was labelled 'revisionist' and virtually destroyed. However, the period also saw a considerable expansion of secondary school enrolments, as the figures in Tables 10.2 and 10.3 show.

Policy in the period of reform since 1978 is that education should be geared towards China's modernization. Education has regained a central position in government policy, with a number of legislative measures coming into force to establish a national system that retains sufficient flexibility to adapt to local needs and conditions. Since the late 1970s, the general direction, especially at tertiary level, has been to emphasize quality and content, and to downplay ideology, but without letting it slip too far into the background. In a 1978 speech, Deng Xiaoping said:

> Students must indeed give top priority to a firm and correct political orientation, but that by no means implies that they should abandon the study of the sciences, social sciences and humanities. On the contrary, the higher the students' political

consciousness, the more consciously and diligently they will apply themselves to the study of these subjects for the sake of the revolution.[1]

However, juggling these two demands, content and ideology, has not proved easy. In the late 1980s, marked by two major student movements in 1986 and 1989, students showed signs of losing interest in the Marxist-Leninist ideology espoused by the CCP. After the suppression of the movement in June 1989 they were generally less vocal than before, but the trend in the 1990s was more towards nationalism and consumerist prosperity than Marxism-Leninism.

In the mid–1980s the government undertook major educational reform. One result was that in April 1986 the National People's Congress adopted a law stipulating nine-year compulsory education in the cities and developed areas by 1990 and almost everywhere by the end of the twentieth century. The nine years or so are preceded by three years of preschool education and are followed by an optional three years of senior secondary education and then tertiary education, with technical or vocational education being at either secondary or tertiary level.

China's first *Education Law* went into effect in September 1994. It specified China's basic education principle as follows: 'Education must serve the socialist modernization drive, be combined with productive labour, and cultivate builders and successors who develop morally, intellectually and physically.' The law covered general principles, the basic education system, schools and related institutions, teachers and educational workers, students, education and society, investment in education and guarantees, foreign exchange and cooperation, legal liabilities, and included supplementary articles.[2]

The Sixth Plenum of the Fourteenth Central Committee of October 1996, with its emphasis on ethics and culture, also urged greater attention to ideological and moral education in the schools at all levels. It asked that schools should 'adhere to the socialist orientation in running schools, strengthen work in moral education, and strive to train builders and successors of socialism with an all-round development in moral, intellectual and physical and other aspects'.[3] It was also keen to infuse the curriculum with socialist ideology and ethics, and use the education system for strengthening patriotism among the youth.

FINANCE

In the mid-1980s, education in China began to be privatized. Fee-paying private schools were introduced. More importantly, state schools began to charge fees, first at tertiary level and later at other levels, with a tendency for these fees to rise and spread with time. At the beginning of the twentieth-first century, students pay fees more or less everywhere in the country, and these tend to get higher the further up the education system one rises. As can be seen in Table 10.1, China ranked quite low among its neighbours in the proportion of its gross national product (GNP) spent on education at the end of the twentieth century. This is despite the fact that, in absolute terms, government expenditure on education has been rising.

Since it is obvious that fees charged will run counter to the law on universal education, the government has encouraged measures to help cushion the effects of privatization on enrolments. Many schools provide scholarships in the form of free or cheap education to especially needy students, who are very common in poor areas.

Another mechanism is a series of semi-private initiatives, of which the main one is Project Hope, designed to promote educational development in poor areas of China. In October 1989 the China Youth Development Foundation announced its first 'fund to help school dropouts in poverty-stricken areas' to carry out 'Project Hope'. By the end of 1998, the various implementation organizations of Project Hope had received donations to the value of more than RMB¥1.6 billion, which had been used to help 2 098 700 dropouts back to school and to build 7111 'Hope' primary schools. Ordinary Chinese citizens, of any rank, are encouraged to contribute to the project, as are overseas organizations, enterprises, groups and individuals. It was probably the most extensive and influential social charity in China in the 1990s. A survey carried out in 1998 found that less than 1 per cent of donors complained that their donations failed to reach the children designated to receive the money; and that about 97.8 per cent of the donor groups and 96.4 per cent of individual donors claimed to have provided the funds voluntarily.

ENROLMENT

It has always been CCP policy that all children should receive an education, especially at primary level. The proportion of children who have been able to go to school has risen dramatically under the People's Republic of China. There have been years of exception to this pattern. For instance, at primary level, enrolments dropped quite significantly in the 1980s, as the figures in Table 10.4 (p. 270) show. Reasons for this include:

Table 10.1 Public funding of education as percentage of GNP, 1996[4]

Country	Percentage	Country	Percentage
China	2.3	Japan	3.6
South Korea	3.7	Cambodia	2.9
Indonesia	1.4	Malaysia	5.2
Philippines	2.2	Singapore	3.0
Thailand	4.1	Vietnam	2.6
India	3.4	Pakistan	3.0

- the decline in the numbers of the cohort due to the restrictive population policy introduced in the late 1970s
- the decline of the local community schools, which had been financed by rural collectives but suffered reverses with the decollectivization policies of the 1980s
- the privatization of education and the economy, making it possible, especially in the countryside, to make more money by taking a job than by going to school.

Despite the continuing privatization, endeavours such as Project Hope mentioned above have led to an increase in enrolment rates. According to a report carried out by the China Civil Education 2000 supervisory group and jointly issued by UNESCO and China's Ministry of Education on December 11, 1999, 98.9 per cent of the relevant school-aged children were attending primary schools, an increase from 97 per cent in 1990, with a significant rise also in the progression rate to secondary school.[5] This means that progress towards meeting the law of 1986 has been very substantial, even if it not entirely met. However, the status of the enrolments is not always clear. A child who goes to school very briefly may have met the requirement to enrol, even if in fact he, or more usually she, does not in fact attend school or learn much. She may easily remain illiterate, despite being counted as having enrolled. So by no means all who enrol graduate.

Table 10.2 Enrolment and progression rates

Year	Primary school enrolment rate	Progression rate to junior secondary	Progression rate to senior secondary
1952	49.2	96.0	168.6
1965	84.7	82.5	70.0
1975	96.8	90.6	60.4
1980	93.9	75.9	45.9
1985	96.0	68.4	41.7
1989	97.0	71.5	38.3
1992	97.2	79.7	43.4
1994	98.4	86.6	46.4
1995	98.5	90.8	48.3
1996	98.8	92.6	48.8
1997	98.9	93.7	44.3
1998	98.9	94.3	50.7

Table 10.3 Number of educational institutions

Year	Primary	Junior secondary	Senior secondary	Tertiary
1952	526 964	3 117	1 181	201
1965	1 681 939	13 990	4 112	434
1978	949 323	113 130	49 215	598
1980	917 316	87 077	31 300	675
1984	853 740	75 867	17 847	902
1985	832 309	75 903	17 318	1 016
1987	807 406	75 927	16 930	1 063
1989	777 244	73 525	16 050	1 075
1990	766 072	71 953	15 678	1 075
1992	712 973	69 171	14 850	1 053
1993	696 681	68 415	14 380	1 065
1994	682 588	68 116	14 242	1 080
1995	668 685	67 029	13 991	1 054
1996	645 983	66 092	13 875	1 032
1997	628 840	64 762	13 880	1 020
1998	609 626	63 940	13 948	1 022

Table 10.2 shows the proportion of children of primary school age who have enrolled in a primary school. It also shows the percentage of primary school graduates who go on to junior secondary schools and graduates of junior secondary proceeding to senior secondary schools.[6] Tables 10.2 and 10.3 include only regular secondary schools, that is, they do not include others kinds of secondary school, such as specialized secondary schools.

The rate of attendance at university or college education is very low in China by comparison with countries with more advanced economies, even though rates have gone up in recent years. Table 10.6 compares China with selected neighbouring countries in 1996 in terms of the proportion of the relevant age cohort attending a university or college, and the percentage of tertiary education students who are female. The fact that the figure for the percentage female is lower for China than given in Table 10.7 is due to the fact that Table 10.6 is based on World Bank figures, whereas Table 10.7 is based on the Chinese State Statistical Bureau.

On March 29, 2001, *People's Daily* (p. 1) announced figures on proportions of the total population who had graduated from various levels of schooling, based on the 2000 census. These showed that the percentage in the total population who had graduated from primary school had fallen by 4 per cent since the 1990 census. On the other hand, the proportion of junior secondary graduates in the total popu-

Table 10.4 Total student enrolments (millions)

Year	Primary	Secondary (all types included)	Tertiary
1950	28.924	1.57	0.14
1965	116.21	14.32	0.67
1978	146.24	66.37	0.86
1980	146.27	56.78	1.14
1985	133.70	50.93	1.70
1988	125.36	52.46	2.07
1989	123.73	50.54	2.08
1990	122.41	51.05	2.06
1991	121.64	52.27	2.04
1992	122.01	53.54	2.18
1993	124.21	53.84	2.54
1994	128.23	57.07	2.80
1995	131.95	61.92	2.91
1996	136.15	66.36	3.02
1997	139.95	69.95	3.17
1998	139.54	73.41	3.41

Table 10.5 Overall student enrolment as percentage of population

Year	Total students	Primary	Secondary (all types)	Tertiary
1952	9.47	8.89	0.55	0.03
1957	11.11	9.94	1.10	0.07
1965	18.09	16.02	1.97	0.09
1978	22.18	15.19	6.90	0.09
1980	20.69	14.82	5.75	0.12
1985	17.60	12.63	4.81	0.16
1989	15.65	10.98	4.48	0.19
1990	15.35	10.71	4.47	0.18
1993	15.24	10.48	4.54	0.21
1994	15.69	10.70	4.76	0.23
1995	16.25	10.89	5.11	0.24
1996	16.95	11.12	5.42	0.25
1997	17.24	11.32	5.66	0.26
1998	17.33	11.18	5.88	0.27

Education

lation had risen by 45 per cent over the same period. The proportion of senior secondary graduates had gone up from 8039 in every 100 000 people in the 1990 census to 11 146 for every 100 000 people in that of 2000, up 39 per cent. The 2000 census stated that the number of people with university and higher degrees had increased from 1422 per 100 000 people in the 1990 census to 3611 per 100 000 people in that of 2000, up 154 per cent.

THE EDUCATION OF GIRLS

It has recently become recognized worldwide that there is a special urgency to educate girls. In the rural areas of China, many people still lay far less emphasis on educating their daughters than their sons, with the result that many girls drop out early in their educational career, and a few never go to school at all. In 1989, at about the same time as the Project Hope (discussed above) was inaugurated, several government organizations founded the School Girl Grand Fund with the aim of helping female dropouts return to school. In 1992 the fund was renamed Project Spring Bud. It attracts money from individuals and groups in China, with Hong Kong being particularly generous in contributing. By the middle of 1995 Project Spring Bud had received donations amounting to more than ¥18.5 million, helping 61 000 girls to return to school. This project has made a very significant difference to female education, especially in impoverished and minority areas.

Table 10.6 Comparisons of China with neighbouring countries in tertiary education, 1996[7]

Country	Percentage of age cohort in tertiary education	Percentage of cohort female
China	6	33
Hong Kong	28	43
Japan	43	44
South Korea	60	37
Cambodia	1	16
Indonesia	11	35
Malaysia	11	n.a.
Philippines	35	57
Singapore	39	44
Thailand	21	n.a.
Vietnam	5	n.a.
India	7	36
Pakistan	3	n.a.
Australia	76	51
New Zealand	59	56

Table 10.7 Percentages of female students at various levels

Year	Primary	Regular secondary	Tertiary	Total
1978	44.9	41.5	24.2	43.7
1980	44.6	39.6	23.4	43.0
1985	44.8	40.2	30.0	43.4
1989	45.9	41.4	33.7	44.6
1990	46.2	41.9	33.7	44.9
1991	46.5	42.7	33.4	45.3
1992	46.6	43.1	33.7	45.5
1993	46.8	43.7	33.6	45.8
1994	47.1	44.3	34.5	46.2
1995	47.3	44.8	35.4	46.5
1996	47.5	45.29	36.43	46.8
1997	47.6	45.5	37.3	46.7
1998	47.6	45.7	38.3	47.1

LITERACY

According to the 1964 census, 38.1 per cent of the population aged twelve years or over was illiterate or semi-literate. By 1982, the rate had dropped to 23.5 per cent. The 1990 census claimed that, including only those of 15 years of age or more, the rate of illiterates in the whole population had fallen from 22.81 per cent in 1982 to 15.88 per cent. The figure given in the 2000 census for illiteracy or semi-literacy among those aged 15 or more, was 6.72 per cent.

Meanwhile, the problem of the 'new illiterates' was becoming a serious one. These are young people who leave school because of good employment opportunities, especially in the countryside, which means that this is a problem special to the period of reform. In March 1990, the Chinese representative at a UNESCO Conference on Education held in Bangkok disclosed that the 'new illiterates' totalled 2.7 million, accounting for 3 to 4 per cent of all school-age children, which is more than half the number who throw off illiteracy every year. In 1994 estimates of the age group 15 to 40 showed the illiteracy rate in 1982 as 18.5 per cent, falling to 9.3 per cent in 1990 and 7 per cent in 1993.

Towards the end of 1994, State Education Commission Vice-Minister Wang Mingda

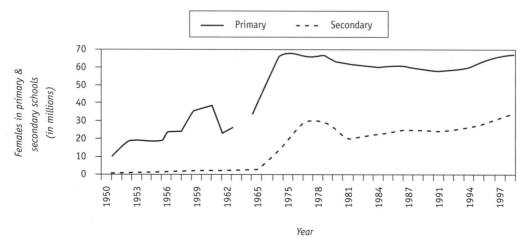

Figure 10.1 Number of female students in primary and regular secondary schools (in millions)

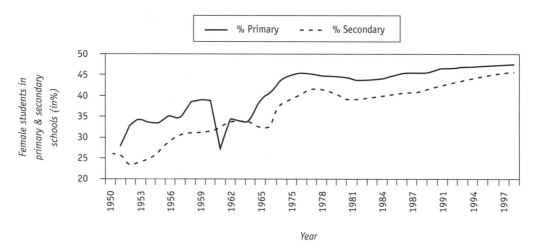

Figure 10.2 Percentage of female students in primary and regular secondary schools

announced that the illiteracy rate of Chinese people born after 1949 and over 15 years old had been reduced to some 7 per cent of the total population, about 84 million people. But he added that there were about 150 million people above 15 who still could not read or write, nearly half of them born before 1949. And an average of 1 million 'new illiterates' was expected to be added to that figure every year. Mr Wang said there were plans to eliminate illiteracy among an average of 4 million people each year during the 1990s. And he noted that by the year 2000 it was planned that less than 5 per cent of young and middle-aged people would remain illiterate.

According to Wang, most of the illiterate population lived in poverty-stricken, remote border regions and in areas inhabited by ethnic minorities; 70 per cent were women. (A 1998 figure puts literacy among males aged 15 and over at 91 per cent, but at only 75 per cent among females.[8]) The government's reaction to this was to establish a high-level national group with the specific aim of countering illiteracy. At its inaugural meeting on November 2, 1994, Vice-Premier Li Lanqing stressed the importance of the literacy campaign, noting that a national working conference on education had declared it among the most important tasks needing attention.[9]

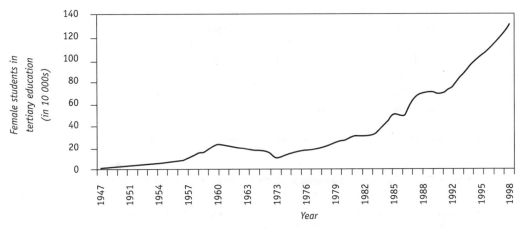

Figure 10.3 Number of female students in tertiary education (in 10 000s)

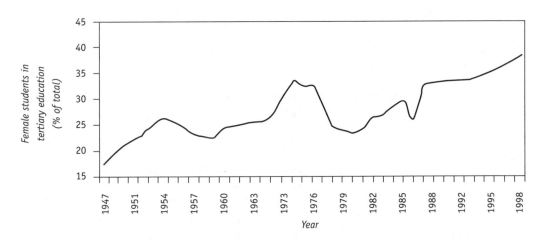

Figure 10.4 Percentage of female students in tertiary education

Literacy

STRUCTURE AND CURRICULUM

Preschool education is widely available to children aged between 3 and 6 years. Areas covered include hygiene, physical education, moral education, language, general knowledge, basic mathematics, music and art. A large part of preschool education is concerned with moral and social training. Most kindergartens offer full-time care for children, and many are boarding schools, run on a weekly basis or for even longer periods of time, with children returning home for weekends or holidays.

Primary school education was reduced to five years during the Cultural Revolution but the trend afterwards was to revert to six-year education at primary level. Six-year primary schools rose from about 40 per cent of the total in 1984 to 60 per cent in 1993, five-year schools being especially common in rural areas, where children often begin school at 7 years of age rather than 6. The drop-out rate is relatively high in rural areas. Subjects taught to primary school children are moral education, Chinese, science, arithmetic, geography, history, physical education, music and painting. Some minority areas also include attention to the local language, culture and history, but this is in addition to, not instead of, the national curriculum.

Outside the formal school system, particularly in the large cities, a network of children's centres and children's 'palaces' provides additional educational and recreational activities for children. Alternative education systems include part-time schools, mobile schools and alternate day schools, many of them found in the minority nationality areas.

The first three years of secondary education are part of the compulsory education system. Other than regular secondary schools, there are vocational schools and specialized technical schools, the latter being either technical or teacher training schools. The specialized technical schools experienced a big expansion from the 1970s on in fields ranging from commerce and legal work to the arts and forestry. In the countryside, agricultural secondary schools educate students in agricultural science and technology. However, the number of teacher training schools was actually slightly lower in 1998 (875) by

Table 10.8 Specialized secondary school statistics by type of institution (students in '000s)

	1952	1965	1978	1980	1985	1990	1995	1998
Total no. schools	1710	1265	2760	3069	3557	3982	4049	4109
Per cent technical	46.4	68.9	62.1	66.9	71.1	74.2	77.8	78.7
Per cent teacher training	54.1	31.1	37.9	33.1	28.9	25.8	22.1	21.3
Total no. students	636	547	889	1243	1571	2244	3 722	4981
Per cent technical	45.6	71.7	59.5	61.2	64.2	69.8	77.2	81.5
Per cent teacher training	54.3	28.3	40.5	38.8	35.8	30.2	22.8	18.5
No. graduating	68	91	232	410	429	661	839	1 293
Per cent technical	60.2	80.2	51.3	49.0	60.8	64.7	70.8	76.3
Per cent teacher training	39.7	19.8	48.7	50.9	39.2	35.4	29.2	23.7

Table 10.9 Specialized secondary school graduate figures by type of institution (students in '000s)

Category of school	1952	1965	1978	1980	1985	1990	1995	1998
Engineering	9.5	40.8	31.3	57.8	84.1	128.9	205.0	356.2
Agriculture	4.4	6.4	27.1	29.1	26.5	30.0	39.8	44.8
Forestry	0.3	1.4	–	3.2	4.7	6.3	10.1	10.1
Medicine	15.8	12.9	43.9	53.5	51.6	94.0	90.9	126.3
Economics and finance	10.5	8.8	13.9	47.1	71.9	126.1	124.4	212.1
Management	–	–	–	–	–	–	65.2	131.9
Politics and law	–	–	–	–	14.8	20.3	28.7	42.4
The arts	0.1	2.3	2.2	2.1	5.3	7.5	14.3	37.3
Physical culture	–	0.2	0.2	1.0	1.6	6.2	11.4	17.6
Teacher training	27.4	18.01	12.7	209.1	167.5	233.7	249.4	314.5

Education

comparison with 1975 (887), and the proportion of teacher training schools to the total specialized secondary schools fell dramatically between 1978 and the end of the twentieth century. The number of students and graduates in the teacher training schools continued to rise, but at a far slower rate than those of the technical schools.

Table 10.9 gives the number of graduates in the various categories of specialized secondary schools. These indicate that the greatest expansion has taken place in fields like economics, finance, politics and law. Newest and most prominent of all is management, for although there may be some graduates in specialized secondary management schools before the 1990s under the category of 'others', this category is not listed in the statistics for the years nominated below until 1995. Moreover, the rise of more than double in just three years (to 1998) shows this as a spectacularly rising field of study.

Table 10.10 shows the number of tertiary education graduates by field of study and reveals the changes that have taken place in student preferences of fields of study in the period of reform. Not surprisingly, they follow patterns similar to those found in the specialized secondary schools. Whereas China under Mao Zedong had a very weak law system indeed—and it is still weak by Western standards—its function within society has grown enormously since the late 1970s and there is also significant profit to be made through the practice of the law. The regrowth of interest in subjects such as literature, history and philosophy in the period of reform has been accompanied by a very significant broadening of the way in which these subjects are taught and learned. Whereas the Cultural Revolution imposed an astonishing narrowness on such subjects, with the content being restricted to a rigid Marxist and Maoist analytical framework, the scope has become enormously broader since the early 1980s, with students learning a range of approaches and having access to a wide range of works translated from European languages.

Table 10.10 Number (in '000s) and percentage of university and college graduates by field of study, 1952–92

Field of study	1952	1957	1965	1978	1980	1985	1990	1992
Engineering	10.2	17.2	80.3	56.5	44.2	97.7	195.8	207.0
Percentage	31.9	30.5	43.3	34.3	30.1	30.9	31.9	34.3
Agriculture	2.4	3.1	15.7	13.9	4.0	17.3	27.7	24.9
Percentage	7.4	5.5	8.4	8.5	2.7	5.5	4.5	4.1
Forestry	0.8	0.8	3.2	2.6	1.2	3.4	5.7	5.5
Percentage	2.5	1.5	1.7	1.6	0.9	1.1	0.9	0.9
Medicine	2.6	6.2	22.0	27.5	17.7	29.2	42.9	45.7
Percentage	8.2	11.0	11.9	16.7	12.0	9.2	7.0	7.6
Teacher training	3.1	15.9	29.0	35.4	61.9	94.1	190.9	179.3
Percentage	9.6	28.4	15.6	21.5	42.2	29.7	31.1	29.7
Humanities	1.7	4.3	8.3	11.8	6.2	22.5	33.7	28.7
Percentage	5.2	7.6	4.4	7.2	4.2	7.1	5.5	4.7
Science	2.2	3.5	20.7	12.7	8.4	18.5	29.9	25.9
Percentage	6.9	6.3	11.1	7.7	5.7	5.9	4.7	4.3
Economics and finance	7.3	3.7	2.1	1.6	1.3	24.1	66.4	65.7
Percentage	22.7	6.5	1.1	9.9	8.6	7.6	10.8	10.9
Politics and law	1.4	0.4	0.8	0.1	0.1	5.4	12.1	12.4
Percentage	4.4	0.1	0.5	0.1	0.1	1.6	1.9	2.1
Physical culture	0.07	0.5	1.9	1.1	0.6	2.6	4.3	3.9
Percentage	0.0	20.1	1.0	0.7	0.7	0.8	0.7	0.6
The arts	0.3	0.6	1.6	1.1	0.6	1.6	5.2	5.2
Percentage	0.8	1.0	0.9	0.7	0.4	0.5	0.9	0.9
Total	32.0	56.2	185.5	164.6	146.6	316.4	613.6	604.2

During the period of Mao Zedong's dominance, philosophy meant Mao Zedong Thought and Marxism entirely, but it is much more inclusive nowadays. Fields of study such as engineering have been popular at all periods, because of its enormous importance in society and for China's economy. Another field that can never be otherwise than extremely valuable to society is medicine, and the number of its graduates continues to rise.

The fields of study listed for the years since the early 1990s are different from the earlier period, necessitating a second table. However, the reader will observe strong similarities.

TEACHERS

Teachers traditionally enjoyed a very high social status in China. Under Mao Zedong, they were in some ways held in high regard but at the same time suffered some of the worst excesses of political campaigns, because of the influence they exercised on society. During the Cultural Revolution Mao Zedong encouraged students to criticize their teachers for ideological and other faults to the extent that many were unable to operate and some committed suicide. One of the first results of the overthrow of the 'gang of four' in 1976 was a reestablishment of teacher confidence. In 1978 the Fifth Educational Work Conference reevaluated the work of teachers upwards. One of the main aims of the long-range development plan for education announced in 1996 was to improve the qualifications of teachers. In his report to the Fifteenth CCP Congress, given on September 12, 1997, Jiang Zemin made a special point of enhancing the social status of teachers, placing it first in the list of items that needed to be done to boost the education system. He said: 'We must see to it that education is given a strategic priority. We should respect teachers and their teaching, and strengthen the ranks of teachers.'

The figures in Tables 10.9 and 10.10 show continuing good numbers of graduates of teacher training and education courses in the reform period, especially from those at secondary levels. And the cohort of teachers continued to rise, as the figures in Table 10.12 indicate. But at the same time, the financial

Table 10.11 Number (in '000s) and percentage of university and college graduates by field of study, 1992–98

Field of study	1994	1996	1998
Philosophy	2.1	2.0	1.2
Percentage	0.3	0.2	0.1
Economics	81.0	127.0	133.0
Percentage	12.7	15.1	16.0
Law	17.7	25.9	29.6
Percentage	2.8	3.1	3.6
Education	35.2	40.6	40.7
Percentage	5.5	4.8	4.9
Literature	92.9	120.1	119.6
Percentage	14.6	14.3	14.4
History	16.8	16.4	14.2
Percentage	2.6	2.0	1.7
Science	87.8	97.3	92.7
Percentage	13.8	11.6	11.2
Engineering	228.9	315.0	308.6
Percentage	35.9	37.6	37.2
Agriculture	27.9	33.0	28.9
Percentage	4.4	3.9	3.5
Medicine	47.1	61.4	61.4
Percentage	7.4	7.3	7.4
Total	637.4	838.6	829.8

status of teachers was not particularly high, because their salaries did not rise at anything like the rate of inflation in the 1980s and the first half of the 1990s, which meant that their standard of living actually fell in many cases. With the additional opportunities of making money which society offered, many good potential teachers could earn more money in other jobs. Just as important, many people looked down on teachers because they did not earn much money. The nationalist revival since the late 1990s has had the effect of strengthening pride in the teaching profession, but, on the other hand, the continuing trend towards Western ideas and consumer goods prevalent among young people may have an opposite impact. The reestablishment of postgraduate studies (see Chapter 1, E. May 27, 1983) improved the qualifications of teachers at tertiary level. On the other hand, there has been a serious braindrain of stu-

dents at tertiary level to Western countries, especially the United States, and to Japan. The number of PhD and other graduates returning has increased markedly since the mid–1990s from a low of 1593 in 1990 following the suppression of the student movement in 1989 to 7379 in 1998, and such returnees frequently find prestigious and well-paid jobs, but at the end of the twentieth century those who stayed overseas still greatly outnumbered those who returned.[10]

The following tables show some statistics relevant to teachers at all levels of the education system.

Table 10.13 shows the number of students per teacher at various levels. It includes all categories of schools at the three levels nominated.

Table 10.14 shows the numbers and percentages of female teachers. Note that there are categories other than those included, such

Table 10.12 Total teacher numbers ('000s)

Year	Primary	Secondary (Regular and specialized)	Tertiary
1952	1435	130	27
1965	3857	709	138
1978	5226	3281	206
1980	5499	3171	247
1985	5377	2967	344
1988	5501	3389	393
1989	5544	3423	397
1990	5582	3492	395
1992	5527	3624	388
1994	5611	3757	396
1996	5736	4040	403
1998	5819	4312	407

Table 10.13 Student:teacher ratio

Year	Primary	Secondary	Tertiary
1952	35.6	24.2	7.1
1965	30.1	20.2	4.9
1978	28.0	20.2	4.2
1980	26.6	17.9	4.6
1985	24.9	17.2	5.0
1988	22.8	15.5	5.3
1989	22.3	14.8	5.2
1990	21.9	14.6	5.2
1992	22.1	14.8	5.6
1994	22.9	15.2	7.1
1996	23.7	16.4	7.5
1998	23.9	17.0	8.4

Teachers

as specialized secondary schools, which explains why the totals are greater than the sum of the three categories nominated. The proportions indicate the percentages of female teachers of all teachers in the relevant category. The figures show generally rising numbers and percentages of female teachers in all categories. Although at the end of the twentieth century the percentages were still short of half in all categories, they were drastically higher than in 1952.[11]

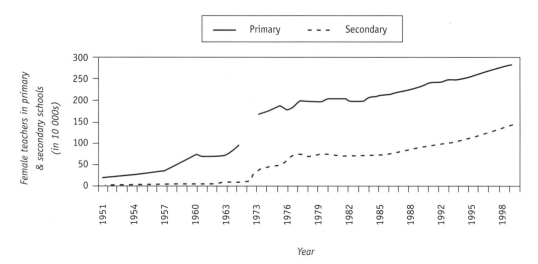

Figure 10.5 Number of female teachers in primary and regular secondary schools (in 10 000s)

Table 10.14 Number of and proportion of female teachers ('000s)

Year	Primary	Regular secondary	Tertiary	Total
1952	246	11	4	264.9
Percentage	18.4	11.7	14.9	16.6
1962	698	78.3	30.4	820.4
Percentage	27.8	19.6	21.1	26.2
1975	1888	505.2	38	not available
Percentage	36.3	24.1	24.4	not available
1978	1977	715.2	52.4	2772
Percentage	37.8	24.4	25.4	31.8
1980	2039	750	63	2889
Percentage	37.1	24.8	25.5	32.4
1985	2128	744	92	3056
Percentage	39.6	28.1	26.7	35.2
1990	2409	956	115	3640
Percentage	43.2	31.5	29.1	38.4
1995	2640	1192	132	4179
Percentage	46.6	35.8	32.9	42.0
1997	2797	1369	142	4557
Percentage	48.3	38.2	35.1	43.9
1998	2846	1454	148	4709
Percentage	48.9	39.3	36.3	44.7

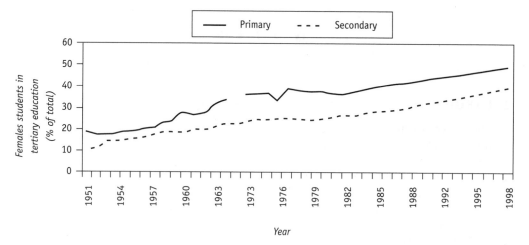

Figure 10.6 Percentage of female teachers in primary and regular secondary schools

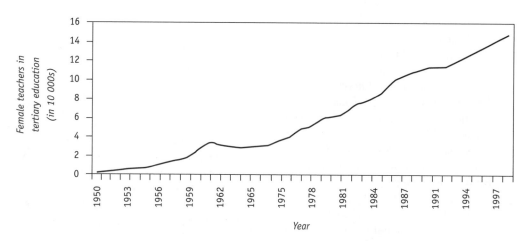

Figure 10.7 Number of female teachers in tertiary education (in 10 000s)

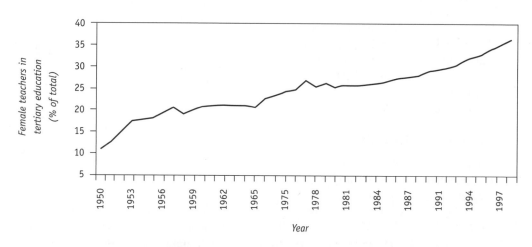

Figure 10.8 Percentage of female teachers in tertiary education

Teachers

NOTES

1 CHRONOLOGY

1 The sources are numerous. For the period to January 1981, Colin Mackerras, with the assistance of Robert Chan, *Modern China: A Chronology from 1842 to the Present* (Thames & Hudson, London, 1982) is the main source. For the period since the early 1960s, the regular 'Quarterly Chronicle and Documentation' in the *China Quarterly*, published by the Contemporary China Institute, School of Oriental and African Studies, London, and *Beijing Review*, an English-language weekly published by Beijing Review in Beijing, are very valuable. For the years since 1979 the *Chinese Encyclopedic Yearbook 1980* (*Zhongguo baike nianjian*) (Chinese Encyclopedia Press, Beijing and Shanghai, 1980 and later years) and the NCNA-sponsored *People's Republic of China Yearbook* (PRC Yearbook Ltd, Beijing. distributed by Economic Information & Agency, Hong Kong, 1981 and later years) have been particularly useful. For those since 1977, John L. Scherer (ed.), *China, Facts and Figures Annual* (Academic International Press, Gulf Breeze, Florida, 1978 and later years) is recommended, but note that from the 1988 edition, a series of editors other than Scherer has worked on this *Annual*. In 1991 the *China Review* began production, being published by the Chinese University Press.

2 POLITICS AND LAW

1 Quoted in 'Quarterly Chronicle and Documentation', *China Quarterly* 131 (September 1992), p. 847.
2 Quoted in ibid. 144 (December 1995), p. 1245.
3 *Beijing Review* XXXIX, 45 (November 4–10, 1996), p. 23.

4 *Beijing Review* XXXVII, 10 (March 7–13, 1994), p. 21.
5 'Quarterly Chronicle and Documentation', *China Quarterly* 143 (September 1995), pp. 945, 955.
6 State Statistical Bureau (comp.), *Zhongguo tongji nianjian 1999* (*China Statistical Yearbook 1999*) (Statistical Press of China, Beijing, 1999), p. 3.
7 Susan V. Lawrence, 'Village Democracy', *Far Eastern Economic Review* CLXIII, 4 (February 27, 2000), pp. 16–17.
8 Todd Crowell and David Hsieh, 'A New Upheaval?', *Asiaweek* XXV, 22 (June 4, 1999), p. 33.
9 *China Daily*, February 16, 1999.
10 Quoted in 'Quarterly Chronicle and Documentation', *China Quarterly* 139 (September 1994), pp. 862–3. The early 1995 8 per cent figure comes from 'Quarterly Chronicle and Documentation', *China Quarterly* 142 (June 1995), p. 646.
11 See Li Rongxia, 'Cracking Down on the Abduction of Women and Children', *Beijing Review* XLIII, 19 (May 8, 2000), p. 14.
12 'Amnesty Criticizes Executions in China', *China News Digest* Global News, No. GL00–016 (February 4, 2000), item 33. This source is published several times weekly on the Internet
13 *China Daily*, September 8, 1986, p. 4.
14 Han Zhubin, 'Report on the Work of the Supreme People's Procuratorate', *Beijing Review* XLII, 17 (April 26–May 2, 1999), p. 29.
15 This is based on a report by the British Broadcasting Corporation's Tim Louard, broadcast over the Australian Broadcasting Corporation's program *World Roundup* on December 13, 1988, itself claiming to be based on *Shanghai Evening News* (*Shanghai wanbao*).

3 EMINENT CONTEMPORARY FIGURES

1 The sources listed for the chronology in Chapter 1 are also useful for the biographical material in the present chapter. See also Editorial Board of *Who's Who in China*, comp. *Who's Who in China, Current Leaders* (Foreign Languages Press, Beijing, 1989, revised edn, 1994) and Colin Mackerras, Donald H. McMillen and Andrew Watson (eds), *Dictionary of the Politics of the People's Republic of China* (Routledge, London and New York, 1998). Several international biographical dictionaries have also been very useful in compiling this chapter, examples including *The International Who's Who*, published annually by Europa Publications Limited since 1935 and *Outstanding People of the 20th Century*, first published by the International Biographical Centre, Cambridge, England, in 1999. In addition, the biographies draw from a list of 50 Chinese regarded as 'shaping China' at the time the PRC celebrated its fiftieth anniversary in October 1999: 'Nation Builders', *Asiaweek* XXV, 38 (September 24, 1999), pp. 74–97. The Internet has also provided much helpful information.

2 See website www.netins.net/showcase/wfp/1993.html

3 See this list in *Asiaweek* XXV, 46 (November 19, 1999), p. 76–117. China Petrochemical Corp. ranked eighteenth in Asia in 1999. In the same year it was the sixth largest petrochemical company in the world.

5 FOREIGN RELATIONS

1 See 'Quarterly Chronicle and Documentation', *China Quarterly* 133 (March 1993), p. 200.

2 'Quarterly Chronicle and Documentation', *China Quarterly* 135 (September 1993), p. 642.

3 See the full speech, among other places, in *China New Digest*, Global News, No. GL99–044 (April 7, 1999), item 365.

4 *Beijing Review* XXXVIII, 26 (June 26–July 2, 1995), p. 21.

5 *Beijing Review* XXXIX, 13 (March 25–31, 1996), p. 8.

6 *Beijing Review* XLIII, 10 (March 6, 2000), p. 21.

7 *Far Eastern Economic Review Asia 1994 Yearbook, A Review of the Events of 1993* (Review Publishing Company, Hong Kong, 1994), p. 116.

8 Quoted in Susan V. Lawrence, 'True Colours', *Far Eastern Economic Review* CLXII, 12 (March 25, 1999), p. 21.

9 Andrew Watson, 'World Trade Organization', in Colin Mackerras, Donald H. McMillen and Andrew Watson (eds), *Dictionary of the Politics of the People's Republic of China* (Routledge, London and New York, 1998), p. 234.

6 CHINA'S ECONOMY

1 There are no absolutely guaranteed economic statistics covering the entire history of the PRC since its inception in 1949 up to the present. However, for this publication the following up-to-date and reliable sources have been used, listed in alphabetical order. *Asia Yearbook* (Far Eastern Economic Review, Hong Kong); *Beijing Review*, various issues; *China Business Review* (US–China Business Council), various issues; *The Economist* (London, various issues); *Economist Intelligence Unit, Country Profile: China, Mongolia*, 1999–2000, and various quarterly issues; *Far Eastern Economic Review* (Hong Kong); International Monetary Fund, *International Financial Statistics, China, P.R. Mainland*, monthly, various issues; *Issues & Studies* (Institute of International relations, Taipei), various issues; *JETRO China Newsletter* (Tokyo), various issues; *People's Republic of China Yearbook 1998/99* (PRC

Yearbook Ltd., Beijing, distributed by Economic Information & Agency, Hong Kong); United Nations, *International Trade Statistics Yearbook, 1997*; United Nations Development Fund, *Human Development Report*, (Oxford University Press), various issues; World Bank, *Global Development Finance, 1999, Country Tables, China* (Washington DC); World Bank, *Entering the 21st Century: World Development Report 1999/2000* (Oxford University Press, 1999); World Bank, *World Bank Atlas*, various issues; and *Zhongguo tongji nianjian (China Statistical Yearbook)* (Statistical Press of China, Beijing). Internet sources include the following: *China and the World* www.chinabulletin.com/indexe.htm; *China News Digest, Global News*, various issues. www.cnd.org/CND-Global/; *China News Economy* www.china.org.cn/English/News/Economy/index.html; *TCFA UPDATE* (A Newsletter of The Chinese Finance Association), various issues, www.aimhi.com/VC/tcfa//update.html; *Yahoo!News—China Economy* fullcoverage.yahoo.com/fc/Business/China_Economy/. Other publications have also proved useful, and a special section is allocated to the economy in Chapter 4.

7 POPULATION

1 The following are the main general sources, in order of importance, for the figures in this chapter: State Statistical Bureau Office of Population Statistics, *Zhongguo renkou tongji nianjian (China Population Statistics Yearbook 1990)* (Science and Technology Documents Press, Beijing, 1991); State Statistical Bureau (comp.), *Zhongguo tongji nianjian (China Statistical Yearbook)* (China Statistical Publishing House, Beijing, 1981–99); and *Asia Yearbook* (*Far Eastern Economic Review*, Hong Kong, successive years).

2 See *Beijing Review* XXXII, 11 (March 13–19, 1989), p. 4.

3 They derive from the successive *Asia Yearbooks,* themselves based on the *Far Eastern Economic Review*'s own sources, the United Nations Statistical Yearbooks, and a range of other sources.

4 *People's Daily*, November 1, 1990, p. 1; Ka Po Ng, 'Chronology of 1997', in Joseph Y.S. Cheng (ed.), *China Review 1998* (Chinese University Press, Hong Kong, 1998), p. xxx.

5 See Ellen Salem, 'It All Depends on How You Count Them', *Far Eastern Economic Review* CLXIII, 9 (March 2, 1989), p. 63.

6 The figures for the 1990 census are based on the detailed figures to be found in *Zhongguo renkou tongji nianjian (China Population Statistics Yearbook 1990)*, p. 49, and for the 1995 sample census those found in State Statistical Bureau (comp.), *Zhongguo tongji nianjian (China Statistical Yearbook)* (China Statistical Publishing House, Beijing, 1996), p. 72.

7 For the late 1980s see *Far Eastern Economic Review* CXLIII, 9 (March 2, 1989), p. 64. In 'Population Policy' in Christopher Hudson (ed.), *The China Handbook* (Fitzroy Dearborn Publishers, Chicago, London, 1997), p. 233, Penny Kane claims the reasons for the imbalance in the markedly high sex ratios to be 'not entirely clear', but cites 'the most exhaustive source', by Zeng Yi and others and published in *Population and Development Review* XIX, 2 (1993), pp. 283–302 to the effect that under-reporting accounts for between 43 and 75 per cent of the missing females. She argues that sex-selective abortion most likely accounts for most of the remaining missing females.

8 See *Beijing Review* XXXI, 3 (January 18–24, 1988), p. 8.

9 See 'Quarterly Chronicle and Documentation', *China Quarterly* 144 (December 1995), pp. 1249–50.

10 One study identifies six categories of people in the floating population, among which only two would normally be classified as migrants. These are 'socially

motivated mobility', which includes people visiting or living with relatives, and children being brought up by relatives, and labour migrants. The first is the one relevant for the issue of restricting population growth. Initially constituting almost two-thirds of the floating population, it dwindled in the mid- to late 1990s to about 10 per cent. See Hein Mallee, 'Definitions and Methodology in Chinese Migrant Studies', in Børge Bakken (ed.), *Migration in China* (NIAS Report Series, No. 31, Nordic Institute of Asian Studies, Copenhagen, 1998), p. 129.

11 The sources for the material on age structure are: *Zhongguo renkou tongji nianjian* (*China Population Statistics Yearbook 1993*) (China Statistical Publishing House, Beijing, 1993), pp. 48–53 and *Zhongguo tongji nianjian 1996*, p. 72.

12 See Judith Banister, 'The Aging of China's Population', *Problems of Communism* XXXVII, 6 (November–December 1988), p. 62.

13 For the State Statistical Bureau figure see *Beijing Review* XL, 27 (July 7–13), p. 34. The United Nations figures are cited in State Statistical Bureau (comp.), *Zhongguo tongji nianjian* (*China Statistical Yearbook 1998*) (China Statistical Publishing House, Beijing, 1998, p. 924.

14 State Statistical Bureau, Office of Population Statistics, *Zhongguo renkou tongji nianjian* (*China Population Statistics Yearbook 1988*) (Zhanwang Press, Beijing, 1988), p. 857.

15 *Zhongguo tongji nianjian 1998*, p. 924.

16 The figures for 1957, 1975, 1978, 1979 and 1981 in this table are taken from Judith Banister, *China's Changing Population* (Stanford University Press, Stanford, 1987), p. 86, the figures themselves deriving from a range of Chinese sources. For the 1990 and 1996 figures see *Beijing Review* XLII, 25 (June 21, 1999), p. 21 and *Beijing Review* XL, 27 (July 7–13, 1997), p. 34. The 1997

figures come from the Information Office of the State Council, 'Progress in China's Human Rights Conditions in 1998', *Beijing Review* XLII, 18 (May 3–9, 1999), pp. 37, 45.

17 This table is taken from successive *Asia Yearbooks*, published by the *Far Eastern Economic Review* in Hong Kong, which, for population figures, are themselves based on the United Nations *Statistical Yearbooks*, the Population Reference Bureau, Inc. in Washington DC, *Far Eastern Economic Review* correspondents and other sources. The 1997 figure is based on the World Bank.

18 These figures are based on *Beijing Review* XXXII, 23 (June 5–11, 1989), p. 26 and *Zhongguo tongji nianjian 1998*, pp. 386, 389.

8 GAZETTEER

1 Sources for this chapter include: *Zuixin shiyong Zhongguo ditu ce* (*Newest Practical Chinese Atlas*)(Chinese Atlas Press, Beijing, 1997), which includes detailed maps, as well as information about each province-level administrative unit and their main cities; State Statistical Bureau (comp.), *Zhongguo tongji nianjian* (*China Statistical Yearbook*) (Statistical Press of China, Beijing, various years); People's Republic of China Yearbook (PRC Yearbook Ltd., Beijing, distributed by Economic Information & Agency, Hong Kong, 1981 and later years); David Munro (ed.), *Chambers World Gazetteer, An A–Z of Geographical Information* (Chambers, Cambridge, 5th edn 1988).

9 THE MINORITY NATIONALITIES

1 The main source for the population figures is the Economic Department of State Ethnic Affairs Commission and Department of Integrated Statistics of State Statistical Bureau, People's Republic of China, (comp.), *Zhongguo minzu tongji nianjian 1995* (*China's Ethnic Statistical Yearbook 1995*) (Ethnic Publishing House, Beijing, 1995), pp. 2–6. There are

minor divergencies among the sources for all censuses, but this source is preferred as being a thorough and up-to-date tabulation of the data.

2 For a detailed treatment of this issue see Colin Mackerras, *China's Minorities: Integration and Modernization in the Twentieth Century* (Oxford University Press, Hong Kong, 1994), pp. 233–59.

3 These were published as *The Question of Tibet and the Rule of Law* (International Commission of Jurists, Geneva, 1960) and *Tibet and the Chinese People's Republic* (International Commission of Jurists, Geneva, 1960).

4 See Zhang Tianlu, *Xizang renkou de bianqian* (*Changes in the Population of Tibet*) (Tibetan Studies Press of China, Beijing, 1989), pp. 9–10. The whole issue of China's Tibetan population is extremely controversial. For a detailed and highly scholarly treatment of the subject, see Yan Hao, 'Tibetan Population in China: Myths and Facts Re-examined', *Asian Ethnicity* I, 1 (March 2000), pp. 11–35.

5 The main source for this list is Wu Shimin, Wang Ping, a.o., *Minzu wenti gailun* (*Outline of Nationalities Problems*)(Sichuan People's Press, Chengdu, 1999), pp. 386–90.

6 *China Daily*, August 26, 1982, p. 3, and November 9, 1989, p. 1.

7 Information Office of the State Council of the People's Republic of China, 'China's Policy on National Minorities and Its Practice (September 1999)', *Beijing Review* XLII, 42 (October 18, 1999), pp. 19, 23.

8 *Renmin ribao, Haiwai ban* (*People's Daily, Overseas Edition*), June 28, 2000, p. 1.

9 'Focusing on Western China', *Beijing Review* XLIII, 15 (April 10, 2000), p. 14. On economic disparities between Han and minorities see also Colin Mackerras, 'The Impact of Economic Reform on China's Minority Nationalities', *Journal of the Asia Pacific Economy* III, 1 (1998), especially pp. 69–71.

10 The main sources for the figures in the Table 9.3 are the *Statistical Yearbooks of China*, especially State Statistical Bureau (comp.), *Zhongguo tongji nianjian 1986* (*Statistical Yearbook of China 1986*) (Statistical Press of China, Beijing, 1986), pp. 81–2, and *Zhongguo tongji nianjian 1999* (*Statistical Yearbook of China 1999*) (Statistical Press of China, Beijing, 1999), pp. 40–1, and Information Office of the State Council of the People's Republic of China, 'China's Policy on National Minorities and Its Practice', pp. 16–33. The sources for Table 9.4 are *Zhongguo minzu tongji nianjian 1995*, p. 372 and *Zhongguo tongji nianjian 1998* (*Statistical Yearbook of China 1998*) (Statistical Press of China, Beijing, 1998), p. 44.

11 *China News Digest* Global News, No. GL99–009 (January 20, 1999), item 36, quoting *China Daily*.

12 For the figures on literacy in Tibet and Yanbian see Information Office of the State Council of the People's Republic of China, 'China's Policy on National Minorities and Its Practice', pp. 23–4.

13 Information Office of the State Council of the People's Republic of China, 'Fifty Years of Progress in China's Human Rights', *Beijing Review* XLIII, 9 (February 28, 2000), p. 48.

14 See Li Xing in *China Daily*, June 28, 1999, p. 3.

15 'Fifty Years of Progress in China's Human Rights', pp. 48–9.

16 Quoted from BBC Monitoring Service, Asia-Pacific, May 9, 1996, itself taken from the evening report of May 6, 1996, Xinjiang Television, Ürümqi, in Modern Standard Chinese.

17 *Xinjiang ribao* (*Xinjiang Daily*), October 27, 1997, quoted in 'Quarterly Chronicle and Documentation', *China Quarterly* 153 (March 1998), p. 202.

18 See *China News Digest* No. GL99–053 (April 23, 1999), items 32 and 72 (1).

19 The main sources for the information in this section are Baoerhan et al. (comps), *Zhongguo da baike quanshu, minzu* (*The*

China Encyclopedia, Nationalities) (China Encyclopedia Press, Beijing, Shanghai, 1986); and Shi Zhengyi et al., (comps), *Minzu cidian* (*Nationalities Dictionary*)(Sichuan Nationalities Press, Chengdu, 1984), especially pp. 404–10. See also Ma Yin (ed.), *China's Minority Nationalities* (Foreign Languages Press, Beijing, 1989) and Lunda Hoyle Gill and Colin Mackerras, *Portraits of China* (University of Hawaii Press, Honolulu, 1990), pp. 122–8.

10 EDUCATION

1 Deng Xiaoping, 'Speech at the National Conference on Education', April 22, 1978, *Selected Works of Deng Xiaoping (1975–1982)* (Foreign Languages Press, Beijing, 1984), p. 120.

2 See *Beijing Review* XXXVIII, 21 (May 22–8, 1995), p. 13.

3 *Beijing Review* XXXIX, 45 (November 4–10, 1996), p. 26.

4 See these figures in Michael Westlake (ed.), *Asia 2000 Yearbook, A Review of the Events of 1999* (Review Publishing Company, Hong Kong, 2000), pp. 14–15, themselves based on the World Bank.

5 *China News Digest* No. GL99–166 (December 13, 1999), item 70 (4).

6 The main sources for the tables in this chapter, unless otherwise stated, are the State Statistical Bureau (comp.), *Zhongguo tongji nianjian* (*Statistical*

Yearbook of China) (Statistical Press of China, Beijing, various years), especially *Zhongguo tongji nianjian 1999* (Statistical Press of China, Beijing, 1999), pp. 637–74.

7 Westlake (ed.), *Asia 2000 Yearbook*, pp. 14–15.

8 Cited in Choong Tet Sieu, 'A Caring System', *Asiaweek* XXVI, 29 (July 28, 2000), p. 39.

9 *South China Morning Post*, Hong Kong, November 4, 1994.

10 See the figures in *Zhongguo tongji nianjian 1999*, p. 644, and Robin Paul Ajello and Rose Tang, 'Homeward Bound', *Asiaweek* XXV, 28 (July 16, 1999), pp. 32–7.

11 For these figures and for those in Figures 10.1 to 10.4 see Research Institute of All China Women's Federation and Research Office of Shaanxi Provincial Women's Federation (comp.), *Zhongguo funü tongji ziliao* (*Statistics on Chinese Women 1949–1989*) (China Statistical Publishing House, Beijing, 1991), pp. 125, 131, 136, 152, 168 and 174, *Zhongguo tongji nianjian 1993* (Statistical Press of China, Beijing, 1993), p. 729, *Zhongguo tongji nianjian 1995* (Statistical Press of China, Beijing, 1995), p. 597, *Zhongguo tongji nianjian 1998* (Statistical Press of China, Beijing, 1998), p. 692, *Zhongguo tongji nianjian 1999*, p. 651.

INDEX

Page numbers in bold type (e.g. **262***) indicate detailed treatment of a topic.*

Index

Miao people, 262, 263, **264**, 265
  autonomous areas, 254–6
  bibliography, 163–4
  population, 252
Michiko, Empress, 45
Micronesia, 184
Miles, James A.R., 142
Military Commission. *See*
  Central Military
  Commission
military events: chronology,
  1–84
Miller, Arthur, 23
Milosevic, Slobodan, 64, 71
Min River, 47
minerals, 188
mines, 51, 83. *See also* coal
Minhe Hui–Tu Autonomous
  County, 256
ministries and state
  commissions, 49, 98–9
minority nationalities, **251–66**
  autonomous areas, 25, 59,
    98–100, 251, **253–4**
  bibliography, 161–3
  characteristics, **262–6**
  chronology of events, 19,
    25, 51
  economic and cultural
    indicators, 253, 257–9
  map, 257
  politics and government,
    19, 90, 96, 98–9
  population, **251–3**
  religion, 51
  secessionism, **259–62**
minzhu dangpai (democratic
  parties), 85, 97, 99
Mitterand, François, 22
modernization, 17, 53, 85, 92,
  153
Mohe, 66
Moi, Daniel T. Arap, 52
Moinba people, 252–3, **264**
Mojian Hani Autonomous
  County, 256
Moldova, 168, 184
Mon-Khmer languages, 262,
  266
Mongolia, 265
  chronology of events, 6–7,
    37, 41, 52, 62, 72
  diplomatic relations, 184

political relations, 167
Mongolian languages, 262, 265
Mongolians, 262, **264**
  autonomous areas, 254–6
  population, 253
  religion, 259
Mori Kazakh Autonomous
  County, 256
Morin Dawa Daur
  Autonomous Banner, 256
Morocco, 8, 21, 184
Mosuo people, 264
motorways, 39, 60, 65, 76
Mount Emei, 246
Mount Everest (Jomo
  Lungma), 6
Mount Qingcheng, 67
Mount Tai (Taishan), 228
mountain ranges, 224
Mozambique, 63, 184
Mubarak, Husni, 37, 71
Mugabe, Robert, 48
Mukden. *See* Shenyang
Mulam people, 252, 255, **264**
Muli Tibetan Autonomous
  County, 255
Murray, Geoffrey, 142
museums, 7
music, 14, 17
Muslims
  Chechnya, 168
  minority nationalities, 162,
    259, 261–3, 265
  political activities, 36, 38,
    49, 81, 260
Myanmar (Burma)
  chronology of events, 6, 57
  diplomatic relations, 184
  minority nationalities,
    262–3

N
Nagano, Shigeto, 52
Nagy, Imre, 4
Namibia, 57, 184
Nanchang, 84, 95, **241**
  population, 217, 218
Nanjiang Yi Autonomous
  County, 256
Nanjing (Nanking, Jiankang,
  Jinling), **237**
  chronology of events, 1, 11,
    32, 48, 65, 67, 84

massacre (1937), 62, 80
  population, 217, 218
Nanking. *See* Nanjing
Nanning, 65, **245**
  population, 217, 218
Nanpu Bridge, 43
Nanzhao kingdom, 262
Narayanan, Kocheril Raman, 80
narcotics. *See* drugs
Nathan, Andrew J., 146, 152
*National Economic Atlas of
  China*, 155
National Games, 6, 23
National Missile Defence
  (NMD), 81, 174
National People's Congress
  (NPC)
  bibliography, 146
  corruption, 84, 93
  economy, 3, 22, 26–7,
    29–31, 42–3, 46, 50, 65
  education, 20, 26
  elections, 100
  government, 95, **96–7**, 98
  leadership: (1954–65) 3, 6;
    (1966–88) 15–19, 22–3,
    26, 29, 31; (1989–91)
    35, 40, 43–4; (1992–96)
    50–51, 56, 61;
    (1997–2000) 69, 82, 84
  legal system, 81, 101–2,
    104, 107
  legislation adopted:
    (1977–88) 18, 20, 22,
    25, 27, 29, 31;
    (1989–91) 38, 42;
    (1992–96) 46–7, 49, 56,
    59; (1997–2000) 64, 81
  politics and international
    affairs, 6, 28–9, 37–8, 53,
    64, 71, 74, 78
National Women's Congress, 1,
  17, 23
National Work Conferences,
  8–9, 60, 69
nationalism: bibliography, 153
nationalities. *See* minority
  nationalities
nationality, dual, 20
NATO. *See* Belgrade Embassy
  bombing
natural disasters: chronology of
  events, **1–84**

air routes, 35
borders, 11
minority nationalities, 26, 159, 162, 163, 254, 256, 265
natural disasters, 6, 62, 67, 70
politics and government, 4, 36, 39, 61
population, 215–18
protests and separatism, 26, 38, 49, 64, 84, 107, 163, 260–1
railways, 25, 75–6
reform through labour system, 147
religion, 259
Xinping Yi–Dai Autonomous County, 256
Xinzhou County, 69
Xishuangbanna Dai Autonomous Prefecture, **248**, 254
Xiushan Tujia–Miao Autonomous County, 255
Xiuyang Tujia–Miao Autonomous County, 255
Xiuyuan Manchu Autonomous County, 254
Xu Beihong, 3
Xu Caihou, 76
Xu Chi, 62
Xu Deren, 61
Xu Gang, 158
Xu Guoming, 36
Xu Haifeng, 25
Xu Jiatun, 43
Xu Kuangdi (Hsü K'uang-ti), **132**
Xu Shiyou, 26
Xu Tun, 42
Xu Wenli, 68
Xu Xiangqian, 41
Xu Xiaoping, 158
Xu Xinghu, 78
Xu Yongguang (Hsü Yung-kuang), **132–3**
Xu Yongyue, 98
Xu Yunhong, 76
Xu Zhihong, 83
Xuanhan County, 79
XUAR. *See* Xinjiang Uygur Autonomous Region
Xue, Litai, 152

Xun Huisheng, 11
Xundian Hui–Yi Autonomous County, 256
Xunhua Salar Autonomous County, 256

Y
Yalong River, 76
Yan Jiaqi, 143, 149–50
Yan Xishan, 6
Yan Yiyan, 7
Yan'an, 86, 230
Yanbian Korean Autonomous Prefecture, 254, 258
Yancheng, 217
Yang Baibing (Yang Pai-ping), 35, 47, 66, **133**
Yang, Benjamin, 150
Yang, Dali L., 143
Yang, Gladys, 79
Yang Jingren, 24
Yang Ju-tai (Yang Rudai), **133**
Yang Liqing (Yang Li-ch'ing), **133**
Yang Mingjie, 61
Yang Mo, 5
Yang Pai-ping (Yang Baibing), 35, 47, 66, **133**
Yang, Richard H., 152–3
Yang Rudai (Yang Ju-tai), **133**
Yang Shangkun, 97, 133
chronology of events, 31, 35, 37–8, 41–4, 47, 50, 70
Yang Yibang, 22
Yang Zhong, 29
Yangbi Yi Autonomous County, 256
Yangpu bridge, 50
Yangqi Hui Autonomous County, 256
Yangshuo, 245
Yangzhou, 237
Yangzi (Yangtze) River (Changjiang), 224, 239
See also Three Gorges Dam
bibliography, 159–60
chronology of events, 3–4, 10–11, 24, 50, 57, 70, 79–80
Yanhe Tujia Autonomous County, 255
Yantai, 80

Yao (people), **266**
autonomous areas, 255, 256
bibliography, 163
population, 252
Yao Jingyi, 57
Yao Wenyuan, 9, 15–16. *See also* gang of four
Yao Yilin, 22, 26, 29, 34, 47, 54, 88
Yaukey, David, 159
Ye Fei, 78
Ye Jianying, 14, 16, 20, 22, 26, 28, 88
Ye Shengtao, 32
yearbooks, **137–8**
Yee, Herbert, 143
Yellow Emperor, 61
Yellow River (Huanghe), 224
chronology of events, 6, 13, 24, 47, 60, 65
Yeltsin, Boris
chronology of events, 45, 55, 57, 62–4, 68, 73
foreign relations, 167–8
Yemen, 186
Yeung, Y.M., 161
Yi people, **266**
autonomous areas, 245, 255, 256
language, 263, 264, 266
population, 252
Yili Kazakh Autonomous Prefecture, 254, 260
Yinchuan, 51, 218, **236**
Yingkou, 15
Yining, 79
Yinjiang Tujia–Miao Autonomous County, 255
Yip, Vincent F., 162
Yitong Manchu Autonomous County, 255
Yiyang, 79
You Ji, 158
Young, Susan, 158
Yu Changxin, 82
Yu Ling, 67
Yu Qinli, 78
Yu Yongbo, 47
Yu Zhengsheng, 98
Yu Zuomin, 79
Yuanhan Group, 95
Yuanjiang Hani–Yi–Dai Autonomous County, 256

Index